C000195843

Sabre

In memory of the thirty
RAF Sabre pilots killed
in the line of duty

Sabre

THE CANADAIR SABRE IN RAF SERVICE

DUNCAN CURTIS

SUTTON PUBLISHING

First published in 2005 by
Sutton Publishing Limited · Phoenix Mill
Thrupp · Stroud · Gloucestershire · GL5 2BU

Copyright © Duncan Curtis, 2005

All rights reserved. No part of this publication may be reproduced, stored in a retrieval system, or transmitted, in any form or by any means, electronic, mechanical, photocopying, recording or otherwise, without the prior permission of the publisher and copyright holder.

Duncan Curtis has asserted the moral right to be identified as the author of this work.

British Library Cataloguing in Publication Data
A catalogue record for this book is available from the British Library.

ISBN 0-7509-4236-3

Typeset in 10/13 pt Sabon.
Typesetting and origination by
Sutton Publishing Limited.
Printed and bound in England by
J.H. Haynes & Co. Ltd, Sparkford.

CONTENTS

ACKNOWLEDGEMENTS

The author would like to thank Tim Barrett, John Barrie, Air Cdre John A. Bell, Bill Bevan, Jim Bignall, P.R. 'Porky' Bond, Rex Boulton, Chas Boyack, John D. Bradley, Reg Bridgman, Tom Broomhead, Robin A. Brown, Air Cdre Desmond Browne, Colin Buttars, Air Cdre Dennis Caldwell, Peter Caygill, Brian Chapman, Don Christmas, George Cole, Alan Cook, Bob Copping, Howard Curtis, John Daly, Roy Davey, Wg Cdr Geoff Davies, 'Moose' Davies, Tony Dawes, Alan East, Trevor Egginton, Graham Elliott, Don Elsden, Don Exley, Peter Foard, Michael A. Fox, Peter Frame, Norman Giffin, John Gooding, H. 'Jimmy' Green, Ron Grey, Paddy Harbison, Gp Capt John Hardwick, Guy Harris, Denys Heywood, Peter Hicks, S. Hodgetts, Bill Holmes, Alistair Holyoake, Mrs Lydia Inkersole, Alan Jones, Bob Jones, Dennis Jones, Charles Keil, Tony Kidd, Richard Knight, Ian Laurie, Snowden 'Snowy' Le Breton, Mick Letton, Roger Lindsay, Tony Lock, Bob Lysgaard, Jock Maitland, Paul Mansfield, Roger Mansfield, Denis H. Martin, Sqn Ldr Bruce McDonald, David R. McLaren, Brian Merifield, MoD Air Historical Branch, 'Pop' Miles, National Archives, Roger Neaves, Ned Neill, Sqn Ldr Vick Nickson, Peter Norris, David Nowell, J.M. 'Oakie' Oakford, John Oxenford, Colin Pardoe, Keith Parker, Keith Payne, John Perrott, Eric Pigdon, Jak Pintches, RAF Museum, Norman Roberson, E.H. 'Ted' Roberts, Robbie Robinson, Derek Rumble, Mike Ryan, Stewart Salmond, Peter 'Tom' Sawyer, Brian Scotford, Ken Senar, James Smith, Ken Sweet, Jim Taylor, Tony Vasey, Harry Walmsley, David Watkins, Bill White, Bob Whitworth, James Wilde, David Wildish, David Williams, Doug Wood and Alan 'Lefty' Wright for their help in the preparation of this book.

INTRODUCTION

The F-86 Sabre began with North American Aviation's project NA-134, an aircraft originally drawn up for the US Navy. The NA-134 was to be a carrier-based jet capable of supporting the planned May 1946 invasion of Japan, and was required to be superior in performance to existing shore-based interceptors.

Work on the NA-134 project began in late 1944, and the North American Aviation (NAA) design team came up with an aircraft featuring a straight, thin-section wing set low on a rather stubby fuselage. A nose intake fed air to the jet engine, which then exhausted at the tail. The US Navy ordered three NA-134 prototypes under the designation XFJ-1 on 1 January 1945, and on 28 May approved a contract for 100 production FJ-1s.

Meanwhile, the US Army Air Force (USAAF) issued a design request for a medium-range day fighter that could also cope with the escort-fighter and fighter-bomber missions. A top speed of 600mph was stipulated, and, on 22 November 1944, NAA put forward its RD-1265 design study for a version of the XFJ-1 to meet the USAAF requirement. On 18 May 1945 the USAAF ordered three prototype aircraft, to be known as XP-86s (XP = 'experimental pursuit').

Both fighter types were designed around the General Electric J35 axial-flow turbojet, but their jointly developed design soon led to compromises. The naval version required strengthening to cope with carrier landings, and the Air Force aircraft emerged with a thinner, straight wing and slimmer fuselage, though it shared its tail surfaces with the XFJ-1. Armament for both aircraft would be six .50 calibre machine guns arranged around the nose intake.

Critically, though, at a gross weight of 11,500lb, the XP-86 was estimated to be only capable of reaching 574mph at sea level and 582mph at 10,000ft. Clearly, further design work would be necessary if the XP-86 was to meet the Air Force's ambitious requirements. At this point in the life of the XP-86 design, a decision was made to sweep the wing and tail surfaces in order to achieve the USAAF's

The first XP-86 prototype on a test flight over California in late 1947. The basic day fighter F-86 design changed very little throughout its production life. (*Author's Collection*)

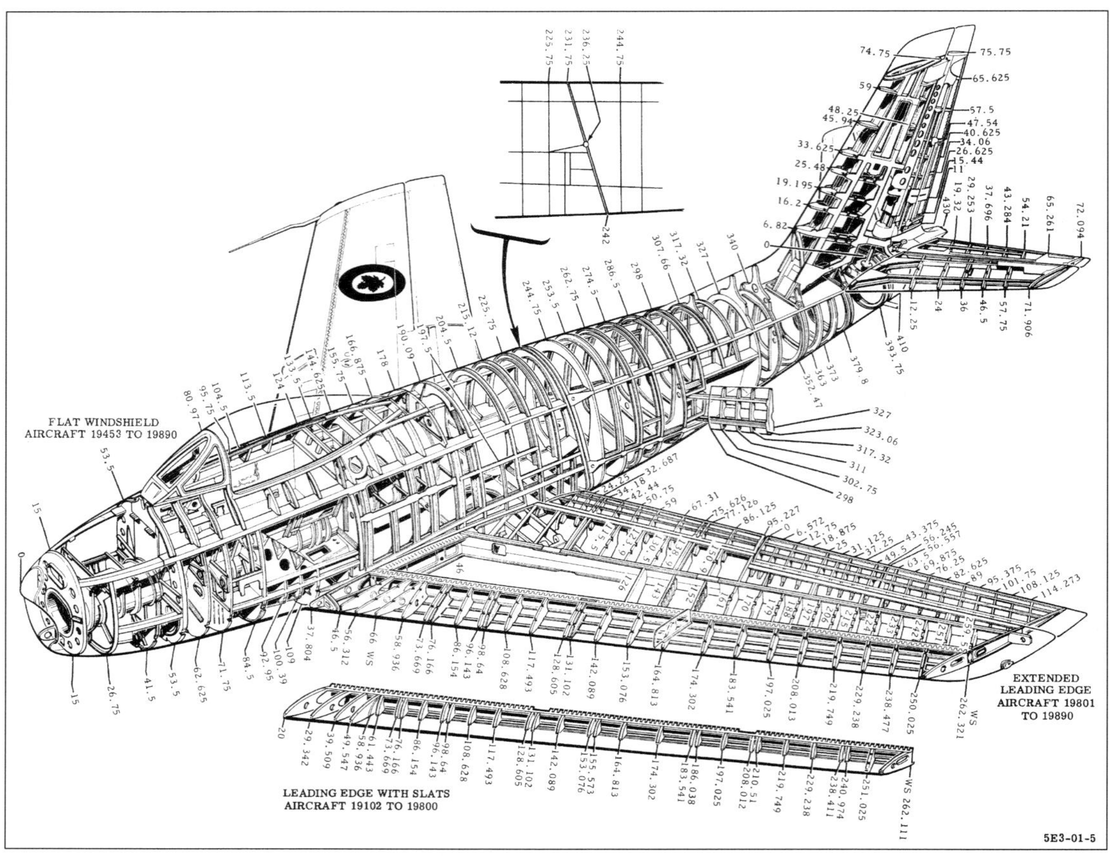

The internal structure of the Canadair Sabre is shown in this diagram. The earlier slatted leading edge is shown separately; it was factory fitted to all aircraft up to s/n 19800/XD779. (*Author's Collection*)

higher speed requirement. The radical redesign of the XP-86 evolved from one simple fact: even with a thinner aerofoil section, the straight-winged aircraft would still not be able to reach the 600mph stipulated.

On 1 November 1945, NAA received permission from Lt-Gen Laurence C. Craigie, Head of Air Force Research and Development, to proceed with the swept-wing XP-86, even though this would put the XP-86 programme back by six months compared to the Navy's XFJ-1. The Air Force agreed that the massive performance gain justified the wait. In the event, the XFJ-1 took to the air for the first time on 27 November 1946, the first XP-86 nearly a full year later.

On 20 December 1946, Letter Contract AC-16013 was approved for 33 production P-86As, though the 'P' ('pursuit') prefix was changed to the more recognisable 'F' for fighter on 1 June 1948; the XP-86 thus became the XF-86, and production P-86As were redesignated as F-86A aircraft. All were constructed at NAA's Inglewood, Los Angeles plant.

The XP-86 prototype, serial number 45-59597, was initially powered by a 4,000lb-thrust Chevrolet-built J35C-3 engine, but production versions would feature the higher-powered General Electric J47 engine. Company test pilot George Welch took the first XP-86 into the air for the first time on 1 October 1947, and this basically unchanged design then went into production as the F-86A.

North American went on to build further day-fighter versions of the Sabre – the F-86E and F, as well as a dedicated fighter bomber, the F-86H. Ultimate versions, F-86D and L, were powered by reheated versions of the General Electric J47 engine and equipped with radar and rocket armament for bomber interception.

THE CANADAIR SABRE

In early 1949, the Canadian government had begun talks with North American Aviation to procure a number of Sabres. With NAA working flat out to meet USAF contracts, however, it became obvious that the company would not be able to produce surplus aircraft for the Canadians. The answer was simple: Canada would obtain a licence to build Sabres itself, and for an initial payment of just US $1,000,000 licence production of the aircraft would be undertaken by the Canadair company of Montreal. The first instalment of the agreement was paid to NAA on 14 May

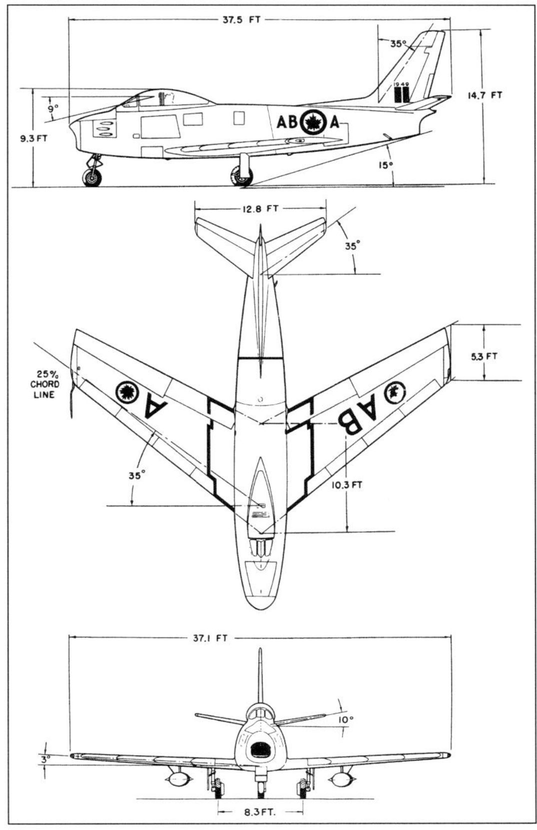

The Canadair Sabre general arrangement. (*Author's Collection*)

Gleaming in its polished metal finish, this is the first – and only – Canadair Sabre 1. The aircraft was basically a Canadair-built F-86A, assembled from US-supplied parts. Aircraft 191-010 was also unique in being the only Canadair Sabre without the 'all-flying' tail. (*Author's Collection*)

A J47-GE-13 engine in its transport stand. The starter/generator can be seen at the left, in the centre of the engine air intake; it was usually encased in a streamlined shroud. Further to the right, the large black casing encompasses the compressor section, and to the rear of this the combustion chamber 'cans' can be seen. Immediately to the right of these is the turbine and exhaust section. (*David B. Wildish*)

1949, and in August a contract was signed for Canadair to produce 100 F-86As.

Based at Cartierville, the Canadair complex comprised a number of separate factories. Plant 1 was where Sabre components were manufactured, and it was soon extended by 200,000 square feet to cope with increased Sabre production. The actual assembly of manufactured components was accomplished inside Plant 2, from where the first Canadian-built F-86 – officially designated the Canadair CL-13 Mk. 1 – was rolled out in August 1950. Though this aircraft was basically a Canadian-built F-86A, developments at North American had overtaken this design, and all subsequent Sabres to emerge from Canadair were based on the F-86E, with its 'all-flying' tailplane.

The prototype Sabre 1 flew for the first time on 8 August 1950 from Dorval, Canadair's chief test pilot Al Lilly taking the aircraft on a 30-minute check flight, followed by a further 15 minutes the next day. The first production Canadair Sabre, the CL-13 Mk. 2, flew on 31 January 1951, and this machine was based on the F-86E-1 with J47-GE-13 power. Sabre 2 production ran to 350 examples, initially ordered for the Royal Canadian Air Force (RCAF), and the first were delivered in April 1951.

Concurrent with Sabre 2 production, Canadair was planning a CL-13 to be fitted with the new indigenous 6,000lb-thrust Orenda 3 jet engine. The Orenda had earlier been tested in a modified F-86A airframe, and the engine had shown great promise. Canadair followed this up with a single modified Sabre 2 to serve as its test bed, and the redesignated CL-13 Mk. 3 took to the air from Cartierville on 25 September 1952 with Scotty McLean as pilot. Subsequent Orenda-powered Sabre 5 and 6 aircraft formed the backbone of RCAF fighter squadrons into the 1960s.

The Sabre which the RAF would receive was the Canadair CL-13 Mk. 4, an interim J47-engined aircraft roughly equivalent to the North American F-86E-10, and referred to in RAF parlance as the Sabre F. Mk. 4. This version did not benefit from the Orenda engine, but the proven design was available 'off the shelf' at a time when the Orenda-powered versions were still some way in the future. The prototype Sabre 4 flew on 28 August 1952.

CHAPTER ONE

BRITAIN'S INVOLVEMENT

Almost from inception, Great Britain had taken an interest in the new Sabre aircraft, and in the spring of 1948 test pilot Roland Beamont travelled to the United States to fly the machine. During his visit Beamont sampled a number of other American aircraft, and finally, on 21 May 1948, he was able to fly the XP-86. His mount on this occasion (the second prototype, 45-59598) was still fitted with the 4,000lb-thrust J35 engine, but Beamont nonetheless found the cockpit layout, performance and handling of the aircraft to be a revelation. His report concluded that not only could the Sabre break the sound barrier, it was also a pleasant and straightforward aircraft to fly.

The first production F-86A Sabres were delivered on 14 February 1949 to 1st Fighter Group at March Air Force Base (AFB) in California. During this period, 1 FG had played host to an RAF pilot, Flt Lt Paddy Harbison, who was on an exchange tour with the USAF. He was ideally placed to report back on the new wonder fighter, since it was logical that he would convert onto the new type. In fact, he was one of the first in the Group to fly the Sabre:

I first checked out in the F-86 on the 17 February 1949. At the time I was an exchange pilot with the USAF [equivalent rank – Captain], having been assigned to the 1st Fighter Group in July 1948 in the early days of the exchange programme. When I joined the Group it was equipped with the Lockheed F-80B, and it was the first USAF Fighter Group to be re-equipped with the F-86. Those were exciting days and indeed a story in its own right. I was thus fortunate to be the first serving RAF pilot to fly the F-86 and as a bonus to routinely exceed Mach 1. During my tour with 1st Fighter Group I served on both the 71st and 94th Fighter Squadrons.

Paddy Harbison returned to the UK in late July 1950 and found it hard to convince fellow RAF pilots just how good the F-86 was; they just could not believe that it could be far superior to the RAF's contemporary Gloster Meteor. It took the Korean War to highlight the Meteor's deficiencies, and also to bring the Sabre to the attention of RAF top brass. In early confrontations with Russian-built MiG-15s, the Meteors in Korea

These fiscal-year 47 F-86As were the first Sabres assigned to the 1st Fighter Group. Paddy Harbison took 47-627 (third in line) on his first solo on 17 February 1949. (*Bruce Robertson*)

(operated by an Australian squadron) came off second best, and they were quickly relegated to the role of fighter bomber. Clearly, to compete against the MiGs, Britain needed its own swept-wing fighter. But with no British design immediately available, provision of a foreign aircraft seemed to be the only interim option until Hunter and Swift fighters finally came off the production lines. The Sabre was the obvious choice.

On 13 September 1950, Chief of Air Staff (CAS) Sir John C. Slessor requested a briefing on the Avro Canada CF-100 all-weather fighter, which was in the running to fulfil the F. 4/48 requirement. In response, AM J.N. Boothman at the Ministry of Defence appraised Slessor of the entire aircraft-production set-up in Canada, including Canada's licence production of the Sabre, and this marked the first official mention of the type as a candidate for RAF service. Slessor, however, was reluctant to accept any form of 'stopgap' fighter and decided to wait for the long-term (British) alternative, even though there was none.

Despite this, the aircraft favoured to meet the shortfall was still the F-86 Sabre, and, although he had opposed procurement of the aircraft, in early October 1950 Sir John Slessor left for a tour of production plants in North America to see what was on offer. On 11 October he arrived at the Canadair factory to see the licence-production facility. Slessor was impressed by what he found at Cartierville: ample floor space, modern machines and vast resources of manpower left him with the abiding impression that Canadair could deal with the RAF's fighter shortfall faster than any factory in the UK. To quote Slessor's report: 'Their F-86 looks like being far the earliest answer to our most unpleasant problem.' However, he urged that Fighter Command take the F-86E (Sabre 2 with American J47 engine) rather than the Orenda-powered version because of the expected late delivery of Orenda power plants.

First Sabre Trials in the UK

Even prior to Slessor's visit to Canada, Britain had already been assigned two Sabres, and the impressions gained from these machines had a direct input into subsequent procurement of F-86s for the RAF. With the signing of the Air Standardisation Coordination Committee Combined Test Project Agreement on 14 September 1950, an initial assessment of two loaned USAF F-86As was begun. These aircraft, F-86A-5 s/n 49-1279 and 49-1296, were delivered to the Central Fighter Establishment (CFE) at West Raynham on 14 October 1950 and put through evaluation by service crews. Under the terms of the Project Agreement, no commercial test pilots were allowed to fly the Sabres, and so the RAF personnel assigned to fly the aircraft often had to field highly technical questions from their civilian counterparts.

Fresh from his attachment to 1st Fighter Group in America, Paddy Harbison returned to Great Britain in July 1950 and was posted straight to CFE at West Raynham. He later remarked: 'I was unaware then that the RAF was to be loaned two F-86As for trial purposes – hence my assignment there. In due course the aircraft arrived at Burtonwood and I picked up the first one – '279 – on the 14 October 1950 and flew it to West Raynham.'

CFE testing involved a full tactical trial of the aircraft, the test being divided into three main areas: general handling and performance, engine handling, and tactical handling. In the final phase, the two aircraft were flown in high-, medium- and low-level mock combat against Gloster Meteor fighters and B-29 bombers. Against the Meteor, the F-86A was found to be superior in roll, climb, dive and straight-line speed. CFE's conclusion was simple: the F-86A was superior in performance to any British fighter.

For the pilot, the Sabre's cockpit was extremely comfortable and its canopy gave an almost unobstructed view outside. When F-86A 49-1279 was tested at Boscombe Down, however, many pilots felt that the instrumentation was not laid out in a logical fashion. In truth, the Sabre represented a massive leap forward from contemporary RAF fighters. (*Bruce Robertson*)

The reservation concerned the machine-gun armament: the RAF favoured 20mm cannons on its day fighters.

On 1 March 1951, with CFE testing complete, both F-86As were transferred to the Aeroplane and Armament Experimental Establishment (A&AEE) at Boscombe Down in Wiltshire, where 49-1296 was briefly assigned to a weapon-test role while '1279 took part in instrument-error measurements and engine-thrust experiments. Both were then used in handling trials, which were concluded in July. The A&AEE generally agreed with the earlier CFE findings, but concluded that the ailerons lacked feel and were unduly sensitive at low speeds. Cockpit layout also came in for criticism, being thought of as confused when compared to British standards.

On 23 April 1951, 49-1296 was transferred to the Royal Aircraft Establishment at Farnborough and was put straight into research work, some of the first projects including an investigation of the aircraft's lateral stability and rudder-trim-tab effectiveness. Another early project involved a profile-drag analysis along with Supermarine E. 41/46 and Hawker E. 38/46 experimental types. Whilst at Farnborough, 49-1296 was lost in a crash on 14 August 1952 following an elevator runaway. The pilot, Flt Lt 'Taffy' Ecclestone, ejected safely.

To continue Farnborough's testing schedule, 49-1279 was transferred to RAE on 21 October, though, after a brief 10-minute flight on the day of its arrival, it was grounded for an aileron-trim problem until 15 January the following year. However, by this point other unserviceabilities had cropped up, and when spare parts arrived on 12 February 1953 it was discovered that these were incorrect. Finally, at the end of the month all spares were in place, and following installation the aircraft flew a 35-minute sortie on 6 March. Three days later, 45 minutes into a sortie the aircraft experienced hydraulic-system failure and, though recovered safely to Farnborough, 49-1279 was grounded until 17 June. During June and July of 1953 the F-86A managed to accomplish thirteen days of flying for a total of thirteen flying hours.

On 18 July 1953, 49-1279 was grounded for a major inspection, and the aircraft did not fly again until 10 February 1954. The aircraft then took part in a project to investigate modifications to improve the high Mach-number characteristics of the F-86A. The aircraft's slats were fixed in the retracted position and all gaps were sealed prior to addition of a number of aerodynamic modifications. First to be tested were vortex generators. Arranged at 35 per cent wing chord, the generators were found to reduce wing drop above M = 0.92 and increased the aircraft's longitudinal stability by about 0.13 in the M = 0.9 to 0.94 speed range. Drag was negligible for this installation.

Next the RAE team experimented with wing fences. These were five inches high and extended from 18 per cent chord on the lower wing surface, around the leading edge, to 63 per cent chord on the top surface. They were placed at 36 per cent, 53 per cent and 71 per cent of span on each wing and were found to delay nose-up pitching in the M = 0.88 to 0.94 range. They did, however, cause an unspecified reduction in performance.

To complete this test, '1279 was fitted with a simple wing leading-edge extension. This was accomplished by locking the outer two segments of the leading-edge slats in the two-thirds extended position. The remaining inner two segments were locked shut and this arrangement was found to alleviate nose-up pitch at M = 0.80 but was found to be ineffective by the time the aircraft had reached M = 0.92. It is interesting to note that the

RAF Sabre F. 4 cockpit. Items are: 1 – undercarriage selector, 2 – machmeter, 3 – altimeter, 4 – undercarriage emergency ground-lock override, 5 – parking brake, 6 – radio compass indicator, 7 – fuel filter de-icer button, 8 – fuel filter de-icer warning light, 9 – accelerometer, 10 – airspeed indicator, 11 – inverter failure warning light, 12 – hydraulic pressure gauge, 13 – inverter failure warning light, 14 – hydraulic pressure gauge selector, 15 – inverter failure warning light, 16 – control surface alternate system 'on' warning light, 17 – A4 gunsight, 18 – oil pressure gauge, 19 – take-off trim indicator, 20 – jet pipe temperature gauge, 21 – artificial horizon, 22 – fuel pressure gauge, 23 – fire warning lights, 24 – standby compass, 25 – fire warning system test push-button, 26 – tachometer, 27 – fuel flowmeter, 28 – cockpit pressure altimeter, 29 – rudder pedal adjuster release, 30 – rudder pedal indicator, 31– fuel contents gauge, 32 – vertical speed indicator, 33 – clock, 34 – loadmeter, 35 – generator failure warning light, 36 – voltmeter. (*Author's Collection*)

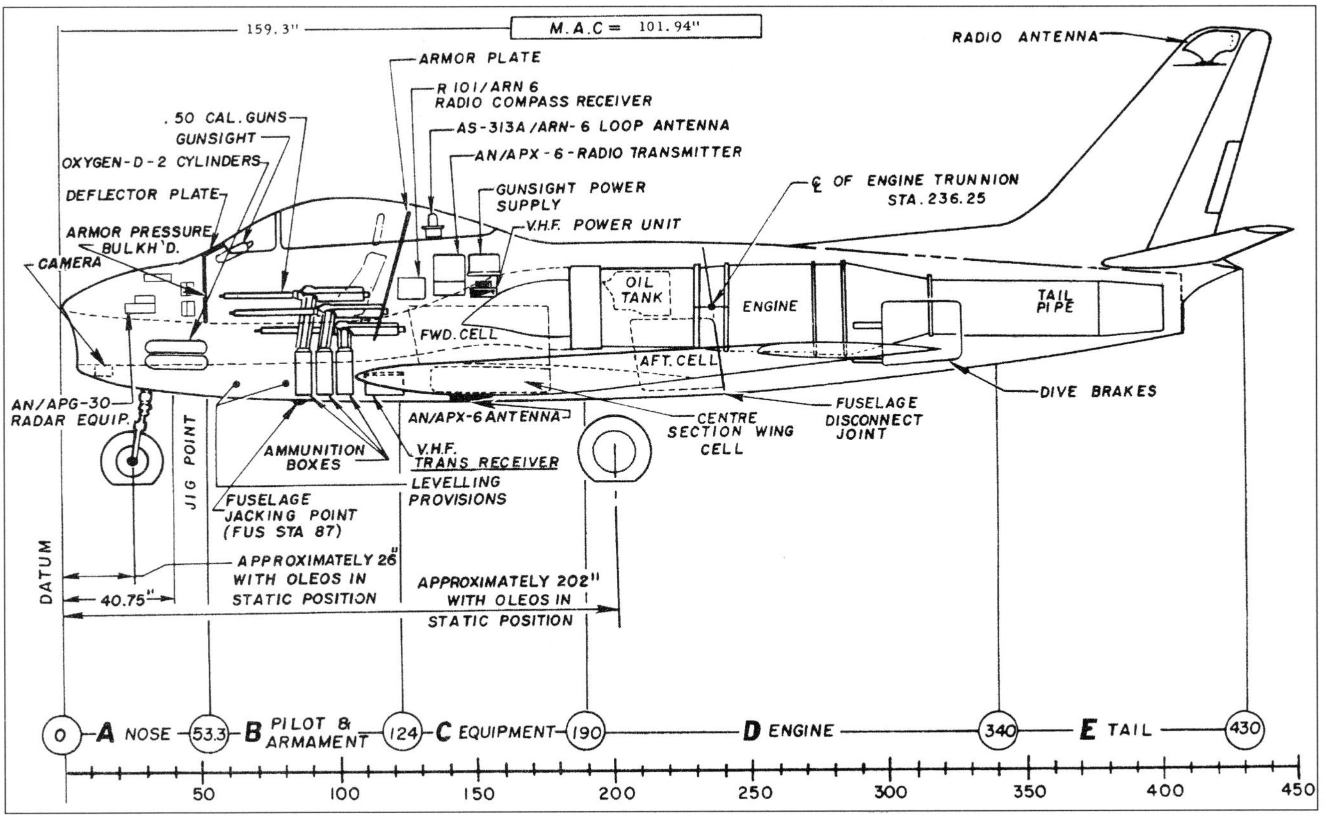

Sabre F. 4 weight and balance data sheet. (*Author's Collection*)

three areas under investigation – vortex generators, wing fences and extended-wing leading edges – were all items that North American was trialling back in California.

Given the previous delays in the test programme, on 15 May 1953 a one-year extension to the loan agreement had been granted. Further to this, in March 1954 a further extension request was made to Washington and this was approved by Brig-Gen B.K. Holloway, Deputy Director of Requirements, to terminate 'on or before 14 November 1954'. With testing complete, 49-1279 was duly ferried out to 7559th Maintenance Group at Burtonwood on 11 November 1954 for return to the USAF.

CHAPTER TWO

THE ROCKY ROAD TO PROCUREMENT

Once the Sabre had been selected as the RAF's 'stopgap' fighter, there remained a considerable amount of diplomatic wrangling to actually procure the aircraft. It was hoped that US military aid would assist in this process, and on 4 October 1950 the British Joint Services Mission (BJSM) in Washington was informed of the United States' attitude to future military aid to Europe. The Americans expected the NATO nations of Europe to assume full responsibility for production of fighter aircraft, devoting any excess production to tactical air forces. Thus, US aid under the provisions of the Mutual Defense Assistance Program (MDAP) and Military Assistance Program (MAP) would be in the form of tactical aircraft. This policy would initially be a thorn in the side of those wanting to procure Sabres for the RAF's fighter squadrons, since the F-86 was not a 'tactical' aircraft in the true sense.

By 18 October 1950, the Chief of Air Staff had already reached a precise figure for how many Sabres he wanted for Fighter Command, despite the US declaration of 4 October: 200 aircraft would support 6 squadrons of 22 aircraft each by the end of 1951, plus a further 180 Sabres as a three-month war reserve, giving a total of 380 aircraft for this 'stopgap' fighter force. While conceding that such an arrangement was fraught with disadvantages, Chief of Air Staff Sir John Slessor stated that, 'None of them compare with the disadvantages inherent in the fact that on present form it will be at least two years before we have a single squadron in the RAF equipped with a type that is not outclassed by the MiG-15.'

On 21 October Slessor contacted the Canadian and US governments to confirm that Great Britain was in the market for 300 Sabres (strangely at odds with the 380 calculated three days earlier) and that delivery would need to be made as soon as possible. Further, on 23 October the ministry cabled Washington to ask for a clarification of the term 'tactical aircraft' in the Americans' 4 October declaration. The response from Washington on the 28th was simple: the term applied to fighter bomber, light bomber and tactical reconnaissance fighter aircraft. Thus, if Sabres were to be supplied to the RAF under MDAP rules, they could not be used as fighters by Fighter Command.

At a meeting of the Western European Air Advisory Committee on 26 October, the Canadian representative disclosed that Canadair Sabres could be made available, and supplied under the US Mutual Defense Assistance Program. He also stressed that as such they could only be used in a tactical role. Thus, it seems incredible that on 30 October 1950 an application for Sabres to equip RAF fighter squadrons was made to MDAP. The application comprised three possible options for the allocation of aircraft:

One of the last Sabres delivered to the RAF, XB995 is one of those that received the '6–3' wing at the factory. It was ferried across the Atlantic on Bechers Brook 10 in December 1953 and was then assigned to 4 Sqn in 2 TAF. (*Check Collison via Larry Milberry*)

Equipment to be supplied from 1951 Funds	Option 1	Option 2	Option 3
To equip operational forces by 1 January 1952 (22 aircraft per sqn)	132	132	154
To equip training units by 1 January 1952	14	20	16
3 months' wastage at war rates	103	162	134
2 years' wastage at peacetime rates (repair/write-off)	16/35	18/70	20/78
Total	300	402	402

Inevitably, this request was declined the next day, on the grounds that it contravened the US policy that interceptor fighters should not be supplied under MDAP to Europe. The UK government had undoubtedly expected this response, for on the day that the MDAP's refusal arrived Slessor declared that if purchased outright (rather than loaned under MDAP), Britain could use the Sabres for whatever purposes it wanted. He already knew that Canadair could sell Sabres at US $323,000 per aircraft and North American for US $200,000 each. Slessor therefore suggested that 300 Sabres be ordered from North American, presumably the F-86E version.

The US Under Secretary of the Air Force, John McCone, immediately responded, saying that Sabres for the RAF should be manufactured at Canadair since North American was simply too busy to spare any production for export. McCone stated that Canadair could produce 84 RAF Sabres in the last half of 1951 followed by 246 in the first half of 1952 and a final 72 by the end of the year – a total of 402. He again stressed that these aircraft would have to be

Huddled together in the hangar at Goose Bay, these Sabres are part of Bechers Brook 5 in May 1953. The aircraft at the left is XB599, which was initially allotted to 71 Sqn, but was damaged in a heavy landing at Benson on 23 October 1953 while being ferried by a 147 Sqn pilot. (*Check Collison via Larry Milberry*)

purchased outright because of MDAP limitations on fighter export. On 17 November McCone suggested that even if the British did buy the aircraft outright, many components included in the Canadian-built Sabres could be supplied under US aid, and would therefore make the aircraft cheaper. This 'government-furnished equipment' (GFE) included machine guns and radios.

The Canadian Chief of Air Staff, AM W.A. Curtis, informed Slessor on 5 December that the US government had been in contact with a view to supplying the GFE for 384 RAF Sabres in the 1951 and 1952 time frame. Clearly, the United States government wanted to help as much as it could, and so Slessor's remarks to the BJSM in Washington on 27 November 1950 therefore seem churlish: 'It hardly seems wise that the US should confine themselves under MDAP to supply of fighter-bombers which we and even France can produce and withhold high-performance interceptors which at present we can not.'

The case seems to have stood there until 12 December, when the personal secretary to John Slessor suggested in a letter to Canada's AM Mills that if Sabres were procured for re-equipment of overseas (tactical) RAF squadrons, the case for supply under MDAP might be strengthened. Despite some reservations, things moved quickly, and on 21 December Col Sam Agee of the US Military Aid Advisory Group (MAAG) in London met with Mr G.S. Whittuck, UK Director General of Equipment. Agee brought good news: MDAP would indeed accept a bid, this time for 392 Canadian-built Sabres. They would be for use in overseas RAF squadrons as top cover for Vampire and Venom fighter bombers. Not strictly tactical, but agreement

This line-up of Sabres awaits the start of Bechers Brook 8 at St Hubert, Canada in September 1953. Many of these aircraft, which have '6–3' wings, were reallocated serial numbers once in the UK: for instance, XB965, second in line, became XB941 in RAF service. (*Check Collison via Larry Milberry*)

had been reached. Six squadrons could be equipped, but the bid had to be submitted by 22 December – the very next day.

Fortunately, the bid was placed on time, and late on 22 December Gen Hoyt Vandenburg advised the Joint Services Mission in Washington that MDAP had been instructed to accept the RAF's bid for US-funded Canadair Sabres. The only proviso was that delivery dates could not be guaranteed. Further bugs would need to be ironed out – indeed it was not until 2 October 1951 that the Canadian cabinet approved the deal – but crucially the RAF would after all get its Sabres. Funds for 395 Canadair Sabres (rather than 392) were cleared by the US Budgetary Committee in February 1952, though after further negotiations it was decided that the total acquired initially would be 370. All except for three would be Sabre 4 aircraft, these being J47-engined F-86E-equivalent models.

FIGHTER COMMAND GETS ITS SABRES

Meanwhile, efforts were being made also to provide Sabres for Fighter Command. During early November 1952, Col Abbott of the US MAAG in the UK contacted the Air Ministry to advise that MDAP was prepared to offer a further sixty Sabres to the RAF. These aircraft, Canadair Sabre 4s, had initially been allotted to the USAF but were now surplus to requirements. Crucially, Abbott stated that the aircraft could be used by Fighter Command, and agreed that a few of the 'tactical' fighters could also be used to make up numbers and form three squadrons with twenty-two aircraft each. These would be Meteor squadrons that would re-equip with Sabres. Provisional suggestions made to the Chief of Air Staff on 14 November put forward that the first squadron could re-equip from June 1953, with the remaining pair gaining Sabres from September. The offer was formally accepted on 19 November.

After further negotiation, by mid-1953 the RAF had laid plans for its Sabre fleet: two squadrons of Fighter Command Sabres, rather than three, would come into service during September 1953 and be phased out in March 1955. On 30 December Sir Basil Embry, C-in-C of Fighter Command, suggested that the two squadrons be based at Waterbeach, where they would re-equip 56 and 63 Sqns. In practice, the two units that actually received these aircraft were 66 and 92 Sqns at Linton-on-Ouse.

Released from USAF use, the Sabres were handed over from 5 June 1953 under MDAP Project 3F-420. The Fighter Command Sabres differed somewhat from the 'Germany' aircraft: the original AN/APX-6 radar identification unit was replaced by a British-sourced IFF Mk. 3 GR item, and on 9 February 1953 it was agreed that the AN/ARN-6 radio-compass set would be accompanied by an indigenous Rebecca Mk. 7 box.

FURTHER COMPLICATIONS

Even before delivery of Sabres to the RAF had begun, it was realised that the rate of acceptance would fall short of expectations. This problem was exacerbated on 15 January 1953 when AVM Miller of the Royal Canadian Air Force asked whether a number of Sabres from the RAF order could be loaned to RCAF squadrons in Europe due to a predicted deficit. Miller stated that with 3 Wg undergoing conversion to the Sabre 5, the RCAF would only have fourteen Sabres remaining to begin equipping 4 Wg. Therefore a loan of sixty RAF Sabre 4s was proposed, to be available for the period March 1953 to March 1954. After the latter date, Canadair production would have caught up with RCAF requirements, and the loaned aircraft would be returned to the RAF. Despite the fact that it would disrupt re-equipment of the RAF squadrons, this loan was agreed.

During September 1953, the RCAF stated that the sixty loaned Sabres would be returned to the

This parade at RAF Abingdon on 2 January 1953 marked the ceremonial handover of the first eight Sabres for the RAF, which had arrived on Bechers Brook 1. The aircraft on that mission had actually arrived at Abingdon on 22 December 1952, the intervening period giving ground crews the opportunity to paint the individual OFU/FTU code letters on most aircraft. In fact the parade did not feature all of the eight Sabres on BB1: missing are XB535 and XB548 – their places taken by Sabre F. 2s XB530/A and XB531/B. The latter had been ferried to the UK earlier in 1952 and had formed part of an initial trio of aircraft at North Luffenham, which began RAF training on the type. (*via Mike Fox*)

One of the sixty Sabre 4s seconded to the Royal Canadian Air Force, 19702 (here in 444 Sqn, RCAF colours) was eventually transferred to the RAF as XB864. It saw no squadron service, being stored at 33 MU Lyneham for most of its life before being transferred to the Yugoslavian Air Force. (*Larry Milberry*)

RAF in the November/December 1953 period, and true to their word all were struck off temporary RCAF charge on 1 December. Following overhaul with Airwork at Speke, these machines – still bearing their RCAF serial numbers – were ferried by 147 Sqn pilots to Kemble for onward assignment to the RAF units.

Preparing for Service

The next major step was to decide how to get the Sabres to the UK. Canada's AM Curtis favoured flying them across rather than shipping by sea; the RCAF was already in the process of ferrying large numbers of its Sabres to Europe using the same method. To resolve the problem the Air Ministry convened a meeting on 13 March 1952, chaired by Wg Cdr R.K. Cassells. Although delivery by aircraft carrier and cargo ship was discussed, the groundswell of opinion seemed to back the air-ferry option. Final decision was deferred until further information had been gathered. This meeting also drew up an initial delivery timetable, stating that the first ten Sabres would be passed to the RAF in December 1952. Completing the order, 20 would follow in January 1953, 30 per month from February to April, 40 per month in May and June, 50 per month from July through to September and a further 20 in October. The remaining 25 aircraft, for a total (erroneously calculated) of 375, would be delivered after October 1953, the dates to be decided. In November 1952 the definitive total – 370 aircraft – was arrived at and the tentative delivery schedule arranged so that the first three Sabres would arrive in September 1952 with completion of the delivery in October 1953.

The final decision to air-ferry the Sabres was made on 10 July 1952 and passed to the embassy in Washington. The whole ferry operation was given the name 'Bechers Brook' on 22 October 1952, in honour of a famous jump on the Aintree racecourse. It should be noted that although the RAF would eventually receive 430 Sabres, the loan of 60 aircraft to the RCAF meant that only 370 would need to be ferried across the Atlantic by the RAF. The sixty 'Canadian' Sabre 4s were independently ferried over by RCAF pilots.

In order to train the ferry crews, on 12 August 1952 the RCAF agreed to convert three experienced RAF jet pilots onto the Sabre. The three pilots would begin training at No. 1 Operational Training Unit (OTU) at

An F-86F of 3595th Combat Crew Training Wing, Nellis AFB. The aircraft carries the Crew Training Air Force badge on its vertical tail. This actual aircraft was flown by Trevor Egginton (later of 67 Sqn) while he was at Nellis with Course 53-E. (*via Mike Fox*)

Chatham, New Brunswick prior to 30 August. Additionally, it was agreed that three Canadair Sabre 2s would be allotted to the RAF in the interim to commence familiarisation. The three pilots chosen were all from 1 Overseas Ferry Unit, and comprised Sqn Ldr T. Stevenson, AFC and Flt Lts Deffee and Edwards. This initial cadre of pilots departed for training with 1 OTU during August, and upon completion of their training took the three RAF Sabre 2s and ferried them to the UK. This trio of Sabres would initially be based at RAF North Luffenham, a Canadian base near Lincoln, where six further RAF pilots would receive conversion training. Ground crews were also slated for conversion training and familiarisation at North Luffenham.

The three Sabre Mk. 2s (designated Sabre F. Mk. 2 in RAF parlance from May 1953) left St Hubert in Canada on 28 September 1952 as part of an RCAF ferry flight to Gros Tenquin in France. The trio arrived at Prestwick on 4 October and flew into North Luffenham on 10 October. The aircraft still bore their RCAF serial numbers on arrival, but were allotted RAF serials XB530, XB531 and XB532. The Sabres remained at North Luffenham until 4 December, when training of RAF ferry pilots began with 1 OFU at RAF Abingdon.

No. 1 OFU began training Sabre ferry crews utilising only experienced jet pilots. The conversion course lasted two weeks, and 10 flying hours were given in the Sabre as well as a ground-school element. Crews then departed for Canada, where ground training and fifteen more hours of Sabre flying were logged as well as a one-week survival course. To cater for the impending ferry operation, sixty pilots were selected from Fighter Command and 2 TAF to join ‘Bechers Brook’. All were required to have more than 400 hours of jet experience.

In Canada, the new Sabres were test-flown and ferried to Bagotville by RAF pilots attached to the Canadian Central Experimental and Proving Establishment. Once at Bagotville, maintenance was carried out and the aircraft were handed over to 1 OFU and readied for the ferry flight to the UK. Ideally, every Sabre was given five hours of 'shakedown' flying prior to being allotted for the ferry mission. About ten days prior to each ferry mission the small party of RAF personnel at Bagotville was augmented by two airborne servicing teams, which were flown in from the United Kingdom aboard Hastings aircraft. These teams accompanied the fighters along the ferry route and provided technical assistance to cover unserviceabilities. One team deployed ahead of the fighter stream on each leg of the mission while the second brought up the rear; the teams comprised around 40 personnel to support Sabre operations plus a further dozen or so looking after the two Hastings transports. This arrangement was set up to cater for a standard thirty-aircraft ferry mission, but would be scaled down for smaller deployments.

The first ferry mission, code-named Bechers Brook 1, began on 9 December 1953, starting at St Hubert, Quebec. It followed the standard ferry route for all Bechers Brook missions, via Bagotville, Goose Bay, Bluie West 1, Keflavik and Prestwick. Nine Sabres were flown across on BB 1, but the full complement of airborne servicing teams accompanied the move to provide experience for all those involved. Unfortunately only eight aircraft arrived safely: one pilot was killed when XB534 crashed on approach to Prestwick. The remaining Sabres were ceremonially handed over to the RAF at Abingdon on 2 January 1953. The eight aircraft delivered on this mission were taken on charge by 1 OFU.

Organisational changes subsequently led to the formation of 1 (Long Range) Ferry Unit and, later, 147 Sqn; both of these units were tasked with ferrying Sabres for the RAF. On Bechers Brook 4 in March 1953, a 'double shuttle' technique was tried for the first time, using thirty-two pilots to ferry sixty-four Sabres. As soon as the first thirty-two Sabres arrived at the first staging post, a Hastings would immediately gather up all the ferry crews and return them to ferry the remaining aircraft. This mission proved a great success and, despite ensuing unserviceabilities, managed to deliver sixty Sabres in just four days. The Bechers Brook missions ended in May 1954, by which time around 372 Sabres had been safely ferried across the Atlantic.

Training the Squadrons

To train RAF pilots in the numbers required to equip numerous squadrons of Sabres, planners now looked at the training set-up. Initially, the problem was solved by sending a core of up to a hundred pilots to the United States for training there. After basic training in the UK, four courses of roughly twenty-five pilots each departed England during 1952 and went through the whole USAF flying-training system. The first courses were completed on the F-84 Thunderjet, but the last two culminated on the F-86F Sabre. These courses passed out as Classes 53-C, D, E and F during 1953. Though courses 53-E and 53-F did receive a very thorough grounding on the Sabre, it was clear that for the RAF a more convenient solution was required.

A draft plan dated 23 March 1953 had 147 Sqn at Abingdon continuing to train pilots until June of that year, when conversion would be transferred to Wildenrath in Germany. With training of the Germany-based units planned for completion in September/October 1953, training would then revert to the UK, where an Operational Conversion Unit (OCU) at Chivenor in Devon (tentatively set to be 229 OCU) would complete all further RAF Sabre pilot training. The draft plan was agreed in August 1953 and revised further on 29 January 1954 to account for the longer-than-expected time required to train all crews; a new date for the move to Chivenor was set at April 1954. In accordance with these plans, the Sabre

Four pilots from Class 53-F pose with their instructor at Webb AFB in Texas. These courses were a mix of nationalities, though most were USAF personnel. L–R: Jerry Welch, Roger Mansfield, Maj Croker (instructor), Roy Davey, Ed Cavanaugh. Both Mansfield and Davey were RAF pilots and both went on to fly the Sabre with 112 Sqn. (*Roger Mansfield*)

Conversion Unit (SCU – later Sabre Conversion Flight/SCF) was established at RAF Wildenrath, Germany in March 1953, and continued training RAF Sabre pilots until June 1954, when it finally handed over the role to 229 OCU at RAF Chivenor.

Camouflage Trials

Sabres for the RAF arrived from Canada in natural metal finish, but, in preparation for their deployment to Germany with 2nd Tactical Air Force (2 TAF), during January 1953 a test programme was set up to investigate what, if any, loss in performance would result from application of a camouflage scheme. Instigated as Central Fighter Establishment (CFE) Trial 163, the test utilised two Sabres, XB538 and XB543, both of which were 147 Sqn machines.

Due to a shortage of spares and ground equipment, the CFE trial was undertaken at Abingdon, beginning on 16 January. Three pilots took part in these trials: Flt Lts B.J. Spragg and Rex Knight plus Maj J. Saunders, a USAF officer on exchange with CFE. Initially, both Sabres were flown in natural metal finish without drop tanks so that

In January 1953, Central Fighter Establishment began a series of trials to ascertain whether camouflage paint would degrade the Sabre's performance. Two natural metal-finished 147 Sqn Sabres were used for the test, and at the beginning of February one of the machines, XB543, was painted in camouflage to provide a comparison. As the application of paint proved to have little effect on performance, the decision was made to paint all RAF Sabres thus; the colour scheme also later became standard on Royal Canadian Air Force Sabres. Note that XB543 (foreground) still retains its individual code letter, 'G', forward of the roundel. (*Bruce Robertson*)

baseline performance measurements could be noted. This practice was started on the first day of the test, with readings being taken for airspeed, climb rate, engine fuel flow, jet-pipe temperature and outside air temperature for a range of altitudes.

XB543 was then painted in DTD 827 camouflage finish by a contractors' working party at the end of January, and a new flight-test programme began on 18 February. During that day, XB543 performed the same mission profiles as for the earlier sorties. A formation climb with the natural metal-finished XB538 was also undertaken. During the whole test programme, eleven sorties were carried out, totalling 8 hours 25 minutes for the two aircraft.

In the climb-comparison test, it was shown that the natural-metal aircraft was able to keep formation using less power and with a lower jet-pipe temperature. However, as no climb comparison had been accomplished prior to application of camouflage on XB543, these results could not be easily quantified. Although a slight degradation was seen in most areas following paint application (notably a 2–3kt increase in stalling speed), there was also a slight increase in indicated speed at 97 per cent power. This was possibly due to the gloss paint slightly smoothing out surface imperfections on the airframe. However, the report concluded that no significant effect was seen after application of camouflage, and the go-ahead was given for painting RAF Sabres.

THE COLOUR SCHEME

Sabres for RAF-squadron use were camouflaged at the Maintenance Unit (MU) before allocation and, once the camouflage scheme had been finalised for RAF Sabres, painting was performed at Kemble and Lyneham by Air Service Training. For RAF

Germany machines, this consisted of gloss dark-green 641 and dark sea-grey 638 uppers, with cerulean (PRU) blue 636 undersides. The upper-surface camouflage demarcation was located so that the underside blue came up to the bottom of the machine-gun blast panel. On Sabres which were to be based in the UK, the same upper-side colours were used, but this time the undersides were painted silver. In addition, the demarcation line was much lower, running forward from the wing root/fuselage junction. This scheme variation was approved on 11 August 1953, and the final schemes for 2 TAF and Fighter Command Sabres, contained in Drawings F-86/1000 and 1007 respectively, were agreed on 10 December. However, a few Sabres assigned to the Sabre Conversion Unit at Wildenrath and to test duties retained their natural metal finish. It is interesting to note that in January 1954 the Canadian government asked if it would be possible to use the same colour scheme on RCAF Sabres; thus the Canadian Sabres in Europe along with those on the production line were finished in the 2 TAF scheme.

Turning to serials and service markings, the RAF Sabres carried 30in-diameter Type D roundels on fuselage and upper wing surfaces, with 18in roundels below the wings. Serial numbers were painted black, and were 8in in height on the fuselage and 16in high under the wings. The starboard (right) wing serial was angled along the mid-chord line and read from the rear, while the port (left) wing serial read from the front. The tricoloured fin flash was 24in high, each coloured band being 6in wide. In standard RAF practice, the red band always faced the front of the aircraft.

Serial Number Allocations

RAF Sabres were originally allocated serial numbers in the ranges XB530 to XB532 (three Sabre F. Mk. 2s), XB533 to XB550, XB575 to XB603, XB608 to XB646, XB664 to XB713, XB726 to XB769, XB790 to XB839, XB856 to XB905, XB941 to XB990 and XD102 to XD138 – all Sabre F. Mk. 4s, for a total of 370 aircraft. The serial number XB551 was later allocated to a further Sabre, which was allotted to Hawker at Dunsfold, presumably as a chase aircraft for air tests of other RAF Sabres.

With the increase to 430 aircraft, serial numbers XD706 to XD736 and XD753 to XD781 were allocated for the additional 60 Fighter Command aircraft. To differentiate between the Fighter Command aircraft and those for 2 TAF, the earlier allocation of aircraft in the XD102 to XD138 range were given 'XB' serial numbers, filling in the gaps from XB647 to XB650, XB770 to XB775, XB851 to XB855 and XB978 to XB999. To confuse things further, the aircraft initially given serials XB901 to XB905 were redesignated as XB912 to XB916, and XB941 to XB990 became XB917 to XB961 and XB973 to XB977. The situation became more confusing because the original serial numbers had been painted on the aircraft in Canada; thus, for example, on Bechers Brook 9, aircraft XD119 and XD120 were ferried across; they were repainted correctly as XB980 and XB981 respectively, when they arrived at 33 MU Lyneham.

The idea that XD-serialled Sabres should only be assigned to Fighter Command units lasted until it was realised that the UK-based units were using up aircraft at a higher rate than expected. By 23 July 1954, only two XD-serialled Sabres remained in reserve at the Maintenance Units, and on that day the Air Ministry approved the issue of XB-serialled aircraft to Fighter Command squadrons. Because of the shortage of Fighter Command Sabres, no XD-serialled aircraft were ever issued to 2 TAF.

One of four 'plain Jane' RAF Sabres placed on static display at Odiham for the Queen's Coronation Review, XB582 had been issued to 3 Sqn just prior to the display. It was flown from storage at Kemble to Odiham at the beginning of July and then rejoined the squadron when the Sabre units returned to Germany after the review. (*A.J. Jackson collection*)

THE SABRES ARRIVE WITH THE SQUADRONS

The RAF's 2nd Tactical Air Force began life as the organisation that was tasked with flying tactical missions over Europe until the close of the Second World War. On 15 July 1945, with the cessation of hostilities in Europe, 2 TAF was disbanded and aircraft and personnel were absorbed into the British Air Forces of Occupation (BAFO). The first major operation for BAFO was in controlling aircraft on the 1948/9 Berlin Airlift, and further exercises with friendly nations in Europe paved the way for integration into the NATO force. USAF Gen Lauris Norstad was subsequently tasked with forming these Allied air forces into a single integrated force, and he decided to split the Rhine area into two halves – north and south – with an Allied Tactical Air Force (ATAF) responsible for each. In the north, 2 ATAF, comprising RAF, Belgian and Dutch units, was responsible for an area running from the Belgian border in the west to the West German border with East Germany in the east. The southern area was controlled by 4 ATAF, and this sector comprised many of the USAF and Canadian units in Europe.

On 1 September 1951, BAFO was renamed 2nd Tactical Air Force and, rather confusingly, placed under 2 ATAF command. AM Sir Robert Foster, KCB, CBE, DFC was appointed as the first Commander-in-Chief of 2 TAF. It is important to stress that 2 TAF was the RAF component of 2 ATAF, and that in 1954 AM Sir Harry Broadhurst, KBE, CB, DSO, DFC, AFC took over control of both 2 TAF and 2 ATAF.

The 2 TAF squadrons began to re-equip with Sabres as they arrived off the Bechers Brook ferry missions. The Wildenrath-based 67 Sqn became the first RAF Sabre squadron, flying its first mission in mid-May 1953. The next to begin operating the Sabre was 3 Sqn, and the final 2 TAF Sabre unit, 93 Sqn, received its first Sabres in March 1954. With the arrival of the second MDAP batch of Sabres, the UK-based squadrons were formed in December 1953 (66 Sqn, converting from Meteor F. 8s at RAF Linton-on-Ouse) and February 1954 (92 Sqn, also at Linton). These squadrons are detailed in the following chapters.

CHAPTER THREE

RAF SABRE PILOTS IN KOREA

The first RAF pilot to see combat on Sabres in Korea was Flt Lt Stephen Walter 'Dan' Daniel, DSO, DFC. He had joined 1st Fighter Group in California during July 1950 as an exchange officer and was then assigned to 71st Fighter Squadron. Daniel had three transition flights in the T-33 jet trainer before performing his first mission in one of the unit's F-86A Sabres.

During January 1951, Flt Lt Daniel was reassigned to 4th Fighter Wing in Korea and joined 334th Fighter Interceptor Squadron (FIS) at Suwon Air Base. At this point 334 FIS was largely tasked with air cover of ground forces following their brief push back into the Pusan Pocket. Daniel returned to his parent squadron in the United States during June 1951.

The next exchange officer to fly Sabres in Korea was Flt Lt Roy Emile Lelong, DFC*, who took part in a ninety-day temporary-duty assignment with 4th Fighter Interceptor Wing (FIW), arranged through the British Joint Services Mission in Washington. Roy Lelong was actually a New Zealander, and had joined the Royal New Zealand Air Force (RNZAF) in January 1942. At the end of the war, Lelong had joined the RAF and, like

This interesting group shot was taken during the CFE team's first deployment to Korea in early 1952. L–R: unknown, AVM C.A. Bouchier (AOC-in-C FEAF), Flt Lt Rex Knight, Col Francis S. Gabreski. Chewing his trademark 'stogie', Gabreski was commanding officer of 51st Fighter Interceptor Group at Suwon at the time. (*National Archives*)

Flt Lt Daniel before him, had been assigned to a US-based Sabre squadron at the time of his stint in Korea. He departed for the Far East from Travis AFB on 3 January 1952. Arriving in Tokyo, Lelong made the usual contact with British Embassy officials before departing for Korea on 10 January. He started flying operational missions with 4 FIW immediately, and between 15 January and his return to the US in April Lelong flew twenty-seven combat missions for a total of 40 flying hours. Promoted to squadron leader, Lelong later commanded 43 Sqn, flying Hunters.

Formal RAF involvement in Korea began in 1952 when a four-man team of pilots from the Central Fighter Establishment (CFE) at West Raynham was deployed to fly Sabres with the USAF squadrons there. Heading the deployment was Wg Cdr John Baldwin, DSO, DFC, AFC. He had gained a reputation as a skilful fighter pilot during the Second World War, and ended that conflict with sixteen and a half kills, mainly flying Typhoon fighter bombers. On the same team as Baldwin in Korea was Sqn Ldr W. 'Paddy' Harbison, who recalls that the deployment was brought about by the need for the RAF to evaluate the latest combat tactics:

> When the Korean Conflict started getting interesting with the appearance of the MiG-15, the CFE Tactics Branch was anxious to obtain some first-hand information on the air war and the tactics being employed. Representations were made to the USAF by the Air Ministry at high level, and the USAF agreed to accept four pilots from CFE in Jan 1952.
>
> I was the only CFE Pilot with previous F-86 experience; the other three pilots had none. The USAF 81st Group was by now at Bentwaters, and the three pilots were checked out there with the absolute minimum sorties. I had two refamiliarisation flights.

The team departed England on 3 February 1952 and arrived at Kimpo Air Base on the outskirts of Seoul ten days later. Half of the team was assigned to fly with 51st Fighter Interceptor Wing (FIW) at Suwon, twenty-five miles south of Seoul. The remaining pair remained at Kimpo and were put under 4 FIW control.

Each pilot immediately went into 'Clobber College', a pre-combat training programme for all incoming pilots designed to appraise crews of escape and evasion techniques and combat flying. The two-day course was followed by a flying phase comprising one or two local-area-orientation flights. Formation flying was then practised, initially in pairs, then as a four-ship and finally with eight aircraft. Once the individual had been considered competent, he was rated as combat-capable, but even then a pilot would still have to fly a 'bomb line' mission; this was flown with an experienced flight leader as far north as Sinanju to point out features and landmarks. Training completed, the pilot would fly ten to fifteen combat missions as a wingman before being considered for leading a two-ship element. By 17 March, Wg Cdr Baldwin had been appointed 51st Fighter Group Operations Officer and had flown twelve combat sorties. Paddy Harbison had flown thirteen Sabre missions as well as a further two with 77 Sqn, Royal Australian Air Force (Meteors). Though considered to be 'new guys', the RAF team was able to offer suggestions where necessary, and the RAF's snake-climb technique was soon adopted by USAF planners to expedite mass take-offs, as Paddy Harbison explains: 'The Snake Climb was an RAF procedure new to the USAF. Instead of the whole squadron or wing forming up on the runway and then taking off in sections of two or four, the aircraft would not form up, but would stream off in pairs without delay and climb to altitude in line astern to join up at cruising altitude. This saved considerable time and fuel. It was also a good method of penetrating cloud.'

On 15 March 1952 Wg Cdr Baldwin was posted missing on a weather-reconnaissance

Taking time out to fraternise with movie star Dinah Shore at Hollywood's famous Brown Derby restaurant, these pilots are from the final group to go to Korea. L–R: unknown USAF officer, Flt Lt R.J.F. Dickinson, Flt Lt John E.Y. King, Dinah Shore, unknown USAF officer, Fg Off C.D. Devine. (*Peter Sawyer*)

mission in north-west Korea. Baldwin was flying F-86E s/n 50-668 with 16 FIS and was last seen diving inverted into clouds at 7,000 feet. The peaks in this area of Korea rise to 5,000 feet; it is thought that he became disorientated and crashed into high ground.

The CFE Team returned to the UK in May 1952 and Paddy Harbison compiled a comprehensive report on the team's findings: '[Our] return had been planned to coincide with the CFE Fighter Convention, where the theme was the MiG-15 versus the F-86. I gave the keynote presentation, which was then very topical and of great interest to the RAF fighter fraternity.'

On 17 April 1952, a second CFE team of five personnel departed the UK for assignment to squadrons in Korea. Their first stop was in the United States, where they undertook six weeks of training on the F-86A at Nellis AFB. The team departed by air for Tokyo on 12 June and arrived in Korea a week later, led by Sqn Ldr J.R.H. Merifield, who was assigned to 16 FIS. The fifth team member was Maj Jackson Saunders, a USAF officer attached to CFE who briefly returned to the USAF fold with 39 FIS. All in this group flew the F-86E.

The CFE team again went through Clobber College, the initiation process being along the same lines as that of the previous team. Sqn Ldr Merifield quickly became a flight commander (in charge of four aircraft), as did Maj Saunders. The remaining team members were assigned as element leaders. One of the team members, Flt Lt Dennis Dunlop, was involved in a crash at Kimpo on 10 September 1952. Returning as element leader from a GCI scramble in F-86E s/n 50-666, he was turning onto final when he noticed a sudden loss in engine power. With fuel flow fluctuating and engine speed down to 20 per cent, an immediate attempt at a restart was made, but, although jet-pipe temperature rose to 600°C, RPM remained steadfastly at 20 per cent. By now, Dunlop realised that he would not make the runway, so he raised his undercarriage and retracted his speed brakes in preparation for a belly landing. The Sabre hit the ground at 85 knots and skidded to a stop in the undershoot area, 500ft from the end of the runway. Though Dunlop was unhurt, his aircraft was a write-off. Subsequent investigation pointed to the main fuel regulator as the cause of the engine problem.

Aside from Dunlop's close call, this RAF team claimed one MiG-15 destroyed (Flt Lt John Nicholls on 7 December) and nine others damaged. They returned to England in December 1952.

John Nicholls was put forward for an award by Gen Otto P. Weyland, USAF Commander-in-Theatre, suggesting that a DFC for his MiG kill and an Air Medal for 100 sustained missions would be appropriate. Nicholls was officially recommended for a DFC on 22 March 1953, his citation reading:

On the 7th December 1952, Flt Lt Nicholls's flight intercepted six MiG-15 aircraft at 36,000ft twenty miles south of the Yalu river. One of the MiGs broke and dived vertically to ground level. Flt Lt Nicholls and his number 2 (wingman) followed him, reaching a speed well in excess of the speed of sound, which resulted in their losing all aileron control. Flt Lt Nicholls managed to pull out behind the MiG, only to find that his gunsight had ceased to function. Although the MiG took violent evasive action Flt Lt Nicholls succeeded in obtaining numerous hits. The MiG burst into flames, broke up and dived to the ground.

Flt Lt Nicholls also on another occasion chased a MiG down to ground level. The MiG took evasive action and while doing so crashed into a mountain and was destroyed.

On another occasion, while leading his flight twenty miles south of the Suiho reservoir, Flt Lt Nicholls engaged two flights of MiGs, one of six aircraft, the other of four, in rapid succession. Flt Lt Nicholls scored hits on one MiG, which poured out smoke and evaded into cloud, and shortly afterwards damaged another. Flt Lt Nicholls's total score was two MiGs destroyed [*sic*] and three damaged.

It is not known why John Nicholls's second kill was not recognised; possibly because there was no corroborating evidence. Nonetheless his DFC was awarded on 2 June 1953.

Aside from the CFE-team Sabre pilots, a further RAF officer had been flying Sabres in Korea from the late summer of 1952. Flt Lt Graham S. 'Blondie' Hulse, DFC had previously been a flying instructor with the Central Flying School at Little Rissington, but in late 1950 he was posted to the United States on an exchange tour with the USAF. Though assigned to a flying-training unit, he managed to get a move to Korea in the late summer of 1952, where he joined 336 FIS, flying Sabres from Kimpo. It took him a while to get into his stride, but he ultimately became the RAF's top-scoring MiG killer of the war.

Hulse's first brush with the MiG-15 came on the morning of 25 October 1952 while he was flying as number four in a four-ship formation. His element leader, 1/Lt Joseph E. Fields, initiated an attack on a MiG-15, which was continued by Flt Lt Hulse. Closing on his quarry, Hulse managed to score hits on the tail cone and fuselage, and the MiG crashed and exploded near Sinuiju. Both pilots received credit for half a kill. Another kill was made on 9 December, and this time Hulse got full credit. He had been flying as number three on a four-ship mission and therefore was element leader. When two MiGs were spotted near Wongsong-dong, Graham Hulse initiated a diving attack and overtook the enemy formation. The MiGs then executed a hard turn to the left to avoid attack, but Hulse still managed to close on one of the jets and scored numerous hits on the tail and fuselage section. The MiG pilot was seen to eject just before his plane hit the ground.

On 8 December 1952 agreement was reached between the RAF and USAF representatives that with immediate effect a total of twelve RAF pilots would be on exchange to the Sabre squadrons in Korea at any one time. Ideally, this number would comprise one squadron leader and eleven flight lieutenants, with conversion of the first group to begin on or after 27 January 1953. In the meantime, a further group of four officers was assigned, led by Sqn Ldr James L. Ryan. He and his group began Sabre conversion with 3595th Training Wing at Nellis AFB during November 1952, and the final missions of the conversion were completed at the end of

RAF pilots that were assigned to 4 FIW pose for the photographer outside Wing Operations at Kimpo, May 1953. L–R: Flt Lt Peter Sawyer, Sqn Ldr E.M. Higson, AM A.C. Sanderson (AOC-in-C FEAF), Col J.K. Johnson (Wing CO), Fg Off John Chick, Fg Off C.D. Devine (*Peter Sawyer*)

December. Following a break for Christmas, the team departed Travis AFB in California on 13 January 1953 aboard a DC-4 bound for Haneda, Japan. The four pilots arrived there on 15 January, and all were then assigned to 51 FIW. One of the team members was Flt Lt John R. 'Jock' Maitland.

Prior to deploying to Korea, Jock Maitland had spent nearly two years lobbying various parties to be allowed to go; he had previously flown Meteors at Odiham with 247 Sqn. After arriving in Japan, Jock was flown to K-13 Suwon in Korea aboard a C-46 transport, and flew his first Sabre-familiarisation sortie there on 26 January 1953. Initially flying F-86Es, Flt Lt Maitland completed his first mission – a four-ship sweep – on 29 January and then took part in further sweeps and escorts during the following months.

Jock Maitland's first claim was put in on 11 April while flying F-86E-10 s/n 51-2838. Tasked as wingman on a two-ship Yalu sweep, his element encountered a number of MiGs. Maitland fired at two, though one 'kill' which took such violent evasive action that it flew into the ground, was not credited. Flt Lt Maitland began leading missions in mid-April, and a number of escort sorties followed: first for RF-80 photo-reconnaissance aircraft up to the Yalu on 15 April, another six days later, and then a series of fighter-bomber cover missions to Chong Chong. MiGs were occasionally seen, but were generally too high to engage.

At last, on 24 June, Jock got his best chance of downing a MiG. Flying aboard F-86E-10 s/n 51-2825 on a Yalu sweep, he chased his quarry north, loosing off round after round and downing the aircraft. Though Maitland's logbook states, 'Shot down a MiG south of Uiju', the claim was downgraded to a 'probable'. Post-flight scrutiny of his gun-camera film showed that the kill had been made north of the Yalu – a situation that was officially frowned upon. 'Jock' Maitland survived the war and later gained fame as the brains behind the world-renowned Biggin Hill Air Fair.

The action was not all one-sided, however. On 5 June Sqn Ldr Ryan ejected from his aircraft while on a combat mission over North Korea after experiencing technical problems. He had been flying F-86E s/n 51-2762 at the time and was rescued from the water at the mouth of the Chong Chong river. Ryan's group remained in Korea for the rest of the war, eventually returning to the UK in September 1953.

A further RAF pilot had been lost on 22 March 1953. Flt Lt Graham Hulse was shot down while flying F-86F-5 s/n 51-2935 with 336 FIS. Some controversy surrounds Hulse's death, with some claiming that his wingman, Maj Gene Sommerich, had actually mistakenly shot him down. According to Sqn Ldr Max Higson's later report,

> Graham attacked a MiG and set it on fire but expended his ammunition before the MiG was completely destroyed. He pulled off to the right and his number 2, a major, started to fire at the MiG. His film, which I have seen, shows the MiG quite clearly. First of all it's flying straight and level with smoke pouring from it. Then it banks to the right and you see Hulse's aircraft cross the screen from right to left, slightly above and in front of the MiG. Then the MiG straightens out and fires three shots; you can see the puffs of smoke. Suddenly about three feet of his, Hulse's, port wingtip breaks away and he disappears off the screen rolling onto his back. The major [Hulse's wingman] was not firing at the time the incident happened.

Jock Maitland also backs this up, saying, 'He was at K-14 and widely supposed to have been accidentally a victim of his own wingman. I saw the cine film [gun camera] and it was not like that.'

Nine days prior to his death, Graham Hulse had scored his last MiG victory. This time he was leading a formation of four Sabres, and it was he who sighted the MiGs first. Singling out one aircraft, he attacked and scored hits on the left wing. Hulse's wingman, Maj Sommerich, then took over the attack and sent the MiG diving to earth near Ch'olsan. Both received a half kill each.

The final group of twelve RAF pilots reported for duty in Korea on 5 April 1953, this time under the command of Sqn Ldr Max Higson; they would be the last RAF pilots to fly the Sabre in action. Fg Off Peter 'Tom' Sawyer was one of this final group, posted to Korea from 203 Advanced Flying School at Driffield. There he had flown various marks of Meteor before pulling some strings with his uncle, who was an air marshal. Before he knew it, Sawyer was on his way to the United States for conversion onto the Sabre. He actually flew out of Heathrow aboard a civil flight on 23 January 1953, arriving at Las Vegas on the 27th. His course began with 3598th Combat Crew Training Squadron at nearby Nellis AFB, where he flew a number of familiarisation flights in the F-80 Shooting Star before starting to fly the Sabre on 3 February. Through the rest of the month and into early March, 'Tom' Sawyer flew more than forty sorties in the F-86E, comprising aerobatics, close formation, cross-country, and mock dogfights. The final period concentrated on live air-to-air and air-to-ground weapon firing and included a number of rocket-firing missions. The course finished on 7 March, his final flight, aboard F-86E s/n 51-13022, being part of a huge

Flt Lt Peter Sawyer in typical Korean War 'hero' pose. The photograph is interesting as it not only shows the standard flight gear and parachute harness, but also the yellow–orange life jacket that was always worn in case of bailout over the Yellow Sea. (*Peter Sawyer*)

160-aircraft 'balbo' formation. After a period of leave, Peter departed for Korea on 30 March and arrived in Seoul on 5 April.

Assigned to 'Able' Flight of 334th FIS at Kimpo, he went through the standard Clobber College induction. He then flew his first mission, a local familiarisation flight, in F-86E s/n 51-2833 (actually a 51 FIW aircraft) on 22 April. After just nine similar flights, on 3 May Fg Off Sawyer went into action, taking part in a patrol around Cho Do Island aboard F-86E s/n 51-2794. The mission lasted 1 hour and 25 minutes. He flew mainly F-86E aircraft during his tour, along with a few F-86F missions, and these comprised patrols, weather-recce flights and a few fighter-bomber escort

Fg Off Peter Sawyer (centre) confers with Col Cosby (left) and Maj Webber (right) in the 334th FIS locker room after a mission. (*Peter Sawyer*)

missions. The unlucky thirteenth combat mission, a Yalu sweep on 14 May, resulted in an early return to base with a hung tank. However, on 26 May, Fg Off Sawyer was in the thick of a big fight, and this time Capt Ryland Dewey of 'B' Flight got a MiG kill.

The closest that Peter got to his own kill was on 14 June 1953. Flying his twenty-fifth combat mission – another Yalu sweep – aboard F-86F s/n 51-2927, he registered several hits on a MiG.

> The most interesting sorties were known as Yalu Sweeps, consisting of several formations (finger fours) climbing to 40,000ft and heading north to the River Yalu, discarding overload fuel tanks when empty. We often saw MiG-15s above us, they usually stayed above us, as – so we later learnt – they had compressibility problems above Mach 0.95. Occasionally, when we found them at a lower height, we were able to engage, usually at a high angle of attack, ending in a tail chase which had to be stopped when the MiG crossed the Yalu (officially out of bounds to us).
>
> Only on one occasion did I have a realistic chance when I was leading a flight of four some fifty miles south of the Yalu heading north, when [we saw] two MiGs descending, going westwards through 40,000ft. After a short chase I was able to fire a few shots from the rear and some hits were shown – appeared on the cine [gun camera] film. After crossing the Yalu I was forced to break off. My number two had left me as he was short of fuel; I managed to land back at K-14 [Kimpo].

This would undoubtedly have given him a 'damaged' had his gun-camera film not subsequently shown the lake at Mukden in the background. He had been well north of the Yalu (a definite 'no-no') and the claim was ignored. In all, Tom flew thity-five combat missions and logged 51 hours in Korea during the war itself.

Part of the same team, Flt Lt 'Dickie' Dickinson, AFC had more luck. Upon arrival in Korea, Dickinson had been posted to 25 FIS at Suwon. His first Yalu sweep was on 13 May, though no MiGs were seen; a further mission three days later produced MiGs, but none were engaged. Then, on 18 May, while flying as number two to Jock Maitland, Dickinson registered hits on a MiG-15 that got between him and his leader. Last seen spiralling down with smoke trailing, the MiG was given as a 'probable'.

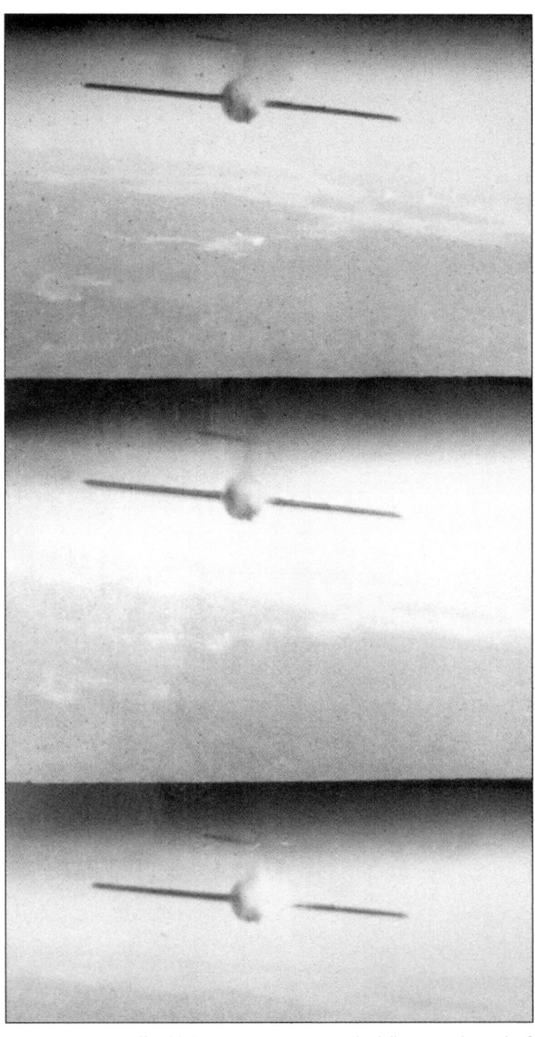

Peter Sawyer's unofficial kill – 14 June 1953. As the kill was made north of the Yalu, it was not counted as a score. Sawyer was flying F-86F 51-2927 at the time. (*Peter Sawyer*)

Flt Lt Peter Sawyer in typical 'hero' pose at Kimpo during the summer of 1953. The aircraft is F-86E-10 51-2831 'Yalu Express', though Peter never actually flew it. (*Peter Sawyer*)

Finally, on 18 June, Richard Dickinson got his kill. Breaking through cloud near the Yalu river, Dickinson saw two MiGs behind him at about 1,000yd. He called the break, and one MiG flew past his tail, the other following the flight leader in a hard turn. Dickinson managed to get on this MiG's tail and started firing, eventually running out of ammunition. However, just as the MiG began to straighten out, it started to burn and spiralled down to crash near Oick-Tong.

The situation in Korea had changed somewhat since the first CFE team had reported its findings. In many cases, the junior pilots in the subsequent RAF team found it difficult to begin their flying training. There were simply so many qualified pilots in the squadrons by this time – and the workload was so high – that the flying officers had to wait it out until their time came. All eventually saw action though, and, aside from Flt Lt Dickinson mentioned above, Flt Lt J.H. Granville-White also downed a MiG, on 29 June. 'Dickie' Dickinson and Flt Lt Colin Downes also had recourse to the use of some of the emergency facilities during their combat missions. Situated on the south-east corner of Cho Do Island off the east coast of Korea was a hard sandy-beach landing strip for use by aircraft in trouble. Both Downes and Dickinson used this 5,000ft strip, which also featured a 2,000ft overshoot area.

More seriously, Flt Lt John King was lost on a mission on 4 June over North Korea, while flying aircraft 51-2838. He is still listed as missing in action. Bob Lysgaard was King's room-mate at Suwon and was on this mission with him.

> What a great guy! John King came from the RAF as an all-weather pilot. On this mission I was flying number four through an awful thunderstorm over North Korea north of the DMZ. John was number three and suddenly hauled back on the stick. I tried hard, but could not keep up with him in that sudden erratic manoeuvre. He did not respond to any radio transmissions and I was lucky to return with the formation to South Korean K-13, Suwon. No one could contact him from the formation or from the base in any way. John never did show up at the base. The investigations considered severe vertigo, oxygen failure or a heart attack. Personally, I never considered the wildest rumour, which was possible defection to North Korea or Vladivostok, USSR.

All pilots in King's group had completed between thirty and fifty missions each by the time of the ceasefire on 27 July 1953. However, the RAF pilots on this team remained in Korea for some time afterwards, continuing to fly patrols to monitor MiG activity. They finally ended their flying commitment in Korea at the end of October 1953. The experience gained in Korea proved invaluable; many of those involved later became flight commanders on the new RAF Sabre squadrons and were able to pass on their knowledge.

RAF Sabre Pilots in the Korean War

Rank/Name	Assignment	Dates
Wg Cdr John Baldwin, DSO, DFC, AFC	51 FIW	Feb 52–15 Mar 52 (KIA)
Sqn Ldr W. 'Paddy' Harbison	4 FIW/335 FIS	Feb 52–May 52
Sqn Ldr E.M. Higson	4 FIW/336 FIS	Apr 53–Oct 53
Sqn Ldr J.R.H. Merifield	51 FIW/16 FIS	Jun 52–Dec 52
Sqn Ldr James L. Ryan	51 FIW	Jan 53–Sep 53
Flt Lt Stephen W. 'Dan' Daniel, DSO, DFC	4 FIW/334 FIS	Jan 51–June 51
Flt Lt Richard J.F. Dickinson, AFC	51 FIW/25 FIS	Apr 53–Oct 53
Flt Lt Colin B.W. Downes	4 FIW/335 FIS	Apr 53–Oct 53
Flt Lt Dennis A. Dunlop	4 FIW/336 FIS	Jun 52–Dec 52
Flt Lt Roy French	51 FIW	Jan 53–Sep 53
Flt Lt Ian Gordon-Johnson	36 FBS	Apr 53–Oct 53
Flt Lt J.H. Granville-White	39 FIS	Apr 53–Oct 53
Flt Lt Graham S. 'Blondie' Hulse, DFC	4 FIW/336 FIS	*c.* Sep 52–22 Mar 53 (KIA)
Flt Lt A.F. Jenkins	51 FIW/25 FIS	Jun 52–Dec 52
Flt Lt John E.Y. King	51 FIW/16 FIS	Apr 53–04 Jun 53 (MIA)
Flt Lt Rex Knight	51 FIW	Feb 52–May 52
Flt Lt Roy Emile Lelong, DFC*	4 FIW	Jan 52–Mar 52
Flt Lt John H.J. Lovell	51 FIW/25 FIS	Jan 53–Sep 53
Flt Lt John R. 'Jock' Maitland	51 FIW/25 FIS	Jan 53–Sep 53
Flt Lt T.J. McElhaw	51 FIW	Apr 53–Oct 53
Flt Lt John Moreton Nicholls	4 FIW/335 FIS	Jun 52–Dec 52
Flt Lt B.J. Spragg	4 FIW/334 FIS	Feb 52–May 52
Fg Off John F.H. Chick	4 FIW/334 FIS	Apr 53–Oct 53
Fg Off C.D. Devine	4 FIW/336 FIS	Apr 53–Oct 53
Fg Off Jim H. Mansell	51 FIW	Apr 53–Oct 53
Fg Off J.N. Murphy	51 FIW	Apr 53–Oct 53
Fg Off P.G. Sawyer	4 FIW/334 FIS	Apr 53–Oct 53

RAF Sabre–MiG Kills in Korean War

Name/Rank	Unit	Kill	Date
Flt Lt Richard J.F. Dickinson	25 FIS	1 x MiG-15	18 Jun 53
Flt Lt John H. Granville-White	39 FIS	1 x MiG-15	29 Jun 53
Flt Lt Graham S. Hulse	336 FIS	0.5 x MiG-15	25 Oct 52
		1 x MiG-15	9 Dec 52
		0.5 x MiG-15	13 Mar 53
Flt Lt John H.J. Lovell	25 FIS	1 x MiG-15	27 Jun 53
Flt Lt John M. Nichols	335 FIS	1 x MiG-15	7 Dec 52

CHAPTER FOUR

3 SQUADRON

Based at Wildenrath, 3 Sqn was flying the Vampire FB Mk. 5 when word arrived of the impending conversion to the Sabre. Commanding the squadron at this time was Sqn Ldr W.J.S. Sutherland, with Flt Lt E. Trees as 'A' Flight commander and Flt Lt T.A. Warren leading 'B' Flight.

During March 1953 a number of 'bone dome' helmets were borrowed from the Dutch Air Force unit at Florennes in order to prepare for receipt of the first Sabres. Suitably attired, Flt Lt E. Trees checked out in the Sabre at SCU on 17 March, followed on 1 April by Flt Lt B.N. Bennett of 'B' Flight plus three others. By that date all squadron pilots had completed the ground-instruction part of the course with SCU, and by 8 April nine squadron pilots had completed the flying phase. On 14 April the squadron completed training with the SCU, though still no Sabres had been delivered. Throughout this busy period, Vampire sorties continued to be flown at the rate of ten to twenty per day.

The first pair of Sabres for 3 Sqn arrived at Wildenrath on 11 May 1953, flown in by ferry pilots from 147 Sqn in spite of poor weather in Germany, which precluded all other flying. Low cloud bases over the Continent kept the Sabres grounded until 19 May, when on the unit's first day of Sabre operations, Sqn Ldr Sutherland led four aircraft on a formation sortie. This was the first formation put up by a front line Sabre squadron, though 67 Sqn had managed to achieve the 'first actual sortie' record – by a matter of one day. However, 3 Sqn flew nine Sabre sorties on 19 May, and 10 hours and 45 minutes went into the logbooks. A further twenty-eight Vampire missions were also flown, the unit continuing to fly this mix of aircraft for some time.

By 20 May, squadron strength was at ten aircraft, and during the next week a further six were delivered. The final four aircraft were flown in on 27 May by squadron pilots; Flt Lt Warren and Fg Offs Hayes, Crisp and Day began the day at 5 MU, Kemble, stopping at Benson before flying directly to Wildenrath.

Unfortunately, the weather conspired to keep flying to a minimum during this period, and it was not until 26 May that further sorties were flown, despite thunder showers in the area. From the end of the month rehearsals were flown for the Queen's Coronation fly-past over Düsseldorf on 2 June. The fly-past itself comprised six Sabres from 3 Sqn and a further half-dozen from 67 Sqn.

Concurrent with the Düsseldorf fly-past, the squadron was informed that the next six weeks would be devoted to practising close-formation flying in preparation for the Coronation Review at RAF Odiham in England. The squadron was ordered to provide twelve aircraft and pilots for the review, which would be flown in three sections of four aircraft. Almost immediately flying was restricted due to the proximity of minor inspections on many of the Sabres, but by limiting the flying hours accrued on each airframe, it was planned that these inspections could be deferred until after the review. On 12 June the last Vampire sortie was flown, a four-ship battle formation.

The following day, preparations for the deployment to England began. Temporarily based at Duxford would be 3 Sqn, with

On 19 May 1953, Sqn Ldr 'Black Jack' Sutherland led this four-ship sortie, the first formation mission by RAF squadron Sabres, and the first Sabre mission by 3 Sqn (he was beaten to the 'first mission' target the previous day by Sqn Ldr Paddy Harbison of 67 Sqn). Aircraft in the formation are: XB614 (lead), XB550 (Sgt Ken Chapple, right wing), XB633 (Ken Bruce, left wing) and XB590 (George Cole, slot). (*Guy Harris*)

squadron markings being applied to the Sabres just prior to flying to the UK . The first personnel to move out of Wildenrath were the ground crews and support staff; they left by rail and sea on 18 June. Two days later Gp Capt Johnnie Johnson led sixteen Sabres across the Channel to Duxford, arriving there at lunchtime. The squadron immediately stood down for a well-earned rest.

On 22 June the first sorties were flown from Duxford, and these comprised sector-reconnaissance missions to familiarise pilots with local landmarks, culminating in a mass dogfight with Meteors from the two resident units, 64 and 65 Sqns. Unfortunately, much of the time in England was characterised by poor weather, though better conditions on 26 June enabled the first full rehearsal to be flown over Odiham, utilising twenty-four Sabres, including aircraft from 67 Sqn. The latter unit had also deployed to Duxford for the review.

Further rehearsals were flown on subsequent days, using varying numbers of aircraft from each unit to make up the required twenty-four, but the weather closed in again and the flying plan was abandoned. On 2 July a number of squadron pilots were taken to Kemble to ferry Sabres to Odiham for the static display there. Two ferry flights were carried out the next day, though the bad weather continued. Cross-country missions were flown on a few days, but the important task of formation practice was still impossible.

From the first week in July, close-formation missions were resumed, and on 15 July a dozen Sabres from 3 Sqn left

In the first months of 3 Sqn's Sabre period, XB747/B was the CO's aircraft. In this photograph, only the nose band and tail code have been added; the aircraft would later gain a squadron commander's pennant on the forward fuselage. (*Dennis H. Jones*)

Duxford for the full review. The fly-past was successful and on 16 July the Sabres returned to Wildenrath. Three Valetta transport aircraft were requisitioned for the ground crews, who returned to Germany in some style and comfort on 17 July. The squadron was finally able to get down to real business.

The first of the maintenance inspections was completed on 19 July, though further work was immediately suspended: 3 Sqn had been detailed for a permanent move to Geilenkirchen and the ground crews moved out on 19 July. The Sabres followed the next day, but there was no time to relax: on arrival, personnel were briefed for the impending Exercise Coronet. This would be the largest postwar exercise by Allied forces in Europe up to that date, and involved fighter-bomber units pressing 'enemy' attacks on NATO airfields (including Geilenkirchen) from the east. Thus, with no time to settle into the new environment, the squadron was being thrown into a full-scale test of its effectiveness.

At 0400 hr on 23 July, 3 Sqn was put on standby for the first day of Coronet. Tasked with providing interception and airfield-defence sorties from dawn until dusk, the squadron completed sixteen sorties on the first day. Fine weather over Germany meant that 'enemy' attacks were intensive, with activity around the Geilenkirchen area on 24 July accounting for thirty-two sorties, including a number of high-level interceptions. During this period it was discovered that the lengthy Sabre start procedure was jeopardising swift scrambles, so in future all alert pilots sat in their cockpits waiting for a 'scramble' call, rather than sitting at readiness in the crew room. This procedure, already adopted by USAF crews in Korea, managed to cut down scramble times.

Continued fine weather meant that the airfield was again under attack on 25 July, when twenty-seven sorties were flown. The following day saw a change in tactics: 3 Sqn Sabres flew long-range fighter sweeps to airfields in southern Germany, supporting fighter-bomber missions flown by 2 TAF Vampires. Similar profiles were flown on until the busiest day of the exercise, 29 July, when four squadron Sabres were scrambled to intercept a formation of thirty-six Meteor F. Mk. 8s coming in from England. The Sabres were successful in pressing their attacks at 33,000ft. That afternoon four Sabres supported fighter-bomber Vampires on a mission to the Canadian base at Gros Tenquin in France; this developed into a large air battle over the base. A further fighter sweep that day took the Sabres to the USAF base at Bitburg. Coronet finished on 30 July, with twelve sorties being flown by 3 Sqn. During the month the unit had completed 345 sorties for a total of 264 hours and 45 minutes; this was more than twice the amount flown the previous month. John Daly recalls this hectic period:

Our final close formation trip was to deploy to Geilenkirchen on 20 July – and what a hairy trip that was. The Squadron was moving base, Geilenkirchen newly built, the boss decides to go in a box of boxes [sixteen aircraft] but led us into a cu-nim, and we came out to arrive as sixteen by one!

The best and most realistic exercise kicked off immediately – Exercise Coronet, wonderful, dangerous and as far removed from close formation as it is possible to be. It came to an end on 1 August [*sic*], everyone exhausted from lack of sleep (we were flying from dawn to dusk – i.e. about 4 a.m. to 10.30 p.m.)

At the beginning of August, runway resurfacing began at Geilenkirchen, and for the following nine days all flying was cancelled and aircraft servicing given top priority. It was a useful break, though lack of spare parts for the Sabres meant that full advantage could not be taken. Flying recommenced on 10 August, with twenty-two sorties flown in fine weather. The squadron flew back to Wildenrath briefly on 3 September to practise mass take-offs and landings with 67 Sqn before a further exercise began one week later.

Exercise Monte Carlo started on 10 September and was aimed at testing the signals and organisation of NATO forces. It was hoped that the Sabres would be used in their intended (high altitude) role but, since most attacks were made below 10,000ft (by Vampires), this was not possible in most cases. The exercise finished on 13 September with a midday interception of twelve Vampires at 12,000ft; this was typical of the missions flown during Monte Carlo.

Almost immediately the unit began preparing for deployment to the Armament Practice School (APS) at Sylt. Gun harmonisation of the unit's Sabres had begun on 30 September with one aircraft per day being checked, firing approximately

To remove its J47 engine, the rear fuselage of the Canadair Sabre was detached in its entirety just aft of the mainplane. XB740/M (here without its engine) was stripped down for a major inspection inside 3 Sqn's hangar. (*Brian Chapman*)

While on the squadron's first Sylt detachment, XB670/S skidded on landing and ended in the overshoot area. The undercarriage dug into the sodden soil, but little damage was incurred. (*Dennis H. Jones*)

120 rounds a time. Drop tanks and gunsights were installed on 6 October and most of the aircraft flew out to Sylt on 11 October. The Sabres would fire on air-towed fabric banners, scores being counted by use of paint-tipped bullets. Each aircraft in a firing mission would have its own distinctly coloured shells, and when the banner was recovered the presence (or not) of a hole of a particular colour would indicate each individual pilot's score. By totalling the number of rounds fired against the number of hits on the banner, a percentage of hits would be given.

The first day of APS sorties was flown on 12 October, comprising twelve successful missions and six aborts; the scoring average was poor due to unfamiliarity with the aircraft's gunsight, itself attributable to a complete lack of operation and maintenance manuals. Further missions yielded slightly better results, but by mid-month a civilian technical representative had been sent to Sylt to address these problems, and he noticed that the aircraft had been harmonised incorrectly. He was also able to give useful gunsight information to pilots and ground crews. With guns correctly harmonised, it was hoped that better scores would result once the weather had cleared.

After a twelve-day layoff, 3 Sqn was able to return to APS flying on 30 October, but the changes seemed to have little effect: 10 November was the unit's final day at Sylt, when the daily score of 1.8 per cent only matched the overall average for the detachment. Highest scorer was Fg Off J.C. Sprent of 'A' Flight, who had managed 16 per cent.

At this point, a number of personnel changes began. On 14 December Sqn Ldr D.C.H. Simmons, AFC took over as the new squadron commander; he was posted in from the CFS Examining Wing. Sqn Ldr Sutherland returned to England on 15 December. Also on 15 December, Flt Lt K.S. Peat took over as 'B' Flight commander, Flt Lt Warren being posted back to the UK. As the squadron dispersed for Christmas leave, it could be rightly proud of its record: in the eight preceding months it had converted to the most advanced fighter in the world and had experienced no serious accidents. During 1953, 3 Sqn had flown 2,137 missions in the Sabre, comprising 1,555 flying hours.

The beginning of 1954 was marked by the arrival of heavy snow, but this did not prevent flying. Six aircraft were scrambled on 8 January to intercept a large formation of 234 Sqn Sabres inbound to Geilenkirchen. On 14 January, 3 Sqn was able to complete its night-flying programme, though the last aircraft landed with its undercarriage up. Geilenkirchen's runway was blocked for recovery of the Sabre and the airfield was closed to further flying. The pilot, George Cole, was unharmed. Subsequent investigation indicated that a g-switch in the electrical system might have failed. Cole, like many on the squadron at the time, was night-flying without a valid instrument rating since the squadron's Meteor had been unserviceable for so long. The aircraft involved in this incident was XB684; it was classified as Cat. 3 (R) and returned to England for rectification with Airwork.

The advent of bad weather on 16 January prompted a new system of operation: in future, the squadron would fly at weekends – clear weather permitting – and stand down in lieu when further inclement weather arrived. Thus the unit would be able to use every day of fair weather to continue its training commitment. Taking advantage of fine days at the end of the month, on 23 January a twelve-aircraft 'balbo' exercise was planned with the intention of flying a 'figure 3' formation for the first time; sadly, one of the Sabres went unserviceable and this was not possible. Instead, fly-pasts in a variety of formations were performed over the airfield.

The cold spell continued into February 1954; further sorties to the Monschau range were limited, though some sorties were authorised for practising cloud flying on 10 February. Inevitably, the weather on this mission deteriorated and all aircraft were recalled to Geilenkirchen. Fg Off James W. Tate requested a GCA into base but, unfortunately, he overshot the runway and wrote off his Sabre, XB681. Tate was uninjured, but two weeks later he was not so lucky.

The enviable accident record of 3 Sqn came to an abrupt end on 24 February 1954 when Fg Offs John Adair and J.W. 'Bill' Tate suffered a mid-air collision near Henri-Chapelle in Belgium. Neither survived the accident, wreckage falling near the Liège–Aachen road. Aircraft involved were XB643 (coded 'K') and XB667 (coded 'D'). Both pilots were buried with full military honours on 3 March. 'Ned' Neill was Acting Squadron Adjutant at the time and attended the crash scene:

> I was hurriedly co-opted by [Sqn Ldr] Simmons and Ken Peat to accompany them to the scene in the Boss's Land Rover. The crash scene was in Belgium and consisted of two craters only a few feet apart, which seemed to indicate they had tent-pegged in formation.
>
> I remember John Adair very well, but Bill hardly at all (he wasn't with us for long). But I remember they had served together before (John had been Secretarial and Bill, I think, RAF Regiment) and seemed to share some kind of bond from that period. Also, just to add to the intrigue, John had only recently returned to flying after spending some time under close arrest – I think for financial irregularities. (As you will know, it was enough to bounce a cheque in those days.) It has always intrigued me as to how they came to hit the ground in a near vertical attitude and so close together.

Despite this serious setback life went on, and firing at Monschau started again on 9 March. Incredibly, many missions had to be scrubbed because of a lack of light bulbs for the aircraft's A4 gunsight. Fg Off R.M. Taylor of 'A' Flight

The remains of one of a pair of Sabres that crashed near Henri-Chapelle in Belgium on 24 February 1954. Both pilots, Fg Offs John Adair and John Tate, were killed. (*Dennis H. Jones*)

had a lucky escape on 19 March: his aircraft sustained a birdstrike and Taylor was fortunate in being able to recover to Geilenkirchen. His Sabre 'H' suffered considerable damage, but was at least repairable.

Practice scrambles continued throughout this period, usually against known 'friendly' targets. Four Sabres were alerted on 30 March for a 'bogey', this time a USAF B-45 medium bomber flying at 42,000ft. To the dismay of many, the Sabres had difficulty in intercepting the bomber, the 'indifferent climbing qualities of the Sabre above 35,000ft' being criticised by the squadron pilots. This was worrying, especially since the aircraft had experienced trouble in catching a 'known' target. How would they cope with a 'real' target? It is perhaps fortunate that the occasion never arose.

Three further urgent STIs grounded the Sabres again on 5 April, but flying resumed the next day; a number of formation fly-pasts were practised in the following days, beginning with one of sixteen aircraft on 21 April in preparation for the AOC's parade. Air-to-ground firing switched to the Helchteren range on 11 June, and good weather enabled a full day's practice to be carried out. Fg Off Wood was the day's high scorer with a 29 per cent hit record; clearly, the practice was having a positive effect. Further bouts of poor weather meant that by 23 June the squadron was still 125 hours short of its monthly 700 flying-hour target, and continued bad weather made it impossible to achieve. With the unit still many hours in arrears, on 28 June it was decreed that the monthly target would be

XB984/K was the squadron commander's aircraft and carried unique markings comprising a green tail band, fuselage bands and nose area, all of which were bordered by a thin yellow line. The fuselage bands predated the adoption of similar schemes on other 2 TAF Sabres. (*Brian Chapman*)

reduced to 600 hours. Even then, this was only met by including Meteor flying hours in the statistics.

The annual UK air defence exercise for 1954, code-named 'Dividend', was planned to begin in mid-July, with 2 TAF units acting as enemy forces. The exercise was broken down into two phases, running from 16 to 18 July, and then from 22 July until the exercise finished on 25 July. The personnel of 3 Sqn received a briefing on 16 July, prior to the first full day of the exercise. Unfortunately, inclement weather precluded any flying on 17 July, and it was not until the following day that the Sabres were able to join in. Six raids of four aircraft each were then launched on England, flown at 35,000 to 40,000ft altitude. Sadly, further bouts of poor weather meant that Geilenkirchen's Sabres played no further part in the first phase. Nonetheless, other aircraft were able to press home their attacks and 1,784 sorties were flown against the UK in Phase 1.

Better weather conditions at the start of Phase 2 meant that the unit was able to launch three formations of four aircraft over south-eastern England on 22 July. On the following day three sections of four Sabres and a further six pairs were flown in support of Dividend. Bad weather on the final day of the exercise meant that only five of six planned four-ship sorties could be flown. For the whole phase, 3,942 raiding sorties were flown, and these demonstrated that high-level attacks by American B-47 bombers were almost impossible to intercept. Only 30 per cent of attacks were intercepted before they reached the coast of the UK.

Then, from 10 August, 3 Sqn began air-to-air firing on towed targets. Gun-camera footage was used to validate these missions, and crews were criticised for firing beyond the effective range of their guns. Any further chance to improve the squadron's effectiveness was cut short by the month-long visit to the Sylt armament-practice camp.

The advance party under Fg Off Allsopp left for Sylt by road on 19 August, and Sqn Ldr Simmons briefed the squadron about the detachment two days later. Twenty-five pilots would deploy, leaving five crews at Geilenkirchen. Once the first five pilots had completed the camp at Sylt, they would swap with the remaining pilots, ensuring that some fighter coverage was always available 'back home'. The working day at Sylt would run from 0600 to 1800 hr, Monday to Friday, a shift system enabling air and ground crews to be relieved in the morning or afternoon. The main rail party left Geilenkirchen on

When 3 Sqn moved into Geilenkirchen in July 1953, it inherited far more spacious hangarage than at Wildenrath. This early 1955 photograph shows aircraft with the '6–3' wing, but without the definitive green fuselage bands. (*Brian Chapman*)

22 August for the fourteen-hour journey to Sylt and arrived at dawn the next day. Typically, poor weather then intervened, meaning that the Sabres, which had planned to arrive on 23 August, did not get to Sylt until two days later. Even then, two Sabres had to be left back at base when they failed to start.

Fine weather prevailed at the end of August, though early morning mists prevented much flying before 0900 hr. From the start, pilots were still found to be firing out of range and, though many missions were flown daily, it was not until 6 September that all pilots firing on a single day managed even to hit the flag. Initially, the squadron was flying with gunsights only in the 'manual' mode; they began using radar-ranging from 10 September. John Daly had a lucky escape during the deployment whilst flying XB582:

'On 8 September 1954, I did an air test in which the nose-wheel actuating strut sheared with a loud bang, leaving the nose-wheel undercarriage assembly dangling in the breeze and indicating unlocked. I landed safely by momentarily (with plenty of speed) touching the nose wheel to the ground so it swung back; I raised the nose so it swung forward like a pendulum, where it reached the stops and locked into place. Interesting trip.'

Squadron average was just 3.5 per cent by the end of the detachment, with aircraft returning individually to Geilenkirchen on 14 September. After a well-earned stand-down, work resumed at Geilenkirchen a week later.

Immediately, work began on preparing for Exercise Battle Royal, which commenced on 22 September. Two sections of four aircraft were launched on the first day, and these performed dummy attacks on Wildenrath to provide gun-laying practice for the RAF Regiment. The squadron was placed on standby in the subsequent days, and it was not until 27 September – the last day of Exercise Battle Royal – that 3 Sqn was involved again, when one section of four Sabres flew a sweep over Oldenburg at 35,000ft. Further 'non exercise' sorties kept crews drilled, though. On 21 October a quartet of squadron Sabres, led by Flt Lt Crisp, were scrambled to join an eight-ship sweep over France and Belgium at 23,000ft; no intercepts were made. The following day, five sections of four Sabres were scrambled, managing to intercept a B-45 Tornado jet bomber escorted by USAF Sabres. Previously both types had proved difficult to catch.

November began with poor serviceability, but further bad weather meant that little flying was possible in any case. On 25 November, twenty-two night-flying sorties were scheduled, and all went well until the last sortie, when XB612/F ran off the runway on take-off. The aircraft received Cat. 4 damage, though the pilot was unharmed. XB612 was returned to the UK for repair with Airwork.

A further bout of maintenance problems at the end of the year – specifically due to the incorporation of STIs and SIs – decreased effectiveness. A typical example of this occurred on 20 December. Servicing Instruction (SI) 22 had been issued as a repetitive check of Sabre wings for cracking – a fault that had occurred on Sabres operated by other air forces. On this occasion, ten squadron aircraft were found to have Cat. 4 cracks, and these were grounded until in-depth repair and strengthening had been carried out.

During this period a change of command took place. On 8 December, Sqn Ldr T.H. Hutchinson arrived at Geilenkirchen, allowing Sqn Ldr Simmons to be posted out to the Staff College. However, Sqn Ldr Hutchinson's arrival brought no change in the weather, and further sorties planned at Monschau for mid-December had to be cancelled.

The following year, 1955, began with a long period of adverse weather; ice and snow in particular caused a number of sorties on the ranges to be cancelled. Flt Lt Fargher, the long-time commander of 'A' Flight, was promoted at the start of the month and posted to Sylt as a squadron leader PAI. His place was taken by Flt Lt Fitton, who was posted into the squadron from 234 Sqn on 13 January.

At about this time the first '6–3' hard-edge wings were fitted to the Sabres of 3 Sqn. The hard-edge wing dispensed with the leading-edge slats of the narrow-chord wing, enabling the Sabre to turn tighter at altitude. Unfortunately, the downside was that handling at low speed was less forgiving; stall speed was raised too. Thankfully no accidents were attributed to unfamiliarity with the new wing, but squadron pilots did take a while to get used to the new flying characteristics. By the end of March 1955 most of the squadron's Sabres had had the new wing fitted.

Exercise Sky High began during April and, from the 25th, the squadron's Sabres were involved. On the first day, Bomber Command Canberras and Lincolns began attacks on targets in north-west Europe. However, although this exercise began at 1230 hr, only three sections of four Sabres were scrambled in the afternoon and evening of 25 April. The following day, 'A' Flight removed the drop tanks from its aircraft and then easily managed to intercept a B-45 bomber flying at 35,000ft. Pilots agreed that this configuration finally gave a realistic indication of the Sabre's combat performance. The experiment was repeated on 29 April when three sections of 'hard-edge' Sabres were scrambled for Exercise Sky High.

Though May of 1955 began on a high – 'A' Flight managed to get eight Sabres serviceable and performed a fly-past on

Brian Chapman sits in the cockpit of Sqn Ldr Hutchinson's Sabre, XB984/K; note the CO's name painted in white on the canopy rail and the red ejection-seat warning triangle. By the time of this photograph, XB984 had been modified with the extended '6–3' wing, which is evident in the small detachable wing-root fairing that is visibly resting on the wing. (*Brian Chapman*)

3 May to celebrate the fact – the serviceability of the squadron's Sabres again took a dive. On a good day, the squadron struggled to generate more than fifteen sorties, and towards the end of the month a problem was found in the undercarriage uplock system of one of the aircraft. Subsequent investigation revealed that a number of Sabres had been rigged incorrectly, and flying was restricted further while the ground crews rectified the problem.

During this difficult period the squadron was dealt an additional blow. Fg Off Roger M. Taylor had just returned from leave when he flew the Sabre again on 16 May, a day when the squadron managed to put seventeen sorties into the air. Taylor, in XB699, was leading a flight on a tail-chase mission when, just as the aircraft were joining up, Taylor's Sabre rolled suddenly to starboard, pulled sharply across his number two and rolled into cloud. The Sabre was seen diving out of the cloud at a steep angle from which the pilot appeared to make no attempt to recover; it crashed and exploded at Vaals, just inside the Dutch border close to Aachen, West Germany. No reason for the loss of control could be established. Fg Off Taylor's body was flown back to the UK on 20 May for burial.

One of the largest NATO exercises was 'Carte Blanche', which began in June 1955. In preparation, all of the squadron's Sabres were painted in exercise markings on 16 June (presumably the distemper fuselage bands seen on 112 Sqn Sabres). For Carte Blanche, 3 Sqn would deploy to Beek in Holland, so on 21 June the advance party left by road. Twelve Sabres were flown out the same day, and these aircraft managed to fly eight sorties on local flying from Beek. Conditions on this deployment were basic, as all crews had to live in tents; at least the weather was mild.

During Carte Blanche, pilots stood by for 'skittle' operations in support of a supposed atomic attack. The squadron's objective was to saturate 'enemy' radar, and thus the focus was on generating the maximum amount of sorties. Fifty-one Sabre missions were flown on 23 June alone, comprising mainly intercepts, and the busy atmosphere at Beek was heightened when 112 Sqn's Sabres landed to refuel after an atomic attack was declared on Geilenkirchen.

The following day's action began early: 'A' Flight scrambled White Section at 0445 hr on an interception, and just 35 minutes later an atomic attack was declared and all squadron pilots were ordered to scramble and divert. These orders were almost immediately cancelled as the bomb was reported to be a 'dud'. Nonetheless, Black Section was then scrambled at 0605 hr and a further pair of Sabres took off at 0855 hr.

Later that morning, three sections of Sabres were scrambled and Black Section managed to intercept a large formation of French Ouragan fighters. A false attack alarm was given at 1115 hr, and the airborne aircraft were diverted back to Geilenkirchen. They then flew another sortie, this time joining the Sabres of 234 Sqn on a sweep over Strasbourg before returning to Beek. 'B' Flight completed a number of sorties in the afternoon, the final four scrambling on an interception at 2040 hr.

Carte Blanche continued through 25 June when an intended move to Eindhoven was begun, the ground party leaving Beek for its third different base in a week. Unfortunately, many of the Sabres – of which fourteen were taking part in a fighter sweep – were diverted from landing at Eindhoven, and the main move was cancelled until the following day. Nonetheless, despite an early morning fog eight Sabres were launched at 1115 hr on a sweep over the Luxembourg area, and a second, ten-Sabre sweep by 'A' Flight was flown at 1515 hr in the same area. The final sortie on 25 June was scrambled at 1930 hr, ending in a successful intercept. Severe cumulonimbus cloud formations split up a number of the later missions, resulting in some of the aircraft diverting to alternative airfields.

This left the squadron with Sabres spread across central Europe at dawn on 26 June, but twelve aircraft were nonetheless flown on skittle operations, landing at Eindhoven on completion. A further skittle operation was planned for 1435 hr, but only two Sabres got airborne before further missions had to be curtailed. Unfortunately, Fg Off Mike Line of 'A' Flight brought this mission to a less than successful conclusion when he hit his leader's wake turbulence on take-off from Eindhoven. Line had just raised his undercarriage, and as the aircraft sank back it began to scrape the runway; he then lowered his undercarriage again but was unable to prevent his aircraft running off the runway. It came to rest in the bomb dump and exploded. Line was thrown clear and rushed to hospital in Eindhoven, still unconscious. The two Sabres that had already scrambled were diverted to Geilenkirchen while the runway was cleared. Line recovered from his injuries but to this day recalls nothing of the accident. Line's Sabre, XB633/W, was a total loss.

On 27 June the squadron moved onto the defensive when 'enemy' Sabres attacked Eindhoven, rendering three aircraft out of action. 'B' Flight then launched six Sabres on a sweep at 0615 hr and the two aircraft at Geilenkirchen also returned. 'A' Flight managed to perform a four-ship mission and redressed the balance by claiming five 'enemy' F-84s destroyed and several damaged. At 2000 hr, the eleven remaining Sabres at Eindhoven were flown back to Geilenkirchen, the ground party leaving

Eindhoven the following day to end the squadron's involvement in Carte Blanche.

After a brief rest period, the squadron was again in action at the beginning of July in preparation for armament-practice camp (APC) in Cyprus. On 6 July the first personnel left aboard Hastings aircraft along with any pilots that were not ferrying aircraft; the squadron would take twelve Sabres with it to Cyprus. Unfortunately, though the transport aircraft managed to reach Cyprus safely, bad weather on 7 July prevented any of the Sabres from taking off. Next day the dozen Sabres left for APC, routing from Geilenkirchen to Istres, France and on to Rome-Ciampino airport for a refuel and night stop. On 9 July, ten Sabres flew via Larisa in Greece to Nicosia, Cyprus, leaving two unserviceable aircraft at Rome.

Hot conditions in Cyprus meant that the normal working day began at 0615 hr and ran through to early afternoon, one flight being on the range each day. 'A' Flight started firing on 12 July, sixteen air-to-air sorties being flown against towed flags to the north of Kyrenia. Unfortunately, gunsight problems intervened on the following day and only nine sorties were possible; it was also noted that pilots were still firing too early. On 16 July the two Sabres left at Rome finally joined the squadron in Cyprus; they were flown in by Fg Off C.A. Neill of 'B' Flight and Fg Off G. Jonas of 'A' Flight. Fg Off Neill was immediately into his stride, and managed to score a record forty hits on the flag when 'B' Flight flew sorties on 18 July.

Not all pilots were that fortunate. Brian Scotford, the unfortunate victim of circumstance, spent much of the detachment lazing in the sun. 'The APC in Cyprus in July '56 brings back interesting memories. I had two trips while I was there, and each time I burst a tyre on landing (thank God for nose-wheel steering!). Our OC Flying, Wg Cdr Clive Baker, was less than impressed (and refused to take account of the large bits of stone that were scattered on the runway threshold, one of which I managed to hit each time) and grounded me for the rest of the detachment. Sadly, it meant that I could do nothing but put in more time snorkelling off Kyrenia!'

On 18 July, four Sabres were deployed to Jordan for a three-day visit. One of these aircraft became unserviceable on arrival and Sgt Thornton was flown out in a Vampire to fix it. The quartet of Sabres was based at Amman, and they performed a number of bomber 'stooge' missions for the 249 Sqn Venom fighter bombers based there. Pilots reported that the Venom could easily outfly the Sabre in anything other than a vertical dive. The Sabres returned from Jordan on 20 July, the last day that gunnery missions were flown in Cyprus.

The first section of four Sabres left the island for return to Germany on 24 July led by Sqn Ldr Hutchinson; two other sections of Sabres deployed at twenty-minute intervals. This time the route went via Eskisehir in Turkey and Larisa in Greece; all aircraft arrived in Rome the same day. On 25 July the Sabres left Rome and transited via Fürstenfeldbruck in Germany on to Geilenkirchen. One aircraft was left at Fürstenfeldbruck for a wheel change; Fg Off Challen of 'A' Flight flew it back the next day.

After the hectic days in Cyprus, August 1955 was, by contrast, a quiet month. Some turnover in pilots was experienced, and five junior pilots from the Command Support Unit at Bückeburg were posted in; all had Sabre experience. Exercise Loco began on 24 August, but as with many of these exercises 3 Sqn played only a small part. Two pairs missions and two single simulated bombing attacks were flown on the first day in the 69 Gp area with no signs of opposition. Bomber stooge missions were flown on 25 August, but there ended the unit's involvement in Loco. A similar low-key

Armourers from 3 Sqn swarm over XB871/E as they prepare to harmonise its machine guns in the stop butts at Geilenkirchen. This photograph was taken just prior to the squadron's March 1956 Sylt detachment. (*Mrs Lydia Inkersole*)

involvement was noted for Exercise Argus, which began on 1 September.

Improving air-to-ground scores on the Monschau range were noted in September, though it should be stated that the range targets had been enlarged to a 15ft diameter; a new 20-degree dive angle was also trialled. It should therefore come as no surprise that, when the first large-scale air-to-ground sorties were flown on the range, scores were judged as being 'better than normal'!

The main UK air-defence exercise, 'Beware', began at the end of September, four Sabres flying a 'skittle' radar-saturation mission over the UK on the 23rd to begin the squadron's involvement. Flights planned for the following day were cancelled because of rain and low cloud, but two Sabres managed interceptions over England on 25 and 27 September. Seven Sabres took part in a sweep over the UK on 1 October as the final part of the Beware commitment, noting no action.

The squadron flew to Sylt again on 10 October, though from the beginning of this deployment fog, rain and low cloud played their part and no missions were possible for the first week. It was not until 18 October that it became possible to get the Sabres into the air, and sorties were then flown on the flag at 20,000ft. Sqn Ldr Hutchinson laid down his marker on 19 October with a 47 per cent score, which remained unbeaten during the Sylt detachment. The squadron average had improved since the last Sylt visit, however – to 6.9 per cent in the low range and 12.3 per cent high. The Sabres returned to Geilenkirchen on 10 November.

The low flying rate was relieved somewhat at the end of December when missions were flown on Exercise Sid Fine, which was concerned with the interception of bombers at high altitude. On 20 December two battle formations of four aircraft were flown and five Canberra bombers were claimed, all flying at altitudes above 30,000ft.

The exercise commitment continued into 1956, with four Sabres standing by on 5 January for Exercise Argus. However, at 1045 hr on that day the squadron was informed of the cancellation of the exercise, and normal flying resumed. Fog and snow then intervened for much of the rest of the month and many personnel instead went skiing in the Monschau range. The lack of flying did prove a bonus for the ground crews during this period, and on 13 January 'A' Flight reported that it had achieved 100 per cent serviceability for nearly two weeks, with 'B' Flight reporting a similar achievement.

The first air-to-ground missions at Monschau in 1956 began on 1 February, though fog and snow were still in abundance. On the following day an eight-aircraft sweep was flown over the Canadian base at Zweibrücken before the snow and fog closed in again, precluding any more flying until 11 February. Even then, just a solitary day was possible before weather again stopped play until the end of the month.

A further deployment to Sylt began on 25 March, the advance party leaving by road on that day. Again the weather intervened, with many of the Sabres also requiring STIs before they could be declared airworthy. It would be 6 April before the aircraft finally arrived at Sylt to begin live firing. Incredibly, once flying did begin, sorties were limited by a lack of oxygen-replenishment trolleys. Good results were almost immediately noted in any case: Fg Off M.S. Holtby pegged the best score of the detachment at 43 per cent, and the squadron average ended at a reasonable 12 per cent.

On 1 May, four sorties were flown against air-to-air target gliders, all four being shot down in the process. Brian Scotford was one of those fortunate enough to shoot at these glider targets: 'My particular memory of the April/May '56 detachment concerns the towed gliders. I believe four glider sorties were flown for the whole detachment, and we fired on them in fours with all guns loaded. I was fortunate to be leading one four, turned in on my first pass, placed the pipper on the target, opened fire way out of range and watched the glider disintegrate in front of my eyes. Needless to say the remaining three hopefuls were not impressed and never got another chance.' All Sabres returned to Geilenkirchen on 4 May and the squadron stood down for three days.

Upon return to work, 3 Sqn entered a new era. The personnel had known for some time that Hawker Hunters would be replacing the faithful Sabres, but when lectures started on the new type on 7 May, it became official. These lectures detailed the Hunter's ejection seat, oil and fuel systems, as well as fuel-management and electrical-system operation. Pilots and ground crews were all involved in these lecture periods.

Almost immediately, Sabre flying began to wind down, and on 15 May four of the squadron's Sabres were ferried back to the UK for overhaul. On 24 May a visit by the British press was arranged at Geilenkirchen, and nine Sabres were put into the air for a fly-past, followed by a Sabre-Swift-Hunter formation fly-by. The final Sabre mission on the Monschau range was flown on 29 May, and by 8 June six Hunters were on squadron strength. At this point there was very little Sabre flying other than in performing test flights for aircraft being ferried back to the UK. The squadron was declared non-operational on 12 June 1956 to begin conversion to the Hunter.

On 13 June, five Sabres were ferried to England, with another four on 15 June. The involvement of 3 Sqn with the Sabre was finally drawn to a close on 19 June when the final air test was completed on XB670/S. On the same day, the unit flew its first Hunter sorties. XB670 was the last RAF Sabre in Germany; it was ferried out to Benson by a 147 Sqn pilot on 21 June 1956.

Aircraft Assigned

XB536, XB541/L*, XB547/H*, XB550, XB581/T*, XB582/R*, XB585/F*, XB589*, XB590/V*, XB609/H, XB612/F, XB614, XB617/C*, XB619/L, XB621/K, XB629/X, XB633/W*, XB640/P*, XB643/K, XB644/K, XB646/W*, XB667/D, XB670/S*, XB672/G*, XB673/Q*, XB681, XB684, XB685/Y, XB699, XB703/Y, XB704*, XB707, XB731/B*, XB736/X*, XB738, XB740/M*, XB744/A*, XB745*, XB747/B*, XB749/A*, XB790/M*, XB792*, XB858, XB859*, XB871/E, XB913/L, XB938/D*, XB949, XB953, XB957, XB973/U*, XB984/K*.

* = '6–3' wing (all conversions).

Markings – 3 Sqn

These initially comprised a gloss mid-green intake ring with the squadron badge placed on a white disc either side of the forward fuselage below the forward windshield. The forward nose undercarriage door was painted in the flight colour (red for 'A' Flight, blue for 'B' Flight) with the individual code letter painted in white. 'A' Flight aircraft wore early alphabetical letters, and 'B' Flight those later in the alphabet. The code letter on all aircraft was red with a white outline.

When the later 'bar' markings were adopted by 2 TAF Sabre squadrons, these were applied either side of the fuselage roundel and comprised mid-green bars with a thin yellow outline. There was no yellow outlining on the nose band. Most aircraft carried the pilot's name in white on the port-side (left-hand) canopy rail.

Prior to adoption of the latter scheme the CO's Sabre, XB984/K, had the nose band and fuselage bars, but this time with a thin yellow outline to the rear of the nose band. To further distinguish the aircraft, a broad green band, again with yellow outlines, was painted on the aircraft's vertical tail fin above the fin flash.

Squadron Motto

Tertius primus erit (The third shall be first).

CHAPTER FIVE

4 SQUADRON

Part of 122 Wg at Jever, by early 1954 4 Sqn was commanded by Sqn Ldr Peter W. Gilpin, DFC. The squadron had flown Vampire fighter bombers for a number of years, but on 26 February 1954 plans for their replacement were finalised: conversion onto Sabres would begin the following month.

Initially there was a slow changeover to the new type. Quizzes were held on 1 March to test crews on the Sabre, and the following day sixteen pilots were transferred to Wildenrath to begin flying with Sabre Conversion Unit. All pilots completed the ground-school phase on 4 March, which culminated in an eighty-six-question test. Bad weather prevented any flying training for a few days, though on 5 March supervised engine starts were possible; crews appreciated the opportunity, since the procedure was more complex than the Vampire.

Sqn Ldr Gilpin and Flt Lt Eric Hughes of Jever Station Flight made their first Sabre solos at SCU on 6 March, Peter Gilpin recalling that he was fined £1 for exceeding the minimum flap-extension speed on his sortie. Further bad weather precluded any of the other pilots from flying that day, and when sorties were possible again on 8 March it was again only 'The Boss' and Flt Lt Hughes who flew. However, things did improve and by the time of the CO's return to Jever on 11 March most of the pilots on this course had soloed. Due to the short runway at Jever, pilots undergoing training at SCU were constantly reminded of the need to stop in the shortest-possible distance. To

Early squadron markings comprised just the squadron code letters either side of the fuselage roundel; this Sabre is coded 'F-B'. (*Chas Boyack*)

drive this point home, on 11 March flags were placed beside the runway at Wildenrath at the 2,000yd point to simulate the end of Jever's runway. Ominously, a number of pilots on the SCU course overshot the flag.

With the squadron due to equip entirely with '6–3'-winged Sabres, at least one SCU flight for each pilot was made in an unslatted Sabre. For example, when Norman Giffin went through SCU conversion, he flew XB688, XB952 and XB675 – all slatted machines – but also did one mission in XB935, which was one of a few '6–3'-winged Sabres held by SCU. The following course, comprising mainly 'A' Flight pilots, departed for SCU on 14 March and this time included a number of maintenance personnel, who were brought up to speed on technical aspects of servicing the aircraft. Meanwhile, at Jever the squadron began to prepare the Vampires for ferrying out.

The first Sabres for the squadron were delivered by 147 Sqn ferry pilots on 8 March 1954. It was an ignominious start, as Flt Lt Blair, an ex-4 Sqn pilot, ran off the runway in the first Sabre to land. Chas Boyack was at SCU when the first Sabres arrived, and recalls that this was not the only incident in those early days: 'While we were at Wildenrath, the Boss (Peter Gilpin) received a phone call about our first Sabre, which had arrived at Jever. When the engineers had played with it for a day or so, the Station Commander [Gp Capt George Powell-Shedden] decided that he would get in a spot of taxiing practice with this new-fangled toe-braking and nose-wheel-steering machine. Unfortunately, he got a bit carried away and burnt out the brakes, only coming gently to rest because the grass was fairly long and the ground fairly soft. The Boss was not impressed.'

Fortunately, damage to both aircraft was minimal though Jever's flying was restricted for the remainder of the day. The four aircraft delivered that day were XB647, XB921, XB980 and XB996, all flying in from Benson. As a result of these problems, a hasty runway-lengthening programme was put into action, and in the meantime the runway was resurfaced. Thus, while the first Sabres were put through acceptance checks, the remainder of the squadron deployed its Vampires to Ahlhorn on 12 March. No Sabres were transferred at this time as the first group were still on course at Wildenrath. Considerable upheaval now followed, with freshly converted pilots from 'B' Flight arriving at Ahlhorn on 15 March despite having no aircraft other than a few Vampires to fly. To add to the problems, three personnel who had been detached to Geilenkirchen to ferry Sabres into 4 Sqn were informed that the Sabres were not for allocation to the squadron after all. It therefore fell to the Vampires to keep the squadron flying: on 22 March, range firing was carried out, with twenty-eight sorties being logged; concurrently, high-level missions were launched to prepare pilots for the Sabre.

Most of the second SCU course returned to Ahlhorn on 24 March, except for a few stragglers, who took a further day to finish their conversion. On 25 March the next pair of Sabres for 122 Wg, XB773 and XB856, arrived at Ahlhorn. One of these went immediately to 93 Sqn, the sister Sabre unit in the wing, but deliveries to 4 Sqn continued for the next few weeks. Six Vampires were ferried out to the UK on 26 March and a further half-dozen three days later. This left three on strength. During this period, personnel would travel back to their accommodation at Jever on weekends, returning to work at Ahlhorn on the following Monday.

The arrival of Sabres for the squadron now began to gather pace: five were delivered to Ahlhorn during the weekend of 27/8 March and a further four were transferred from Oldenburg on the 30th, this time by

Fine air-to-air shot of XB773/C-B in early 4 Sqn markings. These codes were 'handed', so that the opposite side of the fuselage read, 'B-C'. (*Norman Giffin*)

squadron pilots; these were the first Sabre sorties carried out by 4 Sqn. Further flying was not possible, however, as this batch was immediately placed on acceptance inspections. By the end of the month, including SCU time, the squadron had logged 146.25 hours on the Sabre.

With runway work finally completed at Jever, twelve Sabres and one remaining Vampire were flown back on 5 April. The Sabres arrived in some style, flying past in formations of four aircraft at a time. Some taxiway work remained to be done at base, but the crews worked around this inconvenience, glad to be back at home. Once back at Jever, the squadron was finally able to commence a concerted working-up period on the Sabre, the first missions being flown with the aircraft in 'clean' configuration without drop tanks. Each flight completed four low-level, close-formation sorties on 7 April, the same day that the final three Vampire missions were launched. Wg Cdr West, who had been watching the early attempts by the squadron to fly neat circuits in the Sabre, put a halt to close-formation sorties on 8 April and decreed that the squadron should concentrate on general handling and aerobatic missions.

When on 21 April the squadron returned from its Easter break, many aircraft were declared unserviceable by an STI requiring strengthening of a cartridge locking pin on the Sabre's ejection seat. Only one sortie was flown that day, but the ground crews managed to have aircraft available on 22 April, when twenty-eight sorties were launched. This marked the squadron's first 'stream' take-off and landing, and was a welcome change in the light of OC Flying Wing's earlier restrictions. For these sorties, drop tanks were fitted for the first time. Continuing to expand their abilities, pilots flew cross-country missions via Hannover, Cologne and Groningen at 35,000ft on 27 April.

The first of many exercises began at 2359 hr on the night of 29 April. 'Wild Goose' was a station-level exercise, designed to test Jever's defences against attack by saboteurs. The squadron deployed to the south-east dispersal and maintained a 24-hour watch. Meanwhile, a full flying programme was maintained for what was planned as a five-day exercise. During the first day, three saboteurs were flushed out, while airborne 'enemy' attacks also began. These were poorly forecast, as the squadron's forward lookout posts were only five miles from the airfield

Like many of the buildings at Jever, 4 Sqn's hangar dated from the Second World War. (*Norman Giffin*)

and gave little time to warn of fast-flying aircraft. Weather on this day was wet, and on the squadron's last sortie Fg Off Laycock and Fg Off Watson ran off the end of the runway during a pairs landing. They ended up side by side in the overshoot area, unharmed and thankfully with no damage to either aircraft. Wild Goose was ended on 2 May.

Aside from these overshoots, further problems began to highlight that Jever's runway was too short. On 3 May, a shortage of Sabre brake units began to be felt, and by the following day only two Sabres were serviceable on each flight. Heavy braking on the short runway was taking its toll. Again, the maintenance personnel managed to overcome this problem by stealing serviceable parts from long-term unserviceable aircraft, and this at least allowed the flights to begin flying three-ship close-formation practice missions.

During May, a number of unusual sorties were flown, beginning on the 10th when the squadron's navigation officer, Flt Lt Bowen, used five Sabres and crews to fly different mission profiles. These were designed to gain knowledge of time-to-height, power settings, and fuel consumption at a variety of speeds. Six hours were devoted to this test, though results were not as expected – very little difference was noted between each profile. Meanwhile, a signals unit had arrived on station, and they began attempting to jam radio signals in order to monitor the effect on Sabre operations. Their efforts were considered a success when the GCI channel was effectively blocked, but negligible jamming was evident on VHF channels.

Training missions continued, and the squadron's first 'barrage' exercise was launched on 11 May when four aircraft flew a mock bombing raid against Cologne with the Sabres of 93 Sqn. On 14 May, various formations were practised, including a stream of five boxes of four Sabres and one formation with six aircraft. These flights were flown at 25,000ft and practised battle-formation tactics as well as tail chases.

By mid-May, pilot manning on 4 Sqn stood at thirty, and with so many flying personnel on the squadron it became difficult for each to achieve the requisite number of flying hours per month. In addition, the squadron's total flying hours were proving difficult to attain because of aircraft unserviceabilities. This situation became so bad that on 24 May, with the squadron 200 hours short of its monthly flying target, an 'early to late' full-day flying programme was put in effect until

XB854/T-B begins its take-off run at Jever. (*Norman Giffin*)

the end of the month. This had an immediate effect, with the forty-two sorties flown on that day alone contributing over 50 flying hours towards the target. However, the problems persisted into June and, with a 420-hour monthly target, it was decided to make Tuesdays and Thursdays 'late flying' nights.

Following earlier criticism by OC Flying, 4 Sqn's circuit procedure had improved greatly by the end of May, but further problems still cropped up. On 3 June, battle formations, aerobatics and dogfights were practised by 'A' Flight, but on one of these missions Fg Off Bradley burst a tyre, though he managed to hold the aircraft on the runway nonetheless. On 8 June, Fg Off Jack lost his drop tanks in flight due to an unspecified electrical problem. By mid-June, these and other aircraft-related problems meant that pilots were averaging between 10 and 12 flying hours per month. As if this were not enough, a number of aircraft were concurrently destroyed or badly damaged in flying accidents.

The first involved Fg Off Ron Gray, who was detailed as number four on a high-level battle-flight mission on 22 June. Chas Boyack was on the squadron at the time:

> [He] lost visual contact with the rest of his four-ship formation, in wispy cirrus at very high level, then decided to return to base using the (new) radio compass. Unfortunately, that lot who paint red stars on their vehicles had sited a beacon on a very similar frequency up on the Black Sea. Our hero went thataway for a while before realising his error – his TX/RX [transmissions and signals received] with Jever were getting fainter. He let down on an estimated heading for base and when clear of fairly low cloud, recognised an autobahn. He pressed on and came to a very large city with lowering cloud and increasing rain. Fuel now became an issue, so he returned to his autobahn (Hamburg/Lübeck) and landed on it. On the right-hand lanes, of course. Right at the end of his landing run, the aircraft turned off the autobahn into an entry to a field. A Beetle pulled up and the American Major greeted our aviator warmly, saying he had seen F-86's in some funny places but never before on an autobahn.

Fg Off Gray's Sabre was XB940, and unfortunately it had hit a tree on the landing run; damage was severe enough to write off the aircraft. More serious for the squadron was Fg Off John Jack's accident of 8 July. Approaching Jever in XB647, Jack's aircraft overshot with its dive brakes extended. The Sabre flicked over at slow speed and rolled into the ground killing Jack instantly. His body was returned to the UK for burial on 13 July, accompanied by two officers and an NCO from his squadron. Incredibly, the squadron did not always get to learn from these accidents as Chas Boyack indicates: 'He crashed doing a break into the circuit. We did not get as much information on accidents then as later became the case, but it would appear that he overcooked the "g" for the rapidly reducing speed approaching the beginning of the downwind part of the circuit.'

The squadron's first battle flight was programmed at the end of June 1954. This meant that during daylight hours one flight was always at standby to intercept intruding aircraft. Many of the scrambles launched by battle flight were against known targets, testing the squadron's readiness.

Exercise Dividend, planned for mid-July, was a major test of the UK's defences, and a large number of 2 TAF units were detailed to act as 'intruder' aircraft. As a result, from 14 July, 4 Sqn began preparing for Dividend, notably by concentrating on dinghy and ditching drills. Dividend itself began on 17 July, though the first raid by 4 Sqn, planned for 0400 hr was cancelled due to very bad weather. Subsequent raids were also cancelled, and rain, a low cloudbase and one-mile visibility continued into the following day. An afternoon raid did manage to take off on 18 July, despite being depleted by one unserviceable Sabre. Norman Giffin flew one of these missions (in XB938) and recalls that confusion reigned when the various formation leaders declared communications problems. Though the mission was being led by Wg Cdr West, it was actually his adjutant who finally took control of the situation and diverse attacks were eventually sent against Sculthorpe, Neatishead and Coltishall. Following the successful return of the ten Sabres on this mission, the squadron stood down for the weekend of 19/20 June.

The second phase of Dividend, subtitled 'Dividend Bonus', began on 22 July with the objective of saturating the UK's air defences. Twelve Sabres from 4 Sqn flew in formations of four aircraft, and all of these were intercepted by Fighter Command aircraft, comprising mainly Meteors, plus a pair of Hunters. On the following day, the first Sabres were airborne at 0430 hr on missions to Bawburgh, Seething, Hardwick, Neatishead and Coltishall – all on the coast of East Anglia. A further wave of fighters was launched on the same area at 1300 hr in the afternoon, flying at heights of between 30,000 and 40,000ft. Twenty-one sorties were flown on this, the squadron's final participation on Dividend, as further sorties planned for 24 and 25 July were cancelled because of bad weather.

There then began an intense period of gunnery practice, which started on 26 July when Fg Offs Beaton and Clayton flew to Fassberg to rehearse an air-to-ground firing demonstration for Iraqi chiefs of staff. Meanwhile, air-to-ground firing at Meppen ranges continued and air-to-air quarter attacks were practised in preparation for a Sylt deployment. With this in mind, on 11 August a lecture was given to squadron personnel by Mr Goliva, the A4-gunsight technical representative. Flt Lt Tony Vasey, 'B' Flight commander, carried out the first air-to-air target-sleeve towing missions by 122 Wg Sabres on 26 August, and two further Sabres performed dummy attacks on the target sleeve. To improve radar lock-on performance, metal foil was later attached to the fabric target sleeve, though subsequently a series of metallic reflectors were found to be more effective.

Exercise Lucifer, a three-day test of Dutch defences, began on 31 August. The squadron's task was to simulate high-level bombers and low-level intruders. However, in similar circumstances to Dividend of the previous month, the first raids of Lucifer were cancelled due to bad weather. Fortunately the weather cleared on 1 September and two raids were launched on the Hague and Brussels as well as targeting airfields in Holland. These missions lasted up to 1 hour and 20 minutes, though little opposition was noted. Similar raids were flown on 2 September.

The squadron's Sylt deployment began on 16 September, when the advance party left by road. The main party left for Sylt in the early morning of 19 September, though the transit of aircraft to Sylt was a fraught affair. When the weather finally cleared on 20 September, six Sabres were able to get airborne but, even then, conditions at Sylt were marginal and only four were able to land; one of these aircraft, XB773/C, had already exceeded its airframe 'g' limits on the ferry flight and was landed in the undershoot, causing further damage. XB773 took three weeks to repair. The remaining Sabres finally got into Sylt on 21 September, and cine and demonstration flights were immediately programmed. Throughout the detachment, bad weather continued to curtail gunnery missions, including those by 'B' Flight on the morning of 22 September. 'A' Flight faired better in the afternoon, though still completed only cine attacks. Further bad weather then intervened, but by 7 October the average was up to 8 per cent.

Unfortunately, this run of excellence was interrupted on 8 October by the death of Fg Off Ken A. Richardson, one of the squadron's two pilot attack instructors. Detailed for air-to-air gunnery on the Amrum high range, Richardson had been flying a pairs mission with Fg Off Dave Clayton. When they got onto the range, the flag was unserviceable, so they elected to carry out a tail-chase exercise with Richardson leading. Richardson had often bragged that he could invert a Sabre and pull through to recover in 3,000ft; squadron pilots doubted this, but what followed may have been proof that he had previously tried such a feat. Soon after the tail chase started, Fg Off Richardson inverted his Sabre and started to descend. At this point, Fg Off Clayton felt uneasy and pulled away from the chase; he lost sight of his leader. Richardson's aircraft, XB937, was subsequently seen to dive into the sea nine miles south-east of Sylt. The pilot was killed instantly. Richardson's funeral on 13 October was attended by eighteen pilots and nearly one hundred airmen from the squadron.

On 12 October a double rearm practice was carried out at Sylt, with aircraft planned to fly firing sorties in between. Typically, this exercise had to be cancelled part-way through because of a rainstorm. Though further firing missions were completed, many other sorties were devoted to QGH and GCA flights until the end of the detachment. The advance party left Sylt by road on 15 October, this time bound for Wunstorf, where the squadron would operate while further work was carried out on Jever's runway. The Sabres, again delayed by bad weather, flew to Wunstorf on 19 October.

Many Sabres were put on primary servicing as soon as they arrived at Wunstorf, which meant that not much flying was possible in the first days there. However, on 21 October a number of sector-recce missions were launched, and five Sabres flew a barrage to Koblenz and Geilenkirchen. They were not intercepted. Further to this, on 26 October the squadron launched a successful strafing attack on Fassberg as part of Exercise Red Rover, but this appears to have been the squadron's only involvement in that operation.

A 4 Sqn Sabre line-up in front of the CO's aircraft, XB996/B-A, at Sylt in September 1954. Back row L–R: Fg Off Mitchell, Fg Off Danny Daniels, Fg Off Les Bradley, Fg Off Bob Smith, Fg Off Chas Boyack, Fg Off Ken Maycock, Fg Off Ray Langstaff, P Off Alan Armitage, Fg Off Ginger Friend, Fg Off Norman Giffin, Fg Off Ron Gray, Fg Off Brian Watson. Front row L–R: Fg Off Les Swart, Fg Off Danby Laycock, Fg Off Bob Molden, Fg Off Dad Sanders, Fg Off Snowy Ewens, Flt Lt John Wallace, Fg Off Dougie Bridson, Fg Off Dave Clayton, Fg Off Peter Phillips, Fg Off Ken Richardson, Fg Off Pete Smith. Ken Richardson was killed in a Sabre crash soon after this photo was taken. (*Tony Vasey*)

For a change, there was a bout of good weather at the beginning of November, and air-to-ground missions were programmed on the Ströhen range. Unfortunately at 1130 hr on 1 November, 2 Gp issued a signal grounding all Sabres for generator-terminal inspections and further flying was curtailed until 4 November, when the first Sabres were passed as serviceable. For the rest of the period at Wunstorf, the range programme was given top priority, and squadron average scores hovered around the 10 per cent mark. Fg Off Bob Molden was highest scorer with 30 per cent.

After weeks of nomadic operations, the squadron left by rail for Jever on 13 November. On 15 November the Sabres successfully departed Wunstorf, but their arrival at Jever was less problem-free. After a long period of rainfall, the runway at Jever was very wet, and further rain and low cloud did not help. One of the first to land was Fg Off 'Snowy' Ewens, who could not bring his aircraft to a stop in time and ran off the runway into the overshoot. Fortunately, his Sabre was not damaged. Some time later, Fg Off Mitchell was not so lucky: his Sabre, XB983/S, ran off the side of the runway and was severely damaged. It could not be repaired on station and was eventually returned to the UK for repair with Airwork.

A further grounding of Sabres was ordered on 20 November, this time for inspection of tailplane actuator brackets, and fourteen Sabres were immediately declared unserviceable. Locally manufactured brackets were subsequently produced, and these were fitted from 4 December as a temporary fix; modified aircraft were then programmed for replacement of these items with Canadair parts at their next minor servicing.

While these aircraft were grounded, pilots were detached to Sabre Ground Training Unit (part of SCU) at Wildenrath for short

The 4 Sqn fuselage markings were probably the most exuberant of all the Sabre squadrons, comprising black upper portions with red areas beneath. The lightning flash and thin surround were yellow. (*Robin Brown*)

courses. 'A' Flight was detached on 22 November, followed by 'B' Flight pilots the next day. As aircraft became available, training missions resumed. For the remainder of 1954 bad weather prevented any form of concentrated flying programme, and only on 6 December did any large-scale sorties get launched. Many of these were low-level missions as a result of low cloud, and a few air-to-ground sorties were also accomplished. On 22 December, in a change from the norm, Sabres were scrambled to search for ships in distress in the North Sea.

When flying resumed in the New Year, the squadron immediately began to prepare for another Sylt deployment. Ground crews departed immediately and ten Sabres left Jever on 3 January 1955. The squadron began gunnery sorties, initially using the dual-control Vampire for demonstration missions, and in the first few days cine attacks were flown. Averages on the gunnery missions were immediately excellent, with a 9.7 per cent average being reached at the end of the detachment, which was the best by a Sabre squadron up to that point. Unfortunately, in mid-month a large amount of snow fell on Sylt island and further flying was not possible. By 21 January personnel were so fed up with kicking their heels that construction of a land yacht began, built from the remains of old target gliders. With so much time on their hands, they also attended lectures on the Hunter aircraft and its Aden cannon armament.

The snow abated on 28 January and flying finally resumed at Sylt; 4 Sqn flew seventeen gunnery sorties on this first clear day. On 4 February the first group of five Sabres departed for Jever, though weather stranded the rest of the squadron at Sylt until 7 February. Despite the problems they had experienced, squadron personnel could be rightly proud of their achievements.

But the squadron was also sidetracked by thoughts of re-equipment, this time with the Hawker Hunter. Ground lectures on the type began at Jever on 16 February and on 1 March, a number of Hunter F. 1s arrived on station. These aircraft were from the Day Fighter Leaders School, and one of the pilots was Tony Vasey, previously a flight commander on 4 Sqn. According to Norman Giffin, it was Vasey who had persuaded the DFLS hierarchy to bring the Hunters to Jever. The plan backfired slightly, however, as Tony Vasey managed to put his aircraft off the end of the runway on arrival at Jever; fortunately, there was no damage done. DFLS personnel briefed 4 Sqn on the new fighter, and a short talk was given by Wg Cdr Merryfield of DFLS on 2 March.

Many hours in March were given over to ground-defence lectures and training, though the squadron managed to maintain its battle-flight and training commitment. On 10 March, Fg Off Blake had a generator failure on the last sortie of the day. He landed in the overshoot and his aircraft, XB993, sustained Cat. 3 damage. It was eventually repaired on station, briefly returning to the squadron in August. Meanwhile, battle flight's aircraft were kept on alert, managing nine successful interceptions of Canberra and Venom aircraft on 22 March alone. Though the customary bad weather intervened throughout this period, on 16 April Wg Cdr 'Hammer' West, Jever's Wing Leader, led sixteen Sabres from 4 and 93 Sqns on a sweep via Ahlhorn and Oldenburg.

In order to make room for the arrival of two Hunter squadrons at Jever, on 18 April 4 Sqn moved out of its spacious Second World War hangar. The squadron's new base was situated across the airfield on the northern side, in less-than-ideal accommodation: the old hangar was used by the RAF Regiment to store various armoured vehicles. Shortly after the move, someone suggested that, in order to get as many pilots as possible enrolled into the 'Mach Busters Club', it would be a good idea to take four Sabres up to do the deed. To ensure that the bang was heard, these aircraft would then dive on Jever, using the old squadron hangar as the target. With their mission completed, the crews expected subsequent phone calls of complaint from the RAF Regiment to add to their sense of achievement, but none came. Indeed, the only call of complaint came from the nearby Malcolm Club, where ceiling plaster had been dislodged and had fallen into a vat of cooking oil. However, on the following day it was reported that the RAF Regiment couldn't open the doors to the hangar: the Sabres' shock waves had damaged the door runners, and the Regiment were stranded for some time.

The squadron was briefly involved in a further exercise, 'Sky High', on 26 April, sending eight Sabres to intercept Canberra and Lincoln bombers as well as F-84 Thunderjets. Only the first four aircraft managed to intercept their targets, claiming two Canberras destroyed. On 29 April more intercepts were launched and, though results were deemed to be less successful, ten Canberras were claimed. These missions were interspersed with practice quarter attacks against towed flags in preparation for another Sylt detachment in May. Intercepts were flown on 4 May, this time against DFLS aircraft, again led by Flt Lt Tony Vasey.

This squadron began its reduction from twenty-two to fourteen aircraft on 12 May with the ferrying of XB990/X to Westland. On the same day the advance party left for Sylt, stopping at Hamburg for the night. The rail party left Jever on 15 May and on the following day the Sabres departed. On arrival at Sylt, XB923, piloted by Ron Gray, hit the pronounced 'lip' at the near end of the

A proud Norman Giffin poses with his new Ford Prefect (right) on the taxiway at Jever, with Bob Smith aboard his MG 'Y' at left. The squadron hangar can just be seen to the left. (*Norman Giffin*)

runway. The impact severely damaged the port undercarriage and ripped off the port drop tank. Somehow Gray managed to get airborne again and released his remaining drop tank, which at the relatively low speed tipped up and rolled off the end of the wingtip, taking the pitot probe with it. Now with no airspeed indication, the pilot began orbiting to ascertain his options; at this point the port wheel finally fell off. Meanwhile, many of the squadron personnel, alerted to Gray's predicament, had run outside to witness the drama. The aircraft was eventually brought in to land at Sylt, but the damage was declared as Cat. 4 and XB923 was returned to the UK for repair. It never flew with the RAF again.

Despite this less-than-auspicious start, 4 Sqn performed well on this Sylt deployment, but could undoubtedly have done even better – bad weather, flags shot off and 'pilot staleness' were thought to be giving mixed results. Therefore, on 17 June flying was brought to a halt and a game of softball was played to raise spirits. On the following days, high-level battle formations at 35,000ft were practised to vary life slightly.

Unfortunately, the crews had little opportunity to gain any benefit from this break in the routine. Adverse weather and limited time until the end of the deployment contrived to prevent any improvement in gunnery scores. On 28 June a rearm turnaround exercise was scheduled, which entailed the Sabres flying at 30,000ft before diving and firing all six guns at once. The exercise was completed successfully, giving many pilots their first opportunity to fire all guns at once; it was usual on firing exercises to fire just one pair. Many expressed surprise at the noise, smoke and deceleration experienced.

On 29 June, 4 Sqn's advance party left Sylt, with the aircraft following on the 30th. The squadron's average for the detachment was 13.77 per cent, the highest achieved by an RAF Sabre squadron (by 0.1 per cent, from 93 Sqn). High-level scores were 14.3 per cent and 13.6 per cent at low level. These scores are particularly notable when one considers that the squadron had for some time been flying with defective ammunition. The problem only came to light back at Jever when an armourer managed accidentally to fire the guns on the ground. The bullets only flew for a few hundred yards before falling to earth, which was just as well, since the aircraft had been pointing directly at OC Flying's office.

The first pair of Hunter aircraft for 4 Sqn were delivered to Jever on 11 July, having been delayed at Oldenburg for three days because of bad weather. 'B' Flight concurrently stood down to convert to the Hunter, a process that went quickly. Pilots' notes for the new type had been issued on 9 July, and personnel from DFLS arrived on station to aid in the conversion process. The first Hunter sorties were flown on 13 July.

The squadron had meanwhile begun preparing Sabres for ferrying back to the UK. On 11 July, four aircraft were ferried out by 147 Sqn crews and a further Sabre was flown out by a 4 Sqn pilot. 'A' Flight had carried on flying missions throughout this period, doing high-level battle formations, including fifteen sorties on the last full day of Sabre flying, 19 July 1955. Ironically, inspections had grounded the Hunters so that the emphasis was entirely on Sabre flying for a few days. 'A' Flight stood down for Hunter conversion on 21 July and was declared non-operational on Sabres. Chas Boyack flew one of the final Sabre missions on the same day, a cine quarters and tail-chase exercise in XB938/D.

Six Sabres departed Jever on 28 July, three for 130 Sqn, two for 3 Sqn and one for 71 Sqn. These aircraft were all ferried out by 4 Sqn pilots. Final air tests on the few remaining Sabres were done on 9 August, and by the end of the month all had departed.

XB931/G was damaged on 10 August 1955 after its oxygen cylinders exploded while being replenished. It was air-freighted back to Lyneham aboard a Bristol freighter and then transferred to Airwork at Dunsfold for repair. However, the damage was deemed too great and it was scrapped. (*via Roger Lindsay*)

A fine in-flight view of XB981/Q in the squadron's definitive colour scheme. (*Tony Vasey*)

Aircraft Assigned

XB647, XB770/L, XB773/C, XB775/M, XB854/T, XB921, XB923, XB931/G, XB935/W, XB937, XB938/D, XB940, XB941, XB955/W, XB961, XB973, XB974/O, XB977/H, XB980/P, XB981/Q, XB983/S, XB989/X, XB990/X, XB993, XB994/R, XB995/W, XB996/A.

All aircraft initially coded 'B' followed by individual code letter – e.g. XB773 was B-C – were later just 'C'. All aircraft had '6–3' wing from manufacture.

Markings – 4 Sqn

Early squadron markings were very simple, comprising the individual code letter on either side of the fuselage roundel, accompanied by the squadron code letter ('B') on the other side of the roundel. Codes were applied in white so that the individual code letter preceded the squadron code letter on the port side and followed it on the left – e.g. XB854 read 'T – roundel – B' on the port side and 'B – roundel – T' on the starboard.

The introduction of 'bar' markings either side of the fuselage roundel, entailed a yellow outline with a yellow lightning flash bisecting a black (upper) and red (lower) sector. The lightning flash was inclined downwards at either side towards the roundel. The squadron code letter was deleted at this time, and the individual code letter was applied in pale blue in the middle of the fuselage. The individual code letter was repeated on the forward nose-wheel door. On the tail fin, against a black sunburst design, the red number '4' was imposed, cut through with a further yellow lightning flash.

Squadron Motto

In futurum videre (To see the future).

CHAPTER SIX

20 SQUADRON

By the Autumn of 1953, 20 Sqn was flying Vampire FB. 9s at RAF Oldenburg, commanded by Sqn Ldr Ian MacDonald. Flight commanders were Flt Lt D.F.M. Browne ('A' Flight) and Flt Lt R.J. Saker ('B' Flight).

The squadron had just completed its Sylt gunnery camp when word came that the squadron would receive its first Sabre F. 4. As a result, on 11 October nine pilots, mainly from 'B' Flight, along with twenty-six airmen, were sent to Wildenrath's Sabre Conversion Unit. Introductory lectures began on the following day, though for the aircrew a bout of poor weather meant that they were grounded for the time being. First solos on the Sabre were finally completed on 18 October. Having completed the course, the ground crew of 'B' Flight returned to base on 21 October, the aircrew four days later. Meanwhile, the personnel of 'A' Flight had begun SCU training on 21 October, and this was completed before the end of the month.

With the pilots and ground crew successfully converted onto the Sabre, it only remained for aircraft to be assigned to the squadron, and the first five arrived in the late afternoon of 28 October 1953. Six more were expected for delivery two days later, but bad weather meant that, reduced in number to five, they did not in fact arrive until 2 November. With the arrival of the Sabres, ground-support equipment also began to arrive with the squadron, though at first it was painfully slow in coming through. By the end of October, with five Sabres on strength, the squadron could only boast one towing arm, one energiser (ground-power set) and one borrowed servicing manual.

Despite this inauspicious start, the maintenance personnel got to work performing acceptance checks on the new aircraft, and by 2 November the first aircraft were available for air test. It was only right that the squadron commander should take the first sortie, though instead of performing a check flight on one of the initial batch of aircraft he instead took XB899, which had arrived on station that same day. The flight nearly ended in disaster: no-one had thought to add ballast to the unarmed aircraft, and as Sqn Ldr MacDonald came across the airfield to perform a high-speed run, he experienced a violent pitching motion which caused him momentarily to black out. Fortunately, MacDonald quickly recovered and landed safely. His Sabre was found to have sustained +11g and -6g, easily exceeding the aircraft's 7.33g limit. Subsequent inspection revealed no permanent damage, and the aircraft was returned to service.

On 5 November, the squadron's sixteenth – and for now final – Sabre was delivered, and on the following day the squadron was able to log its first full day of Sabre flying; all pilots managed at least one flight. The transfer of Vampires to other units continued during this period, and five were flown out to Jever on 27 and 28 November, leaving just four on the squadron. All were allotted for storage, departing for the UK in January 1954.

At the end of the year, a number of personnel changes occurred. On the credit side, Fg Offs Croucher, Leitch and Galpin arrived with the squadron on 9 November. All were USAF-trained and fully converted to the Sabre. Sadly, on the debit side, Flt Lt R.J. Saker, the 'B' Flight commander, was killed in

XB899 was the first Sabre to fly with 20 Sqn and was taken aloft by Sqn Ldr MacDonald to perform a high-speed run across the airfield. Unfortunately, incorrect ballasting of the aircraft caused a violent 'JC' (Jesus Christ) manoeuvre at high speed and MacDonald momentarily blacked out in the -4 g and +10 g bunt. He landed safely, but a lesson had been learnt. Unfortunately, XB899 was later written off in an accident at Schleswigland; pilot 'Flush' Kendall was uninjured. (*Vic Nickson*)

a car crash returning from a squash match at Ahlhorn in the early hours of 17 November. Flt Lt Saker was buried in Hamburg six days later in a ceremony attended by Oldenburg's Wing Leader and the Station Commander, Gp Capt D.E.B. Wheeler, DFC. Saker's place at the head of 'B' Flight was taken temporarily by Flt Lt B.R. Galletly, who was promoted from within the squadron. At the end of November, Fg Off Rigby returned to the squadron from a detachment flying Thunderjets in Korea. He was soon promoted to flight lieutenant and took over as full-time 'B' Flight commander. Another Korean veteran on the squadron was Fg Off W. 'Bill' Simmonds, a Royal Australian Air Force (RAAF) officer on exchange with the RAF. Simmonds was one of only three pilots to have shot down a MiG-15 while flying Meteors in Korea.

On 24 November 1953, 20 Sqn completed its first tactical mission, when Wg Cdr Nelson-Edwards led Sqn Ldr MacDonald and Flt Lt Galletly to intercept a DFLS formation making its way back to England from Wunstorf. It had been a good month for the squadron: they had begun it as novices and ended it with some semblance of operational effectiveness. There were, however, two incidents during the month, with thankfully no injury to those involved. On one occasion, a Sabre ran off the taxiway and damaged a drop tank, and in the second incident a loss of hydraulic pressure resulted in brake failure on landing and a run into the overshoot area.

Though December began in very positive spirits (65 flying hours had been flown by cease of play on 3 December), they were dampened by successive days of poor weather. Allied to this, a continued inability effectively to harmonise the A4 gunsight meant that the squadron could still not be classed as fully operational. And though flying began on 2 January 1954 with a four-ship formation and a number of other missions, the arrival of an STI on 5 January grounded every Sabre while tailplane-trim actuators were inspected;

Vic Nickson brings in XB594/V, devoid of drop tanks, to land at Oldenburg. (*Vic Nickson*)

some aircraft were cleared for flying in the afternoon, but seven were declared 'Aircraft on Ground' awaiting replacement parts.

Fg Off Moran had a close call on 17 January when he experienced oxygen starvation at 30,000ft while on a mission. Fortunately, Moran was alert enough to recover his aircraft, but after the mission the SMO declared him unfit for flying until tests had been carried out. Two days later it was found that all Sabre oxygen regulators had become time-expired, and missions were limited to flying below 12,500ft cabin altitude. It is not known whether the latter was linked to Fg Off Moran's near miss. By the end of the month, replacement regulators had arrived on station, and only one Sabre still had the old type.

Battle flight was first called on 21 January, each flight putting up four-ship formations. Both were successful, with a mixture of 'enemy' Vampires and Venoms being intercepted. The concentrated number of missions led to more than 35 hours being flown on that day alone – a record that stood for just a few days as, during a continued period of clear weather, 37 hours were flown on 26 January. Meanwhile, air-to-ground firing had finally begun on 18 January, when three aircraft flew to the Meppen range to fire the guns. During the month, eight Sabres were harmonised in the butts and a total of four managed to fire at Meppen. In total, there were thirteen range sorties, of which five were aborted for a variety of reasons. The squadron had yet to master the radar gunsight.

A spate of incidents seriously curtailed flying in January, and caused a good few problems. On 27 January, Fg Off Vic Nickson in XB597 had his port main undercarriage door come open in flight. The sudden jolt did serious damage to the underside of his Sabre, which was assessed as Cat. 3. Two similar occurrences at the Meppen range on the following day alerted the squadron that this was no isolated incident and, while maintenance personnel struggled to identify the cause, on 29 January two further doors came open in flight. The more serious of these resulted in the nose-wheel door on XB645 coming unlocked during the break to land, causing Cat. 4 damage requiring return of the aircraft to Airwork for repair. Immediately, all Sabres on station were grounded, pending further investigation. Aircraft were checked to ensure that a nose undercarriage STI had been completed, and after thorough rigging checks they began to return to service. The situation was considerably aided by the fact that 234 Sqn had recently departed the station,

XB594/V gets a polish prior to Princess Margaret's visit to Oldenburg in July 1954. (*Vic Nickson*)

allowing 20 Sqn to spread its aircraft into the vacant half of the hangar. Concurrently, an Intermediate Servicing Team was formed under Chief Technician Codling, and the rationalisation of maintenance manpower helped the squadron through a difficult period. Unfortunately, 20 Sqn had not heard the last of its undercarriage problems.

It was no great surprise that at the beginning of February there were few serviceable aircraft on the squadron. On 3 February, only three Sabres were available to fly, but thankfully these aircraft stayed in an airworthy condition, and by the end of the following day the squadron had almost inconceivably logged 66.35 hours for the month. One of the few serviceable Sabres was lost in an accident on 6 February when XB791 landed heavily in the overshoot area after its engine had been unintentionally shut down before landing; it received Cat. 4 damage. A further Sabre ran off a slippery runway on 26 February, though this time there was no serious result. Fortunately, towards the end of February 1954, serviceability rose once the undercarriage problems had largely been solved, and numerous STIs had been satisfied.

Up to this point, 20 Sqn had received purely slatted Sabres, but at the end of February notice was given that the next two aircraft to be allotted (XB854 and XB977) would be the unslatted '6–3'-winged variety. Both aircraft arrived on station on 4 March, but they remained the only 'hard edge' aircraft assigned to 20 Sqn. Thus, for safety's sake, the squadron standardised on the slatted Sabre, and both XB854 and XB977 were ferried out for reassignment to 4 Sqn at Jever on the afternoon of 30 March.

Concentrated gunnery missions to the Meppen range began on 4 March, twenty-one sorties being flown on that day alone, of which twelve were deemed to have been successful. A further flying record of 39.5 hours for 41 sorties was flown on that day, though bad weather over the next few weeks prevented further inroads being made into the gunnery programme. After the prolonged bout of weather, flying resumed on the morning of 17 March, but the first detail was delayed after Fg Off Harry Capewell aborted his take-off and seriously damaged his Sabre's nose wheel, with the result that XB749 sustained Cat. 3 damage, and thirteen airborne Sabres of the wing diverted to Ahlhorn. The runway was soon clear again and the diverted aircraft returned to base just after lunch. For the next few weeks, flying proved to be a curate's egg – good in parts. On 23 March, the squadron had ten Sabres serviceable, and the battle flight had five scrambles. One of these was the fastest yet – from 'scramble' being yelled to aircraft being airborne in 1 minute 58 seconds. Two days later, the arrival of another STI caused the squadron's first night-flying programme to be abandoned. Towards the end of the month, a further instance of the earlier undercarriage problems occurred, this time resulting in a nose-undercarriage leg coming unlocked while the aircraft was pulling out of a dive. The on-station technical representative from Canadair was enlisted to pinpoint a cause, but even he seemed at a loss.

The squadron began flying its first cine quarter missions on 25 March, though on that occasion only one of the gun-camera films was found to have been correctly exposed, and even this one was out of harmonisation. Only a few Sabres could be fitted with the cine cameras in any case, as it transpired that brackets fitted to XB800 and later aircraft were not compatible with the camera being used. It would take some months finally to procure the spare parts to rectify this situation. As if this were not enough, it was still proving impossible to get the gunsight radars serviceable, and as a result all gunsights were for the time being used in the 'fixed' mode, with deflection computed for 1,000yd range.

But it would be wrong to think that the squadron was an unhappy place during this challenging period; far from it. In general, both air and ground crews saw the Sabre as a quantum leap over the Vampire, and liked it in spite of the teething problems. And there were signs of improvement: on 5 April the night flying finally got underway, and two days later XB797 and XB808 arrived from the Brüggen Wing to bring 20 Sqn back up to full strength again.

The squadron's first Sabre detachment to Sylt cropped up in April, and flying was reduced to ensure maximum serviceability. Led by Wg Cdr I.R. Campbell, AFC, Oldenburg's recently arrived Wing Leader, the Sabres departed for Sylt on 21 April in three 'finger four' formations. Making the most of good weather (unusual at Sylt), 'B' Flight began air-to-air firing on the range on the morning of 22 April, and was relieved by 'A' Flight after lunch. Scores were initially not good, but in light of the serviceability issues, and with new aircraft, they were considered acceptable. In the following days a gradual improvement was noted. Poor weather later in the month, along with gunsight problems and a bout of target flags falling off meant that the squadron average was just over 6 per cent by the end of the deployment. On 12 May Fg Off Simmonds set a new target with a 32 per cent score, though unfortunately a further run of low cloud began on 4 May and few other meaningful scores were logged.

'B' Flight's Sabres returned to Oldenburg in the afternoon of 17 May, those of 'A' Flight following that evening. The squadron immediately ran into further serviceability problems, and by 25 May only five Sabres were available. Of the remainder, no less than a dozen were grounded awaiting brake spares; the requisite parts finally arrived on station on 4 June. With few aircraft available, 'A' Flight removed drop tanks from its aircraft on 28 May and flew short-range missions to rack up sorties rather than hours. Practice fly-pasts for the Queen's Birthday celebrations in Hamburg began at the start of June, and the fly-past itself was performed on 10 June. Three days after this fly-past, Fg Off Moran and Fg Off Christmas began painting squadron crests on the side of the aircraft. The crests were initially quite muted, comprising a yellow rising sun upon which was imposed the squadron's eagle, perched on a sword.

Twenty-five night-flying sorties were completed on 15 June, comprising cross-country missions and local circuits. The following days were punctuated by a number of 'near misses', often quite literally. On 21 June Fg Off Plumb had a very hot start, wrecking his Sabre's engine and leaving just one serviceable aircraft for 'B' Flight. Two days later Flt Lt Rigby was forced to divert into Ahlhorn after his generator failed on a battle flight sortie. Fg Off Lucy was driven over to Ahlhorn in a 3-tonner lorry on 28 June to ferry the repaired machine back to base. Bad visibility on 25 June resulted in a near mid-air collision when Flt Lt W.C. 'Flush' Kendall almost flew into a Sabre formation led by Fg Off Davies. Kendall had only arrived at the squadron on 14 June, and completed his first Sabre solo two days later. 'Flush' Kendall later took over as 'A' Flight commander when Desmond Browne was posted out.

In spite of these distractions, 20 Sqn flew 400 hours in June 1954 – its highest total yet on Sabres. The accent then changed for July, with the impending presentation of the squadron standard by Princess Margaret. Drill became the order of the day as squadron personnel practised for the parade, and on 5 July a full dress rehearsal with band was attended by Harry Broadhurst, AOC of 2 TAF. Princess Margaret arrived at Oldenburg on 13 July to find a well-drilled ceremony, thanks to these efforts. The parade square was flanked by three 20 Sqn Sabres, appropriately coded 'R', 'A' and 'F'. Following the ceremony, the princess took lunch and departed for Ahlhorn in the afternoon. An informal squadron reunion was then held, attended by many 20 Sqn personnel from the interwar and Second World War period.

In line with most other 2 TAF squadrons, 20 Sqn gained an engineering officer on 9 July with the arrival of Fg Off Jurdon. He was attached to the unit on a trial period, and positive results led to this becoming a permanent post. Concurrent with this, the squadron took part in Exercise Dividend, the annual test of the UK air-defence system. Though the exercise actually began on 17 July, 20 Sqn launched its first missions the following day, when twelve Sabres departed for the English coast in formations of four aircraft. These missions saw the formations routing across the Channel to East Anglia at altitudes of up to 40,000ft. Few were intercepted. The squadron stood down from Dividend on 19 and 20 July, and no sorties were flown on the 21st. The next input into the exercise was therefore on 22 July, when a mass raid went in during the afternoon. The final missions were completed the following day, when 'A' Flight put on a dawn raid of eleven Sabres at 0430 hr. A second raid was reduced to nine aircraft by unserviceability. These marked the last sorties flown by 20 Sqn on Exercise Dividend; poor weather on the final two days meant that raids could not be launched. Throughout the exercise, very few interceptions on the raiding formations had been made, and squadron personnel were therefore surprised and dismayed to read press reports that declared the British air-defence system to be 'invulnerable'.

With the end of Dividend, drop tanks were removed from the squadron's aircraft on 27 July, and twenty-seven sorties were flown on the Meppen range. Towards the end of the day, one pilot found his aircraft to be suffering from a severe tailplane flutter. He immediately returned to base and the Sabres were grounded, pending investigation; three aircraft were found to be suffering the same (undisclosed) problem, though the remainder were cleared for flight and completed further Meppen sorties on 29 July.

Incredibly, in almost nine months of Sabre flying, the squadron had suffered no write-offs; this was not to last. A night-flying programme on 5 August brought the day to a close but resulted in two accidents for

The aftermath of 20 Sqn's night-flying exercise on 5 August 1954. Fg Off Harry Capewell was flying XB638 and stalled on approach to Oldenburg; incredibly, he was thrown clear, still strapped into his seat, and survived. Note the bent tailpipe, incurred when the aircraft hit the ground nose-up. (*Charles Keil*)

'A' Flight. Fg Off Fitchew was the first. Although detailed for a dusk sortie, he, along with others, got off to a late start and it was dark by the time he came to land. On his approach, Fitchew flew through the top of a tree, landed short, veered to the left of the runway (narrowly avoiding the controller's caravan) and careered across grass and cornfield before he could step, somewhat shaken, from his aircraft. Fitchew's Sabre, XB709, received Cat. 4 damage. Two minutes later, Fg Off Harry Capewell stalled on approach and landed heavily in the undershoot area; the forward fuselage of Capewell's Sabre, XB638, was destroyed in the impact, though the pilot was miraculously thrown clear, still in his ejection seat. He sustained a broken arm and leg, but was otherwise a very lucky man. Meanwhile, four Sabres still flying were diverted to Ahlhorn. Harry Capewell was flown to England in an Anson on 11 August to continue his recuperation. There would be no more night flying for 20 Sqn's Sabres. After the disastrous events of 5 August, two Sabres were loaned from 'B' Flight to make up numbers on its sister flight.

Exercise Lucifer, which began on 31 August, saw 20 Sqn Sabres acting as enemy raiders against the Netherlands. Bad weather on the first day saw no sorties completed, but a number were flown on 1 September, a typical example being that by Fg Off Vic Nickson in XB594 to Apeldoorn and Hook. The following day, a low-level strike was launched at 0500 hr but, as with so many other sorties on Lucifer, few interceptions were noted; the exercise ended later that day. The squadron then began preparations for another Sylt detachment, 'A' and 'B' Flights pooling aircraft to fly cine sorties. Unfortunately, the XB800-series aircraft had still not been modified to accept cine cameras. As a result, only ten aircraft were available, even before unserviceabilities were taken into account. On 10 September Sqn Ldr MacDonald and two other officers travelled to Schleswigland to check out the facilities prior to the squadron detachment. Due to other squadrons being at Sylt, 20 Sqn would base its Sabres at Schleswigland and fly up to Sylt daily to use the range. Just prior to the detachment, on 11 September further squadron markings were applied, having only just been approved. These comprised medium blue rectangles each side of the fuselage roundel, divided by thin red, white and green stripes. At around the same time, the squadron badge on the forward fuselage was modified slightly, so that the emblem was applied against a white shield.

The advance party left by road for Schleswigland on 17 September and the main party departed by rail two days later. Poor weather meant that no aircraft movements were possible until 22 September, when, upon arrival at Schleswigland, Flt Lt Kendall landed wheels-up in XB899; the aircraft was a write-off. 'Flush' Kendall had just taken command of 'A' Flight after Desmond Browne had left on promotion to command 93 Sqn at Jever.

The squadron lost no time in getting onto the Sylt ranges, 'A' Flight commencing its air-to-air firing at 0630 hr on 23 September. Sgt Lee immediately set the bar, with an excellent 21.5 per cent individual score, but alas the inevitable Sylt weather then intervened; it was often the case that even when the weather was within limits at Sylt, the Schleswigland weather prevented the aircraft taking off. In any case, the squadron's stay on detachment was extended by runway work at Oldenburg. The squadron ended its detachment with a 6.9 per cent average, and the advance party left for Oldenburg on 21 October. The Sabres arrived back the following day. While it had been at Schleswigland, on 20 October, Sqn Ldr MacDonald had handed command of 20 Sqn to Sqn Ldr L.C. Glover.

A small-scale exercise, 'Cornwall', started on 26 October and required the squadron to provide three pairs of Sabres on two low-level attacks against the airfield at Fassberg. A further strike was launched during the same exercise the following day. October's poor weather meant that just 162 hours were logged for the whole squadron that month. November proved no better, as on the first day of the month all Sabres were grounded for a generator inspection. Three aircraft were readied for flight and air-tested on 4 November, with a further three the following day. And though brackets had finally arrived to enable the XB800-series to be fitted with cine cameras, electrical connections to complete the installation had not. This typified the exasperation felt by the ground crews on occasion. Flying was then restricted from 24 November due to the start of a ground-defence exercise called 'Combine Four'. This period was one of increasing frustration for the squadron pilots, and even battle flight had few other commitments.

The start of 1955 was typical for a German winter – it was bitterly cold and icy. On the night of 16/17 January, six inches of snow fell at Oldenburg, but continued efforts by the station personnel meant that the runway and taxiways were soon cleared again. A rare day of fine conditions on 21 January allowed the squadron to fly the unprecedented number of sixty sorties. This proved to be the high point, as fog and poor visibility prevented much more in the way of flying thereafter. Again at the start of February a solitary day yielded a new sortie record, with sixty-nine missions flown before the weather again closed in to ground the squadron for nearly a fortnight. This cycle continued for a number of weeks, though the squadron made the most of short periods of clear weather, so that on 15 February fifty air-to-ground firing sorties were completed, resulting in an excellent 22.5 per cent average.

A taste of the future was provided on 23 February when a number of Central Fighter Establishment Hunter jets arrived at Oldenburg. Lectures on the type were given over the following days, but it would be many months before 20 Sqn got its first aircraft.

Meanwhile the day-to-day missions continued. By removing drop tanks from its aircraft in February, the squadron had managed to log an incredible 687 sorties, though actual hours were considerably less than that. And fortunately the weather held, so that on many occasions from the end of February and into March, more than fifty sorties were flown daily. From this point onwards, a great deal of effort was put into live firing, both air-to-ground and air-to-air. On 22 March the squadron used the Ströhen range for the first time, Fg Off Gould coming out on top with a 40 per cent score. On the same day, Fg Off Williams, one of the squadron's Pilot Attack Instructors, left for Sylt as part of a small detachment from the squadron that was tasked with evaluating the radar gunsight for the Oldenburg Wing. While at Sylt, the aircraft fired on radar-reflective target flags. Continued use was made of Ströhen in the meantime, and Flt Lt Kendall was often the sharpshooter. The squadron's better fortunes continued into April, when the magic 500 flying hours for the month was finally exceeded; this was declared to be a first for a 2 TAF Sabre unit.

Flying was then restricted at the start of May, so that airframe hours could be preserved for the squadron's forthcoming live-firing detachment in Cyprus. At the same time, the hours had to be juggled so that continued effort could be put into flag-towing and cine sorties in order for crews to be up to the required standard. These sorties were flown without drop tanks so that maximum use of the aircraft could be achieved; by 16 May the emphasis had shifted toward fitting drop tanks for the deployment to Cyprus. In the midst of this activity, Oldenburg was inspected by the AOC Gp, AVM J.R. Hallings-Pott, CBE, DSO, AFC. His inspection was followed by the customary wing fly-past, 20 Sqn contributing eight aircraft for 'Charlie' and 'Dog' sections.

The long-awaited departure to Cyprus finally began on 23 May, when three waves of aircraft left for Rome via Fürstenfeldbruck at half-hour intervals from 0800 hr. First away was Blue Section, led by Sqn Ldr Glover; he was followed by White Section under Flt Lt Galletly and Yellow Section under Flt Sgt Howell. The Vampire, flown by Fg Off Williams and Fg Off Owen, had meanwhile departed independently at 0800 hr. Fg Off Leitch, as 'White 2', suffered an

Fg Off P.G.C. 'Jimmy' Edwards (left) and Fg Off W.H. 'Bill' Simmonds (right) pose in front of a squadron Sabre bearing the early-style squadron markings. Simmonds, a Royal Australian Air Force pilot on exchange with the squadron, was one of only a handful of pilots to have shot down a MiG in Korea while flying the Gloster Meteor. (*Vic Nickson*)

undercarriage problem on departing Fürstenfeldbruck, and was forced to return there for rectification. The rest of the squadron continued safely on to Rome's Ciampino airport for a night stop; Fg Off Leitch followed six hours later. Meanwhile, four other pilots and the ground-crew element had taken Hastings transport aircraft from Wildenrath for the trip out to Cyprus. On 24 May the Sabres departed Rome at 1000 hr bound for a refuelling stop at Athens, before arriving over Nicosia late in the afternoon. Following a fly-past in a vic of three boxes, the squadron landed at around 1715 hr.

Working hours in Cyprus ran from 0615 to 1230 hr due to the midday heat; this gave squadron personnel an opportunity to relax in the afternoon – a system that was universally liked. The squadron began live air-to-air firing on 26 May, the aircraft firing in pairs on towed flags. On the first day, ten effective sorties were logged for a squadron average of 8.4 per cent; the squadron was in high spirits, and Flt Sgt Howell broadcast this to the world on 3 June by placing a sonic boom on the Venom dispersal at Nicosia. However, continued problems with gunsights and with target flags that fell off prematurely did temper the mood slightly.

The squadron sent four Sabres on a further detachment, this time to Amman in Jordan on 6 June. Sqn Ldr Glover, along with Fg Off Leitch, Fg Off Waite and Fg Off Galpin, used the opportunity to fly with the Venoms of 249 Sqn based there before returning to Cyprus on 8 June.

While the gunnery missions continued, and scores rose, the squadron also contributed aircraft to an eleven-aircraft Wing fly-past over Nicosia on 9 June to mark the Queen's Birthday. By the end of the following day – the squadron's last day of firing – the average had risen to 9.6 per cent.

The Vampire began its return journey to Oldenburg on 12 June, and at 0825 hr the following day the Sabres departed, though two aircraft were left at Nicosia with tail-trim actuator problems. A further Sabre, XB889, made a heavy landing at Athens on the return trip and had to be left there for rectification. The surviving Sabres arrived back at Oldenburg on 14 June. On 17 June, Fg Offs Williams and Entwistle departed for Athens to retrieve XB889, but on finding it still not fixed they were forced to return to base. Finally on the following day a crew departed in the Meteor trainer and the errant Sabre was back at base by that evening.

Following a short break, the squadron was back in the thick of things on 22 June, when Exercise Carte Blanche began. This exercise tested Continental defence procedures in a wartime scenario, and the squadron was put on alert to intercept 'enemy' intruders, which would be identified by special exercise markings. The squadron's first scramble came at 1235 hr, and four Sabres managed to intercept a Canberra bomber and claim the first 'kill'. Unfortunately, this aircraft was not carrying 'enemy' markings and was determined to be friendly; a further scramble did, however, net an enemy Canberra. On the following day, 'A' Flight was ready at daybreak, but the exercise umpires declared Oldenburg to have been atom-bombed, and there was no flying until 'B' Flight came on shift at 1200 hr. Then, four scrambles were called, including a number of fighter-sweep skittles. Enemy fighters were engaged by seven Sabres from 20 Sqn over Wiesbaden, and for the first time the RAF came off worst. Their adversaries this time were USAF F-86Fs and Canadian Sabre 5s: both types showed significant superiority over the Sabre 4s, and six of 20 Sqn's aircraft were claimed as kills for the loss of two enemy.

Further scrambles, this time for Dutch GCI, were made on the morning of 24 June by the aircraft of 'A' Flight, and this time a Canberra was claimed at 40,000ft. Further skittles were made over the Wiesbaden and

The port wing of 'Flush' Kendall's Sabre, XB808, lies on Meppen range after his fatal crash on 16 August 1955. The wing section was found 60yd from the main impact crater. (*National Archives*)

Frankfurt areas, two more enemy Sabres being engaged, though with no confirmed kills on either side. In the afternoon, 'B' Flight completed sixteen sorties, again mostly for Dutch GCI, but there was little traffic. 'A' Flight again took the early shift on 25 June and received no scrambles, but were relieved by 'B' Flight at 0700 hr who were airborne fifty minutes later. Few intercepts were made, and after 'A' Flight again took over at 1700 hr no further scrambles were called.

'B' Flight was again active on 26 June when it contributed eight aircraft on a Wing sweep over the Wiesbaden area; twelve enemy aircraft were engaged and four were claimed to be destroyed. Following another atom-bomb attack on Oldenburg, three Sabres were diverted to Gütersloh. Oldenburg was then out of action for eight hours, and no further sorties were flown. The final day of the exercise was 27 June, with 'B' Flight yet again getting the best part of the action. They had four Sabres on standby from 0400 hr and got the scramble call just an hour later. The airfield then became fogbound, and all four aircraft had to divert to Amsterdam's Schiphol airport. In the meantime, Oldenburg was again bombed, which put the airfield out of action until the exercise ceased at 2000 hr that evening.

Thankfully, Exercise Carte Blanche had been a safe period of intensive flying for 20 Sqn, though just three days after the exercise finished XB900 had a birdstrike and was placed Cat. 3 for repairs on station. By this point the reduction in squadron size from twenty-two Sabres to just fourteen had taken place, so any unserviceabilities were more acutely felt. As well as the reduction in aircraft,

XB594/V was the personal aircraft of Fg Off V.J. Nickson; it carried his name in white on the canopy rail. The notice on the hangar wall informs all that 'The hangar floor is not a salvage dump.' (*Vic Nickson*)

pilot strength was also reduced, to nineteen crews. However, this situation did not last long: from August a number of Sabres were returned to the UK and swapped with fresher examples recently phased out by 26 Sqn.

A further day at Meppen range was programmed for 16 August, and it was on one of these sorties that Flt Lt W.C. 'Flush' Kendall was killed. Kendall had been briefed to carry out a practice air-to-ground firing sortie over the range, and was airborne at 1034 hr aboard XB808; he joined the circuit at Meppen nine minutes later. Kendall then made one safety run to check his approach height, followed by three dummy runs. On his fifth approach he began his firing passes, completing six passes on the target with no problems. On his seventh pass, however, Kendall's aircraft was seen to pull out at 300ft before rolling to port. The Sabre's nose then dropped noticeably and the aircraft struck the ground and exploded; the pilot was killed instantly. Kendall was 30 years old, with 137 hours on Sabres. The subsequent investigation produced no evidence of aircraft defect, and it was thought that Kendall had suffered a 'g' stall in marginal conditions. As a result of this accident, all scoring at the ranges in Germany was stopped until a full investigation into range procedures could be carried out. 'Flush' Kendall was buried in Hamburg on 19 August.

For many, the first sign of re-equipment had come on 13 August, when Hunters from the Central Gunnery School arrived on station. Battle flight on that day had an interesting time, as they not only attempted to intercept the Hunter formation but also another group of Canadian Sabre 5s that had come across to see the new fighters. CGS staff gave Hunter lectures to the squadron on 18 August.

Exercise Loco, which began on 26 August, was a test of Dutch GCI procedures; 20 Sqn was at readiness from 0330 hr. Fog prevented the first few missions being flown, but later in the day, seventeen sorties were launched, all acting as 'intruders' for interception by fighters vectored in by the Dutch GCI network. Most were intercepted on the return leg. Further missions on Exercise Loco were flown on the following day, and one section was intercepted by USAF F-86s. The exercise ended the same day.

Two more of the squadron's aircraft were lost in August, both to cracked fuel tanks; XB889 and XB915 were deemed to be serviceable for one flight to the civilian contractors, and XB915 departed for Airwork on 10 August, XB889 going to Westland at Yeovilton eight days later. Fortunately, replacements were soon received from 26 Sqn, which was concurrently converting to Hunters. With the re-equipment of its sister unit at Oldenburg, 20 Sqn stood by on battle flight for most of September, which was thankfully a quiet month; Fg Off E.H. Williams had meanwhile taken over as 'A' Flight commander. He was promoted to flight lieutenant in October.

By now the squadron was enviously eyeing the Hunters being flown by 26 Sqn, and, though re-equipment with the new fighter had been expected on 15 September, that date came and went with nothing in sight. On 1 October, 20 Sqn commited eight Sabres to Exercise Foxpaw, acting as simulated bombers against the UK air-defence network. The aircraft, which had been flying in 'clean' configuration for some weeks, were refitted with drop tanks for Foxpaw and departed Oldenburg for the English coast at 1230 hr. This marked the squadron's only input into the exercise.

Towards the end of October, rumour began circulating that the first Hunters would soon arrive. The rumours were further strengthened on 28 October when it was decided to fire off the majority of the remaining .50-calibre rounds on air-to-sea missions. In total, 9,000 rounds were fired during the day, using all six of the Sabre's guns for the first time in many cases. Unfortunately, 'A' Flight suffered three birdstrikes in the process, XB646 being placed Cat. 3 after sustaining a shattered canopy and various airframe dents. A further Sabre lost its fin cap to what was thought to have been a toy balloon. Thankfully, there were no injuries.

For variety, on 18 November, squadron pilots took part in an escape-and-evasion exercise, which began at 0300 hr. The evaders were dropped thirteen miles west of the airfield and tasked with getting to a rendezvous point on the Oldenburg–Varel road at a set time without being captured. The defending force consisted of RAF Regiment personnel and, though nine pilots were eventually captured, four more evaded capture. All unfortunately missed their rendezvous time.

On 23 November, the squadron's first Hunter arrived, and two days later the first Sabres were transferred out. Lectures and practical training on the Hunter began immediately, and on 29 November 20 Sqn was withdrawn from the front line to begin its conversion onto the new type. On 2 December Sqn Ldr Glover and the two flight commanders performed taxi checks on the first few Hunters, and on 8 December Flt Lt Galletly completed the squadron's first Hunter mission. By the end of the month, fifty-five Hunter sorties had been flown against less than twenty on the Sabre.

Most of the Sabre sorties were dedicated to test-flying aircraft prior to ferrying out, and on 19 December three more of the type were ferried away, this time to 234 Sqn at Geilenkirchen. The squadron had ten Hunters on strength by the end of 1955, and six Sabres remained. The last few Sabres were test-flown in the early part of 1956, though even by

A late grouping of 20 Sqn's Sabre aerobatic team. Back row L–R: Fg Off K. Fitchew, Flt Lt W.C. Kendall, Fg Off W.E. Waite. Front: Fg Off D.M. Croucher. (*Vic Nickson*)

February the squadron had four left to get rid of, and three of these were transferred to 3 Sqn.

The final Sabre proved less straightforward to dispose of. On 15 February Fg Off W.E. Waite was test-flying XB914 when the aircraft's port drop tank fell off, hitting the underside of the fuselage as it did so. Waite recovered the aircraft to base, where it was discovered that the tank had been incorrectly fitted. XB914 received Cat. 3 damage, however, and was eventually transferred to the UK for repair at the end of May. The aircraft became not only the last Sabre on squadron strength, but also the last Sabre in RAF service to suffer a flying accident.

Aerobatic Team

Flying aerobatic formations with jet fighters was not an unusual activity for 20 Sqn. Squadron pilot J.R. Griffiths remembers practising such displays prior to the Queen's Coronation fly-past in July 1953. At this point, the unit was still flying the De Havilland Vampire FB. 5s and 9s, and, although these were ideal aircraft for formation flying, lack of spare time for practice caused the idea of a 'team' to be shelved. A short-lived 20 Sqn Sabre aerobatic team was then formed when the 'B' Flight commander, Flt Lt Desmond Browne, was given permission to practise formation aerobatics – limited to three aircraft – so long as it was not to the detriment of normal squadron training and commitments. The team was initially approved by the squadron commander, Sqn Ldr Ian MacDonald, DFC.

According to Desmond Browne, 'We practised first on 4 December 1953, 1 and 17 February 1954, 25 June, 18 and 28 July, 5 and 7 August. We gave our first demo practice over the airfield on 25 June 1954.' The 20 Sqn record also states for 24 June 1954 that 'certain pilots carried out formation aerobatics'. The team comprised Flt Lt D. Browne (leader), Fg Off Derek L. Davies and Fg Off Don Christmas, and there were also one or two other pilots involved at this time. However, the team was never authorised at anything other than squadron level, and with the posting of Flt Lt Browne in September 1954 to command 93 Sqn, it briefly disbanded.

The chance to re-form a team would not come until late in 1954, and this second 20 Sqn aerobatic team, enlarged to four aircraft, included the following pilots: Flt Lt David Williams (leader); Fg Off Derek L. 'Moose' Davies (number two); Fg Off Dennis H. Lucy (number three); Fg Off David 'Crumb' Crowe (number four); Fg Off David B. 'Screech' Leitch (reserve?); Fg Off Nick J. Galpin (number two, replacing Davies). Team Leader David Williams recalls that the second 20 Sqn team began more as a spur-of-the-moment idea than anything else:

20 Sqn's second Sabre aerobatic team from about late 1954. L–R: Fg Off Derek 'Moose' Davies (no. 2), Fg Off Nick J. Galpin (reserve), Flt Lt David Williams (leader), Fg Off Dennis Lucy (no. 3), Fg Off David 'Screech' Leitch (reserve?). Kneeling: Fg Off 'Crumb' Crowe (no. 4). (*David Williams*)

On 20 [Sqn], I think our formation aeros evolved from our fondness for tail chases where, usually on the way home from another exercise, it was routine to put everyone at 200yd line astern and then go into as many manoeuvres as possible and see how many of the section could hold on. In fact, I remember leading six Sabres tail-chasing over Oldenburg at about 2,000ft, for some sort of formal occasion. I am quite sure that we were doing formation aeros throughout this time, but I see from my logbook an entry stating: 'First flight of aeros team' on 20th December 1954, with Fg Off 'Moose' Davies as number two, Fg Off Dennis Lucy as three, and Fg Off 'Crumb' Crowe as four. Since I clearly remember that it was customary to be very careful about notes and details in logbooks then – they were checked monthly – this must have been quite official.

The aircraft used for these practices were all 'normal' squadron aircraft, with no provision for trailing smoke. The display was carried out mainly with the aircraft in a diamond formation, but a five-aircraft arrow take-off was practised a few times before officialdom intervened. The team did, however, regularly demonstrate an echelon starboard take-off, from which the four Sabres would perform a roll while moving into the diamond formation. These displays were flown over the airfield for visiting VIPs. Before the end of 1954, 'Moose' Davies was informed of a posting to 66 Sqn at Linton-on-Ouse, back in England. Davies's place on the 'team' was taken by 'Nick Jack' Galpin. Some idea of the keenness of the squadron to perform is given in David Williams's recollection of their next practice sortie: 'The next 'official' [practice] note is for 31 December (between Xmas and New Year!!), and shows Fg Off Galpin as number two, with Lucy and Crowe as three and four. In January 1955, there are six entries for formation aeros – though no mention of team members – and several more in February and March. In this latter month, it seems I went to Sylt [Island, off the German coast] to practise some air firing so we could use the Sabre for flag-towing back at Oldenburg, and, interestingly, I note two formation aeros trips there – one in a Meteor 8 and one in a Venom!'

During April and May of 1955, the squadron was busy with air-to-air gunnery practice, but at the end of May, when 20 Sqn deployed to RAF Akrotiri in Cyprus, the team finally had the opportunity to put on its first 'official' display. At this time, the rival 26 Sqn was also in Cyprus, so the spirit of competition was high. However, the 26 Sqn 'team' was far less organised, and it seems that some of its team members were away in Iraq at the time. As a result, 20 Sqn flew its first display over Nicosia on 7 June as part of the Queen's Birthday celebrations.

The squadron returned to Oldenburg in mid-June of 1955, taking part in NATO Exercise Carte Blanche for the remainder of the month, with only one further display of note, according to Williams: 'After return to Oldenburg, we took part in Exercise Carte Blanche, and there are only a few entries of the team until October, when we seem to have put on a six-aircraft-formation aerobatic show for "visiting MPs". By December we were obviously too involved in converting to the Hunter to fly the aero team.'

By mid-1955, the team appears to have included Flt Lt 'Flush' Kendall, the 'A' Flight commander, along with Fg Off K. Fitchew, Fg Off W.E. Waite and Fg Off D.M. Croucher. If this is the case, then Kendall's death in a Sabre crash on 16 August would have seriously affected the rest of the team. In any case, the first Hunters for the squadron arrived at Oldenburg on 20 November 1955, and from that point onwards the emphasis was firmly on the new type.

AIRCRAFT ASSIGNED

XB575/Q, XB588, XB589/P, XB594/V, XB597/F, XB638/N, XB645/W, XB646/M, XB707, XB709/Q, XB731/J, XB749/H, XB752/Y, XB755/B, XB790, XB791, XB797/E, XB803, XB808/L, XB815/N, XB854/W*, XB861/K, XB862, XB886, XB888/T, XB889/D, XB892/G, XB895/C, XB899/B, XB900/A, XB914/S, XB915/R, XB977/H*.

* = '6–3' wing (all conversions).

MARKINGS – 20 SQN

Markings initially comprised the unit emblem (an eagle carrying a sword, superimposed over a yellow rising sun) carried on the forward fuselage below the forward windshield section. Squadron individual code letters were painted in white on the tail fin. A later version of this scheme saw the eagle and sunburst imposed onto a white shield, often outlined in black.

When 'bars' appeared either side of the fuselage roundel, the bars were mid-blue, over which (from the top) thin red, white and green bands were applied. At around this time, individual pilots' names were applied in white to the port canopy rail.

SQUADRON MOTTO

Facta non verba (Deeds not words).

CHAPTER SEVEN

26 SQUADRON

October 1953 found 26 Sqn based at Oldenburg with Vampire FB. 5s and 9s and commanded by Sqn Ldr Ken Smith. On 10 October the unit deployed to Sylt for weapon-firing, and it was there on 3 November that a signal arrived detailing the allotment of the squadron's first Sabres. In preparation for this, Flt Lt Green of 'B' Flight, along with four other pilots, departed Sylt to begin their conversion to the new type with the Sabre Conversion Unit at Wildenrath. Eight more pilots, this time led by Sqn Ldr Smith, left for the SCU on 1 November; this left the remainder of the squadron back at Sylt with few pilots and a large number of Vampires. On 7 November the armament camp was cut short so that the six remaining pilots at Sylt could begin to ferry the eleven remaining Vampires back to Oldenburg. All personnel arrived back at Oldenburg on 11 November.

Meanwhile, the squadron's first three Sabres (XB623, XB636 and XB759) had arrived at 'Oldy' on 4 November 1953, followed by four more the following day, the full complement of eighteen being in place by 11 November. In the meantime, the squadron's pilots continued to be routed through the SCU, a further seven crews being detached there on 8 November. Aside from the number of personnel on courses at Wildenrath, a lack of safety equipment meant 26 Sqn was unable initially to fly any Sabre missions. This situation was finally resolved on 18 November and the first mission, delayed by radio failure, was successfully completed. The weather then closed in, and no further sorties were flown until 21 November, when five missions were launched. Continued poor weather throughout this period limited flying activity, especially as the squadron could only launch these early missions on days when good weather was assured. Initially, the emphasis was on individual handling, but from 2 December formation flying was begun, starting with the more experienced pilots.

Concurrent with the arrival of the Sabres, a number of the more experienced Vampire pilots left the squadron and a whole raft of younger pilots, many trained in the United States, began

Early days on 26 Sqn as XB767 (nearest) is refuelled. Note the lack of drop tanks. (*Charles Keil*)

to arrive. Four pilot officers arrived in November alone: R.D. Cherry and D. House went to 'B' Flight, while Charles Keil and M. Blanford went to 'A' Flight; Keil had trained in Canada and Blanford had gone through US Air Force flight training, culminating on the T-33 and the F-84 Thunderjet. These four were sent through SCU conversion on 3 December, returning to the squadron on 17 December. Though the squadron had largely lost its Vampires at this time, the younger pilots did get the chance to fly them on occasion.

At the beginning of December battle formations began to be practised; one of the first such missions was on the 9th, though again bad weather in the form of mist and low cloud prevented much in-depth flying. Finally, a glimpse of good weather on 20 December meant that forty-five sorties were flown, with a similar amount the following day. Almost inevitably, these concentrated periods of flying then led to increased maintenance activity, and by the end of the year flying was beginning to be limited by the poor availability of aircraft.

The following year, 1954, kicked off with further bad weather, and heavy falls of snow; flying was limited, so the opportunity was taken to send a number of pilots on courses. Sqn Ldr Smith and Fg Off Ridout drew the short straws and were sent on a Winter Survival Course at Ehrwald on 2 January; they returned two weeks later. If flying proved impossible for the other pilots, lectures were often laid on, covering subjects as diverse as aircraft recognition and weather.

The squadron's first Sabre accident occurred on 4 January when P Off Blanford experienced problems during one of his first sorties and had to abort on take-off. The Sabre ran off the end of the runway after Blanford had raised the undercarriage. He was unhurt, but the aircraft, XB759, received Cat. 4 damage; it was eventually returned to the UK for repair but saw no further RAF service.

The squadron saw little further flying in early January. Initially this stemmed from a number of technical issues, particularly the unspecified inspections which grounded the Sabres on 5 January. Concurrent with this, 26 Sqn was preparing to move from 4 Hangar to the neighbouring 3 Hangar, previously home to 234 Sqn. In future, 4 Hangar would be shared with 20 Sqn for maintenance purposes. The move was completed on 11 January and three days later the squadron managed to take part in a barrage exercise.

Up to this point, all the squadron's Sabres had operated in standard trim, with drop tanks fitted, but on 21 January a number of sorties were flown on aircraft in 'clean' configuration. Immediately the aircraft's performance was improved, crews praising the time-to-height times in particular. Thirty-eight sorties were flown on this day alone, the squadron averaging six sorties per available aircraft per day at the time.

Though the cold spell persisted into February, flying did continue, and on 25 January Fg Off Shippobotham and Fg Off Wood ferried two of the squadron's last Vampires back to the UK. Back at Oldenburg, battle flights were rehearsed, practice interceptions against the Jever Vampires being flown on 2 February. These exercises were deemed 'ridiculous' by the squadron historian, as the Sabres were forced to fly below 25,000ft with air brakes out and engines at half throttle. On 4 February similar missions were flown for the Wunstorf Venoms, again at low speed and altitude to enable the slower jets to intercept the Sabres. One wonders at the point of these exercises – 'enemy' MiG-15 jets would hardly have been operating in these conditions.

Due to the lack of two-seater Sabres for flying training, all 2 TAF Sabre squadrons were assigned at least one Vampire T. 11 and one Meteor T. 7 for the purpose. Their usefulness was questionable, and the Meteor in particular displayed some alarming flying characteristics. On 16 February the squadron's Meteor, WL430, yawed and crashed on take-off from Oldenburg on its last roller circuit. Aboard were Fg Off K. Harvey and P Off G. 'Paddy' Stewart, and both were seriously injured. Both pilots were taken to Rostrop General Hospital and eventually returned to fly again with the squadron, but for Paddy Stewart this would be a short and tragic period.

The squadron suffered its first Sabre fatality on 24 February. Though visibility on the day was moderate, most sorties were 'general handling' in the local area. Flt Sgt Jack Swales, the only NCO pilot on the squadron, had just learned of a posting back to the UK and was flying Sabre XB866 to reach the magic 50 hours in Sabres. After transmitting that he had lost his compass he was put on a controlled descent, but no further transmissions were heard from him. With no reports forthcoming of crashed aircraft it was presumed that Flt Sgt Swales had crashed into the North Sea. Immediately, an air search was begun using Anson aircraft which continued into the following day. No trace of pilot or aircraft was ever found. It is possible that Swales had been flying one of the Sabres without drop tanks and had run out of fuel.

It is worth noting that the majority of Sabres flown by 26 Sqn were of the slatted variety. However, in February 1954, two aircraft with the '6–3' unslatted wing were assigned straight from 5 MU at Kemble. In order to standardise on one type, both machines, XB931 and XB961, were transferred to 4 Sqn at Jever within a month. For the rest of the time it flew Sabres, the squadron would operate only slatted aircraft.

In March good weather returned to Oldenburg and a concentrated flying programme was commenced. There were odd days, however, when things just didn't go right. On 17 March, one of 20 Sqn's Sabres crashed at the end of the runway and all

The role played by NCO pilots in the air force of the 1950s is often overlooked. Flt Sgt Jack Swales was posted missing on 24 February 1954 while flying XB866 with 26 Sqn. (*Charles Keil*)

airborne aircraft were diverted to Ahlhorn. The squadron's Sabres returned to base later in the day, but with so much disruption to the flying programme a stand-down was ordered. On 23 March the squadron's first night-flying missions were flown, and with better weather on the way, night missions were regularly programmed.

With the squadron coming up to speed on the Sabre, air-to-ground firing was begun on 25 March, initially at the Meppen range. By the end of the month the squadron average was a paltry 4 per cent. Further missions to Meppen were flown in April, by which time the results were deemed 'much better'. A programme of air-to-air quarter attacks was also begun at the beginning of April in preparation for the forthcoming Sylt deployment; results here were not good. Because of the previous bad weather and poor aircraft availability, squadron pilots were averaging 12 hours per month at this point, a situation that was below a satisfactory figure.

A changeover of aircraft occurred in the spring of 1954 as Sabres were flown out for repair and others were assigned as replacements. Fg Off Christey ferried XB877 to Dunsfold on 29 March; the aircraft had been grounded since a Cat. 4 incident on 1 December the previous year! Fg Off Richardson then collected XB700 from 71 Sqn as a replacement on 31 March, but on the same day the squadron temporarily lost one of its aircraft after a burst tyre on take-off holed a flap shroud. This machine suffered Cat. 3 damage, requiring a mainplane change, but was still returned to the squadron. On 6 April another pair of Sabres, XB800 and XB818, were collected from Brüggen by squadron pilots and throughout the summer further aircraft were transferred to 26 Sqn to make good attrition losses.

Sqn Ldr Smith departed for Brüggen along with Flt Lt Woodcock on 6 April to take part in Exercise New Alliance, which was a 'paper' exercise. Seven further pilots left for Essen the following day in conjunction with New Alliance. They all returned on 12 April. While this was going on, Sabres from the squadron flew escort sorties on 8 April for RAF Canberras flying through the Oldenburg zone. After a confused join-up over the Frisian Islands, the bombers were escorted all the way to Frankfurt.

For the remainder of the month flying was slackened off as the aircraft were put through primary servicing before the Sylt deployment. At 0600 hr on 20 April the road party left for Sylt, and at 1020 hr on the following day a dozen Sabres departed Oldenburg, performing close formation fly-pasts over the base and also on arrival at Sylt. Having seen off their aircraft, the main party of the squadron left by rail at 1300 hr. They arrived at Sylt at 1500 hr the next day.

No time was lost once the unit was in place at Sylt: the first aircraft was firing on the flag at 0740 hr on 22 April, and a continuous programme was flown until fog stopped flying at 1630 hr. As the days passed by, scores inevitably improved – Fg Off Wilkinson registered 30 per cent on 23 April – but bad weather then intervened, and it was not until 3 May that the squadron managed to restart its programme fully. This culminated in a 5.4 per cent average score, with Fg Off Wilkinson from 'B' Flight achieving the highest average at 14.7 per cent. Just prior to the end of the deployment, the squadron's four top-scoring pilots were given the chance to fire on a towed target glider; they destroyed it.

On 18 May the Sabres flew back to Oldenburg, the final formation of six performing a fly-past over Sylt before arriving back at base at 2000 hr. The road party got back to camp two days later.

Back at Oldenburg, a lack of brake parts for the Sabres was immediately felt, which meant that little flying could be done despite fine weather in the area. The problem reached a climax on 26 May, when only four Sabres were serviceable on the whole squadron. Nonetheless, somehow on 28 May a battle flight was flown against the Jever Wing Sabres, and Sqn Ldr Smith managed to perform a practice fly-past over Hamburg to finalise timings for the impending Queen's Birthday celebration. Still experiencing problems with brake spares, 26 Sqn managed to get eight aircraft airworthy on 29 May and flew in formation over the Hamburg route before completing several runs over the base. Two days later the brake spares finally arrived and the unit could get back to some form of normality. A further fly-past practice was flown on 5 June, with the actual Queen's Birthday fly-past departing Oldenburg at 1130 hr on 10 June to coincide with the Army parade in Hamburg at midday. Eight aircraft from 26 Sqn were included in the sixteen-Sabre wing formation which flew past in four boxes of four.

Low-level cross-country flights were practised beginning in mid-month, and on

This group photo was taken at Sylt in the spring of 1954. Much to the dismay of Sqn Ldr Ken Smith, when the prints arrived it was discovered that most of the squadron were 'doing a Spud' – caricaturing Flt Lt 'Spud' Murphy, who had a habit of closing his eyes and drawling when talking to anyone. Back row L–R: Pete Perry, Brian Cleathero, Ted Bearman, Tony Welch, Charles Keil, Mike Blanford, Ian Dray, Ron Higgs, Stan Drysdale, Alan Biltcliffe, Gordon Statham, Ron Cherry. Front row L–R: Dave Hunt, Trevor Wood, John Christey, Mike Haggerty, Flt Lt Alan Woodcock, Sqn Ldr Smith, Flt Lt John Murphy, Fred Richardson, Dave House, Tony Funnell, Keith Mack. (*Charles Keil*)

14 June a Sabre returning from one such mission burst a tyre on landing back at base, damaging a flap. The aircraft was repaired on site. A more serious incident occurred on 23 June during the first detail of the day. One of the squadron's pilots suffered anoxia over the Hamburg area, his aircraft descending into the Russian Zone before the pilot fortunately regained consciousness. He promptly diverted into Fassberg, and somehow an international incident was avoided.

Fg Off Harvey, who had been seriously injured in the Meteor crash on 16 February, finally returned to the squadron on 11 June and immediately began flying the Sabre. His co-pilot in the accident, Fg Off 'Paddy' Stewart, returned to the squadron on 4 July; he flew the Sabre again on 16 July.

The end of June brought a fair frenzy of activity; on the 24th, eight Sabres and a spare scrambled on a barrage exercise, ostensibly to intercept aircraft flying out of the UK. Unfortunately, the intensity of the effort and resulting interceptions were poor. The 13 July saw Princess Margaret visit the station for 20 Sqn's standard presentation, and 26 Sqn supplied a large number of personnel for the customary parade and inspection that went with it. The departure of the Princess allowed the squadron then to begin preparation for the large UK air-defence exercise, named 'Dividend'. On 15 July, drop tanks were fitted to all of the Sabres, and the following day recrystallisation of aircraft radios was undertaken for the exercise.

Dividend began on 18 July with the squadron flying sorties to the UK acting as 'enemy' aircraft attacking the mainland. During the first day, one section of four, led by 'Wilkie' Wilkinson, had to divert into the US Air Force base at Manston due to a navigational error. Charles Keil recalls that Wilkinson received a lot of ribbing for this indiscretion:

> Wilkinson led a four-Sabre formation to a 'target' somewhere in East Anglia as part of Exercise Dividend. Sabres of 26 Sqn were simulating Russian bombers. Fighters of Fighter Command were vectored up to intercept. The 'attackers' flew at altitude from Germany to overhead the 'target' in the UK, then turned round and flew back to Oldenburg. Very boring really, because once at altitude, we flew in open 'finger four' battle formation more or less straight and level for well over an hour. Radio silence was observed unless there were emergencies.
>
> Wilkie and his formation somehow finished up well south of East Anglia, i.e. off track at least a hundred miles, and their fuel state became a matter of concern (difficult to understand when in theory he had enough fuel to fly to the UK and all the way back to Oldenburg). He and his number two finished up diverting into Manston. Wilkie also somehow managed to 'lose' his number three and number four, who separated at some stage, and also landed in the UK short of fuel – but at another airfield.
>
> There was always the possibility that Wilkie had deliberately not actually flown the prescribed mission, and knowing his predilection for doing his own thing, it is just conceivable that the whole thing was set up to allow him to spend an evening with ex-USAF pals (he flew F-84s in Korea with the USAF) at Manston. The 'deliberate' theory does not really stand examination because he had hazarded the other two aircraft in the four-Sabre formation, so the assumption must be that due to carelessness, faulty instruments or extremely bad weather he became hopelessly lost – hardly comprehensible for such an experienced pilot and flight commander.

From 19 July the Oldenburg flying wing stood down from the exercise for two days, flying its next Dividend sorties on 22 July. The following day further sorties were flown, as well as local flying operations. Twenty-three-year-old Fg Off G. 'Paddy' Stewart was programmed to fly as number two on a two-ship mission to practise high-level battle formation, followed by a mild tail chase at 30,000ft. The mission would end with close-formation flying then a break and landing back at base. Flying in Sabre XB865, Stewart took off from Oldenburg at 1447 hr GMT on 23 July and climbed in close and battle formation up to 28,000ft before commencing the tail-chase part of the mission. His leader levelled out at 15,000ft and carried out two slow rolls, then looked for his number two. Stewart called that he was below cloud and that he had no airspeed indication and that his height was 6,000ft. He then requested a homing from approach control and, after checking this, advised that his engine had flamed out. This message was received at 1518 hr GMT.

Shortly afterwards the aircraft was seen on fire in the air by witnesses on the ground, and began to break up at about the same time as the pilot ejected, at approximately 1,500ft. Sadly, Stewart failed to separate from his seat and was killed. His Sabre crashed four miles west of the German town of Hude. As it hit the ground, a severe fire engulfed the forward fuselage, which made investigation into the reason for the accident more difficult. However, examination of the engine, which fell to earth away from the airframe wreckage, revealed no signs of internal fire; indeed, fire damage on the starboard exterior of the engine indicated that the fire had started in the area of the oil tank. No precise cause was ever determined.

An interesting postscript to Fg Off Stewart's crash is given by Charles Keil: 'I flew at least three sorties on Exercise Dividend. It was on the third flight – my logbook doesn't reveal the target, but the date was 22 July – that I was aware of slight engine surging and fluctuation in the jet-pipe temperature. I put the aircraft unserviceable after we landed and the ground

The tail section of Paddy Stewart's Sabre, XB865. Evidence of an in-flight fire can be seen from charring of the paintwork. (*Charles Keil*)

crew took it out onto the airfield and ran it at full power but could not replicate the surging or temperature fluctuation. This was the aircraft in which Paddy Stewart was killed on its next flight.' Further Dividend sorties were cancelled due to bad weather, and Fg Off Stewart's crash marked a sad end to the exercise.

For some of the squadron, a welcome break was the deployment of aircraft and crews to the USAF base at Chaumont in France for a squadron exchange. Led by Sqn Ldr Smith, eight Sabres with the call sign 'Inkstain Red' departed Oldenburg in four-aircraft formations at 1300 hr and 1330 hr. Two aircraft in the second formation were temporarily delayed by unserviceability, but all arrived safely at Chaumont after 1 hour and 20 minutes of flying. Charles Keil was one of the lucky pilots to fly on this detachment, though his arrival at the USAF base was slightly mistimed:

> When we made our approach to land at Chaumont, I was flying in close formation with Ken Smith and touched down first. Having committed myself to land, he for reasons I cannot recall decided to go round again. The other pair (Jimmy Ridout and Dave Hunt) on approach behind us also went round again. I completed my landing run, turned off at the end of the runway and followed the truck to the hardstanding and shut down. Which was all somewhat embarrassing because the big USAF top brass came out to meet me while our boss was doing another circuit. And before my colleagues landed and taxied in, I had removed my Mae West, flying suit, etc. and was ready for the champagne on ice which awaited us in front of the hangar.

Sorties from Chaumont began on 27 July, suitably late after the previous evening's excesses. Local flights were carried out, along with two runs to Paris on 28 and 29 July. The eight Sabres returned to base on the 29th. On the way home, Sqn Ldr Smith's formation flew a number of formations for the camera of 'Wilkie' Wilkinson, flying in another Sabre. These photos appeared in a number of publications and have become well-known. It is interesting to note that aircraft on this deployment carried individual fuselage-code letters, a system that had only recently come into force.

Meanwhile, as part of the exchange, ten 492 Fighter Bomber Sqn F-86Fs from Chaumont had arrived at Oldenburg on the evening of 26 July. They performed similar missions to the aircraft at Chaumont before completing their stay with a battle-formation mission at 0700 hr on 30 July, after which they flew back home.

Many of 26 Sqn's aircraft were put through primary servicing at the start of August, and as a result not much flying was possible. However, the situation had improved by 12 August, when two days were spent firing on the Meppen ranges. Nevertheless, unseasonably bad weather punctuated life throughout the month, preventing flying to such an extent that it started to affect morale. Sadly, when good weather returned on 25 August, flying was still pretty much out of the question, as many Sabres were unserviceable or again on primary servicing. One piece of good news was that XB613, classed as Cat. 3 damaged since the previous February, was finally repaired by the 3 MRSU party on 16 August and was placed on minor servicing.

A further exercise, code-named 'Lucifer', was planned for the beginning of September, and thus at the end of August the Sabres were prepared. In fact, the first day of Lucifer was planned for 31 August, but a warm front prevented any flying on that day. Therefore the squadron flew its first missions of the exercise on 1 September, when mid-morning raids on Holland were launched. The Sabres were limited to speeds of Mach 0.75 and a maximum height of 20,000ft, so it is perhaps surprising that no intercepts were reported. Confusion reigned on this first flying day, because the squadron call sign had changed to 'Stovex', but as exercise call signs were also in use, no one seemed to know who was who. Further missions were flown in the morning and evening of 2 September, again with no reported intercepts.

The squadron lost a further Sabre on 3 September, though thankfully this time the pilot was unharmed. Fg Off Bob Chase was flying XB734/E and found that when

Chaumont's USAF station commander greets 26 Sqn pilots on their arrival there on 26 July 1954. RAF pilots L–R are: Sqn Ldr Ken Smith, Fg Off Jimmy Ridout, Fg Off Dave Hunt and a rather awkward-looking Fg Off Charles Keil. The latter had unexpectedly touched down first, and had already removed his flying gear by the time the rest of his formation had landed. Note the squadron commander's pennant below the canopy rail. (*Charles Keil*)

On return from the squadron's detachment to Chaumont on 29 July 1954, Fg Off 'Wilkie' Wilkinson took the opportunity to photograph the aircraft in a number of formations. The Sabres were flown by Sqn Ldr Ken Smith (XB883/A), Flt Lt Ridout (XB818/M), Fg Off Hunt (XB708/T) and Fg Off Charles Keil (XB577/V). (*Charles Keil*)

preparing to land, though he selected the undercarriage down, it would fail to lock and immediately retracted again. Unfamiliar with cockpit procedure (pulling a circuit-breaker would have solved the problem), he was forced to perform a belly landing. Fortunately, he brought the aircraft in on the grass beside the runway so that flying could continue despite the mishap. Despite performing a very skilful landing, Chase's aircraft was assessed as being beyond economical repair.

Sqn Ldr J.A.G. Jackson, DFC, AFC arrived at Oldenburg on 6 September to take over command of the squadron; Sqn Ldr Ken Smith, his tour completed, was posted to the Army Staff College, departing on 8 September.

Following a station parade on 15 September to mark the fourteenth anniversary of the Battle of Britain, the entire squadron deployed to Ahlhorn on 17 September. First to set off was the road party, followed by the main body of the squadron on 20 September. Fourteen Sabres plus the Meteor and Vampire trainers flew across at 1000 hr that morning, the rear party leaving at 1330 hr. Once the aircraft were deployed to Ahlhorn, Exercise Battle Royal commenced, half an hour late, on 21 September; the squadron flew no missions on this day. However, on 22 September the dozen Sabres flew in six pairs on morning raids at 30,000ft over the Düsseldorf and Ruhr area. Charles Keil flew on this mission, logging one hour of flight time in XB580/D.

On the following day six further pairs missions left Ahlhorn from 0930 hr on

The aftermath of Fg Off Bob Chase's accident on 3 September 1954. Chase was forced to land wheels-up after his undercarriage kept cycling to the retracted position when selected as 'down'. (*Charles Keil*)

penetration flights, but the squadron's commitment to Battle Royal was deemed as 'hazy'. Twelve pilots were again available at 0500 hr on 24 September, but were not used. Instead, training flights were flown, including a squadron mass 'balbo' formation routing via Oldenburg, and Schleswigland. In the afternoon further penetration raids were launched. The final phases of Battle Royal were low-key: on 25 September two sections were again available but not used and the remainder of the day was spent flying anti-aircraft cooperation exercises as well as short cross-country missions at altitudes of between 12,000 and 2,000ft. On the following day further AA cooperation flights were flown, but no other exercise missions; 26 Sqn stood down from Battle Royal on 27 September but remained at Ahlhorn.

Low-level sweeps were flown on successive days until 29 September, when eight Sabres took part in practice strikes on the airfield for the benefit of RAF Regiment gunners. A change from the routine on the same day saw squadron pilots off on a 36-hour escape-and-evasion exercise, the last stragglers arriving back at Ahlhorn at 0800 hr on 1 October. For the rest of their stay, 26 Sqn Sabres flew mainly battle-flight missions, though an air-to-ground detail to the Meppen range was squeezed in on 12 October after a spell of bad weather. On 21 October the advance party left for Oldenburg with the aircraft following at 0815 hr on 22 October.

By 1 November all but four of the squadron's Sabres were grounded for aileron bungee inspections. The four serviceable aircraft were heavily utilised on air-to-ground firing sorties during the day, but by that evening even these machines had been grounded, this time by a generator-defect inspection. Incredibly, even 26 Sqn's Vampire and Meteor aircraft were unserviceable at this time and thus no flying was possible. The Sabres finally began to return to the air on 4 November.

Some variety was introduced on 10 November when twenty-two Meteor F. 8s from the Day Fighter Leaders School at West Raynham staged a raid on the airfield at Jever. The battle flight of Sabres from 26 Sqn's 'B' Flight this time managed successfully to intercept the Meteors, and further aircraft from 'A' Flight also joined in on this occasion. Conditions were far worse for battle flight on 24 November, when bad weather led to the aircraft of 'B' Flight diverting into Wunstorf.

December 1954 brought bad weather, though the disruption was mitigated by a lack of aircraft. All Sabres had been grounded on 27 November for defect inspection, but this time the ground crews worked miracles and by 6 December the unit was able to declare sixteen Sabres airworthy. Two days later, a mass-formation 'balbo' was launched, and several sorties on short-range Sabres (those not fitted with drop tanks) were also completed. The joy was short-lived. On 21 December many of the Sabres were again grounded, this time so that maintenance personnel could inspect the aircraft for wing-root cracks. Though cracks were subsequently found on a number of the Sabres, they were all deemed to be minor in nature and the aircraft were returned to flight status. The squadron then stood down for a well-earned Christmas break.

Flying recommenced on 4 January 1955, with 'B' Flight taking up battle-flight duties. On the second sortie of the day, Fg Off Funnell (call sign 'Black 4') lost his normal hydraulic system, followed by most of the utility-system pressure, and had limited recourse to the alternative (emergency) system. Through skilful piloting, Funnell was able to return to base, shepherded by Fg Off Wilkinson: a lucky break indeed.

On the same afternoon, drop tanks were removed from all Sabres, an occasion that led the squadron diarist to write, 'Blessed relief! Quite a pleasant change to be able to look down at a Venom.' Their performance thus improved, morale among the pilots was high.

For their first air-to-ground sorties of the year, 26 Sqn changed venue to the range at Ströhen, ten miles east of the town of Damme, on 12 January. This range was used a number of times in the coming months, but almost immediately heavy snow falls halted further sorties. With flying impossible, ground lectures were given to many of the squadron personnel, and off-station visits began, such as when pilots visited the US aircraft carrier *Corregidor* at Bremerhaven on 27 January. Ironically, when the snow did begin to thaw at the end of the month, further sorties to the Ströhen range had to be cancelled because of flooding!

A number of incidents punctuated squadron life during February 1955. The bad luck began on 7 February when XB682/R suffered a tailpipe fire on shutdown from a mission. Luckily, the fire was put out by alert ground crews and no damage was done to the aircraft.

On 10 February the squadron lost its final Sabre in a slightly baffling accident. Fg Off Rickwood was briefed to carry out an aerobatic sortie at 15,000ft, flying XB839/X. Witnesses saw Rickwood's aircraft flying fast at about 1,000ft, when two objects were seen to separate from the Sabre. At this point the aircraft dived steeply to the ground and impacted in a peat bog eight miles from Oldenburg. The two objects seen by witnesses were the aircraft's canopy and Fg Off Rickwood in his ejection seat; sadly he failed to open his parachute in time and was killed.

Investigation of this accident was hampered by the boggy ground at the scene, and most of the wreckage was not recovered. However, from the injuries sustained by the pilot it was determined that he had separated from his seat during ejection and struck the aircraft's tail. Though the Sabre Pilot's Notes advise undoing the harness straps before ejection at low level, the manual also stresses the need to adopt the correct posture to avoid being thrown out of the seat during ejection. It was probably failure to adhere to this recommendation that killed poor Rickwood.

It is worth noting that, though an official investigation was carried out into this crash, its findings were haphazard and often in error: the accident report states that the crash occurred on '11 March 1955', even though the Chief Investigating Officer signed off the report on 8 March 1955! Some time later a feasible explanation was proffered as to the true cause: jamming of the horizontal stabiliser, caused by wear in the front-beam snubber. It was thought that such a problem would have caused the abrupt dive into the ground; Fg Off Rickwood's faulty seat separation was simply a factor in the pilot's death.

The day after Fg Off Rickwood's death, Fg Off 'Wilkie' Wilkinson struck a goose

Fg Off Charles Keil about to board one of 26 Sqn's Sabres, XB535/L. Keil is wearing the helmet he loaned to Fg Off Stewart prior to the latter's fatal crash on 23 July 1954. A shortage of flying clothing meant that the helmet was later returned to Keil, and he wore it for the rest of his Sabre career. (*Charles Keil*)

while running in to break for landing at Oldenburg. Considerable damage was done to Wilkinson's Sabre, though this was confined to the starboard wing slat and leading edge; after leaving the circuit to perform stall checks, the aircraft was recovered safely to base. This run of accidents was brought to an end on 24 February when Fg Off Ferguson's aircraft, XB623/G, yawed on take-off and hit a snow bank. Though Ferguson escaped unhurt, his aircraft was subsequently declared a write-off.

In spite of these incidents, a good deal of flying was accomplished during February, though snowy weather did have its effect. In addition, from 10 February a large number of pilots were away on courses or on sick leave. However, firing sorties to Ströhen were launched on 22 February, and these missions were again programmed in the early part of March, leading to one of the best air-to-ground scores when 'Wilkie' Wilkinson registered an unprecedented 63 per cent on 3 March.

The wind-down of Sabre operations on 26 Sqn began on 24 February when all pilots attended an AFDS lecture on the RAF's new Hunter fighter. The lecture was rounded off by a flying display of a Hunter F. 2 over the airfield. Though Sabre flying continued, it was obvious that the writing was on the wall – in addition, a number of key squadron personnel began to be posted away from the unit.

A further Sabre accident occurred on 11 March after P Off Statham inadvertently landed his aircraft with the undercarriage up. Damage to the Sabre, XB543/Z, was not serious and the aircraft was repaired on unit. However, Statham's accident had blocked Oldenburg's runway, and airborne aircraft had to be diverted to Jever and Ahlhorn while the wreckage was cleared away.

Exercise Lateral Pass took a section of four Sabres to Leeuwarden on 22 April, beginning the squadron's involvement in this exercise, which was to continue through the summer of 1955. On 10 May a further wing fly-past sortie was flown, the squadron again supplying eight Sabres for the sixteen-ship fly-past. A number of formations were performed on this day, comprising box sections of four aircraft and finishing with a Sabre silhouette formation. With these missions completed, ground crews began fitting drop tanks to all the Sabres in preparation for the forthcoming Cyprus deployment. Further maintenance work was carried out to ensure that all aircraft were in perfect shape for departure time, so that maximum use could be made of the good weather in Cyprus for live firing.

On 22 May the squadron's Sabres departed for Cyprus, routing via Fürstenfeldbruck to night-stop at Rome's Ciampino airport. Ground crews and pilots not allotted to Sabre aircraft were flown on the same route in Hastings transports. The first day got off to a

XB839/X gets a top-up at Oldenburg. This aircraft is the one in which Frank Rickwood was killed on 10 February 1955. (*David Watkins*)

bad start with the Vampire trainer being left unserviceable at Oldenburg with a fuel leak, while a Sabre had to return to Fürstenfeldbruck with an undercarriage problem; it arrived in Rome the following day. The squadron flew to Nicosia, Cyprus on 23 May, via a refuelling stop at Athens; again problems intervened and a further Sabre was forced to return to Rome, again with undercarriage problems. The delayed Sabres arrived at Nicosia on 25 May.

Live-firing missions began on 25 May, though the Whitsun stand-down from 27 May prevented any further missions being flown for some time. Returning to work on 30 May, Sqn Ldr Jackson led six Sabres to Habbaniya in Iraq for a further detachment. Meanwhile back in Cyprus, a Command modification to fit Mk. III recorder cameras to Sabre gunsights led to increased accuracy in assessing pilots shooting'.

Sqn Ldr Jackson had led six Sabres to Habbaniya in Iraq for a further detachment on 30 May, the other five pilots involved being Fg Offs Hunt, Richardson and Wilkinson and P Offs Biltcliffe and Statham. This group practised ground-controlled intercept missions in Iraq, and on 3 June Fg Off Wilkinson gave a local flying display, which terminated in the now-customary laying of a sonic bang on the airfield. The five other Sabres at Habbaniya, meanwhile, gave a formation-flying display. The Iraq detachment returned to Nicosia on 4 June, though one of the pilots was forced to jettison his Sabre's drop tanks after experiencing fuel-feed problems. On 9 June the squadron performed a further display, this time a seven-Sabre fly-past to mark the Queen's Birthday.

On 12 June 26 Squadron left Cyprus, reversing its outbound route to night-stop in Rome; they flew back to base on the following day. Inevitably, one Sabre had meantime gone unserviceable and followed a few days later. The ground crews and spare pilots returned to base in the Hastings via a short and entertaining stop in Malta.

The return from Cyprus really marked the beginning of the end for Sabre operations on 26 Sqn; on 16 June, with the arrival of the first three Hunters, the flights were rearranged. Because it was necessary to have some pilots qualified on the Hunter in time for the Duke of Edinburgh's station visit on 12 July, it was decided that 'A' Flight would decrease in size and convert to the Hunter first. All Sabres were concurrently transferred to 'B' Flight so that the squadron could maintain some semblance of operational readiness. Further Hunters were delivered on 17 June, and the first solos by squadron pilots were made on the 20th when five crews took to the air.

Among all this frenzied activity, Exercise Carte Blanche started on 22 June; but though nine Sabres were available on the first day, only one scramble was launched. On the following day, bad weather prevented a number of sorties, but some missions were flown into the American Zone, where formations of 25–30 'enemy' Sabres were engaged. No losses were reported by 26 Sqn on this occasion. On 26 June, two sections of four Sabres provided top cover for a formation of Belgian F-84s on a bombing mission to Frankfurt; on return to base the fighters engaged further formations of Canadian and American Sabres from the opposing forces. Oldenburg was subject to a dummy atom bomb on 27 June, so all airborne aircraft were diverted to Jever. Nonetheless, sorties were launched from Jever before a return to Oldenburg. Carte Blanche finished that evening.

The last formation flight of 26 Sqn Sabres was flown on 28 June, when an eight-ship high-level sweep was completed. The following day, the squadron's first Hunter battle formation was flown, and the Sabres began to be flown back to the UK for overhaul.

The Sabres were sidelined for the Duke of Edinburgh's visit to Oldenburg on 12 July; his aircraft was escorted from the Dutch border by the squadron's Hunters. The Duke presented the squadron standard before departing, again escorted by a formation of Hunters. Six more Sabres left the unit for overhaul in the following few days.

Unfortunately, the squadron's conversion onto the Hunter was not without incident. On 22 July, Fg Off Drysdale, on one of his first flights in the new jet, stalled and dropped a wing on take-off. His Hunter slewed off the runway and ploughed through the runway-control caravan, killing three air-traffic personnel. The squadron was fortunate that no further lives were lost, as a number of pilots had gathered around the caravan to watch the day's activities.

Amid this sadness, the Sabres gradually faded from squadron life. One aircraft was air-tested on 28 July before the last three Sabres were finally transferred to 20 Sqn on 30 August.

AIRCRAFT ASSIGNED

XB535/L, XB543/Z, XB577/V, XB580/D, XB588/P, XB593/Q, XB595/W, XB609/X, XB613/C, XB623/G, XB636/G, XB700/B, XB707/K, XB708/T, XB734/E, XB751/N, XB759, XB764/V, XB767/Y, XB800/F, XB818/M, XB832/E, XB834/J, V, XB839/X, XB862/R, XB865, XB866, XB868/S, XB877, XB883/A, XB886/W.

Only two '6–3'-winged aircraft were assigned – XB931 and XB961 – for only a few weeks in March 1954.

MARKINGS – 26 SQN

The squadron's first Sabres gained individual markings for the first time with the application of the springbok emblem on the vertical tail. This was painted onto a white circle, bordered in mid-blue. The springbok's head faced to the left on both sides of the tail.

With the majority of aircraft now adorned with squadron markings, individual code letters were applied. These were painted in yellow, with a thin red outline, and placed forward of the fuselage roundel on both sides of the fuselage. 'Bar' markings were not applied by 26 Sqn to its Sabres.

SQUADRON MOTTO

'N Wagter in die Lug (A guard in the sky).

CHAPTER EIGHT

66 SQUADRON

In late 1953, 66 Sqn was flying Gloster Meteor F. 8s from Linton-on-Ouse in Yorkshire when preparations began for conversion to the Sabre. Poor weather and a lack of serviceable Meteors provided the perfect opportunity to begin ground-schooling on the new type, and lectures began in November 1953. Concurrent with this training, a number of new pilots were posted into the unit. Meanwhile, Meteor flying continued, the emphasis being placed on practice interception missions and battle formation. Being 'non-tactical', 66 Sqn (and later 92 Sqn) concentrated mainly on air-to-air gunnery. By the end of November, average scores of 51.8 per cent had been achieved on cine missions and 15.2 per cent on live air-firing missions – all on the Meteor, as no Sabres were yet in service.

The first two Sabres for 66 Sqn, XD706 and XD720, were flown in from Kemble on 27 November and put straight through acceptance checks; it would be some weeks before they were actually flown by squadron pilots. No further Sabres would be delivered until mid-January 1954.

The final month of 1953 saw flying again affected by weather, though by now the emphasis was heavily on beginning conversion to the Sabre. During the month Sqn Ldr D.C. Usher, commanding officer of the squadron, completed his Sabre conversion with SCU at Wildenrath. Other pilots attending the course were Flt Lt 'Bush' Barrey, DFC, DFM, AFC ('A' Flight commander), Flt Lt Gray and Flt Sgt Volanthen. The majority of pilots on the squadron did not go through formal Sabre

A 66 Sqn line-up at Linton, with the Wing Leader's aircraft second in line. (*J.D.R. Rawlings*)

conversion, however, and it was down to those that had gone through SCU (and later 229 OCU) courses to disseminate information on the type.

Peter Foard, fresh from a stint ferrying Sabres with 147 Sqn, was posted into 66 Sqn during December 1953, along with fellow pilot P Off Harry Armstrong. Peter Foard's experience of the Sabre put him in great demand:

I was asked to give a verbal introduction to the F-86 and its handling characteristics. After several reconnaissance trips on the Meteor, [on 23 January 1954] I flew an F-86 on a local familiarisation sortie, including a radio-compass let-down, which was a self-conducted type of QGH. The following day, I flew as number two in the first vic formation of F-86s to fly from Linton. It was led by P Off Harry Armstrong, another 'Bechers Brook' veteran, and the number three slot was flown by Sgt Pat Stride, who I believe joined us from 3 Sqn in 2 TAF. The squadron gradually converted from the Meteor 8 to the F-86, some of the newer inexperienced pilots being required to complete a certain amount of hours on the Meteor before flying the F-86.

Aside from the two aircraft delivered at the end of November, the main delivery of Sabres to the squadron began on 14 January. On that day, XD708, 712, 722, 757, 774 and 778 were flown in from 5 MU at Kemble. Sabre-conversion flights at Linton finally began on 22 January 1954, and the 'old salts' on the squadron were the first to fly. One of these was Ian Laurie, a sergeant pilot who had been with 66 Sqn since January 1949, first on Meteor F. 4s and then F. 8s. He took XD706 on a 30-minute familiarisation sortie on 22 January and over the next few days did five further missions, culminating in a 40-minute flight in XD708 on 28 January to finish his conversion onto the type. By the end of the month, 97 hours had been flown on the new type by the squadron, and twenty-two pilots had started their conversion. Crews that had been with the squadron for some time usually flew the Sabre straight after a period of cockpit and Pilot's Notes familiarisation. Any pilots new to the squadron took a different route: they instead completed a number of flights in the squadron's Meteor T. 7 trainer before being let loose on the Sabre. Additionally, a single Vampire T. 11 trainer was heavily utilised to provide instrument flying-check flights for all squadron pilots.

The squadron's Meteor 8s were ferried out by the end of January, with the 20 hours' flying on the type during the month being largely down to providing test flights before the aircraft were reassigned. On 31 January, 66 Sqn possessed twenty-one Sabres, all XD-serialled aircraft.

Conversion onto the Sabre continued into February and, with more crews becoming effective, formation-flying sorties were completed in mid-month, these focusing on close and battle formations. No difficulties were found in adapting the Sabre to these missions. A total of 136 hours were flown on the Sabre in February, rising again to 430 hours in the following month. This was particularly encouraging, especially when one considers that the more experienced 2 TAF Sabre squadrons were struggling to reach these figures at this time, in spite of having more experience on the type. Late in March, live firing was undertaken for the first time, a total of twenty-four guns being fired in the air, though at this point the exercise was simply to give maintenance crews and pilots experience in handling the Sabre's armament. None of these sorties involved firing at a target; the guns were simply fired into thin air in level flight. Cine exercises also began, the resultant film proving far clearer than that obtained from the Meteor's G. 45 camera.

Ground training continued throughout the Sabre period, depending on availability of

On 18 March 1954, 66 Sqn put up a four-ship Sabre formation for the media. A Vampire trainer was used to fly the press photographer as the formation flew over York. Those involved were: (back row L–R) Brian I'Anson, Brian Merifield (Vampire), Nigel Bain, Ian Laurie, press reporter; front row L–R: Ira Fothergill, 'Bush' Barrey, press photographer. (*Brian Merifield*)

personnel. In poor weather, up to fifty hours per month could be achieved, but at times when there was a busy flying programme, the theoretical side often took a back seat. During March 1954, the squadron also managed to spend the day at York swimming baths, practising dinghy drills.

Despite only recently having converted onto the Sabre, 66 Sqn also took part in Exercise Magna Flux during March. The squadron flew sorties on the exercise from 1 March and finished its involvement five days later. 66 Sqn Sabres were deemed to have provided good results in the exercise, which saw them acting as defending interceptors against dummy raids by NATO aircraft coming from mainland Europe. The squadron also flew its first night-reinforcement exercise on 25 March, taking a number of Sabres to Geilenkirchen in Germany. Ian Laurie flew out in XD708, returning to Linton with the squadron the following day.

The last Sabre to be assigned to the squadron in the initial delivery – XD718 – was flown in from Kemble on 8 March. However, it appears that this and one further aircraft had been assigned in excess of the usual complement, as this brought the squadron total to twenty-four aircraft. As a result, on the same day, XD710 and XD719 were transferred to 92 Sqn, re-establishing 66 Sqn's correct 22-aircraft strength.

The final pair of pilots to convert onto the Sabre completed their Meteor check flights in April, and at this point the T. 7 trainer departed the squadron. John Rumbelow was one of these two pilots, with his first Sabre flight with 66 Sqn taking place on 1 April. Better weather during the month allowed a further 505 Sabre hours to be flown, and more than a quarter of these were devoted to practice sorties for the forthcoming Queen's escort. The majority of the remaining missions were on formation and cine practice. Of ninety-five gun-camera sorties, sixty were effective. In addition, a number of firing sorties were completed, these first missions firing into floating targets in the North Sea.

Other than a few similar sorties, 66 Sqn concentrated entirely on air-to-air gunnery.

The squadron deployed through the RCAF Sabre base at North Luffenham on 10 May to complete rehearsals for the Queen's fly-past, having previously used North Luffenham for refuelling stops a number of times in the previous month; 110 hours were devoted to this activity alone. The actual fly-past took place on 15 May over Buckingham Palace, and the squadron returned to Linton the same day. At the end of the month the squadron began live air-to-air gunnery, initially using a fixed gunsight without radar-ranging. Forty-six gunnery missions were considered effective and, in spite of a squadron visit to Sperry Gyroscope, problems still existed with the gunsight. Peter Foard, though an experienced Sabre pilot, had not previously fired the Sabre's guns: 'Apart from routine training and practice interceptions, exercises in air gunnery against a towed 30ft flag target were carried out. We had little success with the radar gunsight, as we found that the radar-ranging of the gunsight tended to lock on to the tug aircraft, thereby supplying a false range. We even experimented by tying a sackful of empty milk tins to the spreader bar of the flag target, with limited success. We therefore reverted to the old proven method of "fixed" gun sighting and assessing our own deflection.'

On 6 May 1954 the squadron had lost its first Sabre, XD722. Flt Lt Jed Gray had experienced an engine flameout at 18,000ft and, unable to relight, was forced to look for a landing field. Though he eventually managed to bring his aircraft onto the approach to the airfield at Langham, he just could not stretch his glide far enough and the Sabre landed in the undershoot area; it was written off. Peter Foard had a similar problem around this time:

On 13 May 1954, while carrying out an air test for ASF, I had completed the test and ran in to the airfield for a break and landing, lowered the undercarriage on the downwind leg and then discovered the engine had flamed out. Frantic efforts to relight were unsuccessful and I found myself committed to a 'wheels-up' landing on the grass alongside the runway. I'd had to stretch my glide, and even then I'd scraped my wing tanks off on the airfield boundary hedge. When the aircraft was hoisted on to its wheels again and an attempt was made to start it, it only achieved 60 per cent of idling revs. The fault was a broken fuel-metering rod in the fuel-control system.

Sadly, Peter Foard's Sabre, XD773, was a write-off. Two further Sabres were lost on 16 June when XD711/U and XD716/K collided four miles west-north-west of Hornsea. Both pilots, Fg Off John Sweet and Fg Off John Rumbelow, ejected successfully. John Rumbelow remembered it distinctly:

On 16 June 1954 I was flying number four position [in XD716] in a section, part of a flight of twelve aircraft, in loose battle formation, climbing to 35,000ft, expecting to be bounced. At approx. 15,000 a break to port was called by my section leader, John Sweet. I entered the break, but almost immediately the aircraft went into an inverted spin. This surprised me as it had never happened before and the aircraft was not cleared for spinning.

I attempted standard spin recovery, to no avail, and had resorted to other non-orthodox procedures when a voice over the RT said, 'Get out, John, get out'. At the same time smoke entered the cockpit, and it was only then that I became aware that something was seriously wrong and started the ejection procedure. This involved pulling three levers. Pulling the first on the right-hand side locked the harness and revealed another, lower lever which operated the ejector seat, to be pulled only after operating the no. 2 lever on the left, jettisoning the canopy. I only pulled the first lever but found myself out in the fresh air. I freed myself from the seat, pulled the ripcord and came down in a field at Beeford, still gripping the ripcord but minus the bone-dome. This was found and had a lump missing from the brow section. I assumed that I had exited at the same time as the canopy blew. It was not until the helicopter picked me up that I realised another aircraft was involved.

The forthcoming UK air-defence exercise, Dividend, planned for July, meant that minimal hours were flown during June 1954; the target of 200 hours was easily met by mid-month, at which point many personnel were sent on leave. Nearly half of the flying was devoted to air-to-air gunnery.

During Exercise Dividend, 66 Sqn was tasked with defending the UK from attacking aircraft at high and very high levels, among them the Canadian Sabres from Germany. Dividend would test the air defences against attacks that would be likely in the first few days of a war. Among the aircraft raiding the UK were USAF KC-97s, B-47 Stratojets, F-80s, Canadian F-86s and Thunderjets. In addition, aircraft from the Fleet Air Arm and the French Air Force also took part, as well as further RAF Sabres from 2 TAF in Germany. The high-level B-47 attacks in particular proved almost impossible to intercept, and highlighted the superiority of this bomber, whose speed was a match for most fighters of the day. The UK air-defence system fielded 877 fighters during the exercise, including the RAF Sabres from Linton, USAF F-86Ds from the USAF at Manston, plus RAF Meteors, Vampires, Venoms and Canadian Sabres. Around 30 per cent of attacks were intercepted before they reached the coast of the UK.

Some idea of the busy nature of Dividend can be gained from a single pilot's missions during the first few days. Ian Laurie flew XD725 twice on 45-minute sorties on 17 July, followed by similar missions aboard XD721 and XD770 on the following day. Further sorties of similar duration were completed in Phase 2, starting on 22 July; Ian flew no less than ten times in the following four days.

Sadly, on the first day of Phase 2, 66 Sqn lost three further Sabres. Fg Off Glyn Owen was fortunate to be able to eject from XD758/L when his fire-warning light illuminated north-east of Helmsley. However, on this occasion, there may have been extenuating circumstances, according to Peter Foard: 'The one big problem with the F-86 was that it had no Graviner or fire-extinguishing system, and if the fire-warning light lit up it could be a matter of seconds before the aircraft blew up. This was no great problem whilst flying in formation, as your wing man could carry out a visual inspection. I personally experienced a couple of spurious fire warnings which proved to be electrical faults. One pilot flying alone at 40,000ft [Owen] was convinced his fire-warning light was flashing and ejected. We came to realise that it was possible to believe the warning light was "on" when the sunlight reflected on it.'

The other two aircraft lost on 22 July took their pilots with them. Flt Lt Green and Fg Off Horne had been letting down through cloud as part of a four-ship formation and flew into Kinder Scout, one of the highest peaks in England. Their aircraft were XD707/B and XD730/X. Flt Lt Green had only arrived on the squadron earlier in the month, having previously flown Sabres in 2 TAF. John Rumbelow adds more to the story: '[They were] doing a high-level descent through cloud. Descent is made by splitting into two separate pairs, numbers three and four descending 25yd behind numbers one and two. Descent should be made in the safety lane or sector. Numbers one and two broke cloud, saw the high ground and pulled up. Numbers three and four did not see the high ground – their descent was not in the safety lane.'

The post-exercise scrutiny of Dividend highlighted the lack of 'Tu-4' (B-29/B-50) aircraft in the scenario, but more importantly conceded that the chances of intercepting the high-altitude (B-47) jet-bomber raids was, at

XD730/X of 66 Sqn taxis out for another sortie. This aircraft was one of three lost by the squadron on the same day, 22 July 1954. It crashed into Kinder Scout during Exercise Dividend; pilot Flt Lt A. Green was killed. (*Bruce Robertson*)

best, marginal. Clearly, Soviet bombers of this type could also have raided with impunity. Bad weather thwarted many missions during Dividend, and the need for all-weather fighters was evident.

Air-to-air gunnery practice was very much the order of the day in early August, and high-level practice interceptions continued. Results were mixed. The inability of ground controllers to appreciate the large radius of turn required for the Sabre's increased speed came in for particular criticism. Late in the month, wing practices for September's Battle of Britain Day celebrations took up a lot of time. With the wing scheduled to fly over London, full dress rehearsals meant a refuelling stop at the Canadian Sabre base at North Luffenham on the trip south.

On 27 August 1954, a flight of 66 Sqn Sabres was tasked with a cross-country mission prior to commencing one such Battle of Britain fly-past rehearsal. The formation of three aircraft was led by 30-year-old Flt Lt Gerald 'Jed' Gray, an above-average pilot with 70 hours on Sabres; the first leg would take them to the RCAF base at North Luffenham. Leaving base in mid-morning, the flight to North Luffenham took them 25 minutes, but just as Gray began to orbit and burn off fuel for landing, he heard an intermittent crackling noise from the front end of the cockpit. All indications appeared normal, however, and his number two was ordered in close to inspect for anything suspicious; nothing was seen from outside. Shortly afterwards, smoke began to fill Flt Lt Gray's cockpit, and the canopy was opened to aid forward visibility. As Jed Gray contemplated his options, flames appeared at the left-hand side of the cockpit and his decision was made: he ejected, landing safely. Gray's Sabre, XD776, crashed in a grass field three-quarters of a mile north-north-west of Blatherwycke Church and five miles south of North Luffenham. It was destroyed, having flown just 68.5 hours from new.

An official inquiry was later convened, with AVM W.J. Crishan, CB, CBE as president. Intervening examination of the wreckage had revealed that the source of the fire was in the left-hand forward ammunition tank; empty soot-blackened cartridges in this area explaining the 'crackling' sound that Gray had heard – the sound of the ammunition 'cooking off'. Though no certain cause could be found for this occurring, it was felt very likely that high-temperature air used to heat the gun compartment could lead to such a situation. Normally this heated air, tapped off the engine compressor, was controlled by thermostatic switches, with an overheat lamp in the cockpit indicating any problems. The

A 66 Sqn line-up with the uniquely painted XB542/Z at the front. This machine had the higher 2 TAF camouflage demarcation line, but was painted with Fighter Command silver undersides. (*Peter Foard*)

inquiry decided that one or more items in the system had failed and caused the overheat. The loss of this Sabre, along with others, prompted the assignment of a number of XB-serialled aircraft into the unit from September 1954. First to be sent to the squadron was XB542, which was coded 'Z'. Unusually, this machine was painted in the silver-underside scheme peculiar to the 'XD'-serialled Fighter Command aircraft, but retained the higher camouflage-demarcation line of the 2 TAF Sabres. It is thought that XB542 was the only Sabre to wear this colour scheme variation.

Despite a number of aircraft being grounded for unspecified modifications in September, a number of high-level practice intercept missions were flown, and several were successful against Canberra targets. The squadron deployed to Coltishall on 9 September, so that the aircraft could be within unrefuelled flying range of the Battle of Britain fly-past over London. While at Coltishall, aside from fly-past practices, a number of high-level sweeps were also flown. The fly-past was completed over Buckingham Palace on 15 September, the squadron immediately returning to Linton. To commemorate Battle of Britain Day further, on 18 September Linton's gates were thrown open to the public and 66 Sqn's Sabres were put on display. The squadron also performed formation fly-pasts over several local airfields, and a number of pilots also gave solo aerobatic displays.

A marked improvement in air-to-air gunnery was finally being felt at this time, and this was put down to improved radar serviceability. Pilots were also getting used to the aircraft and were now closing in on their targets before firing. As if to demonstrate the fact, Flt Lt Dawkins raised the squadron record to 60 per cent midway through October. Ian Laurie was not far behind, scoring 47.5 per cent aboard XD778/R on 12 October.

On 25 October, the AOC 12 Gp presented Linton-on-Ouse with its station badge; 66 Sqn again put on a fly-past, this time as part of the wing in conjunction with 92 Sqn. The feat was repeated on the following weekend, when photographs were taken. The first night-flying sorties with the Sabre were also completed during October. One of the squadron's more experienced NCO pilots was also posted out during the month. Flt Sgt Raymond Volanthen was posted to Aston Down as a maintenance-unit test pilot. Sadly, he was killed in a Hunter crash on landing at Kemble on 6 December.

The squadron's flying target of 585 hours was exceeded by almost 5 hours in November, despite nearly a week being lost to bad weather. Again, several intercepts on Canberras were successful, and the squadron also provided formations of Sabres so that the Church Fenton Meteors could practise intercept missions. The Sabres flew at less than maximum ceiling and speed to enable the slower fighters to have some chance of catching them.

Fg Off Glyn Owen had a lucky escape on 29 November, though the squadron lost its tenth Sabre in the process. Owen had been on a formation exercise aboard XD772/H when his engine seized at 35,000ft; immediately his fire-warning light came on and the cockpit filled with fuel vapour. With the likelihood of his aircraft exploding at any time, Fg Off Owen immediately ejected, opening his parachute at approximately 25,000ft. His Sabre crashed in open ground near to RAF Binbrook. Unfortunately, a strong westerly wind then began to carry Owen out towards the North Sea, and some time later he dropped into the freezing water and climbed into his dinghy. Fortunately for the pilot, however, one of his colleagues, seeing his predicament, had immediately alerted Linton of the circumstances, and a rescue effort was soon in full swing. After an hour, one of Topcliffe's Neptune patrol aircraft spotted Owen's dinghy and an air-sea rescue launch from Grimsby set out to fetch him; he was picked up after two hours afloat in the North Sea. As a result of this rescue, Owen became something of a celebrity and was called upon to brief squadron pilots on his exploits.

Sqn Ldr Usher left the squadron in November 1954, and from 22 November his place as CO was taken by Sqn Ldr A.F. Osborne, DFC. Among other arrivals during the month were P Off J.B. Thornton and Fg Off A.H.G. St Pierre. Unlike most other pilots on the squadron, these two had already completed formal Sabre conversion, this time as part of No. 2 Sabre Course with 229 OCU at Chivenor, having been detached there from the squadron since early September.

Modification of squadron aircraft to accept the '6–3' hard-edge wing began in December 1954; the process was drawn out over the next few months, so a mix of slatted and unslatted aircraft were operated for a while. Ian Laurie flew one of the first converted aircraft, XD757/W, on a 45-minute familiarisation flight on 31 December. There were two

A formal squadron pilot line-up in front of the hangar at Linton. Back row L–R: Sgt Ian Laurie, unknown, Fg Off Kiwi Connell, Fg Off Sammy St Pierre, Fg Off Ned Kelly, Fg Off Ben Gunn, Sgt Pete Foard, Fg Off Brian Thornton, Fg Off Mick Davies, Fg Off Larry Harriman, Sgt Pat Stride. Front row L–R: Fg Off Johnny Rumbelow, Fg Off Glyn Owen, Flt Lt Johnny Morris, Fg Off Pete Riley, Flt Lt Jed Gray, Flt Lt Bush Barrey, Sqn Ldr Sammy Osborne, Flt Lt Tommy Dawkins, Flt Lt Nigel Bayne, Fg Off Harry Armstrong, Fg Off Ray Williams, Fg Off Ira Fothergill, Fg Off Johnny Ditmas. (*Peter Foard*)

Members of 'A' Flight scramble to their aircraft, with XD735/T at the left. L-R Brian Thornton, Norman Glass, Kiwi Connell, Charlie Spinks, Johnnie Ditmas, Ray Williams, Ben Gunn, Pete Riley, Pete Foard. (*Peter Foard*)

instances of drop tanks being lost in flight at the end of 1954, though no particular cause could be found; in both cases no damage was caused. Fg Off A.H.D. Connell also survived a flameout in December, though he was able to relight at 15,000ft and returned safely to base.

The beginning of 1955 predictably brought snow, ice, sleet, heavy rain, fog and low cloud, all of which conspired to prohibit flying throughout January. Compounding the situation, ten aircraft were away all month on modification by a civilian working party, and three more were grounded for lack of spares. Only 366 hours were flown, which was a superb effort under the circumstances. Battle-formation and cine sorties were flown, as well as sector exercises. On the first of these, weather was very bad, but, although one section had to be diverted to Middleton St George, every planned sortie was successful. The snow and ice continued into February, the squadron only logging 294 hours for that month. Nonetheless, on 8 February, a sector exercise saw four pairs scrambled and five Canberras claimed. Additionally, with slightly better conditions at the end of the month, air-to-air gunnery began again, the aim being to get prepared for the forthcoming camp at Acklington. Unfortunately, the squadron's Vampire was unserviceable during the month, and thus unavailable for instrument flights, with the result that five pilots lost their ratings.

With the lack of flying days being felt, Exercise Rambler was launched at the end of February. This was an escape-and-evasion test, simulating a mass breakout from a prisoner-of-war camp. Aircrews from 66 and 92 Sqns were tasked with breaking through static defences two miles deep, defences being manned by station personnel. Very few did manage to get through the defences, many being picked up on the Yorkshire Moors by local police. Only one, Fg Off Armstrong, was able to get to the rendezvous point successfully. Sadly, he was killed the following month.

The squadron continued practising for its Armament Practice Camp (APC) at Acklington during early March, making the change to high-level air-to-air sorties at the same time. To aid the squadron further, two of the Pilot Attack Instructors (PAIs) visited Jever early in the month to discuss air-firing in the Sabre. A number of aircraft were flown down to the USAF base at Shepherds Grove for firing on the 1,000yd butts there, but not all could be fitted in before going to Acklington; this would later be deemed a cause of the squadron's low record there.

Ian Laurie had a lucky escape on 1 March, only his skilled airmanship preventing what could easily have been another black day for the squadron. Programmed for high-level firing at 37,000ft in XD708/A, Laurie experienced a control problem that meant he could only turn right. Upon contacting base to relay his predicament, he was told to descend to 5,000ft and bail out; this he was not keen to do. Letting down over Bridlington, Laurie realised that it was still possible to control the aircraft in some fashion and possibly get back to Linton. He was therefore given an extended GCA approach, and brought his aircraft onto the extended runway centre line by pulling a long right-hand circuit. He began his approach, gear down, from as much as twenty miles out, and eventually landed safely.

Three sector exercises were launched in March, and during these the squadron got its first experience of intercepting the massive USAF B-36 bomber. Crews regularly turned out at 4 o'clock in the morning to catch these 'raiders', and found no difficulty in coping with the bombers at altitudes up to 42,000ft. Compared to the Canberra, the B-36 was an easy target, but it took crews a while to get used to pulling in close enough before initiating their dummy firing run.

On 21 March, the squadron moved sixteen Sabres out to Acklington, along with pilots and support personnel, and immediately tried to start live firing exercises. However, bad weather stymied efforts, along with both a lack of manpower and mobile test equipment at Acklington. In any case, shooting scores were not impressive, as many gunsights were found to be out of alignment. The problem was not corrected until the last day of March.

During the Acklington APC, Fg Off Thornton was forced to divert into Driffield, where his aircraft was grounded because his oxygen system could not be charged; the correct adaptors could not be located on station. Fg Off Harry Armstrong was therefore detailed to take the adaptors over to Driffield on 16 March. Unfortunately, his aircraft, XD755, stalled on approach, flicked over and dived into the ground; Armstrong was killed instantly. Armstrong's aircraft was a 'hard-edge' Sabre, and one feature of the conversion was a small wing fillet which had to be removed when the ammunition door/step was lowered on the ground to allow the pilot to climb into the aircraft. Unfortunately, these fillets had not been refitted prior to Armstrong setting off on this flight, and this was felt to have caused the premature stall. This was the squadron's eleventh Sabre loss, and also the third pilot lost on the aircraft; sadly, it would not be the last.

The Acklington APC finished in early April, 66 Sqn ending with an average 12.9 per cent score. The final week had been marred by a fire in the locker room, though no one was injured; only flying equipment was destroyed. The squadron returned to Linton following a fly-past over York. The remainder of the month was fairly low-key for the squadron and, although Exercise Sky High was initiated at the end of April, only one pair of Sabres was scrambled throughout the exercise because of bad weather. On a more positive note, two other exercises during the last week involved sorties against DFLS Hunters, a number of 'kills' being claimed by 66 Sqn.

Following the loss of a number of key aircrew and a further lack of trained ground crew, the squadron found itself less than 70 per cent manned in May. Coupled with a bout of poor serviceability, there were rarely more than eight Sabres available on a given day. As a result, flying hours were down, each pilot getting less than fifteen hours' flying per month. In spite of this, several sector exercises were flown, against diverse types such as the Lincoln bomber and Vampire, Meteor and Hunter fighters. Most of these sorties were flown as single aircraft.

On one occasion in June the aircraft were scrambled against the Meteors of 264 Sqn, but most intercepting pilots were scrambled too late and thus failed to make contact. It was not a happy time for the unit.

The squadron Vampire was still unserviceable in June, and many pilots had to fly in instrument conditions despite not having current ratings. This may have had an input into the squadron's next fatal accident. On 16 June 1955, XD712 crashed in Elsham Carr Lane, nine miles from Scunthorpe. Fg Off L.M.P. Harryman, a 23-year-old with 110 hours of Sabre time, was killed instantly. He had been briefed to fly as number three in a battle-formation and tail-chase exercise with four other Sabres, though the full formation consisted of three groups of four Sabres each; Harryman's group was at the tail, so he would in effect be number eleven. The aircraft had departed base at 1100 hr local time, and completed the battle-formation exercise successfully. At this point the fifth Sabre left the formation, and the remaining quartet closed up in line astern for the tail chase. The leader commenced the exercise at 21,000ft with a half roll and steep spiral descent; the following aircraft took chase, registering up to 8g on pulling out at 13,500ft. It was at this point that the number three aircraft began to pull out, but as the nose reached horizontal it rolled onto its back, and was last seen entering cloud at about 10,000ft. The aircraft broke up in cloud, and wreckage was spread over a wide area; Fg Off Harryman, unlike the other flight members, had not been wearing an anti-g suit.

Investigation revealed that the Sabre's wings had failed in upload adjacent to the wing root. Detailed examination of the wreckage was carried out at the Royal Aircraft Establishment, Farnborough, though it was difficult to ascertain whether Harryman had blacked out prior to structural failure occurring.

Thankfully, in July the squadron was able to return to some form of normality in spite of the poor manning of ground trades. Better weather meant that exercises were flown for northern and western sectors, the squadron claiming a number of 'kills' against aircraft from Bomber Command. Emphasis was put on instrument flying and air-to-air gunnery; the squadron firing average rose to 18.9 per cent by the end of the month. And, by using the Station Flight Meteor T. 7, the number of pilots with expired instrument ratings also began to decrease. Organisational changes were also made, the flying element of the squadron being split into 'A' and 'B' Flights so that each would be allocated four Sabres each day, thus ensuring that forty sorties could be flown across the squadron. The ground engineering trades were absorbed into the newly formed 'C' Flight under Flt Lt Morris and were responsible for generating aircraft to meet the daily requirement. The airmen under 'C' Flight were happy, as their regular day now ended at 5 o'clock sharp.

The squadron also tried out a novel procedure later in the month – a night-reinforcement exercise, whereby a number of aircraft would deploy at night to a distant base to simulate a rapid reinforcement in theatre. Prior to this, on 5 July, one night was devoted to night flying to familiarise the crews with long-distance navigation in the dark. Peter Foard had an interesting incident aboard XD774 during his night sortie, which was planned to take him from base to Valley, down to Droitwich and up to Hull, before returning to Linton: 'On 5 July 1955 at roughly midnight, at 40,000ft, I observed an orange-coloured "Chinese lantern" shape at the same level, north of Birmingham. Having got permission to investigate, I broke off from the planned exercise and headed towards it. Distance was impossible to judge, but after several minutes the object accelerated upwards at about a 45-degree angle and disappeared. On landing I had to write a full report for the station spy, but heard no more of the incident.'

Peter's experience was typical of many pilots in the 1950s and, equally typically, no explanation has ever been forthcoming. The squadron finally deployed on its night-reinforcement exercise on 19 July, eight Sabres flying over to Oldenburg in Germany. They returned to Linton on the morning of 21 July.

Throughout this period the squadron continued to put the aircrews on instrument-flying checks, but by the start of August, the Station Flight Meteor was unserviceable, Cat. 4. Fortunately, 66 Sqn's Vampire trainer finally became serviceable shortly afterwards and by the end of the month all ratings were completed successfully, the squadron then having twenty-one pilots with Green ratings and seven with White cards. The White instrument rating denoted a pilot who had undergone basic initial instrument training, while a Green card showed that the holder had completed a set amount of flying hours and undergone an instrument-flying check. In addition to these training issues, three pilots from other units were also converted onto the Sabre (229 OCU having long since finished Sabre conversion courses); these were Lt Cdr Williams, a Royal Navy pilot, Flt Lt Pabst and Fg Off Chandler, the last two coming from West Raynham. And, despite a manning level now decreased to 60 per cent, the squadron managed to fly 583.15 hours on Sabres during August 1955.

The annual UK air-defence exercise, 'Beware', was initiated on 24 September. Comprising three phases, each of approximately two days' duration with a break of two days in between, Exercise Beware finished on 2 October. For once the weather stayed fine throughout the exercise, and 66 Sqn managed to launch 174 sorties on interception missions against Canberra, Meteor and Vampire aircraft at heights ranging from 50ft to 51,000ft. The squadron claimed eighty 'kills'.

A further night-reinforcement exercise was also launched, this time to Geilenkirchen, and

XD774/Q taxis past the camera, following a gunnery sortie. Note the soot around the lower gun muzzle; it was usual to fire only one pair of machine guns during practice missions. (*J.D.R. Rawlings*)

A close-up of 66 Sqn markings. (*Robin Brown*)

further missions in September comprised a number of high-level navigation exercises over the North Sea, during which formations of Meteors were vectored onto the Sabres. To celebrate Battle of Britain Day, the squadron also managed to put up a fifteen-aircraft formation, which proceeded over the airfields at Catterick, Thornaby, Acklington and Turnhouse. Other solo aircraft also gave aerobatic demonstrations at Acklington, Thornaby, Hooton Park and Kirkham. One other Sabre was flown down to Biggin Hill and placed in the static park for the air show there.

Air gunnery continued throughout September and October, Fg Off Campbell setting a new squadron record with a 75 per cent score, while several other pilots also managed gunnery scores over the 50 per cent mark. Exercise Phoenix, a sector exercise, started at the end of October and continued into November. During the final stage, on 1 November, six Sabres from 'A' Flight were deployed to Ouston and six from 'B' Flight to Acklington. Successful intercepts against 264 Sqn were achieved before 'A' Flight returned to Linton. 'B' Flight meanwhile was diverted back to Acklington because of excessive activity in the Linton circuit, finally making the flight back later in the day. Two further sector exercises involved long high-level flights to northern Scotland: on 11 November eight Sabres flew to the Royal Naval Air Station at Lossiemouth, with a similar number on 25 November flying to RAF Kinloss. On both occasions the Sabres were successfully intercepted by the Hunters of 43 and 222 Sqns from Leuchars; clearly, the days of the Sabre were numbered.

For the rest of November, further practice-intercept (PI) and cine missions were flown, along with the occasional 'rats and terriers' sortie. These would inevitably involve the aircraft going out over the sea and attacking land targets as 'enemy' intruders ('rats') while other aircraft attempted to intercept them (the 'terriers'). On one of the PIs a Valiant bomber was successfully intercepted for the first time. On 16 November, twelve Sabres were mustered for a photographic sortie for the squadron's Christmas card. Results from the photographs were poor but good colour film of the aircraft was obtained.

With heavy snowfalls in December, only thirteen days were suitable for flying; only 307 hours were flown that month, compared to 487 in November. A number of the

This historic formation was put up on 19 April 1956, just as the Sabres were being replaced on 66 Sqn by Hunter F. 4s and a number of Meteor F. 8s. Spurn Point can be seen below as the formation makes its way along the Yorkshire coast. The Sabre is XD753, the squadron commander's specially painted mount. (*Bruce Robertson*)

squadron personnel also began to receive tuition on the Hunter aircraft, and Flt Lt Barrey and Fg Off Connell attended a manufacturer's course on its Rolls-Royce Avon power plant. The squadron ended the year with a strength of 23 aircrew officers, 13 senior NCOs, 15 junior NCOs and 63 airmen.

Inevitably, 1956 dawned with more adverse weather, though almost 300 hours were flown nonetheless. Also, a new battle flight commitment was instituted, 66 Sqn sharing the duty with 92 Sqn on a week-on/week-off basis. The squadron lost its final Sabre, XD729/J on 25 January when the aircraft lost power on approach to Linton and was belly-landed in the undershoot area. Thankfully, the pilot, Fg Off L.J. Bradley, survived. XD729 was the thirteenth Sabre lost by the squadron, and the last RAF loss.

With Hunter re-equipment in the offing, a number of changes were made to the squadron personnel. During January, Flt Lt Hughes took over as 'A' Flight commander, 'Bush' Barrey taking up a new post as flight commander to one of the Jever squadrons; the following month, Flt Lt R. Goring-Morris took over control of 'B' Flight. Both flight commanders had Hunter experience. At this point the unit had a strength of 19 officers, 13 senior NCOs, 15 corporals and 65 airmen.

Sabre flying continued into the first weeks of March 1956, at which point the aircraft began to be ferried out for overhaul. Concurrently, the first Hunters arrived so that, by the end of the month, a number had been through acceptance checks and five had completed air tests. In addition to the Hunters, 66 Sqn also re-equipped with a number of Meteor F. 8s, to be retained until sufficient Hunters were available to equip the squadron fully. This was obviously a retrograde step – for most of them it meant converting onto two new types – and the maintenance and supply of these aircraft was a nightmare. To assist the Hunter conversion further, Sqn Ldr Neville Duke visited Linton during March and gave Hunter lectures to both squadrons. By the end of the month, 66 Sqn had logged 10.05 hours on the Hunter as well as 24.45 hours on the Meteor 8. The Sabre still took up most of the time, however, with 227.40 hours being flown.

Other than test flying, the final Sabre flights were devoted to getting mixed formations of 'old' and 'new' airborne for photographs to be taken. The last of these was completed on 19 April, when the CO's aircraft, XD753, flew in formation with a Meteor F. 8 and Hunter F. 4, all in the squadron colours. It presented a unique opportunity to capture three eras of the squadron in the air at the same time.

By the end of April, the emphasis had completely changed, with just thirteen Sabre sorties being flown for a total of 10 hours. The Hunters, on the other hand, flew 288 sorties and the Meteors completed 114 missions. Just three hours were flown on Sabres in May 1956, and this marked the squadron's final association with the aircraft. At the start of May, just four Sabres remained on strength, and XD725 departed for Airwork on 11 May. The last trio, XD706, XD753 and XD765, all finally departed Linton on 16 May.

Aircraft Assigned

XB542/Z, XB795/F, XB855/H*, XB941/S*, XD706/D, XD707/B, XD708/A, XD710, XD711/U, XD712/S, XD715/K, XD716/K, XD718/P, XD719, XD720/N, XD721/V, XD722, XD724, XD725/X, XD729/J, XD730/X, XD731/B, XD735/T, XD753/L, XD755/F, XD757/W+, XD758/L, XD761/G, XD762/U, XD763, XD765/E, XD768/X, XD770/M, XD772/H, XD773, XD774/Q, XD776/Z, XD777/C, XD778/R.

* = '6–3'-winged from manufacture.
+ = '6–3' wing (conversion).

Note: XD710, XD719 and XD724 were only assigned for a short time before going on to 92 Sqn.

'A' Flight was assigned aircraft A to L inclusive, while 'B' Flight operated aircraft M to Z (letters 'I', 'O' and 'Y' were not used).

Markings – 66 Sqn

Markings for 66 Sqn Sabres were standardised with the application of white 'bars' either side of the fuselage roundel bordered in a broad dark-blue outline. Squadron individual code letters were applied on the vertical tail fin in red with a thin yellow outline. The squadron crest was usually applied on the forward fuselage, and pilots' names appeared in white on the port-side canopy rail.

When Sqn Ldr Osborne took over the squadron in November 1954, he soon adopted XD753 as his personal mount. It retained the fuselage bars, but had the entire vertical tail painted dark blue with a white lightning flash applied above the fin flash. Superimposed onto the lightning flash were Osborne's initials, AFO, in yellow letters.

Squadron Motto

Cavete praemonui (Beware, I have given warning).

CHAPTER NINE

67 SQUADRON

Based at Wildenrath, 67 Sqn was the first RAF squadron to fly the Sabre in service, though only by one day. Sqn Ldr Paddy Harbison had earlier been headhunted for the job as the new commanding officer after giving his Korean-tour speech for a Central Fighter Establishment convention: 'The RAF was soon to get some 400+ F-86 aircraft and the bulk of these were to be based in 2 ATAF. The C-in-C 2 ATAF [AM Sir Robert Foster] saw me after the convention and told me that I would be joining his Command. Accordingly I was posted to RAF Wildenrath in mid-October 1952 as CO of 67 Sqn. This was a Vampire 5 squadron, but was scheduled to be the first RAF Sabre squadron.'

On 28 January 1953, a team of Canadair representatives arrived at Wildenrath and gave lectures on the Sabre, further lectures and film showings being given the following day. However, for many more months the squadron continued to train and fly on the Vampire FB. 5. Anticipating the arrival of Sabres, a few ground-crew members were detached for Sabre familiarisation, one of whom was Cpl Harry Green: 'My involvement as a F II E [engine fitter] started in March/April '53. I was sent, with one sergeant from 3 Sqn, to RAF Abingdon just for a three-day course to learn all about operating Sabres. I convinced my fellow NCO that I should stay for a couple of weeks to pick up all that I could; the sergeant returned to Wildenrath because he was in married quarters and didn't want to upset his marriage. He told my CO, Sqn Ldr Harbison, what I felt, and he agreed. There were three [Sabres] that were being used for familiarisation purposes for the forthcoming [aircraft] being ferried over.'

The first Sabres arrived at Wildenrath early in March 1953, and Paddy Harbison test-flew and accepted them. His flying logbook records that he flew XB591 on 16 March and XB618 the following day. XB603 was tested on 25 March and XB592 on 10 April. All these aircraft were passed straight to Sabre Conversion Unit (SCU) across the airfield. During this period, Paddy also looked after SCU conversion flying: 'My appointment at RAF Wildenrath was CO of 67 Sqn. The Sabre Conversion Unit upon its formation had some groundcrew but no flying instructors. Until these were established I test-flew and accepted the Sabres which were being delivered to Wildenrath. I also set up a conversion course and checked key Wildenrath personnel on the Sabre, e.g., the Station Commander, Gp Capt Johnson, the Squadron Commanders of 3 and 71 Sqns, plus some of the flight commanders. I checked out Flt Lt Martin Chandler, who was later posted to the SCU as an instructor. I suppose it would be accurate to say that in the absence of anyone else I ran the SCU initially, but it was secondary to my 67 Sqn appointment.'

During periods of bad weather, when Vampire flying was not possible, squadron pilots often utilised SCU Sabres to familiarise themselves with the aircraft, a process that began on 14 March with cockpit familiarisation. Ten days later, three squadron pilots started and taxied Sabres for the first time, still using the SCU machines as none had yet been delivered to 67 Sqn. On 8 April, Flt Lt Turner, Flt Lt Mullarkey, Flt Lt Mellers,

Fg Off Hicks and P Off Reynolds started ground lectures at the SCU; Turner and Mellers flew the Sabre for the first time on 14 April. These five pilots completed their conversion course on 20 April. Meanwhile, Paddy Harbison had been using the unit's Sabres to their fullest and took part in a wing fly-past over Wahn for the Chief of Air Staff; Paddy flew one of four Sabres in the first 'public' formation fly-past by the type.

Six further squadron pilots began SCU conversion on 20 April, and first flew the Sabre the following day. Along with the training, equipment also began to arrive at Wildenrath to support the new type. The first Type F bone-dome helmets arrived with the squadron and, along with anti-g suits, were issued to pilots coming from conversion starting on 11 May.

The squadron took delivery of its first pair of Sabres on 12 May 1953 when XB624 and XB674 were ferried in from Kemble. With acceptance checks complete, Paddy Harbison took XB674 aloft for an air test on 18 May, logging the first Sabre flight by an RAF squadron (this beat 3 Sqn by a day – they flew a four-ship sortie on 19 May). By this time, 67 Sqn possessed five Sabres, XB598, XB600 and XB625 having been delivered in the interim.

Meanwhile, Vampire operations continued very much as before. On 19 May, for instance, a section of four Vampires went north to carry out dummy strafing of a disused airfield near the Rhine, while two others went to USAF airfields around Bitburg to dogfight with any stray aircraft there; one RF-80 was attacked on take-off. Additionally, three pairs flew to Oldenburg, Jever and Celle for a lunch stop, and then returned to Wildenrath. Another Vampire flew to Florennes on a similar cross-country exercise. In the afternoon, two pairs took off at 20-minute intervals and flew to Bitburg again, hoping to entice aircraft up for a fight. Four F-84s were attacked by the first pair. On 22 May, eleven Vampires were put into the air for a formation fly-past and low-level run to mark the official end of operations with the type by 67 Sqn.

The unit stood down for Whitsun on 22 May and when squadron personnel returned to work on the 26th the emphasis was fully on getting the Sabres operational and preparing the Vampires for ferrying out. The following day, five squadron pilots left for Benson to take delivery of further Sabres for the squadron. In many respects 28 May was the first 'real' day of Sabre flying for the squadron; seven aircraft had been acceptance-checked, and these were air-tested and formations of two and three aircraft put up. In the late afternoon four of the squadron's Sabres took part in a rehearsal for the Queen's Birthday fly-past over Düsseldorf – six more performed the following day. On the morning of 2 June, six Sabres plus six more from 3 Sqn took part in the full fly-past.

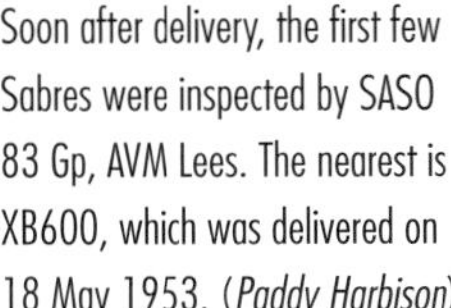

Soon after delivery, the first few Sabres were inspected by SASO 83 Gp, AVM Lees. The nearest is XB600, which was delivered on 18 May 1953. (*Paddy Harbison*)

Tucked up against the winter cold, these aircraft from 'B' Flight are parked outside one of Wildenrath's troublesome low-roofed hangars. The aircraft at the front is XB600/W, one of the first Sabres delivered to 67 Sqn. It was written off in a flying accident on 22 March 1954. (*Peter Hay via Caygill*)

Peter Hicks was one of the first five pilots on the squadron to go through SCU conversion after flying the Vampire with 67 Sqn: 'I had seven familiarisation flights between 17 and 20 April '53, then back to Vampires to let others convert; 67's final squadron formation in Vampires was 22 May '53. Then all Sabre, with almost total concentration on close squadron and wing formation for the Coronation Day Fly-past at Düsseldorf on 2nd June '53 (130 a/c, Sabres, Vampires, Meteors).'

As the first to receive Sabres, the Wildenrath squadrons were detailed to take part in the massive Coronation Review at Odiham in July 1953. The Sabre squadrons would temporarily deploy to Duxford to prepare for the fly-past, and on 4 June Flt Lt V. Woods flew there with OC Flying, Wg Cdr Mike Le Bas, to recce the facilities. The Vampires were meanwhile being ferried out, though a sector patrol was completed by the aircraft from Wildenrath on 5 June. Only two of the type were left on 67 Sqn charge by 9 June, and by the time the unit returned from England they would be history.

Sabre flying was restricted at the start of June to ensure that none were due for 50-hour inspections during the Duxford deployment. This enabled ground crews to prepare the aircraft; on 12 June squadron code letters were applied along with flight-coloured bands to the tail fins of each aircraft: red for 'A' Flight and blue for 'B' Flight. Some flying was carried out, however, and this understandably focused on close-formation flying. In the afternoon of 15 June a formation of twelve Sabres was flown by the squadron; further sorties concentrated on general handling and circuit work. Wg Cdr Le Bas then decreed that all pilots flying Sabres to the UK for the fly-past would need twelve hours minimum of Sabre time before departure, and a number of sorties were programmed to remedy the situation.

Ground crews and support equipment left for England in the late afternoon of 18 June, and two days later twelve Sabres set out for Duxford. Two aircraft had to return to Wildenrath because of undercarriage trouble, one of which was flown by Paddy Harbison. When he landed, investigation of both Sabres revealed the fault: some initially unknown person had stashed contraband cigarettes into the nose undercarriage well, fouling a microswitch and preventing retraction. Customs searches on the aircraft that arrived safely in the UK revealed further smuggled

Though the small hangars at Wildenrath were not ideally suited to housing Sabres, the new aircraft made life easier for ground crews, especially because of the ease of access to the major components. This is XB671/E (note the individual code letter on the nose door), John Perrott's personal mount. (*John Perrott*)

items, and following an investigation a number of individuals were charged. Apart from this black spot, the initial deployment was trouble-free. With the actual fly-past programmed for 15 July, the squadron stood down until 22 June, when sector recces of the Duxford area were completed. The first fly-past rehearsal for the squadron – which was sharing Duxford with the Sabres of 3 Sqn – was successfully flown on 26 June, with two further practices by the end of the month. Bad weather intervened on a few days, and this would be the situation for much of July: sporadic good days punctuated by periods of bad weather unsuitable for close-formation flying. In its first month of Sabre flying, 67 Sqn had flown 116 hours 30 minutes on the type, in 146 sorties.

At the start of July a number of fly-past practices were cancelled due to bad weather, but the spare time was used to good effect. On 3 July Sqn Ldr Harbison and P Off Grant travelled to Wildenrath and returned with their two remaining Sabres on 20 June.

Don Elsden was one of those that deployed to Duxford for the Coronation Review. His usual mount was XB598, and he only did a few training flights before the actual fly-past. One of those missions threw up an unusual problem:

> The incident is not noted in my logbook but the memory of it is clear. On 8 or 9 July I was returning from an extended flight in and beyond the local area, approaching Duxford and flying at an airspeed near the top end of 350–400kt, when I ran into the base of turbulent cloud at about 1,200ft.
>
> Suddenly the aircraft, XB598, went into violent 'porpoising', or severe vertical undulations, and I instantly lost control, with both hands involuntarily thrown off the throttle and control column respectively, and my head, with bone-dome, being pounded against the canopy. The undulations over the next few seconds directed the aircraft increasingly towards the ground and I realised there was little time to act. But I managed to get the throttle closed and cradle the control column, which was moving violently forwards and backwards, with my right arm, and get into a climb, when the undulations immediately ceased.
>
> On recounting the incident to my flight commander and other senior pilots my experience was virtually ignored. However a day or two after this the same happened to none other than Gp Capt J.E. Johnson, Station Commander of Wildenrath, and not surprisingly a report and recommended action to take, should it occur again, was circulated to all Sabre pilots.

The squadron performed its last rehearsal on 13 July when it contributed thirteen Sabres, two further aircraft having been ferried into Duxford on 23 June. With no fly-past rehearsal on 14 July and with a 1,200ft cloud base, Flt Lt Wilson took a Sabre aloft and laid a number of sonic booms over the airfield.

Dawn on 15 July brought broken stratus cloud, which lifted slowly until visibility had improved to 12 miles below a 1,500ft cloud base. Several thunderstorms were forecast over southern England, but fortunately the weather on the fly-past route over Odiham airfield was fair. The wing took off from Duxford at 1100 hr and immediately got into formation. Peter Hicks also flew on the Duxford deployment, recalling that it was a busy time for the squadron:

> [The] wing, led by Wing Commander Flying, Wg Cdr Le Bas, flew from Wildenrath to Duxford on 20 June. Then repeated wing formation over the route with time-check points from Duxford to overhead Odiham (plus/minus five seconds at each checkpoint – not too easy with a topographical map, throttle, ASI and stopwatch) to prepare for the fly-past for The Coronation Review Of The Royal Air Force by Her Majesty The Queen on 15 June '53. With a now unbelievable 631 aircraft in equally spaced wings in line astern, speeds varying from Chipmunks in the lead to us at the tail end, it is not difficult to appreciate the need for making each checkpoint on time before joining up long enough to be in line over Odiham.

With the fly-past successfully completed, the squadron had initially decided to fly straight home to Wildenrath, but thunderstorms over Germany prevented this. Instead they returned to Duxford and flew back to base on 16 July.

There was no respite for the squadron, however, and immediately preparations began for the forthcoming Exercise Coronet. This entailed the squadron deploying to dispersals around the airfield and operating out of tents. On 17 July tents were erected and the area camouflaged so that four fuel bowsers could also be accommodated. The squadron moved into this tented area two days later. Prior to the exercise starting, sorties were launched in the morning of 21 July on high-level reconnaissance missions over the local area, and further sorties were devoted to airfield-defence cooperation. Coronet started in earnest on 23 July, and Peter Hicks was in the thick of it: 'Exercise Coronet took place from 23 to 29 July involving mainly interceptions, armed recces, fighter/bomber escorts, and "anti-rat" patrols. Our main "adversaries" were the Royal Canadian Air Force wing of F-86s based at Zweibrücken. We had much fun, but at that stage had to admit to their greater experience on the '86.'

On the first day of the exercise, six battle-flight interceptions were made, five of which were successful. One further section of four made a sweep down to Bitburg but met little opposition. Twenty intercepts were made on the next day, with attacks made on the Canadian base at Gros Tenquin in France on 25 July in conjunction with the Vampires of 71 Sqn. Opposition was heavy at both Gros Tenquin and Bitburg, the latter being attacked as it was on track to the main target. Heavy 'losses' resulted. During the afternoon, three sections flew top cover for Vampires making low-level attacks, and six airfield and local-defence missions were also scrambled.

Further attacks on French airfields were made on 26 July when Laon/Couvron and Champagne were the targets; undispersed F-84s made ideal targets, and opposition was light. When flying ceased at dusk, drop tanks were removed from the squadron's Sabres, the ground crews working long into the night to achieve this.

With cloud base in the UK down to 300ft, a large bomber force expected on 27 July failed to materialise. Nevertheless, the squadron made several interception scrambles, even though the targets often proved to be 'friendly'.

Further interceptions were made on the following day and this time Canadian and USAF Sabres were caught, along with USAF F-84s. On 29 July several bombers were intercepted between 30,000 and 35,000ft as well as a large number of Meteors. The latter were in formations of up to a dozen aircraft. Through this concentrated period of the exercise, squadron pilots were averaging four sorties per day and, fortunately, aircraft serviceability was generally good. The exercise finished on 30 July, the final day being blighted by bad weather. The last day of the month was spent in clearing the tented dispersals, the squadron then standing down until 4 August.

Exercise Coronet had revealed weaknesses in the squadron's aircraft that had not been appreciated under normal circumstances. One of these was the aircraft's poor interception performance with drop tanks fitted; more successful intercepts had been made following the removal of drop tanks on 26 July. During the exercise the squadron still had four pilots not converted onto the Sabre, and this had raised the workload for the other crews.

Continuing straight on from Coronet, the squadron immediately began preparing for a gunnery deployment to Sylt. Flying was reduced where possible and a great amount of effort was put into getting all aircraft serviceable, particularly the gunsights. While the squadron was away at Sylt, Wildenrath's runways would be resurfaced, and on 8 August eight squadron pilots flew Sabre Conversion Unit aircraft over to Brüggen, where SCU would continue training until the work was completed. In order to get the best advantage from the Sabre gunsights, four aircraft were flown to the USAF airfield at Landstuhl on 10 August for calibration. On the same day, twelve other Sabres left for Sylt, though Sqn Ldr Harbison and Flt Lt Wilson both developed drop-tank fuel leaks and returned to base for rectification. They flew up to Sylt later in the day.

No flying was accomplished on the gunnery detachment until 12 August, when the ground party finally arrived by road from Wildenrath. Ten sorties were immediately launched, using fixed ranging on the gunsight, without radar input. Meanwhile, the four aircraft from Landstuhl also arrived. Sorties then averaged ten per day until 18 August, all firing live ammunition on target flags towed by Tempest aircraft.

Further sorties were hastily curtailed on 19 August after the first six aircraft had flown. Gp Capt Johnson had the nose undercarriage of his aircraft extend in flight, and all aircraft were immediately grounded while microswitch tests were carried out. In any case, weather for the next few days was poor, so the enforced grounding came at an opportune time. As a result of the undercarriage problem, an order was issued limiting all Sabres to gentle manoeuvres until a modified nose undercarriage lock had been installed. By 24 August a Special Technical Instruction had been issued to rectify the fault, three aircraft being cleared for firing on that day.

One of those deployed to Sylt on this occasion was Peter Hicks. He remembers that despite gunsight problems it was still a fairly productive effort: 'In August the Squadron flew to the Air Firing Practice Camp at Sylt for the biannual month's air-to-air firing practice. Our beautiful new machines had radar gunsights, but sadly the armourers hadn't yet got the appropriate instruction manuals, so we "pegged" the radar side of things and used them as fixed sights for the month at Sylt. Despite the teething problems reasonable scores were achieved, and at the end of the month we returned to Wildenrath via Oldenburg.'

On 26 August Flt Lt Mullarkey performed a flag-towing sortie, using a Sabre for this task for the first time; results deemed it a success. Two days later, four Sabres led by Gp Capt Johnson returned to Wildenrath. Johnson used one of the squadron's Sabres on

Pilots of 67 Sqn lined up at Sylt in 1954. Sqn Ldr Paddy Harbison is at centre front, with his flight commanders Flt Lt Arthur Turner ('A' Flight) on the left and Flt Lt A.G.S. 'Tug' Wilson to the right. Derek Birley is to the rear of Harbison and Wilson, with ammunition belt. Aircraft 'A' (XB737) was Flt Lt Turner's aircraft. (*Paddy Harbison*)

Sabres being readied at Sylt for another gunnery sortie. Note that the aircraft being readied for flight have no drop tanks installed. (*Don Elsden*)

this occasion, as his 'personal' Sabre, XB619, was still undergoing rectification after its earlier undercarriage malfunction. Meanwhile, the rest of the squadron's aircraft were air-tested and returned to Wildenrath on 31 August. On this occasion, Flt Lt Mullarkey could not retract the undercarriage in XB586/X and was forced to return to Sylt. He immediately got into XB706/U and flew that back instead.

In spite of the previous months of activity, there was no let-up for the squadron. On 4 September a fly-past was performed for visiting officers from Imperial Staff College. The squadron joined with 3 Sqn to perform a wing formation but, as only twelve aircraft could be mustered, they flew past in a vic instead of the preferred group of three boxes of four. The aircraft then began to be readied for the next exercise, 'Monte Carlo', which would begin at 0400 hr on 10 September.

Exercise Monte Carlo began with four aircraft, as 'Red Section', being scrambled at 1055 hr. Three further sections were sent off throughout the day and three pairs were launched on 'anti-rat' patrols. Several aircraft were claimed. Thirty sorties were flown on the following day, including high-level interceptions, anti-rat patrols and a raid on Florennes in conjunction with 71 Sqn. This set the scene for the next few days of Monte Carlo, which ended at 1130 hr on 13 September. The squadron flew ninety-eight sorties on this exercise alone in just over three days.

The latter half of September brought a downturn in the squadron's fortunes, perhaps inevitably when the previous few months' hectic schedule is considered. Eight night sorties were flown on 15 September – the first on Sabres for 67 Sqn. Two days later, four Sabres were scrambled to intercept a B-29 on its way from the UK. Due to unserviceability, the bomber did not reach Germany, but by the time this was realised the Sabres were already airborne. The section leader, Flt Lt Wilson, flicked into a spin during the climb on this aborted intercept and ejected; his Sabre, XB683/W, crashed six miles from Liège in Belgium. Subsequent investigation revealed that Wilson had removed his flying helmet during the climb to put on his sunglasses. The helmet became jammed behind the control column and, unable to control the spin or remove his helmet, the pilot was forced to eject. Fortunately, he survived. Further B-29 affiliation exercises were more successful; 'B' Flight completed a number of these missions on 1 October and 'A' Flight on the 6th.

On 25 September P Off E.J. Cooper and P Off B.G. Pearce were not so fortunate. While they were practising single-engine approaches in the Meteor, the aircraft pulled into the dead engine and crashed; both men were killed instantly. This was a particularly tragic event, as the single-engine procedure was both unnecessary and irrelevant for Sabre pilots. P Off Cooper was buried in Cologne on 30 September, Pearce's body being returned to the UK for burial there.

A further deployment, this time to the Canadian base at Zweibrücken, commenced on 11 October, when the road convoy left Wildenrath. Typical of the support required for operating away from base, the convoy consisted of sixteen 3-tonner trucks, two fuel bowsers and two Land Rovers. The convoy departed at 0900 hr and stopped overnight with 72 Signals Unit at Adenau before going on to Zweibrücken the following day. Twelve Sabres flew down to the Canadian base on 12 October, and the first sector recce missions were completed the next day. Over the following days, high-level tactical formations and GCA approaches were completed before mist and fog in the afternoon of 15 October curtailed any further flying. On 22 October the squadron continued its nomadic life, the road convoy setting out for the Belgian base at Florennes. The Sabres followed on the 23rd, but were immediately affected by bad weather; the first sector recces at Florennes were launched on 27 October. Unfortunately, by this point the deployment was all but over and on the following day the squadron returned, as part of a wing formation, back to Wildenrath. The poor weather during October meant that only

Pulling into a shallow dive, XB693 is a red-trimmed aircraft from 'A' Flight. (*Peter Hay via Caygill*)

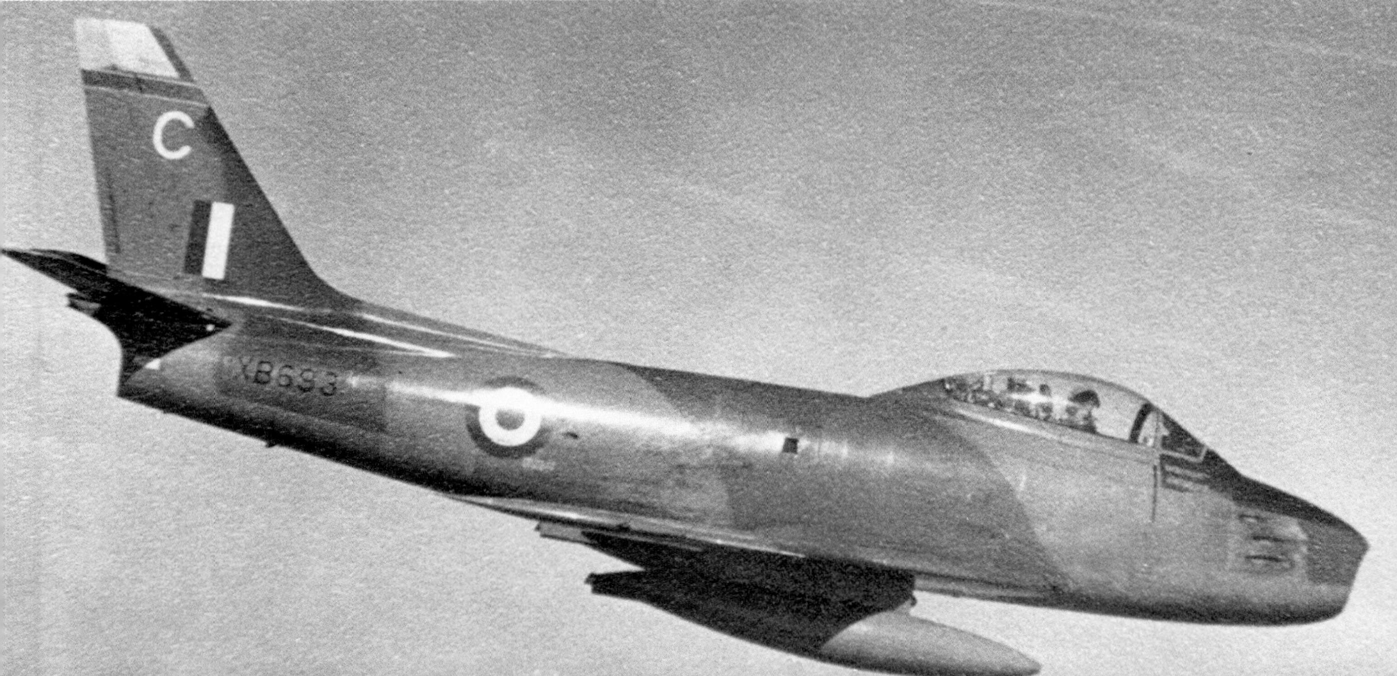

205 hours and 10 minutes were flown during the month – about half of the expected amount.

The Monschau range was used for the first time on 2 November, non-firing reconnaissance of the area being accomplished on this day while other aircraft were having their guns harmonised for the forthcoming Sylt detachment. Unfortunately, one of the aircraft at Monschau (XB706) had an ammunition door detach in flight; though the aircraft returned safely to base it was assessed as Cat. 3 and spent a month being repaired. Worse was to follow.

Battle flight was assigned to the Sabres of 'B' Flight on 6 November, and on the afternoon sortie they were acting as targets for Belgian F-84s. While turning at 15,000ft, the number twos in a formation collided and broke up. P Off Craig in XB690/Z ejected successfully and was soon picked up by Army personnel from Mönchengladbach. However, Fg Off 'Paddy' Pollock, flying in XB730/Y, was killed in the collision. He was buried in Cologne Military Cemetery on 11 November.

The proposed squadron detachment to Sylt was cancelled on 16 November after much hard work had already been expended. It was not entirely wasted, however, and instead a concentrated range programme was started at Monschau. No less than forty-two air-to-ground sorties were flown on the range on 17 November alone. Further missions included dogfighting practice, six Sabres flying as a wing formation with 71 Sqn on 28 November, while a further section was scrambled to 'bounce' the formation.

Fresh from Sabre conversion in the United States, Trevor Egginton joined the squadron during December 1953. However, in contrast to previous US-trained crews, Trevor had done a comprehensive Sabre conversion on his course, and arrived at the squadron fully conversant with the type:

It was a bit of a comedown to go back to the lower-powered F-86E (Sabre 4) after flying the F-86F. Under Paddy [Harbison], with a lot of USA-trained pilots we flew practically the USAF way, modified as we wanted, and not the DFLS way, which was a little antiquated. New tactics were always tried out in the air and modified if necessary. An awful lot of our sorties were: take off, make maximum height, vector 180 degrees and go and dogfight with the USAF Sabres from Bitburg, etc., or the Canadians. Occasionally, the Brits and Colonials (Canadians) joined forces to duff up the USAF. Dogfighting was illegal; it did get a bit hairy at times in a low-speed scissors.

December 1953 proved something of a troublesome month for 67 Sqn: bad weather consisting of low cloud and rain persisted, and there were a number of problems with the aircraft. On 9 December flying had to be abandoned after XB869 ran off the runway and blocked it; the aircraft sustained Cat. 3 (R) damage. On 15 December three gunnery missions were completed at Monschau after which all aircraft were grounded for an ejection-seat inspection. Two aircraft became serviceable in the afternoon, but were soon grounded again by radio and undercarriage faults. Nonetheless, a number of sorties were launched, notably practice intercepts against Belgian F-84s on 21 December and cross-country flights on the 29th. John Perrott flew one of the cross-country sorties in XB538 on 29 December, routing from base to Dorsten, Deventer, Dummer Lake and Venlo before returning one hour later.

The following year, 1954, got off to a bad start, with all Sabres being grounded on 4 January when it was discovered that a number of aircraft had cracked trim drives. Checks were undertaken on the whole fleet and by 6 January five Sabres were declared serviceable. Two more Sabres were airworthy on the following day, but thirteen cracked drives had grounded the remainder. In any case, flying was impossible at this time, with ground temperatures well below freezing and zero visibility. Finally, on 8 January the cloud

'B' Flight Sabre XB706/U in flight; the treatment of the anti-dazzle panel is unusual, as only the electronics bay access panel appears to have been painted the customary black colour. (*John Perrott*)

broke and limited flying was possible, using the small number of serviceable airframes. Heavy snow fell in mid-January and this further hindered the flying programme.

With only five serviceable Sabres, on 14 January the squadron managed to take part in a barrage exercise, a flight of four aircraft making three sorties and intercepting large numbers of Varsity navigation trainers, plus the usual Meteor targets. Night-flying sorties and dummy ground attacks on Wildenrath were also launched, the latter for the benefit of RAF Regiment gunners. However, by the end of the month, the situation was dire: of twenty-two aircraft on strength, one had been allocated for rectification of acid corrosion (XB701), one was Cat. 3 damaged, four were AOG (aircraft on ground, awaiting spares/manpower), two were awaiting minor servicing, six were unserviceable for minor defects and two were on intermediate inspections. This left the squadron with three serviceable Sabres. The worst day came on 25 January, when only one Sabre was in a condition where it could be used for flying. Thankfully over the next few days more aircraft became serviceable, so that by the end of the month a fairly good 254 hours had been logged despite these impossible conditions.

Preparations for another Sylt deployment began at the end of January when flying was limited, and on 1 February the road party, comprising three one-tonners and one Land Rover, departed Wildenrath. The limited flying on 1 February was brought to a premature halt when one of the squadron's Sabres had an undercarriage failure on landing at Wildenrath; two other airborne aircraft were diverted to Geilenkirchen while the runway was cleared.

The main rail party of 67 Sqn departed for Sylt on 3 February, and it was planned to fly the Sabres up on the next day. However, with ice reported on the runway at Sylt, one aircraft was dispatched to investigate; ice was found only on the last few hundred yards and so the remaining ten serviceable aircraft were immediately launched, arriving safely at Sylt, where they landed individually. Trevor Egginton took part in this deployment, his first with the squadron: 'We did virtually no flying; the runway, and particularly the sea, was frozen over. The two SAR range-safety boats were tied up in harbour so could not get to sea – so no flying over the range. I did two sorties only. The causeway was icebound and could not be used. I remember we all drank Sylt dry of anything alcoholic – the cellar bar was actually under water.'

John Perrott likewise saw this deployment as largely a waste of time and effort:

The normal scheme was for each squadron to go to an Armament Practice Camp at Sylt twice a year for practice air-to-air firing on towed targets over the sea. The visits in winter were usually a waste of time as weather conditions were often very poor. Each pilot flew with a PAI (Pilot Attack Instructor) on a demonstration sortie at the start of the detachment, and this was often the most dangerous ride of our time at Sylt. My logbook shows that on 17 February 1954 I flew to Sylt and on 11 March I flew back again. In the interim I had one dual local-area familiarisation flight and one firing-demonstration ride; plus two solo air-to-air firing sorties and one practice formation flight. Total flying time in the 22 days, including flights there and back, was 4 hours 55 minutes, of which 1 hour 15 minutes was spent on air-to-air gunnery in a Sabre. In summer Sylt was famous for its nude bathing beaches, which at least provided off-duty relaxation!

Air firing at Sylt did actually get underway at 0830 hr on 5 February, but of eighteen sorties launched that day only eight were effective. Ice on the runway during subsequent days meant that sand had to be spread to provide a safe surface for the aircraft to operate from; unfortunately, experience showed that this could not be guaranteed. An initial taxi test on 6 February resulted in a burst tyre, and sharp flints in the sand on the runway were found to be the culprit; the same thing occurred after the runway had been swept by hand on the following day. In an effort to get some flying in, the runway was again swept by hand, but with visibility reducing, only twelve sorties were possible, using the List range. A full day's firing followed on 8 February, this time using the Amrum range, but four more tyres were burst by residual flints on the runway.

Unfortunately, the weather then really took a turn for the worse, with high winds and low cloud affecting the area for most of the month. On 15 February the snow fell and firing was carried out sporadically when it could be fitted in. Two Sabres left at Wildenrath on the initial deployment were ferried up on 17 February: one was XB634, flown in by John Perrott and mentioned above; the other, XB679, unfortunately suffered a nose-wheel collapse on landing at Sylt, sustained Cat. 4 (R) damage, and needed to be returned to the UK for repair.

With only three Sabres serviceable on 20 February, firing began at 1030 hr on the Amrum range, shared on this occasion with 68 Sqn, each squadron firing on alternate flags. A further good day of firing was achieved the next day, this time using the List range. With only three Sabres available again, three shoots per flag were flown with Sabres,

Correct harmonisation of the Sabre's machine-gun armament was a key element in ensuring accurate firing. For the ground crew, the Sabre introduced the method whereby the aircraft were adjusted in the stop butts at 1,000ft range and the guns were then fired to verify these adjustments. This is XB701/V. (*Don Elsden*)

the squadron Vampire making a fourth shooter where possible. It was not a perfect solution, but at least pilots did get a few firing missions. The weather subsequently closed in again, and though two Sabres managed to get airborne on 27 February they were soon recalled because of deteriorating conditions; one ran off the runway on landing.

Meanwhile, back at Wildenrath two '6–3'-winged Sabres, XB936 and XB939, had been delivered from Kemble on 17 February. Unfortunately, P Off Phil Rogers overrotated XB936 on take-off on 4 March and hit the approach lights with his starboard drop tank; the aircraft crashed off the end of the runway and was written off, but Rogers survived. The remaining 'hard-edge' aircraft was transferred to SCU; it would be another year before the squadron got its hands on any more '6–3' aircraft.

The Sylt detachment culminated in an escape-and-evasion exercise on 8 March, the squadron forming the defence against sundry evaders. On 11 March the squadron departed Sylt in the eight remaining airworthy Sabres during a brief lull in the weather; two unserviceable aircraft were left at Sylt, a further pair having already departed for Wildenrath on 27 February. The rail party was left to pack up things at Sylt and departed for home on 12 March. It had been a month to forget.

Thankfully, the weather was better at base and for the rest of March a good programme of flying was put together. Battle flight was mounted on a number of days and on 19 March three Sabres made mock attacks on NATO ground forces along the Rhine. They had difficulty engaging the targets because of industrial haze. Unfortunately, amid this activity the squadron lost another Sabre. On 22 March XB600/W experienced electrical failure ten minutes after take-off. Unfortunately the pilot, Fg Off Law, was unfamiliar with the emergency procedure to lower the undercarriage, or with how to operate the generator-reset switch. He did, however, manage to jettison the drop tanks and get to Oldenburg, but the aircraft was written off in the ensuing wheels-up landing. Law was unhurt. Fortunately, with better weather going into the spring, flying became more straightforward and the accident rate fell for a good few months.

A further bout of exercises began on 12 April when the squadron deployed to 'B' Dispersal at Wildenrath to operate in the field on an airfield-defence exercise. Thirty sorties of high- and low-level battle formations were completed on the first day, and a similar number on 13 April. The squadron finished the exercise on the following day and returned to its hangar accommodation. On 20 April the squadron allotted four Sabres to Exercise Mayleaf, and these made dummy attacks on ground targets on the Rhine. Even without the exercise commitment, further offensive operations were launched: on 22 April eight Sabres joined a section of four from 71 Sqn and simulated a bomber raid at 35,000ft; interceptions were launched by the Venoms from Wunstorf, but they got no closer than two miles from the Sabre formation. On the following day a section of four 67 Sqn Sabres, led by Wildenrath's Station Commander, carried out practice interceptions with a formation from 71 Sqn, led by Wing Commander Flying.

Exercise Prune II was designed to test the effectiveness of radio and radar jamming on ground-controlled interceptions, and the squadron was involved from 11 May. In the morning of the first day, the aircraft acted as fighters, and since jamming of the GCI signals proved ineffective, had no trouble intercepting their prey. During the afternoon, roles were reversed and the Sabres acted as bomber formations, with interception missions being launched by Venoms. Only one channel on the HF frequency was successfully jammed and the Venoms again had no difficulty in catching the Sabres. The exercise was repeated on the following day and again no real difficulties were experienced by the interceptors other than with the HF jamming.

At the end of May there was a peak in serviceability of the Sabres, with an unprecedented (and not to be repeated) high of seventeen serviceable Sabres being achieved on 15 June. The aircraft were put to good use. On that day, flying started with high-level tactical formations by six sections of four. Four Sabres then took part in low-level attacks on Army targets north of Krefeld, believed to be 2 (BR) Infantry Division Main Headquarters. Making maximum use of airworthy aircraft, a sixteen-ship mass fly-past was staged and night flying brought the day's proceedings to a close. The situation continued throughout June, and on the 17th some Sabres were flown without drop tanks fitted. A number of high-level formations were again flown, using four Sabres in the 'clean' configuration until drop tanks were refitted on 28 June.

The big UK air-defence exercise for 1954, Dividend, began on 17 July and, though programmed for a number of sorties, bad weather prevented 67 Sqn from having any input on the first day. All sorties involved the Sabres flying in 'box four' formations at around 42,000ft. Flying got underway on 18 July, with the squadron's first attacks all being made on the UK. Most were judged to be successful, since few of the aircraft were intercepted. The squadron stood down from the exercise on 19 July and was not involved in it again until the 22nd, when nine sorties were completed. Seventeen individual missions were completed for the exercise on 23 July, along with three high-level tactical formations as part of the normal training routine. It was now squadron policy to carry cine film in aircraft on every sortie, and when used as a debriefing tool this helped to encourage good tactics and hopefully helped to improve the efficiency of the squadron. The system was adopted for only a few months, however: at the end of March 1954 carriage of film on all aircraft was stopped when it was found to be deteriorating if left unused in the Sabres.

Returning to Exercise Dividend, 67 Sqn cancelled its morning sorties on 24 July because of adverse weather. Two formations of four aircraft were flown against the UK in the afternoon, marking the end of the squadron's involvement. On subsequent days the weather was too bad for any more missions to be flown and one mass sortie on 25 July had to be scrubbed as the squadron had been given incorrect timings. During the exercise the squadron had launched more than fifty sorties against the UK, all limited to Mach 0.74 to enable the generally less capable interceptors in England to catch them. Even so, very few interceptions were made – an alarming revelation.

Returning from the Bank Holiday on 4 August, formations of three aircraft were immediately programmed to practise high-level tactical flying and coordinated quarter attacks. On this mission the pilot of XB538 was unable to lock down his right-hand main undercarriage leg for landing. Despite a number of attempts to recycle the undercarriage, the leg still refused to lock down and collapsed during the landing run. The aircraft settled onto the drop tank, which then burst and exploded after contact with the ground. The pilot was unhurt, but the aircraft required repair. Another case of a main leg not locking down was experienced on 12 August, though this time the pilot performed a roller landing and by bouncing the 'good' leg onto the runway managed to force the recalcitrant leg into its downlock. Subsequent investigation found that the downlock pins had not been greased and all aircraft were grounded while the situation was rectified.

During the latter part of August a number of incidents blighted the squadron, though thankfully no injuries were incurred. On 16 August, just as aircraft were getting back into the air following the undercarriage failures, one Sabre had the top of its fin and rudder come off in flight. Another aircraft had a severe engine overheat and, finally, the squadron's first hydraulic-pump failure was experienced in the afternoon. The utility pump failed on this occasion, and the pilot was able to lower the undercarriage using the emergency handle and return to base. On 29 August, John Perrott was flying XB671 on a sortie to the Monschau range when the nose-undercarriage leg extended in flight; again he was able to regain control and return to base.

A move to new premises was completed on 19 August, the squadron gaining a larger hangar at Wildenrath and finally leaving the low-roofed hangar it had occupied since the Vampire days. The new hangar gave more room for aircraft and equipment, which was just as well because the unit was entering another phase of poor serviceability. During the month there were times when only four Sabres were serviceable, though the squadron was still able to exceed its 500-hour flying target by 8 hours. The poor in-service rate of the Sabres continued into September.

XB627 was lost in an avoidable accident on 7 September, though the pilot escaped injury. Flying on an individual sortie, Fg Off G.E. Thomson had climbed up to 35,000ft to investigate a contrail. When he subsequently dived down to 500ft he was unable to determine his location, and low on fuel was forced to land in a field three miles south of Peer in Belgium. He had been tantalisingly close to the nearby airbase at Kleine Brogel.

A lot of time was spent in preparation for the year's Battle of Britain celebrations. Fly-past practices were flown along with the odd unusual exercise: on 13 September a pair of Sabres flew to Butzweilerhof and carried out trials on the metal PSP runway there. The fly-past itself was completed over Wildenrath on 15 September using twelve aircraft from the squadron. A wing formation was not possible because 71 Sqn was on detachment at the time. Three further aircraft made attacks on a fort constructed on the airfield, and Flt Lt Cornell, OC 'A' Flight, performed an aerobatics routine. Finally, low-level runs were made on the airfield for the benefit of RAF Regiment gunners.

Yet another exercise, Battle Royal, began on 21 September 1954, and though this mainly involved Army formations, the squadron did contribute a number of sorties over the next few days. At the end of each sortie, low-level dummy attacks were made on the airfield by returning aircraft. On 23 and 26 September the squadron was again involved in Battle Royal, sending up a number of formations to patrol the battle area. These comprised high-level tactical formations, acting as top cover for ground attacks. More fly-pasts were flown at the end of the month and into October for the AOC's inspection, the squadron providing up to ten Sabres each time for composite wing formations with 71 Sqn. In the event, the effort was wasted. When C-in-C 2 TAF Sir Harry Broadhurst inspected the station on 5 October, continuous rain prevented the fly-past from taking place, and even the customary parade was cancelled.

Another spate of incidents caused the grounding of all aircraft on 13 October. Air-to-ground firing had begun at Monschau on that day, but the nose-wheel doors of XB639 and XB671 became unlocked in flight on these sorties, and caused serious damage to both. On one of these aircraft, the door was completely ripped off, along with the door jack, and all utility hydraulic fluid was lost. Both Sabres managed to return safely to base. For the next few days ground crews examined all aircraft to ensure that the undercarriage had been rigged correctly. Aircraft gradually became serviceable again and air-to-ground firing was then undertaken on the Helchteren range. On 29 October, the Sabres were loaded with 100 rounds per gun, and twenty-two successful sorties were logged.

The aircraft were grounded again on 1 November for a generator STI; instrument flying was meanwhile continued in the squadron's Vampire T. 11. Three Sabres were airworthy again on 4 November and air tests were completed before they returned to normal service. By 15 November, with Sabre airworthiness rates improving again, tactical formations were flown for the first time in some weeks. At the end of the month, to celebrate having so many aircraft on line, an eleven-Sabre 'balbo' was flown. The squadron also managed comfortably to exceed its 535-hour flying target, with 562 hours and 5 minutes being logged in 554 sorties.

Almost inevitably, this high in November was reversed in the following month. An unusual malfunction occurred on 1 December when an aircraft experienced the loss of both normal and utility hydraulic pressure in flight. Fortunately, the emergency system operated satisfactorily and the Sabre was recovered without incident. By mid-December however, nearly half of the squadron's Sabres were limited to flight below 15,000ft, as the oxygen systems were overdue for replacement, and spares were not available. Adverse weather until 21 December enabled the ground crews to tackle other issues, but the oxygen-system problems persisted into the following year. On 22 December, an airman was sucked into the intake of a Sabre while checking the drop tanks on a fuel-flow test. He was pulled from the intake barely alive, and spent many months recovering.

January 1955 was characteristically cold and snowy, but the squadron did manage to join up with 71 Sqn and perform a fly-past on the 7th. This formation was put together for the Secretary of State for Air, Lord de Lyle and Dudley, VC, who was visiting the station. Members of the formation had considerable difficulty in keeping sight of each other and,

Fg Off John Perrott gives a sense of scale to his backdrop, XB671/E. Squadron markings had been applied either side of the fuselage roundel by the time of this shot, as had the '6–3'-wing leading edge. This aircraft was one of the last three on squadron strength; it departed for the UK on 26 March 1956. (*John Perrott*)

flying in thick cloud, only caught sight of the airfield at the last moment; all landed safely. Further flying during the month was severely limited as more aircraft became grounded because of oxygen-system spares shortages. On 13 January a barrage exercise was flown, but it had to be limited to a formation of three aircraft, these being all that were available. By 26 January only the squadron's Meteor was airworthy, and with all pilots scrambling to fly it, the machine soon also broke.

At the beginning of February, the first aircraft were flown over to Geilenkirchen to have the '6–3' wing modification embodied. Four 67 Sqn Sabres were undergoing modification by 3 February and the first pair of 'hard-edge' Sabres were delivered back to the squadron on 8 February. While at Geilenkirchen, a number of the aircraft were found to have mainplane cracks, and this further decreased the amount of Sabres available for flying. It was also discovered that aircraft received back from the wing-modification programme had inoperative compasses. This problem was soon traced to the sensing unit, which was situated near to the leading edge; it was solved by slightly relocating the sensing unit. Throughout March, aircraft were being routed through Geilenkirchen for modification, and there were rarely more than four Sabres serviceable on the squadron at any one time. Nonetheless, a ground-attack sortie was completed on 24 March, four Sabres attacking Army positions at Menden. A number of formation landings were also practised on 5 April – a first for the unit. This could be a particularly tricky operation, with the 'slot' man in a 'box four' formation positioned a good six feet below and to the rear of his leader to avoid his jet wash. On landing, the leader had to touch down some way along the runway to avoid driving his slot man into the undershoot.

At around this time, squadron markings changed so that squadron bars were placed each side of the fuselage roundel. The tradition had started in the First World War, but in 1954 a Command directive made the procedure all but official. Across 2 TAF, Sabre crews scratched their heads to come up with designs, and 67's process was much the same as those of the other squadrons, in that the aircrew were asked to come up with a suitable marking. John Perrott was involved in the design:

In about late 1954 the squadron was notified that the pre-war system of carrying distinctive squadron markings on either side of the fuselage roundel was to be reintroduced and we could design something suitable for our aircraft. It was a bad-weather day and no flying was possible so the Boss assembled us in the crew room and told each of us to design something which was colourful and, above all, easy to apply using just paint, a brush and some masking tape. None of us were very good at this but eventually someone came up with the final design, which consisted of a blue triangle, with its base next to the roundel, surrounded by a red oblong. Between the red background and the blue triangle was a thin yellow line. The aircraft were duly painted.

One of the squadron pilots, Bob Foulks, who was also the squadron adjutant, received a letter from the Air Ministry asking that we provide a copy of our design and its meaning. Bob decided to pull their legs and, enclosing a picture of the design, explained it thus: 'The triangular shape is to celebrate the fact that this was the first swept-wing squadron in the Royal Air Force. The yellow is to commemorate the award in 1917 of the VC to Lt F.H. McNamara of this squadron for operations in the desert. The red is to commemorate the blood of our fallen comrades, and the blue to represent the squadron's spirit of high endeavour.'

Some time later he received a letter of thanks, together with the comment, 'We were impressed by the thoughts which went into your design. So many patterns appear simply to have been designed in the crew room on a bad-weather day.'

The darkest day for 67 Sqn was possibly 5 April 1955; Fg Off Malcolm Grant had just completed a sortie and was approaching Wildenrath in XB634/B. As he pulled his Sabre onto finals it collided with Anson C. 19 TX238 of 2 TAF Communications Flight, killing Grant and three on board the Anson. As a result of this accident, action was taken to move the Wildenrath Sabre squadrons elsewhere, and 67 Sqn would eventually make its way to Brüggen.

Malcolm Grant was buried on 12 April, the same day that the squadron's new CO, Sqn Ldr Harry E. Walmsley, arrived at the squadron. A week later, on 19 April, he took over command from Paddy Harbison. For Sqn Ldr Walmsley, it was a sort of homecoming:

> After a year at the RAF Staff College in 1954, I attended a jet course at Westonzoyland from January to March 1955 followed by a week at RAF Chivenor converting to the Sabre. I had seven flights totalling 4 hours and 20 minutes. At Easter 1955, I took over 67 Sqn and my first [Sabre] flight was on 14 April.
>
> As a point of interest, I had taken my first squadron, 350 Royal Belgian Air Force, from Celle to Fassberg on 7 May 1945. Ten years of service and back where I finished the War!

At the end of April flying was restricted so that aircraft would have the maximum flying hours for the forthcoming detachment to Cyprus; drop tanks were also removed to ensure that only missions of short duration could be flown. The policy was to ensure that each Sabre had at least 34 flying hours remaining before its next inspection; as each aircraft approached that figure, it would no longer be flown. Understandably, this severely limited the squadron's effectiveness, especially since further cracked mainplanes had been discovered.

The first cine quarter-attack missions were completed on 9 May, flying against flags which were towed along a line running at 2,500ft from Bergheim to Euskirchen. The squadron also towed flags at 8,000ft using Sabres. In an attempt to reduce the time flying to range areas, the squadron prepared for a short gunnery detachment to Fassberg, where the range was right next to the airfield. This would considerably reduce the amount of hours flown by the Sabres and would hopefully also reduce the maintenance effort.

Packing for the Fassberg detachment began on 14 May, and road and rail parties moved out the next day. Eleven Sabres of the air party flew across to Fassberg on 16 May, though some personnel, such as Flt Lt Peter 'Tom' Sawyer had already arrived there in advance; he had flown to the airfield in XB665/W on 14 May.

Heavy rain at Fassberg on the morning of 17 May prevented any flying, but all pilots managed to complete sector recces that afternoon. Further similar missions were flown on 18 May. The first firing sorties on the Fassberg range were launched on 19 May, and because of its proximity to the airfield only 1,925lb of fuel was carried in each aircraft. Flag-towing sorties continued, this time using the Ulzen air range, which was just ten miles from the Russian Zone. The range was shared with 71 Sqn, who towed targets at a different altitude. During the detachment there was a lucky escape for a Belgian airman: unloading the guns from one of the Sabres following a firing sortie, one of the squadron armourers managed inadvertently to fire a round across the airfield. By sheer misfortune, a Belgian F-84 was taxiing by at that moment, and the bullet went straight through the aircraft's drop tank, which jettisoned and caught fire. The bullet ended up lodged in the fuselage just behind the pilot's seat.

Five Sabres flew back to Wildenrath on 26 May, taking a few lucky pilots back to base for the Whitsun grant; the rest of the squadron stayed at Fassberg and went back to work on

31 May. Firing at Fassberg continued until 6 June when the Wing Leader and five squadron aircraft returned to base. The road convoy had already left two days earlier. Meanwhile the weather at Fassberg was showery, but, in spite of heavy rain on the afternoon of 7 June, four Sabres managed to get airborne to give a display for Imperial Defence College personnel. Unfortunately, two of these aircraft had unserviceable airspeed indicators on landing back at Fassberg. The leader did not realise his predicament and led his number two in too fast, resulting in one of the aircraft running off the runway. Three Sabres later departed Fassberg for Wildenrath, but were diverted to Wahn in heavy rain – two slid off the runway there too. Fortunately, damage to all aircraft was restricted to the tyres. All remaining aircraft flew into Wildenrath on 8 June, but even then there were problems. One Sabre experienced an undercarriage problem and was brought into land on the main gear only; fortunately, damage was light.

In preparation for Cyprus, on 10 June all Sabres were air-tested by the pilots that would be flying them. Officers and airmen not travelling by Sabre departed Wildenrath on 12 June aboard Hastings transport aircraft and made a welcome night stop at Luqa, Malta. They were delayed there by engine trouble and made it to Cyprus only two days later.

On 14 June 1955 the Sabres flew out to Nicosia, and on the first day routed via Fürstenfeldbruck to Rome's Ciampino airport. The following day they flew on to Cyprus via a refuelling stop at Elefsis AB in Greece. Unfortunately, two aircraft were rendered unserviceable on the flight out, one making a heavy landing at Elefsis which required undercarriage retraction tests to be completed. The other aircraft had been unable to retract its nose-wheel and was also stuck at Elefsis. They both made it to Cyprus on 17 June.

The working day at Nicosia started at 0600 hr and finished at just after midday, so as to avoid the afternoon heat. Air-to-air firing was flown on the West range, situated three miles off the north coast of the island, and flags were towed at 10,000ft. After a delay while radios were recrystallised, firing began on 16 June, though many sorties were cancelled because of unserviceable aircraft. The detachment would be the squadron's first real use of radar-ranging for the gunsight (previous firing had used a 'fixed' sight), and it caused a number of problems, principally because the radar could not lock onto the flimsy target flag. A typical day was 21 June, when twenty sorties were planned, but, of these, two were abandoned because of aircraft problems, two because of late starts, and twelve because the radar would not lock on to the flag. This left four successful firing sorties for the day. The radar-reflectivity of the flags was subsequently improved and the success rate increased. Amid this activity, Sqn Ldr Walmsley led four Sabres to Abu Sueir in Egypt on 23 June, returning on the 25th. This would be the only time that RAF Sabres visited the country.

The Cyprus deployment ended more with a whimper than a bang; on 27 June one of the Sabres was damaged on take-off when the undercarriage was retracted too soon and the tail struck the overshoot. Undercarriage doors, both drop tanks and the rear fuselage were all distorted as a result. Air tests for the squadron's return to Germany were flown on 1 July, and personnel then stood down for a few days. Twelve Sabres departed Cyprus on 4 July and this time stopped for fuel at Balikesir AB in Turkey. They then went on to Larisa AB in Greece and then to Rome on the same day. The next day the Sabres flew into Brüggen, the unit's new base, via Fürstenfeldbruck.

The return leg was not without its incidents, however. Aside from a broken Sabre and Vampire left at Nicosia, two other Sabres were grounded at Fürstenfeldbruck with oil leaks and generator failure. John

Perrott remembers that the Sabre at Nicosia proved particularly difficult to recover:

On the return journey one aircraft was damaged in a heavy landing in Greece and another had to be left unserviceable in Cyprus. Some time later, Fg Off Bob Foulks went back to Cyprus as a passenger in a Canberra to collect it. His solo return journey with an aircraft plagued with unserviceabilities was the subject of an article he wrote for the magazine *Air Clues*. He received an acknowledgement from the editor, but with the footnote, 'In the office we have read your article with much amusement, but because of the way it reflects on our allies in NATO we dare not publish it.' Among the events was the removal of the tail in Greece using an F-84 tail dolly, which meant that it was the wrong height and the tail simply fell into the dolly. In Turkey, lacking radio contact, he landed in accordance with the direction shown on the landing tee, which turned out to be downwind, as it had not been reset since four days previously; and in Italy, where, because a radio circuit-breaker kept blowing out, the mechanics put locking wire on it to force it to stay in. So much for a safety device!

This Sabre finally returned to Brüggen on 18 August.

On 6 July, 67 Sqn took over its new quarters, the main part of the squadron flying in by Hastings two days later. The Vampire managed to get back at the same time. The first missions from the new base comprised three 'fours' on tactical formations and three more on quarter attacks on 11 July. A number of GCAs were also practised at Kleine Brogel.

Unfortunately, serviceability problems immediately reared their heads. Since June, the squadron had been reducing in strength from twenty-two to fourteen aircraft, along with most other 2 TAF units. This meant that the loss of just one Sabre was felt more keenly, since it represented a greater percentage of the squadron's complement. From 19 July flying was restricted because of a lack of serviceable oxygen-charging hoses; oxygen regulators were also due for replacement at this time, and many aircraft were limited to flying below 1,500ft. On 22 July, flying was further held up by the arrival of an STI which required brackets holding hydraulic lines to the emergency aileron actuator to be inspected. Four were found to be cracked. To alleviate these problems, Sabres were operated without drop tanks for the whole month to allow more sorties to be flown. A further STI arrived on 11 August, this time requiring forward fuselage fuel tanks to be inspected for cracks; four aircraft were affected, reducing available Sabres to just three. Though replacement tanks were fitted, the time-consuming job meant that during much of August 1955 few or no aircraft were available at a given time – even aircraft with cracked fuel tanks were only flown subject to inspection in great detail after each mission. On another occasion, problems with the tailplane gave Trevor Egginton a nasty moment:

I'd done a very rapid descent from height – probably short of fuel. Everything was normal until the flare for touchdown when I couldn't move the stick aft! The touchdown was firm but thankfully not damaging. In the hangar, with rigs on, everything worked normally. I persuaded the crew to disconnect the tail jack – the flying tail could not be moved by hand or full body weight. It looked like the differential freezing and heating had caused it to seize momentarily. It was noted that a lubrication point for the main tail bearing was provided, but lubrication was not in the schedule. We lubricated all our aircraft.

Fortunately, aircraft gradually became available for flying, and on 12 August the first banner-towing sorties were flown on the nearby Weert range, which was used on subsequent days. Other unusual missions were completed on 13 August when four

Sabres made simulated napalm attacks on Belgian positions in the Monschau area. On this occasion the crews were briefed in the air and controlled by an Air Contact Team. Towards the end of August the squadron was briefly involved in Exercise Loco, 2 TAF units providing 'bomber' formations for interception by Dutch and Belgian fighters. Very few interceptions were made against squadron Sabres in sorties on 24 and 25 August. Though the fuel-tank problem was largely resolved by this time, flying hours were again reduced because of a further impending Sylt deployment.

The road convoy for Sylt left on 3 September, the squadron flying up early to take advantage of better weather conditions on the 5th. The rail party also left on 5 September, so the early part of the detachment was made playing catch-up while the various parties made their way to Sylt and set up there. The first air-to-air sorties were flown on 7 September under GCI control and used radar-ranging. This enabled firing to be carried out above cloud at 20,000ft, so fewer sorties than expected were scrubbed. In spite of this, many missions were lost because of unserviceable aircraft and range conditions. In general the squadron was able to log about ten effective shoots on each day.

These missions had thus far been flown on local ranges without drop tanks, but from 24 September these were fitted, enabling the aircraft to use the more distant Western range. By the end of the month, of 593 sorties flown up to that point, only 223 had been effective. On 1 October, four Sabres took off with a full load of ammunition to complete a double-rearm exercise. Firing at glider targets, the Sabres expended their ammunition before landing to refuel and rearm. They then took off to fire further glider-target sorties. When they returned for the second time, a note was made of the stoppage rate, though one Sabre was also declared unserviceable. The time for refuelling and rearming was a very creditable 12 minutes and 10 seconds.

The last day of firing at Sylt was 5 October, the final average being 9.8 per cent. Nine Sabres were flown back to Brüggen on the same day, with two more on 6 October; the rail and road parties left Sylt on 7 October. It had been a very productive deployment.

Once back at base, further air-to-ground sorties were flown at the Monschau range, but conditions had changed because of a number of Sabre accidents on the range at Meppen. Now all aircraft were talked onto the range by radar control, at which point the initial dive was commenced. The attacks were closely controlled by the range officer, who informed each pilot when to commence firing and when to break off. At the same time a 20-degree dive was used, aircraft breaking off at 450yd. Because of the change in procedure, the targets were no longer scored, so the whole process was somewhat pointless.

Much of October and November was characterised by foggy conditions and flying was curtailed as a result. However, the biggest problem by far was now the serious undermanning of ground trades. In the previous months a large number of experienced maintenance personnel had been posted away from the squadron, and were either replaced by inexperienced personnel or often not replaced at all. The situation became so bad that on 11 November all aircraft were grounded for three days while the remaining ground crew tried to repair and service the aircraft.

On 13 December, with better availability of aircraft, twenty-two sorties were flown, including a number of Canberra-affiliation exercises. John Perrott flew one of these on 20 December, logging one and a half hours in XB702. Set against these successes were continuing problems with getting aircraft serviceable. XB626, unserviceable with distortion on all radio channels since 5 December, had been grounded for a month because there were no tradesmen available to fix it. The situation with XB682 was worse: it had been unserviceable since 23 August, awaiting five items to repair it. The spares finally arrived at the end of December, and when crews were available they set to getting the aircraft fixed. Against this backdrop, many of the squadron personnel must have breathed a sigh of relief when pilot briefings on the Hunter 4 began at the end of the year.

Fog and bad weather in January 1956 did not dampen spirits, for on the 11th, the squadron's first Hunter arrived. A second flew in on 19 January and, although Sabre flying continued, the emphasis was now firmly on converting onto the new type. Nonetheless, even at this late date there were still those keen to taste the Sabre. On 12 January, Brüggen's new Station Commander, Gp Capt Dudgeon, made his first Sabre solo with 67 Sqn. And though Hunter lectures took up a lot of ground-training time, the Sabre's commitment was still recognised. On 16 January a number of the squadron's aircraft performed ECM attacks on a Lincoln bomber, and five days later eight of 67 Sqn's Sabres took part in a wing fly-past over 2 TAF Headquarters to mark the departure of Sir Harry Broadhurst as AOC. The new AOC, the Earl of Bandon, was similarly saluted on 23 January, the squadron again supplying eight Sabres for the purpose.

On most days in February, flying was not possible because of snow and ice on the runways; just nineteen Sabre and twelve Hunter sorties were completed. However, the month marked the squadron's final Sabre missions, other than air tests prior to ferrying the aircraft away. Five Hunters were on squadron strength by 23 February and, with weather grounding the aircraft, this enabled maintenance crews to catch up with acceptance checks while preparing the Sabres for departure. This process really got into full swing at the beginning of March, when nine Sabres remained with the squadron. Over the next few weeks, Sabre air tests were flown on most days, as well as ferry flights back to the UK. The final trio of Sabres, XB664, XB671 and XB820, were ferried out on 26 March 1956.

Aircraft Assigned

XB538/Z+, XB550, XB586/X, later Y+, XB596/F, XB598/R+, XB600/W, XB624, XB625/Q+, XB626+, XB627/C, XB632+, XB634/B+, XB639/P, XB664/B+, XB665/W+, XB668+, XB671/E+, XB674/G+, XB678/L, XB679/M, XB682/V+, XB683/W, XB690/Z, XB692/D+, XB693/C+, XB695+, XB701/V, XB702/J, XB705/S+, XB706/U+, XB730/Y, XB737/A+, XB754/D+, XB820+, XB869+, XB936*, XB939*.

* = '6–3'-winged from manufacture.
+ = '6–3' conversions.

Markings – 67 Sqn

Initial squadron markings consisted of a flight-coloured band at the top of the tail fin (red for 'A' Flight, blue for 'B' Flight) bordered in thin yellow bands. Individual code letters were applied in white to the central portion of the fin, usually with a thin black outline. The squadron badge was applied onto the central white band of the fin flash.

When bar markings arrived, these were applied either side of the fuselage roundel and comprised a red bar with a blue elongated triangle superimposed, short side towards the roundel. Each colour was separated by a thin yellow stripe, the whole bar being similarly treated.

Squadron Motto

No odds too great.

CHAPTER TEN

71 'EAGLE' SQUADRON

Vampire-equipped and commanded by Sqn Ldr E. 'Ted' Trees, 71 Sqn, based at Wildenrath, had initially hoped to convert onto the Sabre from mid-1953. In anticipation of this, the first half-dozen squadron pilots went through Sabre Conversion Unit training in May 1953 and a further eight in the following month. Unfortunately, insufficient aircraft were available to equip the squadron at this time, so it soldiered on with the Vampire, taking these aircraft to Sylt for gunnery in August and September.

With Sabres finally in the offing later in the year, on 27 September eight pilots returned to SCU for refresher training; concurrent with this, a number of newly arriving crews also took the SCU course. The process of conversion and refresher training continued into the following month, and on 2 October the first four Sabres for the squadron – XB608, XB628, XB630 and XB880 – arrived at Wildenrath. Over the following weeks, further deliveries were made by 147 Sqn ferry pilots, and the final four Sabres flew in on 16 November to bring the squadron up to its 22-aircraft strength.

At this time 'A' Flight was led by Flt Lt M.C.N. Smart, AFC and 'B' Flight by Flt Lt R.S. 'Dickie' May. The initial period of Sabre operations was a busy one; the ground crews ensured that acceptance checks were completed on the new aircraft, while the old Vampires were readied for ferrying out. The pilots meantime were busy performing test flights on both types. Nonetheless, the squadron felt sufficiently confident to stage a mobility exercise to Florennes Airbase in Belgium on 23 October, using the few Sabres that had been accepted by that time – still less than ten. Unfortunately, on arrival at Florennes, P Off Fisher landed heavily in XB880, burst a tyre and caused Cat. 2 damage to the aircraft. The Florennes detachment was in any case a literal washout, bad weather meaning that only six sorties were completed from there, amounting to 3.5 flying hours. The 71 Sqn detachment returned to Wildenrath on 28 October.

The squadron continued the training commitment through November, flying just 41.25 hours on the Sabre in that month, but easily reached its 200-hour target in December. Unfortunately, the increased amount of flying had a knock-on effect, which meant that the maintenance workload shot up. Minor inspections in particular began to fall behind, and during December a number of pilots were sent on leave as there were so few aircraft to fly. Nonetheless, despite these problems the crews began to come up to operational effectiveness on the Sabre. Though cine sorties could not be flown because of a lack of film-assessing equipment, and with altitude restricted to 15,000ft, during December a start was finally made on air-to-ground work, though in that case all missions were scrubbed because of bad weather. Air-to-air cine missions were finally completed in December, to some positive effect.

Fg Off Roger Neaves arrived at 71 Sqn in late 1953, straight from Class 53-D in the United States:

I first did three F-86 trips with the SCU. My first F-86 flight was on 18 November 1953 in serial no. XB

Just visible on this 71 Sqn Sabre is the flight-coloured nose band applied during the early years. This is a blue-trimmed 'B' Flight aircraft. (*Robin Brown*)

681. The first flight with 71 was on 28 November 1953. I was 19 years old and probably the squadron baby! Having flown the F-84, which had hydraulic aileron boost, I found the F-86 a delight to fly, and it didn't perform the wing-rocking climb-outs experienced by the ex-Vampire chaps.

A lot of our work was PIs (practice interceptions) under the control of the local GCI radar unit, which was just outside Wildenrath. We did plenty of one-on-one cine dogfighting and practising managing four-ships in simulated combats. Apart from the above performance limitations I'd say we would have been able to cope in a hot war.

We did our stint of battle flight in which from dawn to dusk we tried to keep a pair of armed aircraft in the air. The night-fighter chaps had the night commitment, which was rough on them in the winter. I did get the job of chasing a MiG-15 that had blundered across the border, probably lost, but I never got within range and anyway, by the time the Air Ministry could have authorised my firing, he would have been safely home.

It was not until early 1954 that the squadron really began to get to grips with the Sabre. And though the spares problems were never really resolved, maintenance personnel gradually became experienced on the aircraft and the 'in service' rate increased. On 12 January 1954, Flt Lt John H.J. Lovell was posted into the squadron as 'A' Flight commander. Lovell had seen Sabre service in Korea and was one of only five RAF pilots to have been credited with MiG kills in Korea. His presence, and later that of other experienced pilots, helped the squadron immeasurably.

Barrage exercises began in January, although the air-to-ground ranges were still off limits because of poor weather conditions. And even when the Sabres showed good serviceability, the squadron was often let down by its support aircraft, the Vampire and Meteor trainers. By the end of the month, nine pilots were out of date with their instrument ratings because the trainer aircraft were not available for check rides.

Aircraft of 'B' Flight (XB875/W nearest) formate with Gp Capt Johnny Johnson in his second Sabre, XB686. Note the lack of RAF fin flash on Johnson's aircraft; it was painted over by a broad red band. (*John Hardwick*)

Fortunately, though the technical effort still struggled to keep up with the maintenance task, serviceability of the Sabres rose, from 35.1 per cent in January to 49.2 per cent the following month. This meant that the squadron's 400-hour target was exceeded on 24 February. And this was in spite of having eight aircraft awaiting minor inspection and another on intermediate inspection. While the temperature was still hovering around zero, two pilots, P Off C.R. Phillips and P Off Roger Neaves, were detached to Ehrwald in Austria for Winter Survival Training.

The squadron's Sabres took part in their first NATO exercise, 'Magna Flux', which started at the end of February. This involved European-based aircraft simulating bomber attacks against the UK, and 71 Sqn contributed 12 sorties for 14.3 flying hours. It is interesting to note that the two Fighter Command Sabre squadrons – 66 and 92 – were also involved in this exercise, but on the 'defending' side. A further ten sorties were completed by 71 Sqn on Exercise Springboard during March.

In March the squadron managed to complete a few range sorties at Monschau, though results were not good and many sorties were cancelled because of bad weather. Undaunted, they continued the range programme into April, and by the end of the month all pilots had completed one or more air-to-ground firing sorties. Monschau closed for repairs in April and the squadron switched to the Nordhorn range for a while. Good results for some time were stymied by poor gun harmonisation and lack of practice – both for the pilots in firing and for the armourers still coming to terms with the Sabre.

On 23 April 1954, Sqn Ldr L.H. 'Len' Cherry arrived to take over command of 71 Sqn, and after a brief handing-over period Sqn Ldr Trees left on the 28th for a new posting in the UK. Two other pilots posted into the unit at this time were P Off J.M. 'Oakie' Oakford and P Off 'Porky' Bond.

Both arrived on 30 April and were posted to 'A' Flight. 'Porky' Bond had been holding briefly at Bückeburg and immediately on arrival at 71 Sqn went through Sabre Conversion Unit. Like the majority, he transitioned onto the Sabre in six flights and was then put to work on the squadron. Being single, he was in the majority: 'The squadrons were young, largely bachelors apart from the Flight and Squadron Commanders. This made for a lively social life, centred mainly on the Officers' Mess, with probably excessive alcohol consumption at its core. Our elders at work strived to teach us something about being a fighter pilot, and much that could have been taught at an OCU happened on the squadron. Those of us from English [based] training had some advantage over our US-trained brethren, as we were accustomed to bad weather and pilot navigation, but I am sure they were better prepared for the F-86.'

By the spring of 1954, the maintenance situation had not eased at all and, with more in-depth servicing being scheduled, items such as engine stands, lifting slings and other ground-support equipment were found to be in short supply. To make matters worse, the training aircraft were regularly out of service, and by the end of April a dozen pilots were out of date for instrument ratings. In May the squadron missed its 500-hour flying target by over ten hours, though it did manage to contribute some useful night-flying sorties.

For two days from 11 May, Exercise Prune II utilised the squadron's aircraft to intercept 'enemy' bomber formations. Eighteen sorties were flown with limited success, for 15.1 flying hours. A further eleven sorties were devoted to air-to-ground in May, a paltry figure for a squadron trying to get its pilots proficient in this role. For these missions, the Fassberg range was used. Fg Off Cowell and P Off Bond used the squadron Vampire – serviceable for once – on a further air-to-ground demonstration at Helchteren range on 28 May. This 40-minute mission represented the aircraft's only flight of the month.

An attempt to improve the maintenance situation was made in May by amending the intermediate inspection schedule. This theoretically would result in a three to four day reduction in each servicing, but in practice the new scheme increased inspection times by up to thirteen days per aircraft; it really seemed that the squadron could do nothing right. As ever, spare parts represented the worst problem, each missing item meaning that an aircraft was stuck on the ground. When the squadron began rehearsing for the Queen's Birthday fly-past over Düsseldorf in late May, it often averaged less than six aircraft serviceable at any one time.

Unfortunately, the valuable time lost to performing fly-past rehearsals was time that could have been spent on the training programme. Two Sabres were meanwhile flown without drop tanks so that pilots could complete supersonic dives to qualify for their 'Mach Buster' tiepin. Further missions were flown on the Helchteren range, but these were again spoiled, this time by a number of fly-past practices and further bad weather. With more poor results being logged, harmonisation of the guns was placed as top priority before the next range days. Aside from the range missions, a number of dummy air-to-ground sorties were made against ground targets for the Army – two missions at Brackwede and a further pair at Monschau.

Another Korean Sabre veteran, Flt Lt Roy French, was posted into 71 Sqn on 10 June 1954, taking over command of 'B' Flight from Dickie May, who had slipped a disc and was admitted to Wegberg Hospital for observation. Roy French had been on the same Korean deployment as Flt Lt John Lovell, 71 Sqn's 'A' Flight commander.

On the flying side, pilots finally began to get to grips with air-to-ground firing in June, and the one full day at Monschau yielded a

14 per cent average, largely because the guns were finally harmonised correctly. It should be noted that, prior to the Sabre's arrival, gun harmonisation had been done by boresighting the weapons against sighting poles mounted on the ground in front of the aircraft. When the Sabre arrived in service, it introduced a new method whereby the aircraft was parked in front of stop butts and placed on jacks in a rigging position. The guns were then harmonised and fired against the range target to verify their accuracy. The system proved far more effective than the old 'pole' method. June also marked the squadron's first double-rearm practice, where two aircraft would take off, fire all six guns until the ammunition was exhausted, and then return to base. Once the aircraft was on the ground, the armourers would rearm it, and it would take off again to fire all six guns. Any stoppages were noted on this mission, 71 Sqn's first effort resulting in a creditable sub-20-minute turnaround.

The better weather in June allowed more flying to be undertaken, but still the maintenance effort was falling behind. By the end of the month, twenty-eight 'aircraft on ground' demands for spare parts were still outstanding, and a system of stealing these spares from long-term 'sick' aircraft was put into effect. A dedicated 'repair and rectification' section was set up on the squadron to pool resources and, in future, airmen of all trades would undertake servicing on the line, whereas in the past only airframe and engine problems had been tasked there. This meant that time-consuming moves of aircraft into the hangar were reduced, though ground-equipment shortages somewhat

This line-up of 71 Sqn pilots was put together in the early summer of 1954, soon after Sqn Ldr Len Cherry arrived on the unit. Back row L–R are: Fg Off John Akin, Fg Off Lloyd, Fg Off Roger Neaves, Fg Off Tom Whitworth, Fg Off Alan Chalkley, Fg Off 'Porky' Bond. Middle row L–R: Fg Off Don Sly, Fg Off Jimmy Clarke, Fg Off Len Tempest, Fg Off Tony Mead, unknown, Fg Off John Harvey, unknown, Fg Off Tex Latham. Front row L-R: unknown, unknown, Flt Lt Roy French, Sqn Ldr Cherry, Fg Off Frank McClory, Fg Off Johnny Cowell, Fg Off Les 'Basher' Bates. (*Roger Neaves*)

undermined the gains. Many of these initiatives were put in place by Flt Lt I.M. Ritchings, who had just been posted into 71 Squadron as Engineering Officer on a three-month trial. Prior to this, direction of maintenance had been down to the already overworked flight commanders. When Ritchings was posted out at the end of his term in August, his place was taken by Flt Lt J.F. Story.

Two Sabres were damaged in June, though no injuries were caused. On 9 June, P Off R.J. Fisher of 'B' Flight experienced a turbine-blade failure in XB687 and force-landed on the airfield. The Sabre was assessed as Cat. 3 and took a month to repair. The second incident involved 'Porky' Bond in XB550/D: he landed heavily after a night sortie, again causing Cat. 3 damage. XB550 was grounded until October for rectification. A further incident on 1 July, though, involving a 71 Sqn aircraft, was not down to a squadron pilot. Gp Capt R.J. Gosnell, Wildenrath's Station Commander, had taken XB669/V aloft for a flight to Bückeburg, but was caught out by that airfield's short runway, which was also wet at the time. He overshot and slid into a ditch; XB669 sustained Cat. 4 damage and had to be returned to the UK for repair. It saw no further RAF service.

By far the biggest single event on the squadron's calendar was Exercise Dividend, the annual UK air-defence evaluation. In order to test the country's air defences, large numbers of attacking formations of 'enemy' aircraft would be launched from the Continent, and 2 TAF's Sabre squadrons figured to a great extent in this operation. Fifty-one sorties were flown by 71 Sqn on Dividend, which began on 17 July. Travelling in small formations, the squadron was briefed to fly at Mach 0.74 at 30,000–40,000 feet altitude; these performance restrictions at least gave the defenders a chance to catch the Sabres, but even then interceptions were few, with less than 20 per cent of raids being caught. The rare occasions when the defending UK-based aircraft did manage to intercept the Sabre formations only occurred after the 'enemy' had crossed the English coast. Clearly, the RAF desperately needed some better interceptors. 'Porky' Bond flew two missions on Dividend which give some idea of the type of target. On 23 July he flew a 1 hour and 10 minute mission against the USAF base at Bentwaters in XB739. On the following day a similar mission was flown aboard XB850, this time to RAF Wattisham. Incredibly, despite this concentrated period of flying, the squadron comprehensively missed its 500-hour flying target for July, logging only 332.1 hours on 392 sorties.

The long-awaited detachment to Sylt finally began on 24 August. However, with a number of squadrons already on the airfield for gunnery, 71 Sqn flew its aircraft to Schleswigland, launching sorties from there onto the Sylt ranges. Fourteen Sabres and one Meteor T. 7 were serviceable for the deployment on 24 August, with two further Sabres flying over on the 25th and another a week later. Cpl Durrant of the Instrument Section drew particular praise in getting these aircraft serviceable, particularly the work he did on gunsights. Additionally, Technical Wing had performed six minor inspections to ensure that a maximum number of aircraft were available. Unfortunately, on 25 August, when Fg Off Roger Neaves of 'B' Flight brought XB880/B in to land at Schleswigland, he did so with the brakes applied. Inevitably, the port tyre then burst on touching down, causing damage to the lower wing surface.

Aside from the gunnery aspect, moving the squadron served to train the unit in deployed operations, as 'Porky' Bond recalls: 'Our squadron was classed as "mobile" so that the Germany detachments involved a road move. The squadron was equipped with its own transport, Magirus-Deutz trucks, VW Kombis and Land Rovers. The transport included large fold-out truck and trailer bodies, which became crew rooms, locker rooms and testing facilities. Conveniently, the trips to Schleswig and Sylt fell neatly into two sectors with an overnight stop in the Hamburg area, thus allowing the convoy crowd access to the lively and "educational" night life in and around the Reeperbahn.'

Gunnery on the Sylt ranges began immediately, but soon gunsight unserviceability started to affect the squadron's performance. Initially, gunsights were used in the 'fixed' mode, but later in the month, when radar-ranging began to be used, these systems also began to break down. Finally, lamp filaments for gunsight illumination were in severely short supply and, though local purchase of similar items was resorted to, these were found to be too dim to function correctly. Several days were also lost while an undercarriage ground-lock inspection was completed, and more than thirty tyres had to be changed during the deployment because of stone chips on the runway.

Inevitably, this continued upheaval meant that gunnery scores were poor, and only eight sorties per pilot were achieved, rather than the hoped-for target of thirty. As if to reinforce the low morale, when a double-rearm practice was completed on 14 September, it took twice as long as the sub-20-minute exercise back at Wildenrath in June. The squadron returned to base on 17 September, and once back at Wildenrath began moving its operating base from No. 4 Hangar to more spacious quarters in Nos 2 and 3 Hangars.

Exercise Battle Royal started on 21 September and, though the squadron took part on only two days, three sweeps of four Sabres each were launched. The exercise mainly involved ground forces, 71 Sqn's aircraft flying top cover for those down below. On 22 September the squadron's Meteor was again unserviceable after the canopy fell off on departure from Gütersloh. Both of the crew, Fg Off Harvey and Fg Off Tempest, were unhurt. The aircraft, WH117, was assessed as Cat. 2 damaged, and required a number of weeks to get serviceable again.

October 1954 began with seasonably poor weather, and when better weather did allow flying to take place there were often less than five aircraft available per day. Just over 243 hours were flown in the month, the worst since the squadron had converted to the Sabre. Nonetheless, a number of night flights were completed, and 'Porky' Bond's night cross-country on 19 October was typical. The mission took him from base to Brussels, then on via Amsterdam and Düsseldorf to base again. Flying time aboard XB879 was 1.1 hours.

By the end of the month, eight Sabres were with Aircraft Servicing Flight and one more was waiting to be slotted in. A further Sabre was away on repair with 3 Maintenance, Repair and Salvage Unit (MRSU) at Oldenburg. On 21 October the squadron was reorganised so that maintenance personnel came under a third flight, but this appeared to have little immediate effect. Concurrently a number of groundings further lessened the squadron's effectiveness. In early November, a generator STI meant that no aircraft were available for three days, and Servicing Instruction SI/Sabre/22 grounded eight more in mid-December. Meanwhile, the gunsight problems experienced on the Sylt detachment had not improved. Since most were only serviceable in 'manual caged' mode, crews were retrained to use the fixed gunsight.

Further incidents resulted in two aircraft lost, though thankfully with no injuries. On 22 October the port drop tank fell off XB624, just as Fg Off J.D. Clark of 'B' Flight was returning to the circuit. He managed to land safely with no damage done. Four days later, two pairs of Sabres from 'A' Flight were performing dummy attacks on each other at 14,000ft. Fg Off A.J. Chalkeley in XB729 was one of the attacking pair, and on one of his passes he struck the Sabre of Fg Off A.C. Jones, who had been flying XB628 as number two in the other formation. As soon as the aircraft touched they exploded. Fortunately both pilots were blown clear in the explosion and came to earth by parachute despite neither having fired his ejection seat. The accident occurred ten miles from the town of Kronfeld and represented the squadron's first Sabre losses in the twelve months it had been operating the type.

The rest of 1954 proved relatively trouble-free with regard to flying accidents, and a number of barrage missions were flown. On one such sortie on 8 November, six Sabres intercepted twelve Belgian F-84s and eight Dutch Meteors under GCI control. High- and low-level cross-country flights were programmed at regular intervals to maintain proficiency at navigation, and at the start of December four aircraft were detached to Celle to operate from there. It had been planned to fly a number of battle-flight missions from Celle, but with the local GCI inoperative, and with only one Sabre energiser available, in the end just one mission was flown, which landed back at Wildenrath. The year was rounded off by the visit of two CFE Hunters to Wildenrath on 15 December. Talks on the new fighter were given by the CFE team, though it would be nearly eighteen months before the squadron had a chance to get to grips with the Hunter.

The following year, 1955, continued where the old year had left off: just 239.3 hours had been flown in December, and this only rose to 323 hours in January, the cold weather and snow putting paid to eleven days of flying. The squadron did manage, however, to provide eight Sabres for a fly-past for the UK Secretary of State for Air on 7 January 1955, and twelve for a wing fly-past in honour of AM Sir Basil Embry on 27 January.

It was at this point that 71 Sqn's Sabres began to be routed through '6–3' wing conversion at Geilenkirchen; from 7 January, two were dispatched for the work to be undertaken, as well as the Wing Leader's aircraft. Two further Sabres had meantime been 'lost' in Aircraft Servicing Flight for wing changes, and XB728 was nearly lost for good on 31 January. Flown by Fg Off J. 'Oakie' Oakford on an air-to-ground live-firing sortie, XB728 had been hit by a ricochet. Oakford was unhurt and managed to get the aircraft back to base for repair.

And though the weather was fine at the start of February, the squadron lost another Sabre. Wing Adjutant Flt Lt A.J.C. Taylor was killed flying XB760 on 4 February; his Sabre crashed near to the town of Jülich. Fg Off J. 'Oakie' Oakford was flying formation with Taylor at the time, and was fortunate to survive:

We 'leapt into the *luft*' and I did a quick instrument check before entering cloud in close formation. All was OK. The cloud was smooth, but visibility was very poor and I had to fly closer than normal. After a couple of minutes I had a sense of unease that all was not well and I distinctly remember the bristling of my neck hair. The leader seemed to be looking to the right side of the cockpit where our ADF radio aid was positioned. We normally only used it for music on cross-country exercises. He then looked forward. I did a very quick glance at the badly designed panel and saw the artificial horizon at 90 degrees and the vertical speed indicator at the 3 o'clock position. We were out of control, possibly up but probably down, and I had to decide whether to stay with him and let him sort it out or leave him.

I had meanwhile unconsciously dropped back half a length, and just as well. I was extremely alert. The cloud started thinning, then there was the bloody ground rushing up to meet us. I remember seeing a white house above me. We were on our backs, almost vertical, at over 500 kts and about 1,500 ft max above the ground. We both broke, he across my nose, me to the left. The rapid rate of roll was useful as I had to get to the minimum pull-out angle. I then put the stick into my stomach and the 12G-plus made the Sabre judder with a high-speed stall, but at least I had raised the nose a little. As I was reluctantly reducing the stick angle to unstall, I felt a shock wave. 'That's him,' I thought, 'now it's me.' The ground was coming up very fast, but I realised that I might make it. I recovered about tree level and looked over my left shoulder to see a large column of fire where he had crashed on a railway. I almost stalled while circling the crater and making a very garbled Mayday call.

I was guided back to base by radar and, after touchdown, my legs started shaking uncontrollably while operating the foot brakes I was met at the aircraft by OC Wildenrath, the Padre and the Squadron 'Boss'. I was a gibbering wreck. After a cup of tea in the crew room I was taken to the Medical Officer, a drinking buddy, where I demolished a high proportion of a 'medicinal' bottle of brandy. For days I could see that white house at 1 o'clock high. An RAF doctor who attended the crash site said that amongst the other horrid findings on the crater edge was the pilot's wallet with an expired White Card [junior instrument rating] showing. That's the sort of thing you expect in films.

Next time I flew was two days later on my Flight Commander's wing at low level in a snowstorm. Much as I idolised that Korean-experienced 'tiger', I also did rapid checks of my instruments [twitch, twitch]. I learnt that from flying!

The deceased pilot had only eight hours on the F-86. I should have led the pair. The American-designed artificial horizon has the bank indicator on the top segment instead of on the bottom segment as on the British AH. Possibly this added to his confusion. The F-86 wings were bolted on and the excess g on my machine had cracked the bolt holes. An engineer told me that it never flew again, but was used for spares.

Though heavy snow fell in mid-February, the squadron had managed to chalk up 274 flying hours by the 12th; the snowfalls meant that just 70 hours were flown in the rest of the month. However, this did allow the '6–3' wing-modification programme to progress, with six Sabres at Geilenkirchen at most times. During February a further half-dozen Sabres were grounded while wing-root fittings were examined, and the squadron's Vampire was also unserviceable (with the Meteor still grounded for canopy repairs), so seven instrument re-ratings were accomplished in a borrowed Meteor trainer. The wing-modification programme continued into March, when nine more Sabres received the '6–3' wing, but then suddenly stopped. No reason for this was given, and the hasty and unforeseen halt left the squadron with six slatted aircraft. When the rundown from twenty-two to fourteen aircraft came into effect in July, these slatted aircraft would be the first to be allocated out; in the meantime, the squadron had to operate this less-than-ideal mix.

As if this were not bad enough, in March the squadron was alerted for a month-long Armament Practice Camp in Cyprus, and would need to contribute half of the wing's 24-Sabre commitment. The APC was scheduled to begin in the second week in June and thus, on 22 April, it was agreed that the squadron would fly just 400 hours in the period from 23 April to 10 June. With due consideration being given to sidelining the six slatted aircraft, this made planning the move even more difficult.

Nevertheless, in this period a good few sorties were flown, including four air-to-ground against an Army barracks at Minden on 24 March, and a further four on 31 March. On 14 April, seven long-range barrage missions were flown, simulating enemy bombers, and these required fitting drop tanks to the previously 'clean'-configured aircraft. 'Porky' Bond flew one of these sorties, routing from base to Dieppe and Florennes before returning to base. The flight in XB637 took 1.25 hours. Twenty-seven interception sorties were also devoted to Exercise Sky High on 26 April, missions being launched from 0400 hr. No bombers were sighted, though the Sabres flew as high as 45,000ft. Attention then turned to cine attacks and operations above 40,000ft, but six of the Sabres had no gunsight heads (they had been stolen to service other aircraft) and a further half-dozen gunsights could only be used in the 'caged' mode. At least the air-to-ground scores were getting better, though: a 10.4 per cent squadron average had been yielded in March.

Fortunately, there were few incidents during this hectic period. Fg Off 'Oakie' Oakford did have another close shave, however, encountering a high-speed porpoising episode on 13 April. Flying at just 2,000ft, the violent manoeuvre was bad enough to force open the port main undercarriage door, and subsequent investigation revealed the door actuator bracket to be cracked; the aircraft, XB550, sustained Cat. 3 damage. Years later, Oakford recalled the details of the mission:

> One day I went up for an air test. The '86 tested OK so I asked the tower permission for a max. limit 600 kts low-level fly-by, duly given. As I approached the airfield in a gentle dive accelerating through 550 or so knots, heat turbulence and probable overcontrol by me induced porpoising, which got worse. Recommended correction procedure is not to 'chase it' but, near to the ground and in descent, I was reluctant so to do. Suddenly there was a big bang and I stupidly looked back to see if my tailplane was still on. Meanwhile I had instinctively throttled back, aborting the fly-by, and found myself in a gentle climb. After the landing I was a bit twitched. The ground crew told me the main undercarriage doors had been damaged. The speed, porpoising and perhaps non-perfect door fit was the cause of the bang. I was glad that those doors hadn't come off at that speed.

Though no cause for the incident could be found, at around this time Fg Off Parsons also experienced a violent porpoise manoeuvre. While on this occasion no damage was done to the aircraft, Parsons did receive a strained back.

Air-to-air firing really got into full swing in May, when a number of days were devoted to flag missions over the Bergheim range. On these occasions, the squadron Meteor was used as a target tug. In the meantime, 67 Sqn had suffered a horrific accident, when one of the squadron's Sabres collided with a Communications Flight Anson on approach to Wildenrath. It was immediately agreed that the airfield was just too crowded to support these different aircraft safely and, on 16 May, while the problem was resolved, 71 Sqn deployed to Fassberg, along with 67 Sqn. This did have a useful outcome, as the squadrons were then able to use the nearby ranges, thus cutting their flying hours but giving the pilots plenty of gunnery practice. Sector-recce missions were flown from Fassberg on 17 May, and then the squadron began cine quarter and flag-firing sorties. During this period, the squadron completed 196 cine sorties, along with 46 air-to-ground missions, on the Fassberg range. And though less than

Sabres of 71 Sqn huddled inside the hangar at Fassberg in May 1955 during the squadron's deployment there. This is a very interesting shot for modellers, as the aircraft at centre, XB878/X, is midway through receiving the later squadron colours. Thus it has just the yellow and white squadron bands on either side of the fuselage roundel, with no black diamonds yet applied. XB878 also retains the earlier flight-colour band (in this case blue for 'B' Flight) around the intake. (*Bob Whitworth*)

250 hours were flown in the whole month, this was quite an achievement, considering the difficult juggling of aircraft involved. The Sabres had to be routed through periodic inspections to ensure that none would be due while in Cyprus. These same aircraft also needed to have fully serviceable gunsights and radar, and the issue was further clouded by the impending rundown from twenty-two to fourteen aircraft on squadron strength. Nevertheless, Sqn Ldr Cherry still hoped to have twelve Sabres, plus one spare, available. Of the other machines, six were slatted aircraft that would be available for allotment to the UK while the squadron was in Cyprus, and the remaining three would be undergoing maintenance in the same period.

The squadron briefly returned to Wildenrath on 6 June and then began packing for the deployment to Cyprus. It had by this time been decided that the squadron would move its home base to Brüggen, and therefore five officers and two-thirds of the squadron airmen would remain in Germany to prepare the move to the new base while the rest were in Cyprus.

The majority of the Sabres on APC departed Wildenrath on 15 June, routing via Fürstenfeldbruck to night-stop at Rome's Ciampino airport. The next day they flew on to Nicosia in Cyprus via a refuelling stop at Elefsis in Greece; ground crews and a few other pilots followed up in Hastings transport aircraft. It should be noted that, although ostensibly designed to provide fair-weather gunnery practice for the squadron, there were other motives for the Cyprus detachment. The official line was that it would prove and reinforce the Middle East Air Force supply route, but most realised that it was also a good opportunity to show the flag during this period of tensions in the region.

On 17 June, the squadron began its gunnery, firing on the Kyrenia East range, and had logged 164 firing sorties by the end of the month. By the end of the detachment, the squadron average stood at 8.7 per cent, with pilots getting an average of 4.5 firing sorties each. In addition to the gunnery, on 27 June Sqn Ldr Cherry led five Sabres to Amman in Jordan, where a series of exercises were flown with the Venoms of 249 Sqn. These comprised practice interceptions, as well as 'rat and terrier' sorties. On the latter, the squadrons took turns to act as both 'rat' and 'terrier'. Only one airborne incident marred the proceedings when, on 27 June, Fg Off Gasson was performing an air test on XB630 from Amman. Following a high-speed run, on letting down through Mach 0.9 Gasson heard a loud bang behind him, and on looking out saw the port elevator hanging out of position. Understandably, elevator control was somewhat less effective than normal, but Gasson managed to land the aircraft without further damage. Subsequent investigation showed that both elevator linkages had come adrift, one failing completely. It was determined that safety locking of the fastenings had either failed or, more likely, had not been done on the last servicing. XB630 was repaired and returned to Cyprus with the other Sabres a few days later.

Meanwhile, in Cyprus things had been no less interesting. One evening, Fg Off J. Akin of 'B' Flight was returning by motorbike from a social call in Kyrenia when he was met by a number of doubtful-looking individuals waving in his path. Though they ordered him to stop, Akin thought they were terrorists and continued at unabated speed. Unfortunately, they were in fact local policemen, and one of them somewhat over enthusiastically decided to use his pistol to stop the mad biker: five shots were fired and one hit Akin in the leg. He was otherwise unhurt, but was forced to stay behind in hospital when the squadron returned to Germany.

The squadron performed its last gunnery sorties from Nicosia on 1 July, and three days

Bob Fisher's Sabre is hauled out of the overshoot area following a brake failure in 1955; Fisher had stopcocked the engine on his landing run. (*John Hardwick*)

later the Sabres departed. This time the route went via Balikesir in Turkey and Larisa in Greece to a night stop in Rome. The squadron then flew from Rome to Fürstenfeldbruck on 5 July and on to Brüggen.

Just ten days after arriving at its new base, the squadron reached its lowest point with the death of Sqn Ldr L.H. Cherry, AFC. Cherry, flying XB880, had been leading a group of Sabres onto finals and, ironically for one who always stressed the need to keep one's speed up on approach, he stalled and crashed at the end of the runway. Following a service on station, Sqn Ldr Cherry was buried in the British Military Cemetery at Cologne on 19 July. His place as CO was taken by Sqn Ldr Barry N. Byrne, who had been holding at Bückeburg; Byrne was posted into the squadron on 21 July.

As part of the reduction to fourteen aircraft on squadron strength, a number of pilots began to be posted out; and Fg Offs Topham, Jones and Bass all departed for 234 Sqn on 12 July, though this still left 71 Sqn with 25 pilots. By the end of the month, the squadron possessed thirteen Sabres (the fourteenth, XB880, had been lost on 15 July). Throughout August 1955 the squadron's Sabres were grounded by serious fuselage fuel-tank cracks, and the situation became so bad that for one period, 11 to 22 August, there was only one serviceable Sabre in the whole squadron! Of the rest, seven had cracked fuel tanks, one was Cat. 4 with a wrinkled intake, one was Cat. 2 for a wing change, one had its wing removed for an undercarriage repair, two were on minor servicing and one was having its nose undercarriage door replaced. Concurrently a number of aircraft were allotted to the UK and, to make good their loss, four more Sabres – all '6–3'-winged, ex-4 Sqn machines – were transferred to 71 Sqn at the end of August. They proved a mixed blessing. The first two to arrive, XB981 and XB995, required roughly 100 man-hours to get fully serviceable, and one required an engine change. As a result, a paltry total of

146.35 hours was flown in August for just 160 sorties.

Of the sorties that were flown, there were few highlights. On 26 July, Fg Off Fisher led three aircraft on a ground attack mission against Belgian tanks, and three days later eight sorties were flown under the guidance of an MSQ unit during a visit by the RAF Staff College. These missions were directed through solid cloud onto a pinpoint target on the airfield; they were obviously useful, the squadron diarist summing up the experience by saying, 'More of this, please.' On 24 and 25 August, the squadron took part in Exercise Loco, launching mock raids on targets in Holland and Belgium. They met little opposition.

Early in September, the squadron again flew away for gunnery at Sylt, though this was the first occasion that the aircraft had actually been deployed there; the previous detachment had seen the Sabres based at Schleswigland and flying over to the Sylt ranges daily. The squadron departed for Sylt on 5 September – a day early because of forecast bad weather – and this time managed to get twelve Sabres serviceable for the trip. Unfortunately, the gunsight problems again intervened, and it was often found that up to five air tests were required on each aircraft finally to prove the radar sets serviceable. XB974, one of the ex-4 Sqn Sabres, was particularly troublesome. Such interruptions inevitably put paid to a number of sorties, so that of 491 missions launched at Sylt just 188 resulted in effective shoots. By the end of the detachment the average was 12 per cent, each pilot managing to get about ten shoots. On 29 September, the usual double-rearm operational turnaround practice was completed, 'Porky' Bond flying XB739, one of the two Sabres involved. He experienced four stoppages. The squadron returned to Brüggen on 5 October.

On 20 October, Flt Lt John Lovell relinquished command of 'A' Flight on posting out to 234 Sqn. The Korean War veteran was replaced by Flt Lt M.I. Stanway, who arrived on 26 October. Poor weather and low serviceability rates in October meant that just 163 hours were flown – half of September's total. Only one exercise was completed during this period – 'Argus', which saw 71 Sqn supplying a section of Sabres to simulate bombers for Royal Canadian Air Force Sabres to attack. By this time, the Canadians were flying a mix of Orenda-powered Sabre 5 and 6 aircraft and, compared to these, 71 Sqn's seemed decidedly second-rate: they were intercepted with ease before they had arrived at Zweibrücken, and after refuelling were bounced again.

Two incidents rounded off October. On the first occasion, Fg Off D. Lloyd was just rolling along the runway when his Sabre's cockpit filled with dense smoke, accompanied by the smell of burning. Lloyd managed to stopcock his engine and pull off the runway before jumping out. A cable was later found to have burned through, but the damage was extensive and the aircraft, XB739 was assessed as Cat. 4. On the second occasion, Fg Off T. Parsons of 'A' Flight was air-testing XB921 when the ailerons stuck first to port and then to starboard. Parsons gingerly nursed the Sabre back to base, where the starboard aileron shroud was found to be broken. Two nasty accidents had been averted by good skill and a dose of luck.

During the final two months of 1955, less than 400 hours were flown, though finally, in November, eighteen night sorties were completed. These were the first night flights in more than six months. However, poor weather conditions prevailed on many days, and January 1956 continued the trend of less than 200 flying hours per month. A number of effective missions were flown, however, in the early days of the month, commencing on 2 January when four sections of four took part in an ECM exercise against Bomber

With energiser plugged in, XB869/S waits for its next mission in early 1956. This aircraft had only just been transferred from 67 Sqn, and still bears that unit's blue 'B' Flight band on the tail fin. (*Mike Ryan*)

Command Lincolns. A similar exercise on 17 January saw the Sabres fielded against a solitary Canberra. On 12 January, a further section of four deployed on another Canadian 'Argus' exercise. Finally, on 24 January a section of four was detailed to perform an air-to-ground demonstration against ground forces located three miles from the squadron's old airfield at Wildenrath. All of these sorties went off without a hitch and, further to these, the squadron provided eight Sabres for a two-wing fly-past over 2 TAF Headquarters to mark the departure of AM Sir Harry Broadhurst on 21 January. Two days later a similar fly-past was completed for the new head of 2 TAF, AM the Earl of Bandon.

February saw the squadron drop to just 16.3 flying hours in 17 sorties. Most of this was due to heavy snow, and only three full flying days were possible. Sqn Ldr Byrne, who had been away from the unit for much of his time as CO, finally gave vent to his feelings in an open letter appended to his monthly comments in the squadron record book: 'During the month, I was informed that my application for extension of tour had been turned down. So far, out of 233 days total I have held command of this squadron, I have spent only 92 days with it on this unit. The remaining 141 days have been spent on three courses [DFLS, Survival, etc.], one detachment and one exercise. Only five days spent on leave. If I take no leave between now and my date of repatriation in June, I would have only had control of the squadron for six months on this unit.' Little heed seems to have been taken of Sqn Ldr Byrne's feelings: on 5 March he was again detached away from the unit, this time for five days at Wahn on Exercise Bearclaw.

This 'quiet' period, however, did allow squadron personnel to begin preparations for the arrival of Hunter F. 4s on the unit. As far back as April 1955, Flt Lt French had been attached to the Day Fighter Leaders School at West Raynham on the first Hunter course, and on 7 February 1956, Fg Off Tom Whitworth and Fg Off J. Akin travelled to Dunsfold to get further briefings on the

Framed by the underside of the Hunter that was to replace it, XB981/A awaits the inevitable. (*Bob Whitworth*)

aircraft. Though it would be a few months before the Hunters arrived for 71 Sqn, further briefings back at Brüggen would help the air and ground crews to assimilate the new type with a minimum of fuss.

In the interim, the Sabres continued to fly sorties, such as one on 23 March which saw four aircraft performing simulated rocket and napalm attacks in pairs on Belgian tanks near Euskirchen. Continued spares problems still hounded the squadron, however, and by the end of March two aircraft were grounded for engine replacements and a further two for windscreen cracks. Allied to this, there were often no more than ten pilots on squadron strength for much of March and April. More than 270 sorties were flown each month in spite of this situation.

On no less than four occasions during April, Russian Tupolev Tu-104 airliners were intercepted by 71 Sqn Sabres. Rumour had it that one of these aircraft was carrying Marshal Bulganin and Nikita Khrushchev back to Moscow after a visit to Britain. Tom Whitworth, one of those involved, has a mission in his logbook for 7 April (flying aircraft 'M') stating simply, 'Interception of Tu-104 (Malenkov)'; a similar mission was logged in the same machine two days later. Whatever these aircraft were doing, protests were made by the Soviets, and a squadron leader from 83 Gp was dispatched to Brüggen to investigate. He found that no orders had been contravened. Fg Off 'Porky' Bond flew two of the other Tu-104 intercepts – one aboard XB974 on 18 April and another in XB876 on the 23rd. On another occasion, Fg Offs Picking and Oakford managed to intercept an Avro Ashton research aircraft. In his efforts to get a close look at the machine, Picking managed to flame out his Sabre's engine at 38,000ft but was able to restart at a lower level.

On 23 April, 71 Sqn received its first Hunter aircraft, and thus the changeover began. The Sabre's last few days of operations on 71 Sqn were marked by a number of diversions into Volkel, each time by aircraft short on fuel. Fg Off Bond (XB879) and Fg Off Neaves diverted there on

Surrounded by Hunters, Sabre XB869 was the last of the type on 71 Sqn charge; it was ferried out on 5 June 1956. (*John Hardwick*)

Out to pasture. XB632/R only served with 71 Sqn for two months, between March and May 1956; it nevertheless gained full squadron markings. It was then retired to Aviation Traders at Stansted and later served with the Yugoslav Air Force. (*Author's Collection*)

13 April, and Fg Off Sly three days later. On 24 April, Fg Off Bond flew one of the last Sabre missions, aboard XB989 – a low-level flight with practised forced landings and aerobatics. That same day the squadron was declared non-operational on the Sabre; it began full-time Hunter training on 25 April.

The Sabres had begun to be ferried out of the unit in April, and this process accelerated in early May. Ferrying duties were shared by squadron pilots and those from 147 Sqn. 'Porky' Bond's last Sabre flights involved XB974 (ferry to Stansted) on 7 May and XB624 (air test) on 28 May. The final 71 Sqn Sabre was XB869, which was flown out by a 147 Sqn pilot on 5 June 1956. The changeover was not a happy one, with many pilots who converted from the Sabre to the Hunter F. 4 thinking that the new aircraft left a lot to be desired.

Aircraft Assigned

XB550/D, XB599, XB608/P, XB611+, XB624/T+, XB628/O, later V, XB630/P+, XB631/F, XB632/R+, XB635, XB637/E+, XB665, XB669/V, XB686, XB687, XB691, XB700/M, XB710/J, XB728/V+, XB729, XB739+, XB760, XB796/D, XB869/S+, XB870, XB875/W, XB876, XB878/X+, XB879/K+, XB880/B+, XB896/L+, XB921*, XB943*, XB952*, XB974/O*, XB981/H*, XB987/H*, XB989*, XB995*.

* = '6–3'-winged from manufacture.
+ = '6–3' wing conversion.

Markings – 71 Sqn

The Squadron's initial colour scheme comprised red individual code letters on the tail fin, bordered in white. The squadron's eagle badge was painted in black onto a white circle on the forward fuselage. Intake lip areas were painted in flight colours, red for 'A' Flight and blue for 'B' Flight.

Squadron bars, when introduced, were painted either side of the fuselage roundel. Each bar was horizontally divided into white (upper) and yellow (lower) halves, with two black diamond shapes arranged horizontally within each. The painted intake lips had returned to standard camouflage colours by this point.

Squadron Motto

First from the eyries.

CHAPTER ELEVEN

92 'EAST INDIA' SQUADRON

Based at Linton-on-Ouse in the Vale of York, 92 Sqn was operating Gloster Meteor F. 8s at the end of 1953. It would become the second and final Fighter Command squadron to convert onto the Canadair Sabre.

Given the impending arrival of Sabres to the squadron, during December 1953 a number of experienced Sabre pilots were posted in from other units. Among these were Fg Off Mold, Flt Sgt Clayton and Sgt Adams, all of whom came from 147 Sqn at Benson. In addition, a few of the squadron's experienced personnel attended Sabre conversion courses with SCU at Wildenrath in Germany. One of the last to attend was 92 Sqn's CO, Sqn Ldr G. Rennie Turner; he finished at Wildenrath in February 1954, along with P Off R.C. Davis. Once these personnel had done Sabre conversion, they took on the role of trainers back at the squadron, and regular lectures were given on all aspects of Sabre flying and aircraft systems.

Until the first Sabres were delivered, this was as far as the squadron could go to convert to the new type. With neighbouring 66 Sqn receiving its first Sabres in late 1953, morale on 92 Sqn began to wane as they soldiered on with Meteors. Training flights continued, and air-to-air gunnery sorties were flown well into 1954. The squadron ended its Meteor days with a gunnery average of 16 per cent, but would soon eclipse these scores once crews became proficient on the Sabre. Squadron strength at this time stood at 24 officers, 4 NCO aircrew, 6 senior NCOs, 13 corporals and 51 airmen. Towards the latter part of its Meteor period, 92 Sqn experienced difficulties in getting aircraft airworthy, often having less than six available on a daily basis during January 1954.

Further evidence of the impending arrival of Sabres came during January 1954 when the first specialised flying clothing for the type was issued. This included items entirely new to pilots accustomed to flying Meteors; now anti-g suits and bone-dome helmets became the norm. Concurrently, flying was reduced, and the Meteors were readied for ferrying out of Linton. Only air tests were completed, which was just as well because the squadron was running at around 20 per cent less than ideal manning.

Finally, on 23 February the first Sabre, XD727, arrived at the squadron, flown in from 33 MU at Lyneham. By the end of the month, a further six Sabres had been ferried in from Lyneham, and the full establishment of twenty-two aircraft was achieved on 30 March with the delivery of XD764.

On 24 February, squadron pilots had begun checking cockpit drills, and a few taxi tests were completed. The ground-schooling of pilots and ground crew continued throughout this period, a number of exams being set to ensure that the message was getting through. Sqn Ldr Turner and Flt Lt V. Woods completed the squadron's first Sabre sorties on 26 February, with other solos being flown on the following day. By the end of the month only two pilots remained to complete the ground-training syllabus, which, along with conversion flying, continued into March. Within a month of the first Sabres arriving, all squadron pilots had completed conversion, apart from one who was on leave and another who was off sick.

Arriving on the squadron in March from 234 Sqn in 2 TAF, James Smith was an airframe fitter whose previous experience was much appreciated:

> The workload on 92 Sqn was at the least hectic, due to excessive commitments. When the Sabre arrived, it enjoyed instant popularity and was a source of delight both with the ground crew and aircrew. Its advanced technology embraced all trades. Its large, spacious cockpit and its excellent instrument layout was an eye-catching feature.
>
> Its fully powered flying controls served a full-flying tailplane, ailerons and brakes via a hydraulic, engine-driven pump, which also catered for undercarriage and brake systems. The flaps, however, were electrically operated. All controls had emergency back-up systems. Ease of access for servicing was paramount. An engine change could take as little as one hour with its use of hydraulic quick disconnects, plus snap connectors on the servo-control cables operating the flying tail, thus minimising supervisory checks. No adjustments were necessary.

The squadron had a brief involvement in its first exercise with Sabres at the beginning of March. Exercise Magna Flux was a one-week exercise and involved many NATO aircraft launching raids on the UK. Being so new to the Sabre, 92 Sqn's input was limited: the more experienced pilots took part in a number of interception missions. However, the squadron was sufficiently confident to put up a 12-aircraft fly-past during the annual AOC's inspection. The squadron was praised for its precise formation, which was notable, as many of those taking part had never flown the aircraft in formation before.

At the end of March, cameras were fitted to the Sabres so that cine missions could be started, but air-to-air gunnery was still some way off as the guns had yet to be harmonised. Instrument-flying sorties were also started, using the squadron Vampire fitted with American-style gauges. Meanwhile, ground training concentrated on passing out aircrews on flight servicing of their aircraft. This was so that pilots could pre-flight their Sabres in the event of a stopover away from base. All passed the requisite oral exam the following month. One day was also spent at York swimming baths on dinghy drill. By the end of its first full month of Sabre flying, 92 Sqn had logged a creditable 195 hours and 40 minutes.

By now coming up to operational effectiveness on the Sabre, the squadron was set a target of 500 flying hours for April and, thanks to good weather and aircraft availability, managed to surpass this by 18 hours. The squadron began to settle into a normal training routine, and two minor sector exercises were flown against Bomber Command aircraft. These types of exercises invariably involved the squadron being scrambled to make ground-controlled interceptions of aircraft intruding into the sector. One other exercise, 'Adex 1', was completed in April, and good cine films of the interceptions were achieved. These proved useful in debrief situations, where pilots could be coached on their tactics.

Fg Off Alan 'Lefty' Wright was posted into 92 Sqn during April 1955. He came from 3 Sqn in 2 TAF, and his Sabre experience proved useful to the newly converted squadron, especially when problems were encountered:

> I shall not forget that my wheels and doors dropped, unbidden, and all remained down as I was leaving Monschau range in December 1953. My ample fuel state became a critical one in this new uneconomical configuration, but the Sabre got me back to base. Investigation over a day or so revealed the culprit to be swarf in the undercarriage lowering system – hence the doors remaining down after the wheels had dropped. Following a normal 'down' selection, the system operated thus: doors down; wheels down and lock; doors back up and lock. When a year or two later I experienced the

This 92 Sqn formation was most likely photographed during the 19 April 1956 sortie, though XB837/K in the foreground does not appear in the often-seen views of the four-ship formation. (*Author's Collection*)

same malfunction on 92 Sqn, I was able to direct the menders towards the gremlin.

A concomitant problem with this recurring snag was the loss of the usual wheel-brakes power boost from the utility hydraulic system. That was academic after the first failure, followed by a landing on 2,700 yds of dry runway. The second incident required a landing on Linton's 2,000 yds, with icy patches, but this gave the Sabre no trouble either.

First rehearsals for the forthcoming Queen's fly-past over London were begun in April, the squadron committing to three practice missions per week, deploying through North Luffenham to refuel. The fly-past was staged to mark the Queen's return from a Commonwealth tour. For the week prior to the fly-past, the squadron deployed to North Luffenham and flew practices from there, culminating in the actual fly-past on 15 May. While at North Luffenham, two air battles were launched against the Day Fighter Leaders School, which taught squadron pilots a number of lessons in Sabre dogfighting. The first of these sorties was completed on 10 May.

Returning from this sideline, the squadron completed a night exercise for the Royal Observer Corps, Fg Off G. Jones and Flt Sgt M.J. Clayton also demonstrating the aircraft for ROC personnel at a later date. Though they were programmed for Exercise Flamingo, which was subsequently cancelled due to bad weather, other exercises the squadron took part in were successful. At the end of May, live air-to-air gunnery was started and, though scores were understandably low, at least the missions themselves were generally successful. Twenty-one effective target-tow missions were completed, allowing sixty-four effective firing sorties to be flown; 6,669 rounds were fired and only thirteen non-effective firing sorties were logged. Concurrently, a number of air-to-sea sorties were also accomplished, firing 1,814 rounds into floating targets in the North Sea. Cine average for the squadron was 56.3 per cent, actual gunnery scores being considerably lower than this.

By mid-1954 the manpower situation had not improved and, although minor servicing of the Sabres had begun in May, by early June

Close-up of the 92 Sqn fuselage markings. Checks were red and yellow, each square being approximately 9in × 9in. (*Robin Brown*)

flying had to be restricted to allow the maintenance personnel to catch up. The live gunnery training continued through June, and for the first time radar-ranging was used with the A4 gunsight. On several days, radar-reflective flag targets were towed, but in every instance the flags broke away before full use could be made of them. Unfortunately, this meant that only five effective sorties could be flown, all without effective radar-ranging, and the squadron average ended at a fairly embarrassing 1.52 per cent.

During the summer, a monthly flying target of 660 hours was set and successfully exceeded through to the end of July. This was in spite of the earlier manpower problems, which persisted throughout the year, and in spite of seven days that were also lost when the squadron went on block leave in July. With the annual UK air-defence exercise coming up in mid-month, a large amount of training was devoted to interception technique. Practice interceptions were flown up to 40,000ft and crews were also introduced to flying short-range missions without drop tanks fitted. This pre-exercise training was completed on 15 July, and at 1700 hr on the following day Exercise Dividend began.

Phase 1 ran from 16 to 18 July, with Phase 2 running from 22 to 25 July. The squadron, like many others in Fighter Command, was tasked with defending the UK from attacks at high and very high levels. Dividend was designed to 'exercise the air defences of the UK against possible types of attack by manned aircraft likely to be encountered in the first few days of war at the present time'. During Phase 1, the defences were severely stretched, with 1,784 attack sorties being flown against the UK. Attacking aircraft comprised both heavy bomber types and fighters from Europe as well as Fleet Air Arm machines. During Phase 2, 3,942 raiding sorties were flown. In both, high-level B-47 attacks proved almost impossible to intercept, even by the Sabres of 92 Sqn. Around 30 per cent of attacks were intercepted before they reached the coast of the UK. Flying again without drop tanks, the squadron's Sabres did make, however, a number of kills at altitudes in excess of 40,000ft. The record in this respect was set by Flt Lt C. Wilcock, who claimed a PR Canberra flying at 48,000ft. At this altitude, the Sabres were operating close to their ceiling, but this and other 'kills' were verified by examining gun-camera cine film from the attacking fighter. During the exercise, the squadron averaged 20 flying hours per day, despite less-than-perfect weather conditions throughout. Rounding off this period, 92 Sqn Sabres also took part in Exercise Ebb Tide, flying mock attacks against Army positions in the Catterick area.

Three Sabres had been lost by 66 Sqn on the first day of Dividend's Phase 2, and 92 Sqn nearly lost an aircraft too. Fg Off G. Jones had departed Linton on the evening of 22 July on an intercept mission aboard XD714. All went well until forty minutes later, when the aircraft's nose-wheel door unexpectedly opened in flight at 1,200ft, causing an immediate and violent flick. Jones momentarily lost control of the aircraft and only regained it, at low altitude, when the door was finally wrenched off in the airstream. He returned safely to Linton, but his Sabre had been overstressed. Initially assessed as Cat. 3 (R) damaged, the aircraft was soon recategorised as Cat. 4 (R) and despatched to Airwork for repair. Following this incident a trial installation was made on a 2 TAF Sabre to introduce a cockpit switch that would prevent inadvertent operation of the undercarriage in flight. However, this did not prevent a further 92 Sqn Sabre accident in September, and attention then turned to rigging of the undercarriage itself.

After the intensive flying on Dividend, August and September brought the squadron back down to earth: on neither occasion was the monthly flying target met. Poor serviceability and a number of labour-intensive STIs were the root cause of this. Nonetheless, a large amount of practice-interception sorties were flown, and in August rehearsals for Battle of Britain commemorative fly-pasts were begun; the squadron deployed to Coltishall on 9 September and performed the full fly-past with 66 Sqn on the 15th. Continuing the positive note, in air-to-air gunnery during August, Master Pilot E.S. Bannard set a new Sabre record with 53 per cent, and the squadron average was nearly up to the Meteor mark, at 15 per cent. The following month the average had increased to 17.3 per cent – better than with the Meteor – and it continued to improve. A number of trials were flown for RAE at Farnborough to demonstrate operation of the radar gunsight during flag-firing. Finally the squadron began flying until 2000 hr on most evenings in an unsuccessful attempt to catch up on its flying target.

On 21 September 1954, Fg Off C.A. Grabham was killed while on a night-flying training mission. His aircraft, XD733, crashed on Hood Hill near Sutton Bank, three-quarters of a mile north-north-west of Kilburn, Yorkshire and twelve miles north of Linton. Grabham had been airborne for 1 hour 6 minutes and had let down towards base from 34,000ft, calling overhead just prior to the accident; he made no attempt to eject. Subsequent investigation pointed to previous problems with this Sabre's nose undercarriage, and it was thought that the main nose-gear door may have opened in flight and caused a loss of control; the testimony of another 92 Sqn pilot of a previous instance of a nose door opening in flight was used as evidence (XD714 on 22 July). More detailed investigation revealed that a nose-door-retraction bell crank may have been incorrectly fitted; similar problems had been experienced by Sabre squadrons in Germany. This was 92 Sqn's first Sabre loss. A further Sabre, XD771, was written off eight days after Grabham's accident: on this occasion the engine failed, and the pilot, Master Pilot E.S. Bannard, was forced to belly-land in a field. There were no injuries.

To counter these losses, a few XB-serialled Sabres originally slated for 2 TAF were assigned to 92 Sqn. XB757 and XB837 arrived from storage at Kemble on 5 October, and XB677 came in from CFE at the end of the month.

Towards the end of 1954 the squadron was involved in a number of trials. During October two pilots were detached to the Air Fighting Development Sqn, where they were involved in IFF tests. The following month an Army radar

With night falling, crash guards were posted around the site of Master Pilot E.S. Bannard's crashed Sabre, XD771/K, on 29 September 1954. (*Author's Collection*)

unit arrived at Linton and conducted a number of fighter-recovery trials using mobile radar equipment. Finally, in November a number of radar-firing sorties were flown on a new Burgess flag target. Many of these tasks were affected by the poor serviceability state of the squadron's aircraft, a situation exacerbated by the departure of a number of key maintenance NCOs. The fact that so few aircraft were available was also due to many Sabres being grounded while '6–3' wing modifications were embodied. It is interesting to note that, although common parlance for the manufacturer, the term '6–3' was not generally known down at squadron level; instead, the term 'unslatted' or sometimes 'hard edge' were used. Sqn Ldr Turner flew the squadron's first '6–3' modified Sabre on 30 November and, over the next few months, all remaining aircraft were rolled out from conversion. A lot of time was then spent on familiarisation flights, ensuring that the aircrews understood the positive manoeuvring benefits at high altitude while being fully aware that low-speed behaviour, especially at the stall, was less forgiving. Conversion was a slow process, however: as late as March 1955 there were still three slatted Sabres on squadron strength waiting to be modified.

The end of 1954 and the start of 1955 was marked by a long bout of poor flying weather, and the squadron again failed to meet its flying target. On most occasions only short-range sorties were completed and, though the amount of missions flown was quite impressive, flying hours hovered around the 500-hour mark. This was some achievement, but still 50-odd hours short of the minimum required to keep all pilots proficient on the type. Snow, ice and fog in January did not help the situation, and a further Sabre, XD713, was badly damaged in a take-off accident at Linton on the morning of 29 January 1955. Fg Off E.S. Dodds had been performing a formation take-off at the time, and his Sabre's starboard tyre burst on the roll down the runway. Dodds retracted the undercarriage to prevent the aircraft overshooting, but this caused considerable damage to the machine, though the pilot himself was unhurt.

A change of command also took effect in January, with Sqn Ldr Turner departing to a posting in Denmark. His place was taken by Sqn Ldr R.W.G. Freer, who came in from West Raynham.

Sqn Ldr Freer arrived during a particularly bad bout of adverse weather; snow, ice and fog all conspired to reduce the squadron's flying programme so that fourteen days were lost in February alone. Compounding the problem, from 4 February the squadron's Vampire T. 11 trainer, used to provide

North Luffenham was used as a staging post on a number of occasions in August and September 1954, when the squadron flew practice sorties for the Battle of Britain fly-past in London. L–R: Fg Off Eric Mold, Flt Lt Rex Knight, Fg Off Vince Hallam, Fg Off Chris Stone, Fg Off Spike Jones (in intake), Flt Lt Timber Woods, Fg Off A.W.A. Wright, Fg Off Don Cartwright. Sqn Ldr Rennie Turner is perched atop his personal mount, XD779/A, which had three rows of red and yellow checks on its intake area. (*A.W.A. Wright*)

instrument-check flights, was unserviceable. As a result, just when they were really needed, many pilots' instrument ratings began to lapse. Despite this, more than 370 hours were flown during February 1955, and 16 air-to-air gunnery sorties were completed using pegged sights; the squadron average was 18.6 per cent. On the downside, a turnaround exercise using two Sabres was started, which involved firing all six guns and returning to base, where the Sabres were rearmed, refuelled and launched again. During the mission any stoppages were noted. The turnaround itself took 37 minutes (about double the expected time), with six gun stoppages. More work was clearly needed to improve by such a large margin. It should be stated, however, that conditions were far from ideal for the squadron. In particular, the hangar came in for most vociferous complaint: lighting and heating were almost non-existent, and the very few ground-power sockets meant that engine-driven Houchin ground-power units had to be brought into the hangar to get power onto the Sabres being worked on. The resultant noise and exhaust fumes made life almost unbearable at times.

One high point for the squadron came on 25 February, when despite heavy snow and bitterly cold temperatures, the aircrew took part in an escape-and-evasion exercise. Dropped into the wilds of Yorkshire and tasked with getting through heavy defences and back to base, most failed. But a good time was had by most – even those poor souls who got stuck on the Yorkshire Moors; all returned safely eventually.

With the eagerly awaited Armament Practice School (APS) detachment coming up, flying was restricted from the beginning of March to ensure that aircraft could be serviced and guns sighted and fired in on 1,000in butts at Linton. The opportunity was also taken to programme a 'stagger' into the schedule of servicing the aircraft so that all did not become due for maintenance at the same time. Just before the departure for Acklington, on 15 March a team of instructors from Central

Gunnery School arrived on station and spent two days flying with the squadron PAIs and other selected pilots; it was hoped that their input would be passed down to the squadron by the PAIs to improve performance in the impending detachment.

The squadron flew 16 Sabres out to the APS at Acklington on 21 March, landing on a runway only just cleared of snow. The aircraft had performed formation fly-pasts over the base before landing, but soon discovered that further flying was going to be limited. On only two days during the first week was the range safe for firing, and even then further problems intervened. On three occasions, ammunition-bay overheat lights had illuminated in flight – a particularly serious situation, since no fire-extinguishing system was installed in the Sabre. In all three instances a safe return to Acklington was effected. From that point on, the heat to the ammunition bays was turned off on each aircraft and after two clear shoots at up to 20,000ft this modification was used for the rest of the detachment.

When firing did start in earnest, the collective average for many days hovered around the 8 per cent mark. Gunsight serviceability and strict rules for range-firing also meant that many missions were scrubbed. In fact, the aircrews were beginning to have serious doubts about the reliability of the gunsight, especially since there was very poor maintenance back-up for it at squadron level, and almost 20 per cent of missions on the flag were cancelled because of gunsight problems. In support, the squadron only had Cpl H. Barker and one senior aircraftsman in the instrument trade with any experience on the Sabre's A4 gunsight. Indeed, there were only four other instrument mechanics to undertake not just gunsight but all other instrument-related tasks on the squadron. In comparison, USAF-trained pilots on the squadron pointed out that their American colleagues had one master sergeant and eight mechanics on each squadron whose sole job was to look after the gunsight! It should be noted that most missions on this APC involved 'fixed' sighting of the target, without using the aircraft's radar to lock on to it. This was probably just as well, for on the few occasions where radar-ranging was used it often failed to lock onto the flag, tracking the target tug aircraft instead. With these problems and at best eight Sabres available every day, it became impossible to meet the APS requirement of one pair flying on the flag every 20 minutes; instead, the squadron decreed that it would aim to fly four Sabres against the target every hour.

Aside from the gunsight, it was found that the guns themselves were wandering out of harmonisation faster than expected. A number of time-consuming flights back to Linton had to be flown so that firing-in could be completed to test the adjustments. At this point the superiority of 1,000ft harmonisation (where the guns are adjusted to meet at 1,000ft in front of the aircraft – the USAF and NATO standard) was far better than the traditional 1,000in Fighter Command system. Fg Off R.D. Stone, one of the squadron PAIs, flew a Sabre to the USAF base at Shepherds Grove for firing-in at 1,000ft there and the scores improved instantly. Though no further aircraft were able to be harmonised in this way, by being more selective with aircraft on firing sorties, and with further experience, scores began to improve.

Fortunately, the range missions that were successful were well controlled by the GCI personnel, and a number of practice interceptions against Canberra bombers were launched from Acklington, though only one was deemed successful. Three early-morning B-36 bomber interceptions spiced up life, though, somewhat worryingly, the Sabres were not always able to catch these slow-moving beasts.

Meanwhile, the weather at Acklington began to improve, and despite poor serviceability the squadron managed to meet its target of twelve effective firing sorties per pilot by the end of the detachment. These generally comprised eight on the banner target and four sorties firing on target gliders. Concurrent with the proficiency aspect of the APS detachment, the squadron also flew sorties with the aim of winning the Dacre Trophy, awarded periodically to the best squadron score at Acklington. The trophy required shooting to be carried out at between 15,000 and 20,000ft, and proved a novelty for most, as crews had previously been used to firing at 5,000ft or thereabouts. Nonetheless, the squadron excelled itself in this respect, and with gunsights pegged at 1,000ft managed a Dacre Trophy score of 16.3 per cent when the Fighter Command average was just 9.8 per cent.

The squadron lost another Sabre while at Acklington. On 5 April, Fg Off V.H. Hallam in XD710 aborted his take-off run and crashed into the overshoot area. There were no injuries, and, though initially assessed as Cat. 4 (R), the aircraft was later declared a write-off. This left the squadron two aircraft below its twenty-two Sabre establishment.

Led by Wg Cdr E.W. 'Ricky' Wright, DFC, DFM, and in wing formation with 66 Sqn, the squadron returned to Linton on 21 April after a generally good month's firing. In the course of the deployment the Sabres had fired 39,633 rounds and experienced 24 stoppages – a rate of 1,651 rounds per stoppage.

Almost immediately upon return to base, Exercise Sky High started, though only two aircraft were scrambled by the squadron for the whole period. A number of other practice intercepts were launched, however, against the Hunters of DFLS; again, the results were mixed, though the 'hard edge' aircraft did perform better at altitude. To check training standards a team from Central Flying School, led by Sqn Ldr I.N. MacDonald, AFC, arrived at Linton on 25 April. They performed a number of dual-check rides in Vampire and Meteor trainers with squadron pilots and, satisfied, the 'trappers' departed on the 27th. Despite this period of hectic activity, only 253 Sabre hours were logged for April, but thankfully nearly double were achieved the following month. The low amount of flying was in great part because the squadron flew without drop tanks for much of the month of April. This allowed for short-duration gunnery missions to be flown – indeed more than 400 sorties were logged – but it meant that the minimum hours to meet pilot currency requirements were not met.

Numerous sector exercises were completed in May and June, meaning that the air-to-air mission was put on the back-burner. Instead a variety of mission types was flown in respect to the sector commitments; Sabres were launched on 'kingpin' and 'rat and terrier' sorties as well as further PIs with DFLS Hunters. Kingpin exercises simulated Soviet bomber raids, and involved the Sabres being vectored onto a fixed point, from where they were then guided onto the 'raiders'. Enemy aircraft usually comprised RAF Canberras and V-bombers. Aside from this, the squadron was finally busy giving instrument re-ratings, though for this task it used a borrowed Meteor T. 7, as the Vampire trainer was still awaiting repair. In a change from the routine, on 27 May two Sabres plus a complete servicing team and associated ground equipment were deployed to Wymeswold for five days so that Flt Lt V. Woods could do an aerobatics routine for the RAF Association display there.

There were a number of incidents at this time, though fortunately no one was injured. On one occasion in May a Sabre suffered jammed ailerons, and the pilot was both skilful and fortunate in being able to recover to base. Severe engine vibration on another mission resulted in a further forced landing, and this time the pilot was even more lucky, as the engine seized completely just after landing. More seriously, on 14 May the squadron's sixth Sabre, XD780, was lost. Landing in rain off a ground-controlled

With a Lincoln bomber as their backdrop, this group of 92 and 66 Sqn Sabres were visiting Geilenkirchen in Germany during September 1955 on a night-reinforcement exercise. XD724/Y nearest the camera still survives in Honduras. (*Robin Brown*)

approach, Fg Off D. Shelton-Smith stalled his aircraft, which dropped a wing and crashed heavily to the ground. Though uninjured, Shelton-Smith was given a dual check with further observed landings before being allowed back to full flight status.

In addition to these flying incidents, the maintenance side was also busy. One fault that cropped up involved faulty or misreading fuel-contents gauges. To rectify the snag, the wing leading edge had to be removed; seven aircraft were affected in May alone. The Canadair representative later claimed to have a short cut that got around the need to remove leading edges, but months later he had still to divulge what it was. Five engine changes were required during May, some of which were unavoidable; as a precaution crews were given advice on the correct handling of the J47 so as to reduce the instances of engine failure. On the 'unavoidable' side, XD769/J, which had rolled out of minor servicing on 9 May, had flown just less than four more hours by the end of the month due to heavy oil consumption; it had already had one engine change for this problem and was awaiting another. A further drain on manpower was Servicing Instruction (SI) 61A, which was introduced during the month and involved rerouting oxygen hoses on all aircraft. This alone accounted for 10 man-hours per Sabre. Compounding the problems, a shortage of drop tanks meant that three Sabres were not fully equipped.

By the end of May 1955, the squadron had just fourteen Sabres available to fly. Of the others, two had been Cat. 4 since 5 April (XD710) and 14 May (XD780), and two further aircraft were Cat. 3. XB677 and XB837 had been on minor servicing for more than two weeks, and a further pair had just begun servicing. Both Cat. 4 aircraft would later be classed as write-offs, but until that happened no replacement aircraft could be assigned to take their place.

On Tuesday 14 June, the annual AOC's inspection of Linton was taken by AVM W.G. Cheshire, CB, CBE, AOC of 13 Gp. The inspection successfully completed, 92 Sqn put up a twelve-ship formation which performed a fly-past over the station. Two Sabres were later flown up to Leuchars in Scotland to take part in a Royal Observer Corps display on 20 June. Fg Off Cartwright performed an individual aerobatics display there while Fg Off Dodds took his Sabre across the airfield on a number of high- and low-speed runs.

Towards the end of June, Exercise Fabulous had the squadron again launching intercept

XB928/O of 112 Sqn. This aircraft later served with the Yugoslav Air Force as 11104. (*Paul Mansfield*)

Pictured at the time of 234 Sqn's conversion to Hunters, XB752/W awaits one of its final sorties. (*Robin Brown*)

Now fully restored, XB812/U is displayed at the RAF Museum, Hendon in 93 Sqn colours. Restoration was accurate except for the '6–3' wing seen here, which was not present when the aircraft was in RAF service. (*author*)

An element of 112 Sqn Sabres *c.* 1955. The squadron had two distinct iterations of the 'sharkmouth' colour scheme, this being the second, with dark-blue mouth and red outlines. (*Ted Roberts*)

Typical early 3 Sqn markings are worn by XB609/H. Just visible is the squadron's mid-green-painted intake colouration. (*Derek Rumble*)

XB772/P in the dispersal at Geilenkirchen during Exercise Carte Blanche, June 1955. The aircraft wore short-lived pale-yellow bands around the fuselage for the exercise. (*Paul Mansfield*)

A rare shot of 112 Sqn's Exercise Carte Blanche markings, June 1955. This aircraft is XB950/S, which was lost in a fatal crash just a week after this photo was taken. (*Paul Mansfield*)

With newly arrived Hunter XF945 at the rear, XB872/R enjoys its last few days on 234 Sqn. The aircraft has the code letter 'R' in 'B' Flight blue colour on the nose door. (*Robin Brown*)

When 234 Sqn returned from an exchange visit with 494th Fighter Bomber Sqn, USAF in March 1956, XB891 had gained a unique tail colour scheme, a gift from the squadron's American hosts. The 494 FBS 'cougar' was painted on both sides of the fin against a red band. In this May 1956 photo the aircraft (leading the three-ship formation) also sports a natural metal canopy rail. (*Robin Brown*)

XB595/W of 26 Sqn. Barely visible is the thin red outlining to the fuselage code letter. (*via Mike Fox*)

Sabres of 3 Sqn lined up at Geilenkirchen in early 1954 with Trevor Skellington on the left. He is wearing a black-dyed flying suit – a trademark of 3 Sqn. (*Derek Rumble via Alan East*)

Flg Off Clive Haggett proudly poses with his Sabre, XB792/X. The aircraft bore Haggett's name on its canopy rail. (*Robin Brown*)

This is one of 229 OCU's Sabres from 'C' Flight, wearing red trim on its intake and wingtips. XB813/M served with the unit from 29 June 1954 to 30 June 1955. (*author's collection*)

XB672/G, a 3 Sqn 'A' Flight aircraft, has a red nose-wheel door and tail letter in this shot, along with the squadron's green intake band. (*Derek Rumble*)

Sabres from 112 Squadron (foreground) and 130 Squadron share the ramp at Sylt, July 1954. XB939 in the foreground bears the inscription 'STI 14' on its fin cap, indicating that this Special Technical Instruction has been completed. XB928/G to the rear is a 130 Squadron 'A' Flight machine, as indicated by the red disc backing the individual tail-code letter. (*Snowden LeBreton*)

67 Squadron's 'A' Flight aircraft wore a red tail band outlined in yellow, seen here on XB692/D. Note that this machine also has a white-bordered red code letter on the nose gear door. (*John Perrott*)

A vic of 92 Sqn Sabres head out to the North Sea early in 1956. The aircraft bear a mix of 2 TAF and Fighter Command colours. (*Bruce Robertson*)

missions against high-flying intruders. Taking off for one of these sorties on 24 June, Fg Off W.D. Cartwright's Sabre failed to get airborne from Linton's runway 28 and overshot into a field. Cartwright escaped injury, aside from slight bruises, but his aircraft, XB677/H, was a write-off. XB677 was one of a number of 2 TAF Sabres assigned into 92 Sqn. They retained the basic 2 TAF colour scheme of cerulean blue undersides and a higher fuselage camouflage-demarcation line, but often flew with silver 'Fighter Command' drop tanks. 'Lefty' Wright recalls the incident: 'When there was a fresh west or north-westerly surface wind at Linton-on-Ouse, we would routinely reduce the crosswind component by using runway 28 (circa 1,460yd). Soon after our Sabres' wings were modified from slatted to 'hard edge', one of the pilots lugged it off a bit too soon and was stuck at about 10–15ft in an attitude that did not permit acceleration. The cornfield at the end of Linton's runway 28 was on very slightly rising ground, but not quite slightly enough.'

Cartwright's accident meant that the squadron was missing a further aircraft, though this was thankfully only a short-term problem. On 25 July two further XB-serialled 2 TAF Sabres, XB982 and XB998, were assigned to 92 Sqn from 33 MU at Lyneham. Both were among those fitted with '6–3' wings at Canadair prior to delivery to the RAF. Meanwhile a further Sabre had been temporarily lost to the squadron in June when XD779 was handed over to a civilian working party for a mainplane change.

Six aircraft deployed to Oldenburg in Germany on 19 July on the squadron's first night-reinforcement exercise. Valuable lessons in night-time long-range navigation were learned, and the formation also acted as targets for a PI exercise on their return. But there were inevitably incidents during the month as well. One pilot managed to run out of fuel but performed a successful forced landing at Carnaby, while another abandoned a night take-off after swinging off the runway centreline and bursting both tyres. Damage in both cases was minimal.

On the servicing side, things were beginning to improve, though radio problems were now also beginning to surface. No less than three aircraft had what were deemed to be 'untraceable' radio problems, and one particular machine had flown only 18 hours during the previous couple of months because of this. However, changes were afoot which fortunately would assist the maintenance crews. Early in the month Sqn Ldr Freer and Flt Lt Woods visited Duxford to study the 'third flight' scheme in operation. This system, also adopted by 66 Sqn, involved forming a third flight on the squadron to pool maintenance personnel and hopefully increase productivity. One change meant that the third flight would supply a certain amount of aircraft to each of the 'flying' flights and cease work at 1700 hr each day. Providing the commitment was met, this meant fixed working hours and increased morale all round. Fortunately, the system worked and serviceability – subject to spares supply – improved. Flt Lt Woods took over the maintenance personnel as OC 'C' Flight, while the two 'flying' flights, 'A' and 'B', were commanded by Flt Lt Foster and Flt Lt Arnott, respectively.

August 1955 was relatively quiet; two bomber-affiliation exercises were flown with the Canberras of 50 Sqn, plus the usual sector exercises. In air-to-air, Flt Lt V. Woods was highest scorer with 45 per cent and the squadron average was 15.1 per cent. A number of displays were flown, including one at Honiley by Fg Off K.W. Rooney and Fg Off R. Woodward, the former doing runs across the airfield and the latter an aerobatics sortie for the benefit of the ROC. Fg Off P.A. Robert took another Sabre to Chivenor on 21 August for an ROC display there.

Caught at the moment of lift-off from Linton, XD727/D is a '6–3'-winged aircraft, pinning the date to 1955 or early 1956. Prior to the advent of the modified wing, take-off would normally be performed with half flap selected; after '6–3' modification, full flap was mandatory for all take-offs. (*Bruce Robertson*)

There were only two notable incidents during the month, the first when a partial engine failure on approach to Linton caused a complete loss of electrical power; the pilot recovered safely. On another occasion, a Sabre had to be returned to second line for repair after a Houchin ground-power unit produced a reverse current and started a small fire in the aircraft.

One notable exercise was completed on 13 September when Sabres from 92 Sqn, reinforcing Eastern Sector, flew on a Canberra-intercept demonstration for Prime Minister Sir Anthony Eden. As well as this, another night-reinforcement exercise was launched, this time to Geilenkirchen in Germany.

Battle of Britain Day, 1955 saw a great deal of effort put in by the squadron: aside from an eleven-aircraft fly-past on 17 September, five individual aerobatic displays were provided by the squadron's Sabres. These were at Church Fenton (Flt Lt Woods), Binbrook (Fg Off Woodward), Turnhouse (Fg Off Hallam), Horsham St Faith (Fg Off Wright) and Dyce (Flt Sgt Freeman).

However, the main focus of September was on the annual UK air-defence exercise, 'Beware'. On 15 August, Sqn Ldr Freer and Flt Lt Woods accompanied the Station Commander and OC Flying to Driffield with the aim of discussing the squadron's forthcoming ten-day detachment to the base for the period of Exercise Beware. On 21 September eighteen Sabres from 92 Sqn flew over, ground convoys concurrently making their way to Driffield by road. Once at the temporary base, drop tanks were removed and the aircraft flew 'clean' throughout the exercise.

Beware actually started on 24 September and comprised three phases, each lasting roughly two days, with a break of two days in between. The squadron completed 138 sorties on the whole exercise, scrambling to intercept mainly RAF aircraft trying to carry out dummy raids against the UK; intercepts were usually made above 48,000ft, at the limits of Sabre performance. Seventy-eight claims were made, comparing favourably with 66 Sqn, which remained at Linton for the exercise and launched 174 sorties to claim 80 'kills'. Serviceability throughout had been exemplary, reaching 90 per cent on most days. Exercise Beware ended on 2 October, and after breaking camp the squadron returned to Linton two days later, performing fly-pasts over both airfields.

In October the squadron took a detachment of Sabres to Church Fenton and completed a number of missions from there. Further small exercises, such as 'Phoenix' against Canberra bombers, were judged to be of good value in perfecting interception techniques. A number of exercises were flown against the increasingly common Hunters during November, and a further eleven sorties were again logged with DFLS Hunters in the following month. Only one successful intercept was logged on the latter occasion. A 13 Gp interception trial during November had also seen the squadron acting as targets for a change, on this occasion involving a landing at Kinloss in Scotland.

At the end of 1955 the emphasis shifted to completion of operational turnarounds, where aircraft would carry out a series of gunnery missions before returning to base to be rearmed and sent aloft again. In the last week of December this system was practised with four Sabres, though the sorties had to be flown at low level because of poor weather. One aircraft went unserviceable after the first mission, somewhat limiting the exercise. Further bomber-affiliation exercises were also flown against the Canberras of 50 Sqn, and on one occasion in November one of the Canberras landed at Linton and took one of the flight commanders aloft to see the bomber's view of an intercept.

Rounding the year off nicely, air-to-air averages continued to improve, from 19.2 per cent in November to 22.5 per cent in December. Flt Lt M.M. Foster, OC 'A' Flight, ended the year as best shot, with 69.8 per cent, setting a new squadron record in the process. By way of comparison, the 2 TAF Sabre squadrons at this time were struggling to achieve even 10 per cent averages on a regular basis.

Severe weather in the New Year did not halt proceedings entirely; an operational turnaround with four Sabres kept both aircrew and armourers on their toes, and in January alone, forty-six battle-flight sorties were flown. Night-flying missions were also completed, the squadron ending the month with 349.35 hours flown against a target of 480 hours. Despite this less-than-perfect result, serviceability problems on the aircraft were finally being reined in, and rose to a 74 per cent in-commission rate for the nineteen aircraft available. One other Sabre was grounded for spares and another with Cat. 3 damage. At this point the squadron had the full establishment of twenty-four pilots.

92 Sqn's formation sortie of 19 April 1956. The lead aircraft, XD769/J, was flown by Flt Lt V. Woods, with Flt Lt D.A. Arnott (XD719/T) on the right wing, Flt Lt A.W.A. Wright (XB694/N) on the left wing and Flt Lt D.N. Yates (XB837/K) in the slot. Despite a number of contrary references, this did not constitute an aerobatic team – the sortie was a 'one-off' for photographer Mike Chase. (*A.W.A. Wright*)

Aside from the normal routine, 92 Sqn continued to act as an operational conversion unit on an ad-hoc basis. During January, Wg Cdr B.R. Morrison, DFC was converted onto the Sabre prior to taking up a USAF exchange posting, and the following month Flt Lt F.E. Debenham from 12 JSTU at Hatfield completed Sabre training prior to exchange with the Australians. As an aside, Debenham went on to fly the Commonwealth Avon-engined Sabre at Woomera on Blue Jay (Firestreak) missile trials. Sqn Ldr H.S. Horth of Northern Sector also converted onto the Sabre in February.

Though further sector intercepts were flown in February, along with sixteen sorties on a V-bomber-intercept trial, Sabre flying was gradually reduced from this point on. Just over 377 hours day and 5 hours night were flown in March. Ground lectures detailing the Hunter's flying characteristics then began in earnest, as well as talks on the aircraft's systems and its Avon engine. It had by now been agreed that 92 Sqn (and its neighbour, 66 Sqn) would convert onto a mix of Hunter F. 4s and Meteor F. 8s, since sufficient Hunters would not be available initially to equip the squadrons fully. This was an unpopular and retrograde step which highlighted the premature withdrawal of the Sabres. However, the air and ground crews got stuck in, and Meteor conversion began in March.

The Sabres began to be ferried out for overhaul in April 1956 and concurrently Sqn Ldr Freer and the two flight commanders began the squadron's Hunter pilot conversion. Though the official retirement date for the Sabres was set at 15 April, the squadron continued operating the type until 20 April for one special reason.

These are the 92 Sqn pilots that took part in a final formation photographic mission on 19 April 1956, posing with their squadron commander. Back row L–R: Flt Lt Derek Yates, Flt Lt Vic Woods (OC 'A' Flt), Sqn Ldr R.W.G. Freer, Flt Lt A.W.A. Wright, Flt Lt Don Arnott (OC 'B' Flt). At the front is Fg Off Bob Woodward, who piloted a Meteor NF. 14 borrowed from 264 Sqn to fly the photographer alongside the formation. The aircraft at the rear is XB694/N, which carried the name 'Sgt S.J. Adams' on the canopy rail. (*A.W.A. Wright*)

With less than ten Sabres remaining with 92 Sqn, a four-ship formation was put up from Linton-on-Ouse on 19 April 1956 so that Air Ministry photographer Mike Chase could capture the last Fighter Command Sabres on film. Chase flew alongside the formation in a Meteor NF. 14 piloted by Fg Off R.P.V. Woodward while the Sabres put together some basic manoeuvres for the photographer. The four Sabres were flown by Flt Lt V. Woods (lead – XD769/J), Flt Lt D.A. Arnott (right wing – XD719/T), Flt Lt A.W.A. 'Lefty' Wright (left wing – XB694/N), and Flt Lt D.N. Yates (slot – XB837/K).

By the end of April, thirteen Sabres had been ferried out, leaving just seven at Linton, including one final machine that was being fixed by Aircraft Servicing Squadron. Almost 270 hours had been flown on the Sabre that month, a figure that dropped to less than ten in May, when just eight sorties were flown. Of the final four Sabres, XD756 was ferried to Aviation Traders at Stansted on 24 May, with XB757 and XD727 going to Westland at Yeovil on the following day. XD734 was the last Sabre at Linton and was finally flown out for overhaul with Airwork on 11 June 1956.

Aircraft Assigned

XB677/H, XB694/N+, XB757/R, XB837/K+, XB982/B*, XB998/H*, XD709/Z+, XD713, XD714, XD717, XD719/T+, XD723, XD724/Y, XD726, XD727/D+, XD728, XD732, XD733, XD734, XD736, XD754, XD756, XD759, XD760, XD764/X, XD766, XD767, XD769/J+, XD771, XD779.

* = '6–3'-winged from manufacture.
+ = '6–3' wing conversion.

Markings – 92 Sqn

Squadron markings consisted of red and yellow-checked bars either side of the fuselage roundel. The individual code letter was painted in yellow on the tail fin, with a thin red outline.

The only deviation to this scheme was in the case of CO Sqn Ldr Rennie Turner, whose personal mount had three rows of red and yellow checks applied to the intake ring.

Squadron Motto

Aut pugna aut morere (Either fight or die).

CHAPTER TWELVE

93 SQUADRON

Based at Jever under 122 Wing and operating alongside 4 Sqn, 93 Sqn was commanded by Sqn Ldr R.N.G Allen and flying Vampires by early 1954. The squadron, which would be the last unit in 2 TAG to convert to the Sabre, had gained quite a reputation for excellence in gunnery and had won the prestigious Duncan Trophy during its January 1954 Sylt detachment. Runway resurfacing at Jever meant that 93 moved its Vampires to Ahlhorn on 14 March that year, the unit also ferrying aircraft for 4 Sqn, which had lost a number of pilots to Sabre conversion at this time. Concurrent with the move from Jever, Flt Lt H. Iles and four other pilots were transferred to Wildenrath to begin their Sabre course with SCU. They returned to the squadron on 25 March.

The squadron's first Sabre, XB856, was received at Ahlhorn on 25 March 1954, though all of the subsequent deliveries would be made to Jever, once the squadron returned there on 5 April. In the meantime, the squadron began transferring its Vampires to other units, three being flown to Wunstorf on 30 March for transfer to 2 Sqn. Despite this, there were still fifteen Vampires to be ferried back to Jever in April. XB856, still the only Sabre on the squadron at this time, was left at Ahlhorn for the 122 Wing Leader, Wg Cdr West, to fly back.

By the end of the month, 93 Sqn had flown 30 hours and 10 minutes on Sabres, though all of these hours were accrued by pilots under conversion at Wildenrath. Further Sabre deliveries continued with XB576, XB629 and XB746, which were transferred from 112 Sqn on 8 April. By the end of the month, thirteen Sabres were on strength, though the squadron did not have a full complement of aircraft until June.

Sqn Ldr Allen took the SCU course during April 1954, by which time most of the squadron pilots had converted onto the Sabre. This process was completed in May 1954, just before SCU closed for business. One of the last pilots to complete the SCU course was P Off Ritchie; he finished at Wildenrath on 26 May and brought XB802, an ex-112 Sqn aircraft, with him.

XB746/T-C leads a line-up of 93 Sqn Sabres. (*Eric Pigdon*)

Exercise Wild Goose, which started on 29 April, saw the squadron operating from the south-west dispersal. The exercise was designed to simulate operations from a deployed position and the squadron was required to repel ground attacks by 'raiders', many of whom were provided by the Special Air Service. Despite such distractions, 93 Sqn managed to fly just over 180 Sabre hours during the month.

By early May, as pilots became proficient on the Sabre, formation flights were undertaken, along with solo aerobatic sorties and cross-country missions. Barrage exercises also began to be launched; and, once sufficiently confident on the Sabre, the squadron was able to provide a seven-ship fly-past for the AOC's parade on Friday 2 July 1954.

Concerns had been expressed for some time that Jever's runway was too short for safe Sabre operations: indeed, when neighbouring 4 Sqn had received its first aircraft on 8 March, the ferry pilot had managed to run his Sabre into the overshoot. No damage was done on that occasion, but 93 Sqn was not so fortunate on 1 June. On returning from an afternoon pairs sortie, Fg Off Hannah burst a tyre on landing, which brought his Sabre to a sharp halt on the runway. Unfortunately, P Off Whitelaw was landing immediately behind, and the latter aircraft burst two tyres, causing the two Sabres to collide. Though Hannah and Whitelaw were uninjured, Jever's runway was blocked for two hours and the aircraft, XB583 and XB742, received Cat. 4 damage. They were returned to the UK for repair with Airwork. Neither saw any further RAF service.

The squadron commenced its air-to-ground programme in June, the first sorties flying on the range on the 15th. Night flying also began during the month, 11.35 hours going into the logbooks for June. Indeed, the squadron managed very well, despite having few aircraft serviceable during this period – only two Sabres were available on 23 June, for instance. Pilots were also involved in ferrying Sabres for the unit at this time: on 17 June Fg Off Sanderson was flown to Wildenrath in the station Prentice to pick up XB726. Fg Off Pigdon also went down to Wildenrath, this time as back-seater in the Meteor trainer to transfer XB874 to 93 Sqn on 22 June. Both of these Sabres were ex-Sabre Conversion Flight aircraft, transferred to the squadron when SCF (formerly SCU) was disbanded. At the same time, during periods of bad weather or poor serviceability the pilots banded together to apply the squadron markings to the aircraft. From 25 June, code letters and squadron badges were applied.

Battle flight commenced for the first time on Sabres on 8 July, with twenty sorties being

XB874/T-I (code 'I-T' on port side) in flight in 1954. It was unusual for the code letter 'I' to be used on squadron aircraft, due to its easy confusion with the figure '1'. (*Reg Bridgman*)

flown on that day alone. However, the squadron then stood down for four days while the 2 TAF Inter-Station Athletic Championships took place – Jever was placed seventh. Returning to work on 12 July, flying was immediately restricted so that aircraft could be prepared for the forthcoming Exercise Dividend.

Exercise Dividend involved most of the 2 TAF Sabre squadrons flying 'enemy' raids on the British mainland to test air defences. Though slated to start at 0300 hr on 17 July, the squadron's first day of sorties was cancelled due to bad weather. The poor conditions finally cleared in the afternoon of the following day, Sunday 18 July, when two four-ship Sabre formations finally got aloft and raided the UK. Fg Off Ken Senar's involvement in this raid was somewhat eventful. Briefed for an attack on the RAF station at Neatishead, Senar was flying XB701 when, over the North Sea, his aircraft suffered explosive decompression after the cabin seal blew. Senar was immediately in agony as his stomach swelled – the fact that he had been drinking Coke just prior to take-off did not help matters. Managing to put out a Pan call and alerting his number two, George Hickman, Senar diverted to West Raynham, shepherded by Hickman, who was making the necessary radio calls. Once on the ground, Senar saw a medical officer, who advised him not to fly again, but with fine weather across the Channel the temptation proved too much. With the aircraft refuelled and checked over (XB701 could now only be flown at low level), the pair taxied out for take-off. No doubt suffering from little-finger fatigue caused by keeping this digit firmly pressed on the control column-mounted nosewheel steering button, Senar applied full power to take off with the nose wheel slightly cocked. His aircraft then performed a perfect 360-degree ground loop and took off down the runway. The return trip was fortunately without drama, the airfield at Jever having stayed open for the two aircraft. Flying Wing then stood down for two days.

Though Dividend resumed on 21 July, there were no further sorties until the following day, when two raids of three aircraft each flew across the Channel. They were not intercepted. On 23 July there were thirteen sorties for the exercise, two raids setting off at 0430 hr and two more at 1300 hr. Sgt Richard Knight flew XB629 on both days, each raid lasting roughly 1 hour 25 minutes. Unfortunately, the weather then socked in and further sorties were cancelled, thus ending 93 Sqn's involvement in Exercise Dividend.

Up to this point, the aircraft had been flying with drop tanks fitted, but on 27 July 'A' Flight removed the drop tanks from its aircraft, enabling more sorties to be flown along with quicker turnarounds on the ground.

From the second week in August, the accent on flying changed to include a good number of practice cine attacks in preparation for the forthcoming Sylt detachment. Throughout this period, new pilots were being posted into the squadron, but things had changed since the early days of Sabre operations. With the winding down of SCF operations (though 229 OCU was still in existence), much of the conversion task devolved to the squadrons. Most pilots were given a check flight in the Meteor before swotting up on the Sabre Pilot's Notes and being let loose in the beast for the first time. Fg Off Hampton, an Australian officer on a two-year RAF exchange, had arrived early in August, and his first solo, as with many, required a team effort. As Jever's runway was seen to be too short for completing a first solo on the Sabre, on 13 August Sgt Richard Knight flew XB812 (the RAF Museum Sabre) over to Wildenrath so that the longer runway there could be used. Fg Off Hampton was then ferried over in the Vampire T. 11 by Flt Lt Colvin, where he performed his solo before returning in the Vampire. Richard Knight ferried XB812 back

XB712 shows off the squadron's new markings, August 1954. (*via Mike Fox*)

to base, the whole exercise being completed at 1730 hr. A convoluted arrangement, but far safer in the long run.

The squadron was chosen to perform an air-to-ground demonstration at Fassberg on 2 September, and in preparation the five pilots selected (four, plus one reserve) began practice missions on the Meppen range on 30 August. Richard Knight was one of this team flying two sorties to Meppen in XB891 on the first day as well as a dummy attack at Fassberg. The team flew into Fassberg on 31 August to continue training. One other team member was Don Exley, who recalls: 'I flew one of four aircraft that performed a notable occurrence, which was a firing demonstration, air-to-ground, for the IDC at a range near Fassberg, all four Sabres firing all six guns at one time – a very rare occurrence. Normally, guns were only fired in pairs. I still have a copy of the letter sent from AVM J.R. Hallings-Pott at 2 ATAF to Station Commander Gp Capt T.O. Prickett expressing thanks, appreciation and congratulations on what was a jolly good show.'

It is worth noting that Richard Knight again flew XB812, the RAF Museum machine, on the 2 September demonstration at Fassberg. Unfortunately, the return to base from Fassberg was less than perfect. Don Exley's aircraft was unserviceable on start, and Richard Knight returned to base and picked up Sgt O'Neil in the Vampire before flying back to Fassberg; O'Neil decided that an engine change was required on Exley's stricken Sabre. But the fun was not over. On return to Jever, the Vampire's starboard main wheel would not extend and, despite a number of attempts to persuade it down, Richard Knight was forced to land XD535 on the crash strip. There were no injuries.

A brief involvement in Exercise Lucifer began on 1 September, with seven raids comprising twenty-two individual sorties. Only two of the raids were not intercepted. The exercise involved the squadron performing low-level cross-country missions, acting as 'enemy' raiders on key targets. The Sabres flew at reduced speeds and were not allowed to take evasive action. Thus it was not unexpected that most of the raids were intercepted; crews felt the exercise to be unrealistic and of little benefit. With Exercise Lucifer completed, all aircraft were then put on primary inspections, preparing for the Sylt deployment. On 3 September Fg Off Bell brought a Sabre back from repair at Oldenburg, but locked his brakes on landing and burst both tyres. Fortunately, there was no other damage to the aircraft, believed to be XB871.

Bad weather subsequently prevented a great deal of flying prior to Sylt, and thus on 16 September lorries were loaded while aircraft servicing continued. The advance party under Fg Off Ramsay left the same day, with the rail party following two days later. It had been intended to fly to Sylt on 20 September in a 28-ship wing formation, but with adverse weather forecast, it was thought prudent instead to launch in sections of four. Even this scheme was thwarted, however, as a 40kt crosswind at Sylt meant that only five Sabres got there. The conditions were still marginal on the following day, but the rest of the wing still managed to get in safely. Cine missions began immediately and, despite thunderstorms on 22 September, 'A' Flight managed to start its gunnery programme, again only using cine film.

While at Sylt, the squadron gained a new CO, Sqn Ldr Desmond Browne taking over on 22 September; he had been promoted into the post, having previously served as a flight commander on 20 Sqn. He immediately made his presence felt, completing the first live-firing sortie on the day he took over, and setting a credible target of 12.1 per cent. Sqn Ldr Allen meanwhile had been posted to Fassberg and promoted into the Wing Commander Flying slot.

Further poor weather at Sylt meant that only cine missions could be flown up to 27 September, when, with only four gunsights fully serviceable, firing finally began. By the end of the detachment, the squadron average had risen to 4.7 per cent and the CO's score had not been beaten. Unfortunately, there were a number of incidents at Sylt which took the edge off things slightly. On 29 September, Fg Off Ken Senar's aircraft ended up in the overshoot after experiencing an engine problem. Flying XB802, Senar had found that his throttle would not retard below 60 per cent on the landing run but had committed himself to carry on and land. Somehow he managed to radio the tower of his predicament, at the same time cutting his fuel and starting to brake heavily. Inevitably, at higher than normal landing speed, his aircraft ran off the end of the recently extended runway. The recent building activity also meant that the overshoot area was a quagmire, and the Sabre immediately sank up to the top of its wheels in the mire. Senar jumped out and immediately found himself up to his calves in the same muddy swamp. At this point things got comical: first the fire crew Land Rover arrived and got stuck, followed in quick succession by the fire engine and Sylt's Wing Commander Flying. This bizarre scene was too much for Senar, who collapsed in fits of laughter – a performance that did not impress those at the scene who presumed that Sylt's now blocked runway was due to pilot error. Fortunately for the pilot, it was soon discovered that the Sabre's fuel regulator had been faulty. XB802 was beyond the help of mechanical recovery,

Close-up of the placement of the squadron's escarbuncle (shield strengthener) design on the tail of XB913. The disc was dark blue with yellow details. (via Mike Fox)

and so, using wooden planks, it was manhandled back onto the runway by brute force alone. Ken Senar then set about cleaning the detritus from his machine.

Flying at Sylt had switched to the short runway on 7 October because of the wind direction, and on the following day Fg Off Page had a rear fire-warning light illuminate in flight. He made an emergency landing at Sylt, where it was found that his Sabre, XB891, had a number of turbine blades missing. Fg Off Pigdon was less fortunate on 12 October: he fell from his Sabre as he was getting out and broke his arm. Thus, it was with some relief that the detachment ended without anyone else getting hurt.

The number of landing incidents at Jever in the meantime had highlighted the runway problems there, and as a result 93 Sqn was temporarily detached to Wunstorf while runway lengthening at Jever was completed. While the squadron was away, the runway was lengthened by 600yd and again resurfaced.

Fg Off Ritchie left Sylt for Wunstorf with a small advance party on 14 October. A proposed double-rearm practice at Sylt for the following day was cancelled due to poor weather conditions, and the squadron commenced packing. The main party of the squadron moved from Sylt to Wunstorf on 16 October, a cold front at the latter preventing an aircraft move until the 19th; even then the move was delayed by a Venom with a burst tyre blocking the runway. Once at Wunstorf, most sorties for the rest of the month were devoted to battle formation, though the squadron did contribute eight Sabres to a twelve-ship wing fly-past on 23 October. A number of groundings then reduced flying: first an aileron artificial feel inspection on 28 October, and on 1 November an electrical problem. The latter meant that no aircraft were serviceable for five days. Just prior to grounding on 28 October, eight Sabres set off to bounce Fassberg during the station's Saturday morning parade. Ken Senar, flying XB824 as number four in one of the two sections, recalls that one section sped across the airfield at low level and high speed while the second formation dived from high level to lay sonic booms on the station at the same time. With their mission completed, they returned to base for a carpeting, but were suitably impressed by their deeds nonetheless.

An immaculate line-up of 93 Sqn Sabres, with Sqn Ldr Desmond Browne's aircraft XB893/A at the front. Visible below the windshield is the squadron commander's pennant; less visible is the yellow code letter 'A' on the fuselage. Note also the lack of drop tanks on these aircraft. (*Desmond Browne*)

In the final days of the period at Wunstorf, the squadron used the Ströhen range for air-to-ground firing. By 11 November flying was again being restricted to enable the majority of aircraft to be serviced by the ground crews in preparation for the move back to Jever. The rail party departed on 13 November and the aircraft flew across two days later.

Once back at Jever, flying commenced immediately and followed the normal routine of battle flights, formation practices and interceptions. However, as work was still underway in finishing off the runway, flying was at times restricted. Additionally, a number of problems intervened to reduce flying. On 17 November Fg Off Hampton had a flameout at 35,000ft during a battle-formation mission; he managed to glide down to 15,000ft and got a relight. Following his return to base, turbine-bearing failure was diagnosed. Two days after Flg Off Hampton's incident, an inspection grounded the whole squadron while rudder-trim brackets were inspected. A number were found to be damaged and, with replacements taking up to two weeks to be manufactured locally, some aircraft were grounded for that period awaiting spares. Finally, on 24 November two of the squadron's aircraft experienced birdstrikes on take-off; XB726/H sustained damage, and on 29 November Fg Off Hampton took it to Oldenburg for repair with 3 MRSU. The aircraft took three months to repair.

December was largely a washout, with low cloud, ice and fog restricting flying. For example, drop tanks were fitted on 15 December for an intended barrage exercise that was cancelled the following day because the whole of Germany and the Low Countries were blanketed in fog; on this and other occasions, lectures were given. Fg Off Senar suffered an engine flameout on 14 December while flying XB913 and, though the incident was reported in the squadron records as due to 'coarse throttle movement', there is more to it than that. Senar had been taking part in a high-level dogfight when his engine began to resonate, and with jet-pipe temperature rising he was forced to chop the throttle. Now flying at 40,000ft, his engine immediately flamed out and he was forced to look for an airfield within easy gliding range; Oldenburg seemed the nearest option. Having quickly issued a Mayday call, and with another Sabre shepherding him, Ken Senar found his canopy beginning to ice up as there was no heat coming from the engine-supplied conditioning system. Fervently scraping ice from the canopy while trying to navigate, maintain gliding speed and avoid exhausting his hydraulic pressure, Senar got down to about 16,000ft and commenced a relight, to no effect. Fortunately, dropping slightly lower he managed to get the engine going again, and returned to base rather than Oldenburg.

Aside from these flameouts, there was a further grounding on 22 December; on this occasion it was caused by an STI for wing-root cracking. By lunchtime on the same day, two Sabres were declared serviceable, four by the end of the day; but this was incidental, as gusty conditions with further low cloud prevented any flying. However, there were high spots. On 31 December, a particularly fine and unseasonable day, 58 sorties were flown for a total of 37.5 hours – a record for the squadron. This was a particularly notable achievement, considering that 93 Sqn had averaged less than 300 hours per month in the preceding quarter.

After New Year the squadron returned to work on 3 January 1955 and immediately started preparing for another Sylt deployment. Cine quarter attacks began immediately, and soon afterwards the squadron began towing flags for air-to-air sorties. The latter were initially ineffective, owing to the poor performance of the flags' radar reflectors. Air-to-ground missions were also completed on the Meppen range, though heavy snow for much of January and February meant that in-depth training was impossible. Following a particularly heavy fall, on 25 January the entire station was employed in clearing the runway. Their efforts were in vain, because, although in this instance no further snow fell, fog and icy conditions prevented flying from taking place. Nonetheless, the odd day was suitable for flying, and a few battle-formation and QGH sorties were completed. On 9 February, Fg Off Balfour ran off the runway during take-off; disengagement of the nose-wheel steering was the cause. The following day, despite snow on Jever's runway, a number of battle-flight Sabres were launched against Danish Meteor NF. 11s and the Sabres of Oldenburg's battle flight. The wintry conditions also brought another problem: at the end of February a number of aircraft were placed unserviceable because of excessive loads on the accelerometer (g-meter). Following investigation, it was decided that these spurious readings were caused by the aircraft taxiing over the bumpy, ice-strewn taxiways and runways. They were all returned immediately to service. These problems conspired to have a serious effect on the monthly statistics: 208 hours were flown in January and just 165 in February, when only six full days were available for flying.

Thankfully, March proved far less of a problem, though the squadron was informed of a reduction in its establishment. Anticipating conversion to the Hunter aircraft, the squadron would drop from a twenty-two-aircraft strength to just fourteen. Concurrently, some personnel would also be posted away to reflect the new, reduced size of the unit. These changes would take effect over the coming months, though for now no aircraft would be lost. However, from the beginning of March, battle flight operated with just two Sabres, halving the previous commitment in this area. From 1 March, flying was again restricted because of the forthcoming Sylt deployment, though six Sabres were scrambled to intercept a formation of DFLS Hunters incoming from the UK. The interception was aborted because of poor information concerning the Hunter formation's arrival. This DFLS formation subsequently landed at Jever, and on 2 March OC DFLS gave a talk on the new aircraft. Four Sabres then took off to dogfight with a quartet of Hunters, the mêlée beginning at 45,000ft and spiralling down to 20,000ft. Sabre crews discovered that, in spite of the Hunter's superior acceleration, its poor control system – particularly the lack of an 'all-flying' tail on the early marks – was a handicap in high-speed manoeuvring.

Snowfalls in early March grounded the aircraft, but helped the ground crew to get on top of the maintenance task. Guns were harmonised, and on 7 March Sqn Ldr Browne briefed his pilots on the Sylt detachment. Fg Off Revnell left for Sylt the same day in charge of the advance party. The train for the main rail party was loaded on 8 March, and departed the following morning. By 2200 hr on the 9th the ground crew were in place at Sylt waiting for the Sabres to arrive. Fortunately the weather held, and on 10 March, fourteen Sabres flew up to Sylt in squadron formation.

In spite of fog on the range on 11 March, 93 Sqn immediately began live-firing missions, sorties being flown on the flag in pairs. The squadron average rose steadily during this period, from 6.9 per cent after a week of firing to 8.2 per cent at the end of the deployment. Aside from snow and ice on this deployment, the squadron also had to contend with gunsight and radar problems, with radar often giving incorrect ranges. Many target flags also fell off; of these, the flags towed by Sabres were thought detach themselves when the cable was worn away by the aircraft's jet efflux. A change to wing-mounted towing points was suggested but not acted upon. The Sylt detachment ended on 5 April, and personnel spent the day cleaning the aircraft in preparation for a return to Jever. Fg Off

MacKnish and the advance party set off the same day, and both road and air parties were back at base by 7 April. The squadron had flown 231 firing sorties at Sylt (averaging 12 per pilot) and had expended 53,805 rounds.

Returning to work after the Easter grant, serviceability was at a high. On 15 April a new squadron record was set of 47 flying hours during one day, and the continued good serviceability meant that pairs sorties could be launched throughout the day at 20 to 30-minute intervals. A number of 'ceremonial' duties followed: the squadron took part in a sixteen-ship wing formation that flew over Ahlhorn and Oldenburg before returning to repeat the feat at Jever on 16 April; two days later, four Sabres flew into the Dutch base at Soesterberg for a short stay, repaying a number of visits by Dutch Air Force aircraft to Jever.

The long-awaited reduction in aircraft strength began on 21 April when XB697, XB829 and XB856 were flown back to the UK, resulting in an eighteen-aircraft squadron strength. Fourteen airmen were also posted out, but pilot strength remained at twenty-seven for the time being. Just after the departure of these aircraft and personnel, on 26 April the squadron stood by for its first involvement in Exercise Sky High. Only one section of four was scrambled that afternoon; they took 90 seconds to get airborne, by which time the raid was almost over, and thus made no intercepts. GCI had in any case had trouble picking up the raiders, which were flying as high as 45,000ft. A further section was scrambled on the exercise during 29 April, again with no success. However, 93 Sqn ended the month with 464.35 hours in the logbooks, and the large number of missions flown without drop tanks produced 653 sorties – a record for the squadron since it had re-formed in 1950. Squadron commander Desmond Browne's formation of an aerobatic team had resulted in special permission being given to the squadron to fly without drop tanks. This had a rather nice knock-on effect during exercises, the squadron's Sabres gaining a significant performance advantage over those fitted with external tanks. The range limitations without drop tanks were not that noticeable, as Desmond Browne remembers: 'The drop tanks, unless jettisoned when empty, did little to extend the Sabre's radius of action. The tanks slowed the rate of climb, reduced height and manoeuvrability, and limited g allowed to be pulled. On inter-command exercises, the Sabre being used as 'sim bombs' [simulated bombers] against UK Fighter Command, 93 Sqn could still reach the UK coast and return to base with the same fuel reserves as squadrons equipped with drop tanks.'

A further Sylt detachment in May meant that flying in the early part of the month was devoted to flag-towing and cine quarter attacks. The usual gun harmonisation and concentration on gunsight serviceability took up most of the time for the ground crews. Fg Off Sanderson set off for Sylt with the advance party on 13 May, followed by the main party two days later. The ten Sabres flew to Sylt on 16 May, overflying departure and arrival fields in formation. Firing began immediately, though the presence of unauthorised boats on the sea beneath the air ranges meant that many sorties were cancelled in the first few days. Further fishing boats on the range precluded flying on the Amrum high range on 23 May, and flying switched to the South range just in time to meet an incoming warm front. Boats were in the vicinity the following day and stymied further missions.

Trials with a new radar-reflective flag began on 25 May. This new version had metallic spinners attached to it that increased the flag's radar profile. Though initial flights consisted of cine attacks, results were found to be better than with the usual target flag.

By 26 May, the daily average stood at 10.5 per cent on the low range (10,000ft) and 10.6 per cent high. At this point it was decided to extend the detachment to last for seven weeks, two weeks being added to cover the period of Exercise Carte Blanche. A further five days were later added, which meant that the squadron would remain at Sylt until the early part of July 1955. Therefore, a number of changes took effect during the detachment period, making life a little more difficult. The final changes to reach the fourteen-aircraft establishment took place in June, and saw five further Sabres assigned from the unit. XB576, XB812 and XB833 went to 33 MU at Lyneham for storage while XB712 and XB802 were ferried out to 5 MU at Kemble. Three pilots, Fg Offs Harper, MacKnish and Mitchell also departed, though their move was more straightforward: all moved over to the target-towing flight at Sylt.

The loss of so many aircraft and personnel inevitably left the squadron far less flexible than it had been, and serviceability problems invariably had a greater effect than when twenty-two Sabres had been available. However, firing continued at Sylt and, because of the prolonged time available on the range, averages rose. On 7 June firing switched to the low range and, firing at 10,000ft, pilots found that their aircraft were easier to control in the thicker air; tracking of the target improved and scores followed. The daily average immediately rose to 16.9 per cent, with Sqn Ldr Browne managing a 45 per cent score. Within a week the squadron was able to boast eleven pilots easily exceeding the 20 per cent mark. Further changes were made on 16 June, with a switch to firing on a new range area 20,000ft above the sea, 45 miles out from Sylt. On the following day it had been proposed to send off two sections to fire on glider targets but, after the first section had fired, one target was recovered with fifty-odd holes in it, while the second machine had disintegrated on take-off.

Having been at Sylt for such a long time, by mid-June a break from gunnery was taken and more routine training missions began to be flown. On 18 June, battle formations and aerobatics were practised, and the free time also allowed the squadron's aerobatic team to polish its routine. The customary double-rearm mission was performed on 28 June, with four Sabres scrambling to fire all six guns each at glider targets. Both of the gliders were shot down on the first mission, and turnarounds comprising a full rearm and refuel on each Sabre were then performed in less than 20 minutes, before the four Sabres took off again and fired their guns until they either stopped or ran out of ammunition. Fourteen gun stoppages were noted on this exercise. Concurrent with the rearm exercise, all firing stopped for the remainder of the detachment, the overall squadron average ending at 13.76 per cent. The number of effective firing sorties stood at 490, all using radar-ranging, and 91,186 rounds had been fired for the whole period, with 26 stoppages.

The air party flew back to Jever on 30 June, leaving one unserviceable Sabre at Sylt for repair. The final personnel left Sylt on 1 July, spending an enjoyable night stop at Uxbridge Barracks in Hamburg. Though the squadron had not taken part in Exercise Carte Blanche, they did take advantage of the stand-down associated with it and had a few days' well-earned rest.

Upon return to work on 5 July, talk immediately turned to the Hawker Hunter. It was initially planned to re-equip 93 Sqn with the new type by year's end (a plan that subsequently slipped), and lectures started on the Hunter's Avon engine. These talks were given by a Rolls-Royce representative. As if to press the point, battle flight intercepted two Hunters on 14 July, along with six Sabres, two Venoms and a B-45 Tornado. The normal flying programme continued in the meantime, though a more unusual mission on 19 July saw a section of four Sabres flying a low-level cross-country raid, which climaxed at the disused airfield at

Varrelbusch. And despite the final manpower reduction needed to bring it into line with a fourteen-Sabre squadron, morale in the unit remained high. For the fourth month, the squadron exceeded its flying hours target.

This positive mood ended on 3 August 1955 when Fg Off Ted Scott of 'A' Flight was killed in an accident on the Meppen ranges while flying XB548. According to Tony Kidd, a good friend of Scott's, the aircraft suffered an asymmetric slat configuration caused by one slat sticking in the retracted position, and the increased lift from the extended slat caused the aircraft to flip over and hit the ground. Ted Scott – who had been trialled as a spare for the aerobatic team – had been on the first detail of the day, and most of the remaining missions were cancelled. Indeed, in the following days the squadron spent much of its time preparing for Scott's funeral, which took place on 8 August at Hamburg cemetery.

A further Sabre was lost on 25 September when Don Exley landed XB824 hard at Jever, incurring damage assessed as Cat. 4; the aircraft suffered extensive damage to its underside, and one area of fuselage skin was cracked. It was returned to the UK for repair with Airwork.

Eric Pigdon gives an interesting postscript to Don Exley's accident:

> While holding off to land as number four in a stream landing at the end of one of our battle-flight commitments, I found my aircraft thrown up to the right and upside down. With no flying speed and no time to think I instinctively put on a boot full of left rudder and full left aileron; this immediately brought the aircraft the right way up, and it hit the runway hard on the main wheels and continue the landing roll.
>
> I reported a heavy landing, but on the aircraft being inspected it was found to be OK and serviceable for the next flight, which I flew 20 minutes later. On debriefing the incident, we put it down to wingtip vortices, a subject little known at the time, but much reported as a hazard when the [Boeing] 747 started flying. A few weeks later I was away from the station when Don Exley had a similar incident: he continued his flick roll in the same direction and made a heavy landing which I believe put landing legs up through the wings. I never heard of such an incident from any other Sabres; it may have occurred because of the landing separation, with little wind to disperse the wingtip swirl from the preceding three aircraft, which was magnified by our 'soft' [slatted] leading edges.

A number of night-flying missions were flown in the squadron's Vampire on 9 August, the first since March 1954. Four pilots were checked out on this occasion. Following Ted Scott's accident, firing on the Meppen range began again on 11 August, though the whole procedure had been changed in the hope of preventing further accidents. Safety height was raised to 525ft and the range controller now had control of the aircraft to decide when each would break off from its firing pass.

The next few weeks were busy for the squadron, beginning on 16 August when battle flight intercepted a Dakota, two Canberras and four F-84s. Further sorties in the next few days saw battle flight claim three Meteors and a Vampire. Returning from one of these sorties on 22 August, Fg Off Bell hit a bird in the Jever circuit; his Sabre, XB913, required a fin change. Drop tanks were fitted in time for Exercise Loco on 24 August, though the squadron's first input – acting as raiding 'bombers' – took place only two days later. These raids entailed formations of Sabres making attacks on Holland to test the country's defences. The first missions were launched at 0800 hr and six raids were completed during the first day; only one was intercepted and few 'enemy' aircraft were seen. Further raids were cancelled due to bad weather, and of those that were completed none were intercepted. To improve scramble times, on Saturday 3 September two Sabres were put on the flying programme to fly two sorties each.

In between flights, the pilots remained in their cockpits while other pilots pre-flighted and refuelled the aircraft. 'A' Flight achieved a touchdown-to-take-off time of 18 minutes, with 'B' Flight just one minute slower.

On 20 September, a day of good weather with 8/8 visibility, both flights managed to maintain four Sabres each, flying all day and achieving the squadron's best-ever daily figure of 45 hours and 5 minutes. Over the next few days, ground crews concentrated on completing primary servicing on the Sabres to get eight aircraft ready for a proposed exercise on 25 September. Unfortunately, the planned bomber 'stooge', which would have taken the squadron across the Channel almost to the English coast, was cancelled because of a warm front. Subsequent days were also cancelled for the same reason, but on 1 October the morning was spent preparing flight plans for another simulated bomber sortie towards England. Just after midday, a section of four plus two pairs departed Jever on this sortie, evading interception before a return to base. Earlier in the day, Fg Off Davis was lucky to escape with his life after he was forced to crash XB822 over 1,000yd in the undershoot because of an engine failure. The aircraft was a write-off.

Meanwhile, preparations for conversion to the Hunter had continued, and further lectures on the type were given during periods of poor weather. To begin the practical process, ground crews began familiarisation on 118 Sqn Hunters being serviced in Aircraft Servicing Flight from the end of September. During the following month, pilots began training with the 122 Wg Hunter squadrons at Jever, and by 29 October three of 93 Sqn's pilots had taken their first solos in the Hunter. Three further pilots soloed with 118 Sqn in early November, and one of the Hunter pilots was sent off in a Sabre by way of a thank-you. At this point the squadron had just ten Sabres on strength, and this proved to be a sufficiently serious problem that on many days in November only three of the type were serviceable at any one time. To aid the situation, two new Sabres, XB803 and XB886, were transferred from 20 Sqn at Oldenburg on 24 November.

Towards the end of November, a number of the more established figures on the squadron were posted out, part of a large changeover in personnel over the next few months. Concurrently, the first Hunter sorties were flown by the squadron, which had logged five hours on borrowed aircraft by the end of November, encompassing seven

Tony Kidd (left) with SAC Tony Parry (right) survey the wreckage of XB822 after Fg Off Davis force-landed short of the airfield on 1 October 1955. (*Tony Kidd*)

This is how the squadron pilots looked on 9 November 1955, the twenty-one personnel here reflecting the reduction in squadron strength from twenty-two to fourteen Sabres. Back row L–R: Fg Offs D. Exley, J.S.C. Davis, W.B.C. Ritchie, D. Chadwick, T. Balfour, W.R. Clayton-Jones. Centre row: Fg Offs P. Leigh-Lancaster, J.E. Pigdon, B.D.D. Dunbar, R. Garthwaite, Flt Sgt W.R. Shrubsole, Fg Offs G.E. Hickman, J.P. Busby, T. Page. Front row L–R: Fg Offs B.J. Revnell, B.A.E. Sanderson, Flt Lt A.J. Colvin ('B' Flt commander), Sqn Ldr D.F.M. Browne, Flt Lt R.W. Hayes ('A' Flight commander, Fg Offs W.R. Bell, G.J. Couch. Before the end of November, a further three officers – Fg Offs Bell, Couch and Revnell – had also been posted out without being replaced. (*Desmond Browne*)

sorties. This marked a change in emphasis for the squadron, which began reducing Sabre flying in order to prepare aircraft for ferrying out. And though squadron strength of the type was back up to a dozen by 30 November, seven of these were classed as 'AOG' (aircraft on ground) because of unserviceable exhaust cones. Unfortunately, fog, snow and ice curtailed many flying days in December, though an eight-Sabre formation managed to get aloft on 30 December. They flew past in two 'box' formations in line astern and diamond. Further flying on this day stopped when a Hunter ran off the runway. December ended with just 173 hours flown on the Sabre and 2.15 on the Hunter, the latter still flown on borrowed aircraft.

Hunter lectures continued into 1956, and took advantage of enforced quiet periods when flying was stopped by ice, snow and fog. And though battle flight commitments kept the Sabres to the fore, it would not be long before the axe finally fell. By 16 January, only three pilots had still to convert to the Hunter, and the squadron's first aircraft arrived that day. In return for their assistance in converting 93 Sqn to the Hunter, two pilots from neighbouring 98 Sqn completed Sabre solos on 17 January. Sabres then began to be ferried out and, by the end of the month, nine had departed while seven

Most photographs of 93 Sqn Sabres show the aircraft without drop tanks, dispensation having been given for the aircraft to fly 'clean' because of the squadron's aerobatic-team commitments. These aircraft have the definitive colour scheme, with squadron flashes either side of the fuselage, and (barely visible) yellow code letters on the fuselage mid-section. The squadron commander's aircraft, XB893/A, is visible at the far right, with XB701/V next up. (*Desmond Browne*)

Hunters had been assigned in. Sabre flying hours stood at 159 hours and 30 minutes day and 9 hours and 20 minutes night against just 41 hours and 40 minutes for the Hunter. In February the situation was reversed, with only 1 hour and 20 minutes Sabre time against 221 hours and 5 minutes on the Hunter.

The ferrying of Sabres to the UK meant that just eight of the type were on strength by 21 January. Just over a week later, the squadron had reduced to three Sabres, and these flew just five air-test sorties in March, until inevitably they too were grounded in preparation for ferrying out. XB701 was the unit's last Sabre, and on 22 March Fg Off Sanderson prepared to take it back to the UK. Cleared for a low-level beat-up of the airfield, Sanderson brought XB701 in at 500kt and then departed for Benson, leaving only a smoky trail to mark the passing of the Sabre era at Jever.

Aerobatic Team

When Sqn Ldr Desmond Browne (who had started 20 Sqn's Sabre aerobatic team) was posted in to command 93 Sqn in September 1954, he wasted no time in applying his aerobatic expertise to the new squadron. On 21 October, while the squadron was detached to Wunstorf, he led a three-ship formation on a practice sortie; a further mission was flown on 25 October, which marked Don Exley's first flight with the fledgling team. On the following day, another team sortie was performed, as Desmond Browne states:

> On the 26th, after high-level battle formation, we gave, at RAF Wunstorf's request, a demonstration of their first sonic booms in close succession by the four aircraft [as opposed to the three used previously]. As we pulled out of the dive (40,000 to 25,000ft), Air Traffic Control radioed that they had not heard any 'bangs'. With the radio still on, we then heard our own 'booms' arrive (four doubles), with the muttered comments of 'Oh my God!' from the tower! This was perhaps the first and only time RAF Wunstorf heard the 'booms', as it caused some consternation; it was also a unique experience to hear one's own sonic boom whilst in the air.

Further practice missions were flown early on in November, and with the move back to Jever, the team was allowed to 'boom' that station on the 10th, but was never allowed to repeat the feat. The squadron's four-man aerobatic team soon became known as the Golden Arrows, after the squadron marking which bordered the fuselage roundel. The initial team comprised: Sqn Ldr Desmond Browne (leader), Fg Off Dave S. Chadwick (number 2), Fg Off Don Exley (number three) and Fg Off W.E. 'Tinker' Bell (slot).

The team continued to gain experience, flying further sorties in between normal flying commitments. Though a number of practice sorties were completed at the end of November, one of the team's first full displays took place over Jever on 2 December 1954. It was on this day that the Station Commander, Gp Capt Tom O. Prickett authorised the team to continue as the station/122 Wg aerobatic team, with limits reduced to 250ft above ground level. On the same day, the team also practised over a local disused airfield. Don Exley remembers the first sortie as being a fairly simple affair: 'We had been practising at 5,000ft during November, and by December the boss decided (after 25 minutes practice away from base) that it was time to perform over the runway. That was the start of the official squadron team, although it was just a box-four formation loop, followed by a paired landing. The box landing was perfected at a later date.'

All displays were flown without drop tanks, special authority being given by 2 ATAF to this effect. No special colour scheme was used, and regular squadron aircraft were chosen on an ad-hoc basis.

The team amassed more practice missions in December 1954, starting 1955 with a sortie on 19 January. February was largely spent on the ground, as Jever's runway was covered in ice. A brief mission was flown on 4 March 1955 for a visiting Day Fighter Leaders Course, but further commitments to battle flight, plus live firing at Sylt and Meppen, meant that only three further sessions were chalked up in April. Many practice displays were then flown by the squadron team – culminating on 24 June in a display for the press – and air-to-air photographs were taken using the Vampire T. 11. Five more practice missions were flown in the early part of July 1955, and at the end of the day's flying on 19 July the team demonstrated a box take-off and a pairs break and landing, which was followed by a further display over the airfield on the following day.

On 28 July, 93 Sqn's team gave another performance over the airfield, which included a fine clover leaf; nevertheless, this display was considered to have been not quite up to previous standards, owing to gusty conditions. The routine was brought to a close with a box landing. Desmond Browne remembers the aerobatic routine as comprising 'a box take off, steep turn around the airfield, barrel roll along the runway axis, pull up into steep wingover and return for a loop in box formation, wingover and formation change for opposite direction roll, back again for a loop, tight steep turn, into downwind, reducing speed with dive brakes, wheels down, flap in stages, box landing. The spare aircraft, if available, often joined in on an initial loop if the display didn't include a take-off. A full display sequence normally took 15 minutes.'

The team did not fly again until 8 September when it again closed the day's flying. The aim by this point was for the team to practise twice a day in preparation for the AOC's inspection on 16 September. While these practice missions were being flown, the other squadron pilots would retire to the hangar tower, and note any faults. Their feedback after each sortie helped to polish the team's already professional display.

Following his inspection of the station on 16 September, AM Sir Harry Broadhurst viewed a line-up of squadron aircraft in the afternoon, and the day was brought to a close with a display by the Golden Arrows. At the end of its routine, the team's Sabres joined up with 122 Wg's Hunters for a formation fly-past. The four Sabres then broke off and completed what was described as the best box landing yet. At this point the squadron began to push for recognition as the official

93 Sqn's 1955 aerobatic team pose in front of Sabre 'T'. L–R: Fg Off Don Exley (no. 3), Sqn Ldr Desmond Browne (no. 1), Fg Off 'Chad' Chadwick (no. 2), Fg Off 'Tinker' Bell (no. 4). (*Desmond Browne*)

2 ATAF aerobatic team; this would not occur until the Sabres had left 93 Sqn, however. Other displays were flown during September for the Commander-in-Chief of the Italian Air Force and other VIPs.

Very little formation work was carried out for the remainder of 1955, other than a practice session in October and one on 1 November. For the latter, there were only three Sabres serviceable in the squadron, so the three-plane team performed in vic formation.

When Fg Off Bell was posted away from 93 Sqn on 21 November 1955, his position in the team was shared by Fg Off Brian 'Sandy' Sanderson and Fg Off Richard 'Clam' Clayton-Jones (also known as 'CJ'). In fact, it was usually Sanderson that flew in the slot position, but, as reserve, 'CJ' often flew displays when 'Sandy' was not available. Clayton-Jones was trialled by the team on 6 December, when he and Sqn Ldr Browne went aloft to perform two-ship formation aerobatics. The team retained these members for the remainder of the squadron's Sabre period. On 11 November, the team flew its fifth formal display. Desmond Browne recalls that the display was 'for HMS *Diamond*, steaming off the coast north of RAF Jever. We gave its ship's crew sonic booms (allowed over the sea), a formation aerobatic display and a fly-past in her honour.'

With the squadron concentrating on Hunter conversion at the end of 1955, very few further sorties were planned for the team while it retained Sabres. However, as a last hurrah, the Golden Arrows performed the final Sabre display on 16 January, finishing with a line-astern figure of eight. The team's time with the Sabre had been generally safe, according to Don Exley:

During my time with the team, we only experienced two notable incidents. The first, flying Sabres, occurred during a practice pull-up for a loop. As we reached vertical, both wingmen suddenly rolled outwards, and on investigation it was found that one wing slat [on each aircraft] had stuck in the closed position, while the other had extended normally. One can only imagine the devastation had we each flown the opposite aircraft. The second incident happened while performing a bad-weather show at Jever flying Hunters. The cloud base was 8/8 at 300ft [completely overcast], so all manoeuvres had to be horizontal, and we were in four aircraft line astern, but very close together, and pulling 4–5g to stay within the airfield boundary. Because the manoeuvre was going well, the boss decided to continue a second circuit. Due to the low cloud producing calm conditions, we flew into our own jet wash, and a violent 'ripple' came front to rear – I remember counting the rivets on the belly of the number two aircraft just above me, and felt the push up on my tail from the number four below. On parking the aircraft after a successful show, I was asked by the ground chief to look at my aircraft's fin and explain why all the paint was burnt off! The same had happened to the number four aircraft. I think that's when I decided it was getting time to quit formation aerobatics.

The aerobatic team wasted no time in converting to the Hunter, and flew its first mission in the aircraft on 20 March 1956. Personnel were soon posted out, Fg Off Richard Clayton-Jones taking over from Dave Chadwick, and the departure of Don Exley bringing Fg Off Charles 'Taff' Taylor to the team. The Hunter displays included Ken Goodwin of 118 Sqn performing a sonic boom as he brought his aircraft in low and fast. It was the Hunter which made 93 Sqn's team well known throughout Europe; in these aircraft, displays were flown in France, Germany, Great Britain and Norway, often alongside the USAF's Skyblazers F-100 team, as well as the French and Italian national aerobatics squads. The team of 93 Sqn continued to rehearse only when operational commitments allowed, and used only standard squadron aircraft. Its feats are all the more remarkable for this.

Aircraft Assigned

XB548/P, XB576/M, later T, XB583, XB629/N, XB695/X, XB697, XB701/V, XB712/F, later S, XB726/H, XB742, XB746/C, XB755, XB768/T, later Q, XB802/O, XB803/X, XB804/O, XB812/U, XB816, XB822/E, XB824, XB829/D, XB833, XB856/B, XB871/T, later G, XB874/I, XB886, XB891/Q, XB893/A, XB913/S.

All aircraft initially coded 'T' followed by an individual code letter, e.g. XB746 was T-C, later just 'C'.

Markings – 93 Sqn

Initial markings for 93 Sqn were similar to those of neighbouring 4 Sqn and comprised solely the squadron and individual code letters on the fuselage. The individual code letter was applied in white so that it preceded the squadron code letter ('T') on the port side and followed it on the starboard.

When bar markings appeared either side of the fuselage roundel, these comprised yellow-bordered mid-blue boxes with yellow arrows superimposed. The arrows both pointed forward. The squadron badge was applied in blue and yellow on the vertical tail, and as the squadron code letter was not used at this time, the individual code letter was applied in yellow on the mid-fuselage.

Squadron Motto

Ad arma parati (Ready for battle).

CHAPTER THIRTEEN

112 SQUADRON

Famous as a Curtiss Kittyhawk squadron based in the Western Desert during the Second World War, by 1953 112 Sqn was flying Vampires at Brüggen in Germany. During November of that year, while the squadron was deployed to Sylt for gunnery, Sqn Ldr I.D. Bolton, DFC handed command of his unit to Sqn Ldr Frank M. Hegarty, AFC. Hegarty had previously served with the British Joint Services Mission in Washington and had been involved in the RAF's early negotiations for the Sabre.

While still at Sylt the new commanding officer began lectures on the new Sabre aircraft and, when the Vampires returned to Brüggen on 18 December, personnel began to prepare the aircraft for ferrying out. The squadron's first Sabre, XB576, was delivered on 29 December. This aircraft and a further seventeen delivered as the squadron's initial complement were all fitted with the slatted wing. Final aircraft in this batch were assigned at the beginning of February 1954.

The squadron continued to fly the Vampire into early 1954, though no flying was possible in the New Year until 6 January. 'A' Flight then undertook a period of ground-combat training with the RAF Regiment before pilots departed for Sabre conversion at Wildenrath on 15 January. All had completed their first solo flights within two days. 'B' Flight meanwhile had also begun its ground-combat course, and left for the Sabre Conversion Unit at Wildenrath on 22 January; this group had

Close-in view of the early 'red mouth' 112 Sqn markings; even at this early date, paint chips have begun peeling away from the sharkmouth. The aircraft is XB650/U. (*John Oxenford*)

These 112 Sqn Sabres wear the early-style shark mouth, with red infill. XB960/G was being flown by Sqn Ldr Frank Hegarty and XB774/D by 'Dickie' Duke. (*Ted Roberts*)

all soloed by 24 January. Back at Brüggen, 'A' Flight continued to fly the Vampire, logging a number of sorties on the remaining aircraft, including six on the first night-flying programme, on 24 January. The pilots of 'B' Flight returned to the squadron on 28 January, and all had flown more than six hours on Sabres at SCU.

By the end of the month, 112 Sqn had two Sabres serviceable, and these had flown the first missions on 21 January. Within ten days this pair had logged more than 15 flying hours as the squadron slowly changed over to the new type. However, into February 112 Sqn continued to operate with two types of aircraft, and battle flight was still manned by Vampire crews until the type was finally withdrawn on 17 February.

Meanwhile, the so-called Sabre Flight began performing high-Mach sorties on 1 February, and then started to concentrate on radio compass let-downs (a novelty for the unit) and general handling. Fairly early in its Sabre period, the squadron realised that the Sabre's landing run could be appreciably shortened by holding up the nose as long as possible and flying the approach with the canopy open. Both methods served to make the aircraft more 'draggy', and the naval-style landing reduced brake wear. One side effect was unfortunately that a number of tail aspirator sections needed to be replaced when they were scraped along the runway.

Sqn Ldr Hegarty led the squadron's first close-formation mission on 13 February. He was accompanied by flight commanders Flt Lt W.G. Holmes of 'A' Flight and Flt Lt J. McConnell of 'B' Flight. Further close-formation sorties were flown in the following days, but bad weather curtailed much concentrated flying at the end of February and into March.

The new month brought a change to the flying programme, the flights alternating between instrument flying and formation sorties. This working-up phase almost inevitably brought incidents, and the squadron lost its first Sabre in a crash on 4 March. Fg Off L.R. Francis of 'A' Flight experienced a loss of power in XB912 on overshoot at Brüggen from a formation landing. His aircraft crashed into a small wood west of the runway, though Francis was fortunate to escape unharmed. Just over a week later, XB855 received Cat. 4 (R) damage in an unspecified incident; it had to be returned to the UK for repair with Airwork.

These incidents did not help an already poor serviceability record for the Sabres, and by 10 March each flight was still only able to boast three airworthy aircraft apiece. As if to demonstrate the fact, each of the flights put up three-aircraft formations on the same day. Three days later, still with only six airworthy Sabres on strength, 112 Sqn planned a mass-formation mission, but Fg Off David had to abort following undercarriage trouble. The remaining aircraft managed to perform fly-bys in vic formation.

Pilots at this time were eager to join the 'Mach Busters Club', though Sqn Ldr Hegarty had to issue a directive that no further sonic bangs were to be targeted on Brüggen: cracks had begun to appear in a number of walls around the base. Instead, those wishing to break the sound barrier took their aircraft over to the Monschau gunnery range. After asking the range controller to leave his microphone on, a pilot could then aim his bang at the controller's hut and hear himself breaking the sound barrier.

These missions had been performed on slatted aircraft but, with the squadron anticipating conversion to 'hard edge' Sabres, the CO had flown out to the Central Fighter Establishment on 20 February to fly the new version. The first modified Sabre for the squadron, XB958, was accepted on 29 February, and by the end of April 112 Sqn had nineteen of the type on strength. The first missions with 'hard edge' Sabres were flown on 12 March; flying was limited throughout the first week by poor serviceability. But those fortunate to fly the modified aircraft at that time thought it brought no surprises, and comments were favourable. Concurrently, the slatted Sabres were ferried out to other units, most going to 93 Sqn at Jever. The final slatted aircraft on the squadron was XB865, which was reassigned to 26 Sqn on 9 July.

Until the slatted aircraft departed the squadron, sorties were concentrated on using 'hard edge' Sabres where possible, and the majority of hours flown on the slatted Sabres after mid-March were on air tests prior to ferrying them out. Battle-formation practice missions were launched for the first time on 23 March, and dummy rocket attacks were flown against RAF Regiment installations. The Sabres were unfortunately restricted to 400kt and 4g at this time, due to an undercarriage problem. Further to this, while the squadron was still in the transition phase, the aircraft were limited to flying in minimum four-mile visibility and 3,000ft cloud base. As if this were not enough, at the end of March most of the squadron's aircraft were due intermediate inspections and flying was further limited. Inevitably, bad weather going into early April meant that the minima laid down for the transition phase were not met in any case.

Continued bad weather persisted through the month, though the squadron did manage to put up an eight-aircraft formation which flew three fly-pasts on 14 April. The formation flew past in two boxes in echelon, two in line astern and finally in two 'finger four' formations in line astern. With further bad weather halting air operations, on 15 April two USAF officers gave a lecture on the Sabre's A4 gunsight.

Following Easter grant, the squadron found its aircraft grounded for primary inspections, though the situation eased within a few days and the first wing formation was flown with the Sabres of 130 Sqn. The sixteen aircraft flew by in four boxes of four Sabres each. The formation was some feat for the wing, coming as it did during a period of poor serviceability and yet further bad weather.

Coming out of the transition phase, 112 Sqn began mounting battle-flight stand-bys from mid-April. The crews were often scrambled to intercept aircraft passing through the zone, and on 27 April the squadron diarist wrote that battle flight had been scrambled against 'the mythical B-47s'. These speedy USAF bombers were flying at 45,000ft-plus and always proved difficult to reach; their 'mythical' status was gained because the squadron had yet to intercept any and the 27 April missions proved no exception. Aside from these military craft, civil airliners also proved good 'targets' for 112's Sabres. Colin Buttars flew a number of missions against these unwary prey: '[We spent] lots of time doing practice interceptions under radar control – often on civil airliners. Although close to Düsseldorf and using the same beacon used by civil aircraft, there was little or no coordination and we often saw civil aircraft in cloud. No collisions, but lots of near misses!'

With better aircraft availability in May, the squadron was able to initiate a night-flying programme, and 377 hours were flown on 406 sorties. However, the first five days of the month were spent in preparing for the AOC's annual formal inspection. The inspection itself went off without a hitch on 6 May, and four days later, in similar ceremonial fashion, the squadron performed a fly-past over Brussels to commemorate the city's liberation. For two days from 11 May Exercise Prune introduced the unit to its first NATO exercise. The squadron was tasked with intercepting 'enemy' formations, but only one intercept was successful in the whole exercise, the remainder resulting in tail chases with the target hopelessly out of range.

On a more positive note, air-to-ground firing began on the Helchteren range on 12 May. Sharing the range with 130 Sqn's Sabres, 112 completed four sorties, with scores in the 4 to 9 per cent range. The range was again in use on the next day, Fg Off Jenkins receiving a ricochet to his aircraft. XB855 received Cat. 4 damage and it was later returned to the UK for rectification. For the rest of the month there was a marked accent on weapon firing and practice: cine quarter attacks were flown in preparation for a forthcoming Sylt detachment (which subsequently slipped to July) and further range sorties were launched. From 24 May the aircraft guns were harmonised and battle formations were flown. The first dusk and night missions with Sabres were successfully completed on 27 May. The pilots then concentrated on getting passed out for pre-flight inspection of their aircraft under the direction of maintenance personnel. The ability to pre-flight the aircraft was especially useful if a pilot had to land away from base at airfields where ground crews were not familiar with it.

A number of practice wing fly-pasts were flown during the first days of June 1954 in preparation for the real thing – a formation fly-by over Düsseldorf to mark the Queen's Birthday on the 10th. That day was marked by the award of a bar to Sqn Ldr Hegarty's Air Force Cross in the Queen's Birthday honours list. Hegarty was something of an ace in the Sabre, and was approved as the official 2 TAF solo-display pilot on the type.

Flt Lt Denys Heywood took over as 'A' Flight commander on 8 June 1954 and completed his first Sabre flight with the squadron in XB958/J on the same day. Denys had previously completed SCU conversion and had done his first Sabre mission there on 28 May. An experienced veteran of Spitfires and Tempests with 32 Sqn in Palestine, Heywood proved to be an excellent sharpshooter who took over XB774/D as his personal mount.

By mid-June, the majority of the squadron's slatted Sabres had departed, but a few still remained to be air-tested and transferred out. Roger Mansfield air-tested XB884 on 16 June – a mission that did not go as planned:

I taxied out and took off as usual, climbing through 4/8ths of cloud at about 2,000ft. Turning south I climbed up to altitude to carry out the air test. After about ten minutes, when I was at 20,000ft, I noticed a funny acrid smell coming from the air-conditioning system, shortly followed by thick grey smoke. I turned off in turn the radio, generator and battery switches and gradually the smoke subsided. As I was on 100 per cent oxygen I didn't have a breathing problem but now I was left with no radio navigational aids for my return to base. I set a course to the north hoping to spot something which I could recognise, and eventually did so. I had no communication with Brüggen but the weather was clear with good visibility below cloud so they could see me approaching and were able to keep other aircraft out of my way.

At about 500ft I lowered the gear and was nicely lined up with the runway ahead but as I was passing about 400ft the hydraulic controls of the aircraft went solid – I now had no control over the aircraft at all except for the throttle! Luckily, the aircraft was well in trim when the controls failed and continued its shallow approach towards the runway, although there was no way that I could have landed it without an elevator to flare it with once it reached the ground. By this time I was down to 200ft and I thought that if I applied full power on the engine the nose might rise in response to the increasing speed in that trim condition, thereby giving me more height from which to bale out. As the speed increased the nose did rise, gently at first and then quite markedly, so that eventually the aircraft was climbing away almost vertically. I pulled the lever at the side of my seat which blew off the canopy and cocked the ejection seat mechanism. I then turned my attention to the airspeed indicator, which by now was showing a decrease in airspeed as the angle of climb increased. I was now approaching 1,500ft, and when the airspeed fell back to 100kt I squeezed the trigger of the ejection seat and got an almighty kick in the pants, finding myself clear of the aircraft and tumbling over and over first seeing sky, then ground, then sky again.

Firstly, I undid my seat belt and pushed the seat away; now for the parachute D-ring just under the left armpit, or that was where it should have been – but no! Frantically I searched for it as I tumbled over and over with the ground now approaching at an alarming rate. I realised that if I didn't find it in the next few seconds I would be dead. At last my fingers closed round the cold metal of the D-ring, which had somehow been pushed right round towards the back of the parachute webbing strap, and with infinite relief I pulled it with all my strength and the beautiful sight of the parachute unfolding above me appeared before my eyes. I was so low when the parachute opened that I only had about five seconds in the chute before I hit the ground – just long enough for the speed of my fall to be reduced so that when I landed nothing got broken.

This is not quite the whole story as when the parachute opened and slowed me down the seat which I had separated myself from some twenty seconds earlier was falling just above me and, as I slowed down, so it caught me up and crashed into my bone-dome, cracking it and giving me a superficial cut on the head. I was very lucky that it didn't collapse the parachute on its way!

When I reached Flying Wing Headquarters, which was only about a hundred yards from where I had landed, it was decided that we should all adjourn to the Officers Mess bar and get ourselves a few pints of beer, which seemed an eminently sensible idea to me. After we had been in the bar for about an hour someone said, 'Let's go and see where the plane crashed.' So we all piled into a couple of Land Rovers and roared off to the south side of the airfield to an area called the 'bomb dump', where all the ammunition and bombs were stored in underground bunkers. We had to go outside the perimeter fence, and I remember being driven through a sandy area with young pine trees dotted about. As we approached the spot where the Sabre had crashed we could still see small pockets of undergrowth smouldering away, although the main fire had been put out and there were quite a lot of people wandering about examining the wreckage which was strewn over an area of several hundred square yards, mostly broken into pretty small pieces. As we wandered around, my eyes were drawn towards one small piece of the aeroplane which was lying by itself. The force of the impact must have been immense, for there on its own, completely apart from the cockpit, was the handle that I had pulled to lower the gear by the emergency system – it was a short metal rod with a red emergency pull handle on one end and a jagged piece of the shattered instrument-panel coaming on the other, in all only about six inches long. As I stood there my heart went cold, for I suddenly knew exactly what had happened. Situated on one side of the cockpit was the stand-by gear-lowering lever, and on the other side was the stand-by flying-control changeover lever. Both had red handles, and both were only ever used in the case of an emergency. However, the undercarriage emergency lever was attached to a two-foot-long wire cable, whereas the flying-control changeover lever was attached to a metal rod about six inches long! I had pulled the wrong lever and there it was lying accusingly at my feet. In normal circumstances it was only pulled after you had experienced hydraulic failure to the flying-control surfaces, when the lever changed over to an electrically driven system which gave you back control again. However, in my case not only had I isolated a perfectly serviceable hydraulic flying-control system, because there were no electrics to revert to the flying controls had lost all their power and locked solid. All this flashed through my mind as I stared down almost unbelievingly at the lever. No one else had noticed it at that time, and it even crossed my mind to pick it up and dispose of the evidence, so great was my feeling of shame. Then I realised that I could never live with myself if I did this and so I picked it up and walked over to my boss, Sqn Ldr Hegarty, gave it to him and told him the whole sad story.

Before we left the scene of the crime a few of us broke off some brushwood and, for want of anything else to do, began beating out some of the small smouldering areas of vegetation round about. As I was doing this I heard a loud bang and felt something strike the base of my right thumb. It was one of the .5in machine-gun bullets, which had been strewn over the area when the plane had disintegrated on impact and which had been set off by the heat of the fire that I was trying to put out. As that was the third time I had nearly been killed in the last two hours, I felt that discretion was the better part of valour, so returned to my room and went straight to bed.

On the weekend of 19/20 June the squadron began a mobility exercise, deploying to dispersals at the end of the runway to simulate a field operating base. The advance party left the hangar on Saturday and the main party on Sunday; a 100km circuitous route was used by the main party to simulate a convoy deployment, even though the party only ended up at the end of the same airfield. The aircraft taxied down to the dispersals on 21 June, and the mobility exercise was officially commenced at 1330 hr that day. For the period of this exercise, scrambles and practice interceptions were launched. On 25 June the air party moved back to the main hangar and on Saturday 26 June the main party finally returned to normal working.

For much of July the squadron again concentrated on ceremonial work in preparation for a visit by Her Royal Highness Princess Margaret on 15 July. While not rehearsing for the parade, pilots began to paint shark's teeth markings on their Sabres. This was a carry-over from the Vampire markings (the slatted Sabres never received shark's teeth) and continued a tradition which had begun on the squadron's P-40 Kittyhawks during the Second World War. The markings on each aircraft were basically the same, consisting of a red-outlined blue mouth with white teeth. Although some pilots would have preferred the design to be applied aft of the engine intake, these 'mouths' were all applied under the fuselage, just forward of the wing root, and each differed slightly from the rest. To complete the effect, a small 'eye' was painted on either side of the nose. These markings (and permission not to carry the standardised squadron bar either side of the fuselage roundel) were sanctioned by Sir Harry Broadhurst, AOC-in-C of 2 TAF. Broadhurst had a historical link with 112 Sqn, having commanded the Desert Air Force (of which 112 had been part) during the Second World War. Roy Davey remembers the painting of shark's teeth on the Sabres: 'I have memories of painting the shark's teeth on the first aircraft. I seem to remember that several of us went down to the hangar after dinner and masked up the first one. The template was drawn by Reg Crumpton, who had been a draughtsman before joining up. Once again a vague memory that the pilots actually sprayed the first one.'

The squadron's brief involvement in Exercise Dividend – the annual UK air-defence exercise – began on 17 July when the aircraft were placed on stand-by. Bad weather prevented the planned sections of four aircraft from taking off, however, and in any case personnel were now employed in preparing for the Sylt gunnery detachment. The advance party left on 17 July, followed by the main rail party on the 20th and the aircraft on the 21st. Unseasonably bad weather plagued the detachment.

Sector recces at Sylt began on 22 July and a few firing sorties took off the following day. The weather then closed in and prevented further activity until the 26th. This pattern of long spells of bad weather punctuated by the odd day suitable for flying continued until the end of the month. With the arrival of further bad weather, 'A' Flight's crews went up to List in the north of the island to see the RAF's air-sea rescue set-up there. A double-rearm of the squadron's Sabres took place on 16 August – results were not good and on this low note the squadron completed its Sylt detachment. Averages ended at 7.2 per cent for 'B' Flight and 4.4 per cent for 'A' Flight. The air party returned to Brüggen on 18 August with the ground party following the next day. Peter Frame flew on this Sylt detachment and explains the squadron's low scores: 'The problems were twofold: serviceability of the gunsights and poor reflection from the flag targets causing a lack of lock-on when the

Looking rather weary, XB958/J seen at Sylt wears the squadron's initial sharkmouth scheme, with red jaws. Note also the lack of drop tanks. (*Bob Jones*)

gunsight was working. We were able to cage the gunsight and use it like an old-fashioned cross, but were instructed to abort the sortie if all was not well. Additionally, we had no harmonisation boards for the guns and were forced to fire them in at the butts – still a bit of a hit-or-miss affair.'

Thankfully, upon return from Sylt, the weather at Brüggen proved to be a lot better and the squadron immediately got to work on the range. Concurrently, a number of strafing attacks were practised on well-camouflaged infantry units at the end of the month. The latter, often called 'Form D' missions, enabled ground-based units to practise camouflaging their positions and also gave the gunners a chance to track a realistic airborne target.

On 17 September Paul Mansfield (the 'other' Mansfield on the squadron) was flying XB957 on a height climb and Mach run. Asking for a ground-controlled descent through cloud (QGH), Paul received the OK from the ground, but further transmissions from the aircraft ceased at this point. He had little option but to press on through the cloud and hope for familiar scenery when he broke out below. When he did finally break through the cloud, he was met with the sight of pine trees flashing past the aircraft. Paul correctly reckoned himself to be south-east of Geilenkirchen and made straight for the airfield. Unfortunately, the base was undergoing runway resurfacing at the time, and bulldozers and other machinery were strewn across the tarmac. With fuel dwindling, Mansfield was left with no alternative but to land, and after a few passes he brought the Sabre in on a 110kt approach (rather than a more usual 135kt) to ensure a short landing run. With little further incident and with his feet firmly on the brakes, the Sabre was brought to a stop in little more than 500yds – something of a record. Three days later Paul flew back down to Geilenkirchen in the Vampire with wheel and brake spares. With the replacement parts fitted, XB957 was flown back to base the same day.

Unfortunately, not all incidents had a happy ending: on 26 September Fg Off J.E. Jenkins of 'B' Flight was killed in a Meteor crash, along with Fg Off Weir of 130 Sqn. The pilots were buried in Cologne three days later, and a planned wing fly-past in their honour took off but was recalled because of bad weather in the cemetery area. A small squadron formation finally managed to fly over the grave site on 30 September.

September and October were characterised by periods of bad weather, and many range days were lost. However, at the start of October 'A' Flight started performing cine quarter attacks, with 'B' Flight taking part in a number of low-level sorties. The flights regularly swapped these duties. Better weather in mid-month allowed 'A' Flight to perform a number of practice interceptions against aircraft from 10 Wg, Belgian Air Force on 11 October. The following day, Flt Lt McConnell again improved his range score at Monschau, this time achieving 44.8 per cent. The squadron average was now up to 12.14 per cent.

Large formations were put up towards the end of October, a number of these being photographed for the squadron's Christmas card. Nine Sabres took to the air on 18 October before drop tanks were fitted and formations of eleven were flown in the following week. Technical issues contrived to ground the aircraft for a number of days in October and November, not least because of generator problems. As a result of the latter, the aircraft were grounded completely for two days from 2 November. Then on 20 November a planned flying weekend had to be cancelled because of a rudder-trim problem; again all aircraft were grounded, though on this occasion the Station Commander allowed a long-weekend grant, so this particular cloud did have a silver lining.

Continuing problems in harmonising the guns were also felt at this time. Aside from the poor radar reflection of the target flag and the suspect gunsight, it was felt that the gun mountings in the aircraft were just not substantial enough, and in spite of continued efforts it was still not possible to harmonise the guns to fire on one spot. In an attempt to resolve the problem, Peter Frame was sent on a special mission: 'On 8 November 1954 I flew to Hahn Air Force Base (USAF) to beg, borrow or steal a copy of their harmonisation diagram. I seem to remember that I used a combination of the three to obtain the necessary diagram. We were back at Sylt again in April '55, where the results were rather better than previously, but the previous problems with the flags and the sights remained, though to a lesser degree.'

In fact, the gun mountings were still a cause for concern and, just to make sure that the fault was not in the armament fitters' procedure, on 30 November Flt Lt Heywood flew down to the USAF base at Bitburg in XB920. While he was there, USAF fitters harmonised the guns, which were then fired in at the butts; no difference was noted. Denys Heywood returned to Brüggen on 2 December.

Because of these problems, battle flight's ability to commit aircraft also suffered during this period, successful interceptions being reduced as a result. Nonetheless, a number of range sorties and 'Form D' missions against ground targets were launched. Many of the ground-target missions were performed for RAF Regiment gunners actually at Brüggen, so flight times could be kept short. Rounding off the year, many aircraft were being put through primary servicing, but on 29 December battle flight, being manned by crews from 'B' Flight, managed to intercept an American B-45 bomber.

The first sorties of 1955 were completed on 3 January, and comprised the usual battle formation, let-down and practice-intercept missions. From 6 January the range at Monschau was again in use, Peter Frame ending the day with a 35 per cent score. Frame recalls that for a while scoring was suspended because the dive angle had been reduced to 20 degrees and scores were deemed meaningless. The change was brought about as a result of a number of crashes on range work – notably those on 20 and 93 Sqns. In any case, further range work in January was brought to a halt by heavy snow, and many personnel were able to go skiing on the slope at the end of Brüggen's runway.

During this period the ground crews were still busy, and the enforced grounding was used as an opportunity to route aircraft through primary servicings. The aircrew also lent a hand in aircraft servicing, and on 17 January Mr Margeson, the Canadair technical representative, gave a talk that managed to clear up a number of engine-related problems. Sqn Ldr Hegarty performed a taxi test on Brüggen's runway on 18 January, but it was decided that the surface was still too icy to be safely used. Instead, the squadron began building a sledge to race against 130 Sqn. Much of the month was also devoted to ground instruction in an effort to keep people occupied.

After these delays, on 21 January a few sorties were launched, but these had to be hurriedly recalled in deteriorating conditions. Continued ground training was planned in the meantime before good flying conditions finally returned on the 27th. Thankfully, the good weather continued into February, and range missions, battle formations and barrage exercises continued. Barrage exercises involved flying formations against key targets to simulate incoming bomber formations. On 8 February Fg Off Paul Mansfield and Fg Off Al Buckley took off for a check flight in Vampire XD409, though the mission had barely got airborne before the aircraft's compressor exploded. They managed to get the jet down more or less in one piece, and were fortunate to be uninjured. This was

Fg Offs Paul Mansfield and Al Buckley had a lucky escape on 8 February 1955 when the compressor of the squadron's Vampire exploded after take-off. Though the compressor had ruptured the fuel tanks, no fire broke out. (*Paul Mansfield*)

especially true since the exploding compressor had sent shrapnel into all of the fuselage fuel tanks; Mansfield contends that it was only the presence of so much fuel in the crash area that prevented a fire.

Once better weather was on the way in the spring of 1955, the squadron began preparing for another Sylt deployment. On 17 March a number of sorties were flown with Sabres towing gunnery banner targets. Almost inevitably, bad weather then returned to plague the forthcoming detachment. The Sylt advance party departed Brüggen on 4 April, while back at base much time was spent in getting the guns working properly. After the Easter grant, fifteen Sabres and a Vampire finally left for Sylt on 13 April. Taking every opportunity to get onto the flag, sorties began at 0600 hr the following day; twenty-nine missions were flown for an encouraging 12.5 per cent average.

May, however, began with bad weather, and it was not until the 10th that sorties were again flown. These included a double rearm practice, and thankfully this was deemed to be more successful than the previous detachment's effort. The rail party departed for Brüggen on 13 May, in pouring rain, but all aircraft bar one managed to fly out the same day. Fg Off Reeve returned to Sylt on 16 May to pick up the final Sabre, which had gone unserviceable there (probably XB934/X).

Fortunately, the squadron experienced better weather upon returning to Brüggen and the Monschau range was again in use for the rest of the month. From 6 June the pilots' attention turned to repainting the squadron markings, and it seems that at this point the shark's mouth was repainted in black, with white teeth and a red outline.

Further colour-scheme changes occurred briefly in mid-June when Exercise Carte Blanche was begun. On 17 June, in between battle-formation sorties, the exercise markings were applied. In order to identify 112 Sqn's Sabres as 'friendly' forces, yellow distemper identification bands were painted on the rear fuselage, running aft of the roundel up to the forward edge of the serial number. The bands were approximately 38in wide and ran around the entire fuselage. In preparation for Carte Blanche, a number of officers also flew down to Geilenkirchen to view the squadron's intended dispersal area. All pilots were briefed on the exercise on 18 June, and loading of the advance party was completed. Orders were received on 20 June, and the advance party under Flt Lt Heywood left base the same day for Geilenkirchen.

All fourteen Sabres were serviceable and ready to go at 0900 hr on 21 June, taking off shortly afterwards for Geilenkirchen. On arrival, a section of four was immediately turned around and came to an 'at ease' posture at 1030 hr. This section was stood down at midday and the squadron then set about preparing the deployment site and setting up its communications. A further quartet of Sabres was then made available at 1800 hr and scrambled on an intercept at 1950 hr.

On the following day, four aircraft were at 30 minutes' readiness from 0330 hr, though they were not scrambled on this occasion. With no flying on 22 June, after a practice air raid the squadron stood down at 2015 hr. The following day, 23 June, finally marked the beginning of intense flying on Carte Blanche; a dozen Sabres were ready for a 'maximum effort' radar-saturation sortie again at 0330 hr. Just as the pilots were walking to their aircraft, an atomic explosion was called and umpires declared all but one aircraft to be serviceable, with the majority of pilots either killed or injured. Any 'survivors' were put to work collecting the injured and assessing the serviceability state of aircraft and equipment. Understandably, communications had also been disrupted, making the job a lot more difficult. Nonetheless, at 0730 hr orders were received to fly all aircraft to Beek in Holland and operate from there. Miraculously, the injured and dead were resurrected, and at 0830 hr fourteen Sabres departed, five being declared unserviceable for real on arrival at Beek. One Sabre, left at Geilenkirchen because of unserviceability, was flown into Beek during the afternoon.

Despite this slight setback, the squadron managed to launch a radar-saturation sortie shortly after arrival, and upon completion a further five aircraft flew a fighter-sweep mission, landing back at Geilenkirchen. Two sections of four Sabres at Beek had in the meantime been turned round and were sent on a patrol from Marville in France up to Landstuhl in Germany. Three further Sabres were offered to Wing Operations, but these were declined, the squadron having already exceeded its commitment. Additionally, the five unserviceable Sabres at Beek were reinstated, and flew over to Geilenkirchen during the day. This type of concentrated flying programme was typical of Carte Blanche, and it is a great credit to the ground crews that they were able to generate sufficient serviceable airframes.

The pace did not let up: eight Sabres were ready at Geilenkirchen on 30 minutes' standby from 0330 hr on 24 June. At 0530 hr the aircraft were brought to readiness and after some confusion, including a recall when the Sabres were taxiing for take-off, they were

The unusual formation of 112 Sqn Sabres XB960/G and XB774/D with two F-84 Thunderjets of 23 Smaldeel/10 Wg Belgian Air Force over Cologne. (*Author's Collection*)

finally airborne at 0625 hr on a strafing mission. A variety of sorties were flown this day, including ten Sabres on a radar-saturation exercise; Paul Mansfield flew XB950/S on a skittle mission, but Peter Frame had to abort in XB946/R after the main undercarriage 'D' doors stuck in the extended position. Further missions were launched in the afternoon, when four Sabres took off on a fighter sweep at maximum range, and after return and a refuel these were joined by a further quartet to rendezvous with a pair of F-84s over Brussels, the Sabres acting as escort. On 24 June the squadron had fired a theoretical 27,000 rounds; the day was further confused by the arrival of 3 Sqn's Sabres at Geilenkirchen after they had been subjected to a bombing raid at Beek.

Bad weather on 25 June meant that fewer sorties were completed. Two sections of four, which had been at readiness and had taxied at 0430 hr, were recalled as a result. Nonetheless, at 1010 hr four Sabres managed to get away and successfully intercepted four F-86Fs, presumably American. Denys Heywood, 'A' Flight's commander, flew XB958/J on this mission, which lasted 1 hour and 10 minutes. Four further aircraft were scrambled in the afternoon, followed by six more. Upon their return, two sections of four Sabres escorted F-84s and swept the Luxembourg area to finish off the day's flying. Denys Heywood was again airborne for this sortie, this time in XB771/H.

The squadron had a late start on the following day, 26 June and, though one section had been at readiness since 0300 hr with two further sections at 60 minutes, it was not until 1045 hr that the first sortie was launched. The latter had eight Sabres patrolling the Hahn/Bitburg area, a third section of four being scrambled at 1140 hr. In the afternoon, Geilenkirchen was again bombed, 90 per cent casualties being declared by umpires. A section that had been airborne at the time was diverted to Nörvenich, but they were A-bombed there too. At 1700 hr, all aircraft and airfields were declared serviceable again and eight Sabres were able to fly a sweep; Denys Heywood claimed an F-86D shot down, flying XB771 again. Upon return to base his formation was quickly turned around and sent out on a close-escort mission.

The following day, 27 June, was the squadron's final day of flying on Carte Blanche. At 0620 hr eight Sabres took off on a sweep to draw the fighters up prior to an F-84 strike. In the afternoon a further sortie of eight aircraft were called upon for a sweep at 40,000ft, and after another turnaround they were launched again on a further sweep. When they returned to Geilenkirchen these Sabres were yet again refuelled and scrambled on a third sortie, this time an intercept mission. The eight Sabres landed back at Brüggen while others at Geilenkirchen – declared 'unserviceable for combat' – returned separately to Brüggen. The ground crew then began to strike camp and returned to base on 28 June. The next few days were spent unloading equipment and removing the exercise markings from Sabres. A four-day stand-down period was granted to the squadron after Carte Blanche, and flying therefore did not resume until 5 July.

Fourteen Sabres received the Carte Blanche exercise markings, the eleven known examples being: XB650/U, XB771/H, XB772/P, XB919/V, XB920/K, XB939/F, XB946/R, XB950/S, XB958/J, XB960/G and XB979/B.

The only fatal Sabre crash suffered by 112 Sqn occurred on the squadron's first day back from Carte Blanche; the aircraft was XB950/S. Fg Off Mike Smith had been briefed for a low-level flying exercise, followed by a ground-controlled descent through cloud. He took off from Brüggen at 0937 hr and immediately climbed to 25,000ft, but no radio transmissions were heard after 1000 hr; the aircraft crashed one mile east of Heerlen in

XB956/T taxis to the holding point at Brüggen. Note the ejection-seat warning triangle below the cockpit, which was only applied in later years. (*Roger Mansfield*)

Holland ten minutes later. Subsequent investigation revealed that the aircraft had struck the ground at a 30-degree angle on a southerly heading. Wreckage was spread forward in a fan-shaped area for approximately 600yd. Detailed analysis of the wreckage found that the main fuel pump, located 450yd from the main crater, was lying at some distance from a connecting fuel pipe. Both had soil in the threaded mating portions, and it was immediately obvious that they had been disconnected before the crash. This evidence, along with signs of a pre-crash explosion, showed that a fuel leak and fire/explosion had been the cause of the crash. Recommendations were made to safety-lock the fuel connections in Sabre aircraft in future to prevent a recurrence. Mike Smith was buried in Cologne Military Cemetery on 8 July.

Further bad weather and a shortage of tail-cone (aspirator) assemblies caused a reduction in flying during July. At the end of the month, four Sabres were still unserviceable awaiting spare parts. The aspirator problems were caused by 112 Sqn's adoption of the 'naval' approach technique, where the nose was kept high on landing to reduce brake wear. The nose-high attitude inevitably resulted in a few tail scrapes, which meant that the aspirator would often need replacement. Ironically, 112 Sqn had avoided the brake problems experienced by other units, but had instead caused a different spares shortage.

These problems did not prevent Fg Off R. Brown flying out to Rome in a Sabre via Fürstenfeldbruck on 13 July, acting as No. 2 to Fg Off Boulton of 130 Sqn. This was a curious exercise: during 67 and 71 Sqns' Cyprus APC deployment, two Sabres had cut a corner on the taxiway at Rome's Ciampino airport and torn the bottom out of one drop tank each on the taxiway lights. Fg Offs Brown and Boulton were then detailed to fly their Sabres out to Rome and donate one drop tank each to the stricken craft before returning to Brüggen in an asymmetric configuration, carrying just one tank each. The plan would have worked well had not Fg Off Brown cut a corner on the taxiway at Rome himself and torn the bottom out of his own drop tank! After staying in a hotel in Rome for a few days, both pilots flew back on 16 July via Istrana, Fürstenfeldbruck and Wahn. Their return route was dictated by the reduced range of the Sabre with only one external tank.

On 11 August a signal arrived, alerting the squadrons of possible fuel-tank cracks. All aircraft on 112 Sqn were checked, and thankfully just four were found to have problems. These four, XB650/U, XB917/A, XB939/F and XB958/J, were all declared as Cat. 4 and were ferried back to the UK by 147 Sqn pilots for repair at Dunsfold over the following weeks. A replacement 'A', XB995, was assigned to the squadron on 1 September, though the other Sabres were not replaced; this left the squadron with eighteen Sabres. Unusually, 112 Sqn does not appear to have reduced fully from 22 to 14-aircraft strength at this time, unlike most other 2 TAF Sabre units.

One of a number of formations put up by 112 Sqn for photographic purposes, this eleven-ship group is led by XB960/G. (*Peter Frame*)

Exercise Loco began on 24 August, but low cloud on the first day initially prevented aircraft from taking off. In the afternoon six sorties were completed, the squadron's Sabres acting as 'enemy' raiders. None were intercepted. A dozen sorties were flown on Loco during the next day, marking the end of the squadron's commitment. The bad weather continued through the month and, though battle formations and practice intercepts were launched on 29 August, large cumulonimbus clouds over Brüggen forced one pair of Sabres to divert to Wildenrath and three more to Laarbruch. All were safely back at base by 1800 hr. On 6 September a similar occurrence meant that six Sabres had again to divert to Laarbruch.

September 1955 marked the beginning of a hectic period for the squadron, which was exacerbated by the departure of roughly 10 per cent of the ground crew on posting. The majority of these were very experienced on the Sabre, and their loss was immediately felt. By 13 September, only four Sabres were declared as serviceable, though seventeen sorties were still flown on that day. Despite the poor serviceability state of the aircraft, the squadron's flying commitment was only slightly diminished, and further Monschau gunnery missions were flown. On 19 September, a new 15ft-square target flag was introduced (rather than the previous 9ft-square version); inevitably, scores improved.

Exercise Beware, the annual test of the UK's air defences, began on 23 September and involved a number of long-range 'intruder' sorties being flown by the pilots of 112 Sqn. The first day of the exercise brought better weather, and a diversionary thrust on East Anglia was flown by four Sabres from 'B' Flight; there were no intercepts. The following day bad weather stopped flying, but on 25 September further sorties were flown against the English mainland, and this time a number were intercepted by Hunters. Denys Heywood flew XB774 (his personal mount) to Ipswich via Gütersloh on this sortie. During the day one of the aircraft inadvertently lost a drop tank; the fault was later traced to a small metal filing which had shorted across two electrical terminals in the jettison circuit. There was no more flying on Beware until 27 September, when twelve night cross-country flights were also flown. The Beware missions took the squadron to Norwich via Nijmegen and Haarlem in Holland.

On the next day, ten further exercise missions were completed, and these included short patrols over south-east England. Four Sabres on the first mission were bounced by

Hunters. These sorties included a sweep over the Woodbridge and Yarmouth area, while others flew to Woodbridge before orbiting over Dover on the way back.

Exercise Foxpaw, which was also Phase 3 of Beware, took place on 1 October, the last day of the annual air-defence exercise. Seven sorties were scrambled during the day – as part of a gigantic force of aircraft from Bomber Command, 2 ATAF and 4 ATAF – in widespread raids against the UK. The Sabres were airborne for nearly two hours and most were impressed by the interceptions made by Fighter Command Hunters. One pilot reported seeing a Gloster Javelin on this mission. Flying ceased early on 1 October to enable the ground crews to remove drop tanks from the Sabres. The squadron then stood down for a few days.

While the aircraft were in 'clean' configuration, the opportunity was taken to fly four Sabres in formation to get air-to-air photographs for the squadron Christmas card. Photos were taken by a 2 Sqn Meteor, but results were poor. Nine aircraft were subsequently airborne on 12 November for a similar purpose. On this occasion, photos were taken from a Vampire trainer, but these were again of poor quality. It seems that the pictures taken back in October 1954 were used instead.

Poor serviceability rates and bad weather punctuated life at the end of 1955, and fog in November meant that only slightly more than 300 flying hours were logged for the month – just 60 per cent of the target. And the loss of experienced ground crews during September continued to be felt. Because of the heavy workload, one Sabre was flown over to Wildenrath on 15 November to have its minor service completed there. December was only slightly better, though good flying days were interspersed with further bouts of fog. By 20 December, with only four flying days left before the next Sylt deployment, the squadron had flown only 246 hours in 259 sorties. Preparations were made for the forthcoming deployment before the squadron stood down for Christmas.

Following the Christmas break, 112 Sqn returned to work on 2 January 1956 and the road convoy left for Sylt at 1000 hr in a rainstorm. It had been planned to fly the Sabres to Sylt on 4 January, but, when the day dawned clear and bright on the 3rd, it was decided to make the most of the opportunity: eight Sabres flew out of Brüggen that day, leaving two unserviceable airframes to be repaired before they too flew up to Sylt.

The first sorties at Sylt were flown on 6 January, poor weather in the intervening period precluding any flight activity. Even then, the homer was declared unserviceable and two valuable hours were lost while it was fixed; thirteen sorties were flown during the day, none actually being live-firing missions. Unfortunately, snow fell on 8 January, effectively ending the detachment's flying activities. To relieve the boredom, an escape-and-evasion exercise was commenced on 9 January, nearly two-thirds of 'evadees' eluding capture. On the following day, many personnel went to Hornum to see the air-sea rescue launch there, but other than this outing, most activity centred around the bar. Despite the bad weather, Sqn Ldr Hegarty did manage to fly one of the previously unserviceable Sabres into Sylt on 11 January.

Live firing began on 13 January, when twenty-one sorties were completed, though it should be stressed that only one of these was actually a live-firing mission. In a change from the routine, during Sunday 15 January three Sabres were placed on standby to shoot down some errant balloons that were expected to drift into the Sylt area; the balloons were carrying 'special' equipment that could have fallen into the Russian zone, but in the event the Sabres were not needed. The last day of meaningful shooting was 20 January, Fg Off Al Buckley ending the day with 17 per cent. For the month, 112 Sqn had achieved

XB772/P is hoisted back onto its undercarriage after Colin Buttars's incident on landing at Sylt on 16 January 1956. Corrosion of the undercarriage downlock was pinpointed as the cause. (*Roy Davey*)

only thirty-eight firing sorties, split evenly between high level (15.2 per cent average) and low level (12.6 per cent average).

Before the squadron returned to Brüggen, a double-rearm practice mission was flown, though the runway was in far-from-ideal condition, being covered in hard-packed snow. Returning from one of the day's missions, Fg Off Colin Buttars in XB772/P landed with his port main undercarriage leg unlocked; the aircraft ran along on the drop tank for a while before it was ripped off. The Sabre came to rest on its wingtip and, though damage appeared to be superficial, the aircraft was found to be twisted and was declared Cat. 4 (R). The fault was quickly put down to salt corrosion of the downlock, and all flying was stopped while other aircraft were checked. XB772 had been Roy Davey's personal aircraft, and he was less than pleased to see it damaged. Roy remembers that the crew chief was even less impressed:

I was in the Officers' Mess ante-room at Sylt, probably waiting for a meal, when I saw the tail of this Sabre come into view through the large end windows. I knew two things – one, that the runway was not that close, and, secondly, that it was 'my' aircraft. I went out to have a look – it was not very exciting, but I seem to remember that the airman who looked after this aircraft was most incensed that the pilot had wrecked it, told me what the pilot should have done to avoid it, and threatened 'violence'.

Not really part of the story, but this young lad was sort of i/c the aircraft, looked after us both with great care, and was not beyond criticising the way I flew and landed it. On one occasion I had landed on the runway, which was in full view of the ground crew, and as I parked he began to pull two jacks towards the aircraft. Having then helped me unstrap, I asked him what the problem was. He said that he thought I would be reporting a heavy landing and was getting prepared. On another occasion he started taking 'redress of grievance' action against me for doubting his technical knowledge, but fortunately our boss poured oil on troubled waters – at some embarrassment to me.

The squadron flew back to Brüggen on 27 January – with some irony, since the weather that day was bright and sunny. The road and rail parties followed over the next few days. This would be the squadron's last Sylt detachment with Sabres.

Fog and snow in February meant that a pitiful 35 flying hours and 36 sorties were flown throughout the whole month. Only four full flying days were possible, including 16 February, when the temperature dropped to -16°C – the lowest at Brüggen for many years. Thankfully, March proved exactly the opposite, and by the 20th of the month the squadron had reached its monthly flying target – something that had not happened for some time. Serviceability had also improved, and 'B' Flight put up a six-Sabre formation on 9 March, just to show it could still be done. However, changes were afoot: on 12 March, despite the presence of smoke haze from the Ruhr, Fg Off Hillman and Fg Off Little both had flights in the Station Flight Hunter. Further 112 Sqn pilots took the Hunter aloft the following day, and all were impressed by the aircraft's capabilities. More Hunters arrived at Brüggen on 6 April when a Day Fighter Leaders course arrived at the base, led by 112 Sqn pilot Flt Lt Lee Jones. Their arrival was somewhat comical: 112 Sqn had scrambled at 1430 hr to meet the Hunters, but the GCI controllers got mixed up and an intercept was not made until the aircraft were just fifteen miles south of the airfield. The DFLS pilots claimed four Sabres 'shot down' for no losses in the intervening mêlée, but the Sabre crews disputed this.

The final large-scale exercise for 112 Sqn's Sabres was the deployment to Luxeuil in France, home of the French Air Force's Escadre 2/11. Sqn Ldr Hegarty had previously flown down to Luxeuil on 20 March to view the base facilities, and the squadron prepared to move ten Sabres and a Vampire there on 17 April. All aircraft had successfully arrived at Luxeuil by 1600 hr, and the Vampire then returned to Brüggen. The squadron was greeted by Commandant Tatraux of the French Air Force and retired to the Officers' Mess for a champagne reception. The road party had meanwhile left Brüggen and stopped overnight on the 17th at Vauban Barracks in Strasbourg.

Early on the 18th, with the road party still some way away, the pilots performed their own pre-flight inspections, and radios were recrystallised for the local frequencies. Unfortunately, it was then found that the local oxygen adaptor did not fit the Sabres, and only two aircraft had sufficient oxygen already on board to be flown. One of these was XB774/D, and Peter Frame took it on a one-hour local sweep of the area. The road convoy finally arrived at 1600 hr, along with the vital oxygen equipment.

After the necessary maintenance work, all ten Sabres were available on 19 April and sector-recce missions were flown, despite bad weather with 7/8 cloud at 2,500ft and rain showers. By 1600 hr the recce missions were complete and a section of four Sabres took off for a sweep. Low cloud on the following day prevented flying in the morning, but cleared sufficiently for a combined exercise with the French to be flown. Two sections of four Sabres escorted three French F-84s which were simulating a bomber formation at 15,000ft and Mach 0.65. The formation was then attacked by eight further F-84s, the Sabres flying top cover at Mach 0.8 at 5,000 and 10,000ft above the formation. On return to Luxeuil the Sabres were refuelled and launched on an eight-ship battle formation. 'Ted' Roberts flew on both of these sorties, both times in XB979/B, logging 1 hour and 5 minutes on the first and 35 minutes on the second mission.

Poor weather again prevented flying in the morning of 23 April, so crews were given a Hunter questionnaire. That afternoon seven Sabres and a Vampire were airborne; upon their return they were turned around and the Sabres were joined by another machine to be sent off in two sections of four. Next day, seven Sabres were again airborne while the Vampire gave experience flights to members of 112's ground crew. A joint exercise was flown in the afternoon, the squadron expecting opposition from French Ouragans and F-84s; they saw nothing. Denys Heywood flew XB976 on an eight-aircraft sweep from Luxeuil to Stuttgart via Donaueschingen and Karlsruhe.

The final day of the Luxeuil deployment was 25 April. While three Sabres gave an aerial demonstration over the airfield, the rest were prepared for the flight back to Brüggen. All ten Sabres returned to base in the afternoon in formation, with the Vampire bringing up the rear.

Arriving back at Brüggen, the crews immediately began brushing up on the Hunter Pilot's Notes in preparation for their first solos on the type. Sqn Ldr Hegarty made the squadron's first Hunter sortie on 26 April and by the end of the month there were three Hunters on strength. Sabre flying in the meantime took a back seat, being restricted to test hops in preparation for ferrying back to UK. During May the squadron flew only 20 hours and 15 minutes in Sabres for 21 sorties, against 124 hours and 20 minutes on the Hunter in 186 sorties. On 1 May the first three Sabres (XB649, XB774 and XB947) were ferried out by 147 Sqn pilots, and four more departed the following day. Six more Sabres left on 5 May, flown out by squadron pilots Peter Frame, Dicky Brown, 'Boxy' Baker, 'Wilbur' Wright, Pat Reeve and Taff Heath. Peter Frame flew XB976/E to Stansted for overhaul with Aviation Traders. Peter recalls that Stansted possessed no radio and he was therefore talking to nearby North Weald for instructions. On arrival at Stansted he parked XB976, got on a train and spent the night in London before returning to Germany.

By 10 May, the famous shark's teeth markings were already being applied to the squadron's Hunters in time for the AOC's visit on the 15th. The final Sabre on the squadron was XB920/K, a 'hangar queen' that proved difficult to get rid of. On 28 May, Denys Heywood took it aloft on a 45-minute air test, but on approaching the airfield he heard a large bang, which witnesses on the ground saw was accompanied by a large plume of black smoke from the exhaust. Heywood managed to get the aircraft back on the ground, where no fault could be found; a further air test (this time by a nervous Denys Heywood) was fault-free. XB920 was still serviceable for a photographic sortie with one of the squadron's Hunters on 5 June. Lee Jones flew the Hunter while Peter Frame flew the Sabre; Roger Mansfield meanwhile had been given a camera to record the historic formation, flying alongside in the Vampire trainer. The mission completed, XB920 was ferried out to Benson that same day by a 147 Sqn pilot, completing the Sabre story for 112 Sqn.

The squadron did form an informal four-ship aerobatic team in October 1955, with Frank Hegarty as leader, Denys Heywood as number three and Colin Buttars as number four. The holder of the number two (right wing) position is not known at this time. No displays were flown, the idea being to practise until they were actually good enough to perform in public. Richard 'Dickie' Brown took over as number four when Buttars was posted out around March 1956. The squadron later used its Hunters in an aerobatic team, and gained itself quite a good reputation.

AIRCRAFT ASSIGNED

Initial delivery, December 1953–June 1954:

XB576, XB629, XB746, XB802, XB804, XB808, XB812, XB818, XB822, XB829, XB865, XB884, XB893, XB912, XB913, XB914, XB915.

All aircraft had slatted wing, no squadron codes or sharkmouth.

Something of a 'hangar queen', XB920/K was 112 Sqn's last Sabre on strength; when it finally became serviceable, it was flown for this 5 June 1956 'old and new' formation. The Sabre was flown by Peter Frame, while Lee Jones took the Hunter. Roger Mansfield in the meantime took this historic photo from the squadron's Vampire. (*Roger Mansfield*)

Second delivery, March 1954 to end of service:

XB649/C, XB650/U, XB771/H, XB772/P, XB774/D, XB855, XB917/A, XB919/V, XB920/K, XB926/O, XB934/X, XB939/F, XB944/L, XB946/R, XB947/Q, XB950/S, XB956/T, XB957/W, XB958/J, XB960/G, XB976/E, XB978/N, XB979/B, XB995/A.

All aircraft had '6–3' wing from manufacture.

MARKINGS – 112 SQN

Though similar in scheme, 112 Sqn appears to have applied two variants of basic markings to its Sabres.

Inevitably, being a famed 'sharkmouth' squadron, 112 painted its '6–3'-winged Sabres with this motif. The first variant had a blue-outlined mouth with white teeth and red infill. A white eye with mid-blue pupil was applied on either side of the forward fuselage just beneath the windshield. Individual code letters were applied on the tail fin.

Markings for Exercise Carte Blanche are explained in the text, but following on from this the basic sharkmouth colours changed. This time, the mouth outline was red and the infill between teeth was black. At the same time, the eye on either side of the fuselage gained a red outline.

SQUADRON MOTTO

Swift in destruction.

CHAPTER FOURTEEN

130 'PUNJAB' SQUADRON

Based at the new airfield at Brüggen, like the other 2 TAF Sabre units 130 Sqn had flown Vampires in the fighter-bomber role before the arrival of the F-86 in service. While the squadron was at Sylt in November 1953, it was informed that Sabres would soon be arriving, and question sessions based on recently issued Pilot's Notes were undertaken during lulls in the flying there. Two of the first pilots to begin Sabre conversion were Fg Offs Abrahams and Chitty; both USAF-trained, they departed to the Sabre Conversion Unit (SCU) at Wildenrath as soon as they had arrived on the squadron at the end of December. Though it had been decided that these two would be wasting their time by briefly converting onto the Vampire, delays in the arrival of the first Sabres meant that both did in fact fly the older type on a number of occasions.

Vampire flying continued throughout December 1953 and into January 1954, though a number of aircraft were prepared for transfer to the Maintenance Unit at St Athan. At last, on 21 January 1954, six members of 'A' Flight, led by Flt Lt Chapman, departed for Wildenrath and began the squadron's full-time conversion onto the Sabre. Squadron commander Sqn Ldr John G. Mejor, DFC, along with the rest of 'A' Flight and those from 'B' Flight, completed the course during the following month. Tony Lock went through Sabre conversion with the squadron at this time:

The main operational point on the conversion at Wildenrath, and the great difference between the English Vampire/Meteor and other UK-manufactured aircraft from the American/Canadian [aircraft], was the instrumentation and the leap from 'string and wire' to modern hydraulic controls. Footbrakes were also alien to us, being used to control the column lever system. Controls were much lighter and more responsive than the Vampire, and of course speeds were greater (430kt v 135) in the climb and the celebrated Mach run. This entailed a climb to 50,000ft, then rolling the aircraft over into a vertical dive at full power. The aircraft was supersonic for about three seconds as the height loss was swift. Of course, as height was lost, Mach number decreased, severely limiting the time through the barrier.

The squadron's first three Sabres, XB836, XB838 and XB839, arrived at Brüggen on 29 January 1954; their arrival meant that over the following weekend eight Vampires had to be left outside while the Sabres were given hangar space. Unfortunately, temperatures over the weekend fell to -15°C and on the Monday morning all were unserviceable because of frozen grease and perished undercarriage seals. While the squadron was in transition, it was decided that the Sabres would be taken to the ASF hangar and stored there. By the end of January, forty-seven sorties had been flown on the Sabre by pilots at SCU, for a total of 39.5 flying hours. As Stewart Salmond recalls, not all equipment was in place to support a squadron flying the Western World's most advanced day fighter, especially the bone-dome flying helmet:

This newfangled gear, never previously encountered, was supposed to arrive with the aircraft, but didn't. They were in such short supply that stores sent a vehicle to meet the daily BEA

This photograph is unusual as it shows XB858, a slatted aircraft, at the front and a '6–3'-winged Sabre at the rear. Taken during 130 Sqn's changeover to the latter type, XB858 served with the squadron for just two months, from February to April 1954. Note the slightly different camouflage treatment at the wing root of these aircraft. (*Tony Lock*)

flight to Düsseldorf, bringing back each time a few more. Some time later a small party of civil servant scientists visited. They had spent a lot of time and effort developing just the right finish, with maximum fire-retardant qualities, and were horrified to find every helmet had been painted over with a squadron crest to the owner's specification and very artistically decorated. Needless to say, we kept them as they were.

Meanwhile, there was no Sabre flying on the squadron at Brüggen, where all hands were put to getting Vampires prepared for transfer as well as completing acceptance checks on the newly arrived Sabres. The squadron's fourth aircraft was delivered on 1 February, and a further ten on 13 February. All were of the slatted-wing variety. Training of pilots at SCU continued concurrently, and when Flt Lt John Chick was posted into the squadron on 10 February he was immediately detached to SCU to assist in this process. John Chick had flown the Sabre in Korea, and his experience was sorely needed; he would take over as 'B' Flight commander.

With Sqn Ldr Mejor temporarily detached on a winter survival course at Ehrwald, it was only fair that no Sabre flying took place until his return to the squadron on 15 February. However, even then poor weather conditions and low temperatures prevented this from happening, and it was not until 18 February that the first 130 Sqn Sabre flights took place. On that day, both flight commanders performed one air test each. Unfortunately, there were then heavy snowfalls for a few days and, understandably reluctant to risk flying their new aircraft in marginal conditions, the squadron waited for the weather to break. On 23 February the first tentative sorties were flown. These were immediately tempered by the issue of an order which prevented all Sabre flying if the cloud ceiling was less than 3,000ft, or if visibility was below four miles. This order was in place until the squadron had become more experienced on the type and, allied to marginal weather conditions on many days at that time of year, meant that the process of conversion was a drawn-out affair. Thus, though the squadron had logged 309 sorties for February, most of these were in Vampires, which were still present in quantity.

Adding to the hectic pace of life, on 2 March the squadron was ordered to cease acceptance checks on its existing Sabres and prepare for their transfer to Wildenrath. Though initially incomprehensible, the purpose of the order soon became clear; the squadron was to dispose of its slatted Sabres and instead begin to receive unslatted aircraft with the extended '6–3' wing. With neighbouring 112 Sqn also completing the process, this meant that the Brüggen Wing could standardise on 'hard edge' Sabres. The first of this type, XB932 and XB991, were ferried in on 4 March. This period left the squadron with an unbelievable workload. While still preparing Vampires for transfer out of the squadron, the ground crews also had to perform the same feat on fifteen slatted Sabres, while somehow accepting '6–3'-winged Sabres as well. Incredibly, the process went off without serious incident.

Throughout March, the missions changed from individual familiarisation flights to formation practice. Most of these sorties were flown on slatted Sabres, as further deliveries of modified aircraft did not begin until early April. And despite the different low-speed flight characteristics of the '6–3' aircraft, very little in the way of conversion flying was done. For example, Fg Off John Oxenford flew his first sortie in a 'hard edge' Sabre (XB932) on 19 March and, rather than any type of familiarisation flying, he undertook instead aerobatics, radio-compass let-downs and simulated forced landings. In retrospect, it seems foolhardy that the stall characteristics of the new type were not explored more fully, but by good fortune there were no incidents as a result of this; other squadrons were less fortunate. It is worth noting that for a slatted Sabre equipped with drop tanks and at 20,000lb all-up weight, stalling speed was approximately 125kt in the landing configuration. For a similar configuration on a '6–3'-winged Sabre, the stall was a good 10 knots higher. More importantly, the stall on the latter was sharper, with the pilot receiving little warning. Even the Pilot's Notes for the Sabre, which were amended to include '6–3' wing characteristics, did not really highlight the difference, merely stating that 'low-speed behaviour [with '6–3' wing] has been slightly modified'.

For 130 Sqn, there was a spate of undercarriage problems with the slatted aircraft, which initially defied resolution. On 4 March the nose door of XB894 opened in flight during a mission with P Off Chitty on board; he recovered to base but the aircraft was eventually placed Cat. 4 for repair and returned to the UK. Fg Off Brooks had a similar experience aboard XB838 on 22 March – this time resulting in Cat. 3 damage. On the following day, Sqn Ldr Mejor also had an undercarriage door open in flight, this time while he was pulling XB790 out of a 6g turn. This aircraft was also placed Cat. 3 and the squadron commander immediately mandated a 4g limit on all squadron Sabres until the cause could be found. Though rigging checks of the undercarriage locking system were carried out on all aircraft and instances ceased, the undercarriage problem would return to haunt the squadron.

At the beginning of April, more '6–3'-winged Sabres began to arrive on station, and finally the slatted aircraft began to be ferried to other 2 TAF units. At the end of May, most had departed but, with spare parts already required to service the modified Sabres, three slatted aircraft remained on squadron strength for many months to come. Robbed of useful parts, these 'hangar queens' were eventually transferred out, but the last would not leave until early 1955. The squadron had fortunately managed to get rid of its last Vampire in the interim, WA201 departing for 19 MU on 8 April. In the interim, pilots often juggled their time between aircraft: for example, Fg Off Oxenford flew an acceptance check on '6–3'-winged XB927 on 22 April, and later that day completed a 40-minute air test of the slat-winged XB838

This informal group, comprising mainly 130 Sqn pilots, was posed in front of OC Flying Wing's Sabre, XB987. L–R: Fg Off Sam Jeffryes, Wg Cdr G.B. Johns, DSO, DFC (OC 135 Wg), Fg Off Philip Fabesch (OC Station Flight), Gp Capt W.V. Crawford-Compton, DSO, DFC (Station Commander, RAF Brüggen), Fg Off Martin Sommerard, Fg Off Colin Dingle, Fg Off Julian Chitty. (*Tim Barrett*)

prior to its departure to 234 Sqn. By 5 May the situation had calmed down and the squadron then had on strength three slatted Sabres, XB790, XB824 and XB833, plus nineteen aircraft with the '6–3' wing.

With flying now in full swing, the squadron started to perform close- and battle-formation missions from 8 April; concurrently, it used its growing confidence in formation flying to good effect when the first practice fly-pasts for the AOC's annual inspection were put together. These were often in wing formation, with both 112 and 130 Sqns detailing eight Sabres each, while the Brüggen-based Belgian Thunderjets brought up the rear with a further sixteen-ship formation. Thankfully, by this time the maintenance situation had relaxed slightly, and was improved still further with the arrival of Fg Off Chiverton on 12 April. Chiverton was posted in as the squadron's first Engineering Officer, and was delegated responsibility for making engineering decisions that might otherwise have required a lengthy reply to an off-station signal.

The AOC's inspection went off without a hitch on the morning of 6 May; AVM Lees arrived from Wahn in an Anson and first inspected the parade. The squadron's part in the fly-past over Wahn went less successfully.

Joining up after take-off, P Off Martin Sommerard's Sabre, XB959, touched the aircraft of Purple Section leader Flt Lt John Chick. Fortunately, both Sabres remained in the air, but XB959 lost the whole of its starboard aileron and part of the elevator, while Chick's Sabre, XB916, had a badly squashed intake lip and was declared Cat. 4. The fly-past continued using airborne spare aircraft.

With the AOC's inspection behind it, the squadron could now fully concentrate on its true mission. Its first exercise, 'Prune II', began on 11 May and concentrated on electronic countermeasures. During the exercise, 130 Sqn acted first as simulated bombers and then in the interceptor role. At the same time, other stations provided either interceptors or targets. A practice bomber raid was flown early on 11 May and, following a quick turnaround, four aircraft were then ready again at 0930 hr; they scrambled and managed to intercept the 'bomber' aircraft easily. Eight Sabres then joined with four from 112 Sqn taking off in the afternoon to act as bombers, with Oldenburg as the target. No interceptions were made against the Brüggen formation. Exercise Prune II concluded on 12 May.

Range firing had begun at Helchteren on 10 May and, after Exercise Prune II had finished, a good few days' worth of air-to-ground gunnery was logged; the flying usually ceased at 1800 hr to make the most of the better weather. On a roll, the squadron flew 52.4 hours for the day on 24 May, a new squadron record. Inevitably, the increased flying brought incidents, and a further Sabre, XB648, was lost on 3 June after Fg Off Bill Ireland's nose undercarriage collapsed when a tyre burst. The aircraft ran off the runway and most of the nose area was destroyed. Fortunately, Ireland escaped

Extensive damage to Flt Lt John Chick's Sabre, XB916, was caused when P Off Martin Sommerard's aircraft collided with it during the 6 May 1954 AOC's fly-past. Fortunately, both aircraft recovered safely to base. (*Bob Jones*)

Fg Off Bill Ireland's Sabre rests in the undergrowth at Brüggen after his crash on 3 June 1954. Though the damage does not look severe, it was enough to write off the aircraft. (*John Oxenford*)

injury; Tony Lock was there to see it: 'He was lucky the aircraft did not cartwheel as the nose wheel collapsed. He seemed to lose power on the take-off roll at about 100kt, which left him a bit short on the runway (which was 3,000yd long). I suspect a tyre blew and he came off the runway at quite high speed. The aircraft, strong as it was, was not designed for cross-country!'

Mobile operations were accented in June, and on the 4th the squadron departed on its first mobility exercise, deploying in tents to the Möhne See area, without its aircraft, to give experience of operating the domestic side of the squadron in the field. A convoy of ten Magirus 3.5-ton trucks, two Land Rovers and a police escort, along with seventy-six personnel, took part. They returned to Brüggen on 6 June. A further mobility exercise was called on 19 June, and this time the squadron personnel deployed to a tented camp on the north-east side of the airfield, with the aircraft taxiing there on 21 June to begin flying missions. A number of sorties were then launched until all returned to the main hangar on 25 June. John Oxenford recalls that it was a relaxed exercise:

> The whole thing was a half-hearted affair really, because we fed in the mess and used the washing facilities of the permanent quarters. We were lucky, as the weather was excellent during the period and we were able to do a lot of tactical flying, most of which was Battle Flight at 35,000ft.

The vehicles carrying the squadron equipment and personnel had to go on a 100-kilometre run out of camp and back before proceeding to the site. I was driving in the rear party, which did not leave until Monday 21 June. Much to the relief of everyone, our route back when the pack-up came was straight across the airfield and back to the hangars.

In June, flying began to be restricted so that aircraft could be serviced prior to the squadron's first Sabre armament-practice camp at Sylt in July. The main party of the squadron left for Sylt on 20 July, with the Sabres flying in on the following day. Firing began at 1030 hr on 22 July, and on one of the early missions the starboard ammunition access panel came off Fg Off Lees's Sabre, XB991; there was no other damage. Low stratus clouds and mist intervened on the following days and often prevented actual gunnery, even though conditions might have been suitable for flying. Seven shoots were made on the morning of 27 July, but the day's flying was disturbed when Fg Off Dicky Burden ran off the runway in slippery conditions following a rain shower. The aircraft involved was again XB991, and this time the damage was more serious: it was declared Cat. 4 and returned to Airwork for repairs. C.R. 'Pop' Miles was on the airfield at the time of Dicky Burden's accident:

I was with Cpl Vic Kyle, also an instrument fitter, watching from the dispersal as the Sabres broke off to land. The particular Sabre was pretty low and, if I remember, off to the right of the centre line. Then came the crash and we both leapt into the squadron Land Rover and drove down to the crash site. On arrival, there was an almost complete aircraft, but in distinct halves. The wing section had been torn away by the undercarriage from the fuselage, which had continued on for a further 50yd or so, but intact and upright. The pilot was Fg Off Dicky Burden, and he was completely unharmed. I do recall that he directed the crash crew to the site. A few weeks later, Vic and I were invited to Dicky Burden's room in the Officers' Mess (completely out of bounds to Junior NCOs) to have a couple of beers with him.

At 1545 hr that same day, Fg Off Rex Boulton arrived from Brüggen and burst a tyre. This unfortunate spate of accidents did not end there: two days later Fg Off Bill Ireland in XB945 bounced on landing and ran off the side of Sylt's runway; this aircraft was also Cat. 4. On 31 July Fg Off Duncan Bracher had a tyre burst on XB959, the aircraft having only just returned to the squadron following repairs after the mid-air collision during May's AOC's fly-past. Fg Off John Oxenford also had an incident on 4 August, flying XB932. He landed three yards short of the runway and damaged the port speed brake. Fg Off Baker in XB942 then had a tyre burst while taxiing on 17 August. Thus it was with some relief that crosswinds, cloud and rain put paid to range firing on 5 August, and, though some further missions were flown after 13 August, the range was often unserviceable and no further firing was done on this detachment. In the meantime, crews passed the time as best they could, and most personnel paid the cursory visit to the List air-sea rescue boat to relieve the boredom. In an effort to get aircraft serviceable in case the weather should clear, on 17 August Sqn Ldr Mejor took XB933 back to Brüggen to get replacement gunsight bulbs, and the AOC's Anson also arrived at Sylt later that day with replacement tyres.

Unfortunately, the weather didn't improve and on 18 August the first aircraft returned to base from the Sylt detachment. Conditions were no better at Brüggen, and in the following weeks a number of range days and exercises had to be cancelled.

At the beginning of September, better weather finally arrived and, although drop

To facilitate engine changes, the whole rear fuselage of the Sabre was removed; once work had been carried out, engine runs could be accomplished without the need to refit the tail section. This greatly helped the ground crews in leak-checking the engine, and also meant that far less work was required should the engine need to be removed again after a ground run. (*Tony Lock*)

tanks were now in short supply, a concentrated effort yielded an unprecedented 671.1 hours on the Sabres by the end of the month compared with just 250 hours for August. The situation was helped by the use of Geilenkirchen GCA, which meant that even in really dreadful conditions aircraft could still be launched and recovered safely. Helchteren range was again in use by the squadron, and on 10 September a number of long-range attacks were completed. These entailed the Sabres flying a variety of cross-country mission profiles at high and low level, each culminating with attacks on the range. This proved to be a far more realistic and useful exercise for those involved. Exercise Battle Royal kicked off on 23 September, the squadron launching its first section of Sabres at 0820 hr. This routine continued for the next three days. Twelve Members of Parliament visited the station at the height of Battle Royal on 24 September and the squadron managed to put on an operational turnaround exercise for them, while 112 Sqn's Sabres performed aerobatics.

All Sabres were grounded on 9 October for a check of cracks on the compass detector unit. Twelve of the squadron's aircraft were affected and, with more aircraft unserviceable for other problems, this left just four Sabres in airworthy condition. New brackets for the compass detector units were soon fabricated by ASF but, even when these had been fitted, the affected aircraft required compass swings to ensure that compass readings had not been changed.

A string of serious accidents had begun on 26 September when the Station Flight Meteor crashed, killing Fg Off Weir of 130 Sqn and Fg Off Jenkins from 112. Tony Lock remembered what happened: 'Being ex-Regiment, I was always on funeral duty, which can be quite depressing as a young man. A low point in the morale with the aircraft. We lost Jenkins (112) and Stan Weir (130) in a Meteor accident – practising asymmetrics. A lunatic training exercise for single-engine jockeys. That was my first experience of close contact with an accident so close to home. The boss (John Mejor) and myself were two of the first there, but there was little we could do. The fire crews were there before and could not stop the fire, which was fierce.'

During night flying on 19 October, Fg Off Chris Woodruff in XB988 had a fire in flight and crashed seven miles north-east of Kassel. Woodruff was killed in the crash and was buried at Cologne on 23 October. Three days after Woodruff's crash, XB951 was badly damaged after its main nose undercarriage came down in flight. This marked a recurrence of the squadron's earlier problems in this respect, but was especially worrying as STI 11B, a technical instruction to overcome the problem, had already been completed on the aircraft. XB951 was sent to Airwork at Dunsfold for repair. With so many of the squadron Sabres written off or sidelined for repairs, by 27 October only seven Sabres were serviceable. On that day, missions began at 0830 hr, but within an hour the weather had deteriorated sufficiently that all airborne aircraft were recalled. In heavy rain and with a strong 90-degree crosswind, Fg Off Coatesworth then slid off the wet runway on landing, though no damage was done to his aircraft, XB930.

Two days later Fg Off Stewart Salmond experienced an electrical failure in XB918, immediately lowering his undercarriage using the emergency system and returning to base. Turning finals, he was given a 'red' by the runway controller and, presuming that his undercarriage must be unsafe, elected to land on the crash strip. Fortunately, there was no damage to the aircraft, but the incident would have repercussions. Later that day, Fg Off Duncan Bracher's engine failed on approach after a fuel-regulator failure, and the pilot was forced to land in the undershoot area; XB927 was destroyed. Having earlier survived the electrical failure, Stewart Salmond was on hand to see Duncan Bracher's accident: '[He] lost his engine, tried a dead-stick landing but bit a 15 ft (or so) pile of earth just off the end of the runway. By the time we got there the fuselage was on its side, with the whole mainplane ripped off and lying alongside in one piece. Duncan's only injury was a cut on his hand, acquired as he had crawled out through a hole in the partially smashed canopy.'

Incredibly, it was not Bracher's accident that subsequently grounded the Sabres, but that of Stewart Salmond. The order came on 2 November, after investigation into the earlier incident had pinpointed arcing of generator electrical terminal blocks as the cause of the electrical failure. Inspection of the squadron Sabres revealed that several aircraft were suffering from the same problem. During this inspection, XB952 was also found to have a badly cracked exhaust cone; hot gases had already burnt through the insulating blanket and were playing on the fuel-dump pipe. Another near miss. The discovery of this crack led to a further fleet check, and by the end of the day six Sabres were grounded for generator terminal blocks and four for exhaust cracks. As these checks had not been fully completed there were no serviceable aircraft on the squadron. Slowly, aircraft began to be returned to service, the first pair on 4 November.

Sadly the problems did not let up. Though seventeen sorties were completed on the Helchteren range on 9 November, the squadron was still struggling to get back to full strength after the imposed groundings and incidents. Detailed for an air test on that day, Sgt Hughes experienced a severe porpoising moment at 450kt and 6,000ft in XB851; the aircraft sustained an 8g overstress which wrinkled the starboard fuselage skin and resulted in Cat. 3 damage. Two days later, XB953 and XB954 were grounded for mainplane changes after a series of heavy landings. This work was done at squadron level with the assistance of 4 MRSU. On the same day Fg Off Tony Lock hit a flock of birds in XB922, causing damage to the aircraft's nose section. The next problem was uncovered when the aircraft were grounded on 19 November for tailplane artificial feel brackets to be inspected; ten aircraft were found to be cracked. With few aircraft available, on 25 November Fg Off 'Snowy' LeBreton experienced problems keeping straight while landing on a wet runway and skidded onto the grass – only the tyres were damaged this time. Three days later Fg Off Dicky Burden was unable to stop his aircraft on landing and went off the runway into the overshoot. The aircraft's wheels immediately sank into the sodden earth and the starboard wheel struck a raised inspection cover. XB933 received a dented wheel and buckled mainplane skins, but the buckles were assessed as within acceptable limits. The final incidents of 1954 saw Fg Off Lock and Fg Off Lees overstress their Sabres to 8g and 11g, respectively, on 21 December; this left the squadron with just three serviceable Sabres.

It must therefore have been a pleasant change for ten of the squadron pilots to travel to Wildenrath on 16 December to be introduced to the Hawker Hunter. The aircraft, part of a Central Fighter Establishment team, had arrived the previous day. Their pilots, Sqn Ldr Seaton, DFC, AFC and Capt Beck, a USAF-exchange pilot, gave talks on the type to 130 Sqn personnel. But, though the pilots admired the lines and general finish of the Hunter, after hearing the presentations many felt that the aircraft was not as much of a step forward from the Sabre as they had been led to believe. Though it would be some time before they had a chance to find out, their words were prophetic.

The following year, 1955, began with a further incident: Fg Off Coatesworth lost his port drop tank while flying XB943 on 4 January. It was later recovered by the Army detachment at Bracht. Concurrently, most of the oxygen regulators were again found to be time-expired, and the Sabres were restricted to flights below 15,000ft until sufficient spares could be demanded. In any case, there were numerous heavy snowfalls at the start of the year and the effect was minimal. Of the missions that were completed, a number comprised range firing, and on 31 January the Sabres accomplished mock attacks on RAF Regiment observation posts in the south-west and north-east dispersals.

Amid further snow, Fg Off Salmond ferried XB790 out to 20 Sqn on 9 February. This aircraft was notable as being the squadron's last slatted Sabre and had lingered in the hangar, providing spare parts for the rest of the aircraft. It had taken the best part of a year to convert fully onto '6–3'-winged Sabres.

Despite three inches of snow falling on 10 February, work on the station's new harmonisation gun butts was finally completed. A number of Sabres were immediately placed into the butts and adjusted, awaiting a break in the weather. After a week standing idle, the squadron was able to put in a range day on 17 February, firing 1,349 rounds on six sorties; squadron average was 7.4 per cent. Unfortunately, due to further snowfalls there was no more flying until 26 February; in total, only seven and a half days in the whole month were deemed fit for flying.

One of the squadron's armourers had a nasty brush with the Sabre on 1 March. Just as Fg Off Baker was running down his engine after a sortie, SAC Pitchfork was sucked into the aircraft's intake. Bob Jones was a fellow armourer on the squadron and was there at the time of Pitchfork's accident:

A Sabre taxies in after an air-firing sortie; SAC Pitchfork and I, swaddled in the latest fashion of cold-weather clothing, move in to clear any stoppages and reload for the next sortie. As the engine runs down, I take the pilot's report ('clean shoot – for a change') and start on the port side,

In March 1955, 130 Sqn's Sabres still wore muted colours, as exemplified by XB943/L of 'A' Flight. At the time, this aircraft had the best serviceability record in the squadron; Fg Off John Oxenford had been trying to get his name painted on the canopy rail, but the aircraft was never in the hangar! Eventually he succeeded, and the name 'Fg Off Oxenford' was painted in black on the port side. Unfortunately, this was one of the aircraft chosen to return to the UK when the squadron reduced to 14-aircraft strength; it left the squadron in July 1955. (*John Oxenford*)

while 'Pitch' dodges under the nose to see to the starboard guns. I shout, 'All clear, your side, Pitch?' Silence. 'ALL CLEAR, YOUR SIDE??' Even more silence. I go round to investigate . . . no sign of my 'oppo'. The pilot climbs out – 'That engine stopped rather abruptly' – and takes a glance at the intake. 'CHRIST ALMIGHTY!' A brief imitation of headless chickens, the ambulance at the end of the runway hastily summoned, luckily containing a sensible MO, who we shove up the congested intake with his morphine gun. We pull him out; the MO has a firm grip on Pitch's ankles. The poor lad is just alive and off to Wegberg hospital before you could say, '*Noch schnell*'.

The engine rundown had created sufficient suction to snatch the loose hood of Pitch's cold-weather jacket; he, being of slight build, was sucked up swiftly and silently. Down the intake, the Sabre's engine has a rude protuberance aptly nicknamed the 'dog's cock' (from its shape, rather than its function). The unfortunate Pitchfork had fetched up violently on this; his skull was badly smashed, but the hood that had caused his accident also saved his life: stretched tightly over his head by the suction, the thin but tough material had cushioned enough of the impact to prevent brain damage. After six weeks in hospital he was back at work – but got sudden headaches whenever air firing was mentioned!

As Bob Jones mentions, SAC Pitchfork was rushed to Wegberg Hospital; he was out of danger by 4 March. A lucky man indeed.

Meanwhile, despite continued poor weather and easterly winds that brought industrial haze in from the Ruhr, 130 Sqn managed to launch an unprecedented amount of sorties in March. Much of this was down to the shortage of drop tanks, and this meant that sorties rather than hours were racked up. Many of the sorties were radar quarter attacks aimed at building up the squadron for a further Sylt deployment; flag-towing was also practised. And at the beginning of April, 'battle four' formations completed air-to-sea firing, using all six guns for the first time. Crews were particularly impressed by the smoke and noise associated with firing all guns; less so by the 20kt decrease in speed while firing. Snow and bad weather throughout the month still had an adverse effect on flying, and on 28 March the CO decreed that each flying day would begin

XB924/E is refuelled after an engine ground run in March 1955. The 'A' Flight tail code comprised a white letter on a red disc. (*John Oxenford*)

at 0700 hr to recoup the hours being lost; the squadron ended March with 530 sorties flown and just over 512 Sabre hours.

Unfortunately, the minor incidents still blighted life, though fortunately there were no injuries this time. On 9 March a gunnery flag fell off one of the squadron's Sabres near Venlo, and Fg Off Burden lost a drop tank from XB922 the same day. Flt Sgt Vine suffered a burst tyre while landing in XB959 on 23 March.

Preparations for Sylt began at the start of April, when flying was reduced to preserve airframe hours. The main party departed by rail on 11 April, the aircraft two days later. Almost immediately the squadron was hit by further minor incidents, Fg Off Sommerard experiencing a burst tyre on arrival at Sylt due to a brake failure in XB918. Also, on 13 April Fg Off Duncan Bracher landed short in XB929 and hit the edge of Sylt's runway; his Sabre was Cat. 3 and required repair by the MRSU party from Oldenburg.

Already two Sabres down, the squadron began range firing on 14 April, expending 5,262 rounds and starting off with a squadron average of 4.7 per cent. This had doubled by the end of the detachment, even though many sorties had to be cancelled for bad weather or aircraft unserviceability. The squadron also distinguished itself by managing a 13.32 per cent average towards the Duncan Trophy – the best so far by a 2 TAF Sabre squadron. In general, the detachment was successful, and culminated in an operational rearm practice on 11 May. Two sections of four aircraft took part in this exercise, yielding a 19.5-minute best turnaround, which included rearming all aircraft. The squadron returned to Brüggen on 12 May, followed by the main party two days later. XB929 was left at Sylt, still being repaired by the MRSU.

Unfortunately, it was very much back to routine after Sylt, with a recurrence of the undercarriage door problems experienced during the previous year. First to fall victim was Fg Off Ireland, who had his main undercarriage doors come open while performing a 4.5g turn in XB933 on 18 May. Concurrently, two other Sabres, XB924 and XB942, were found to have cracked mainplanes, and XB954 had a fuel leak from its centre tank. Though all were repaired on station, given the planned reduction of Sabre establishment from twenty-two aircraft to just fourteen in June, the opportunity was taken to dispose of many of the more tired airframes.

That the squadron continued to provide battle flight commitments and other missions at this time is a great credit to the ground crews, who as ever were having to cope with spares shortages. On 2 June 'B' Flight managed to provide four Sabres on a barrage bomber mission to Stuttgart, and the squadron was then forewarned of its biggest exercise commitment yet, with 'Carte Blanche' due to be launched in mid-month. Exercise Carte Blanche involved many aircraft from across Europe, simulating a war between 'Northland' and 'Southland', with aircraft divided between each side. As a result, 130 Sqn would initially deploy to Geilenkirchen and find itself providing deployed-fighter interception missions against American, Canadian and French opposition. Special markings were applied to participating aircraft to distinguish 'friend' from 'foe', and like 112 Sqn, which would also deploy to Geilenkirchen, the Sabres of 130 Sqn carried a broad pale yellow band around the fuselage. The 'other side's' aircraft were painted with either a yellow or a black cross on the port wing, depending on whether or not the aircraft was camouflaged.

Preliminary orders for Exercise Carte Blanche were issued on 14 June, and the squadron was given a full briefing four days later. The main ground party of the squadron then deployed to Geilenkirchen on 20 June, and the Sabres at Brüggen were brought to 'available' at 0700 hr the following morning; they took off at 1000 hr and flew a low-level mission straight to Geilenkirchen. The first scrambles took place on 22 June, though not all targets were the enemy: Rex Boulton in XB930 'claimed' a civilian Viscount airliner on that day. The exercise proper began on 23 June, when at 0300 hr 'Northland' was officially declared to be at war with 'Southland'. Later in the morning a simulated nuclear strike disabled the airfield just as eight aircraft were about to be scrambled; with a hasty recovery, first missions of the day began just after midday. These resulted in numerous dogfights with Canadian and USAF Sabres. On the following day, fighter sweeps were completed, ranging as far as Lake Geneva. In turn, the airfield was attacked by American T-33 and RF-80 aircraft. French Ouragans were intercepted for the first time on 25 June, and a further airfield 'atomisation' took place at lunchtime on the 26th, which resulted in 90 per cent casualties for the squadron. After another miraculous recovery the squadron was declared operational again just after 1500 hr that afternoon and then stood down at 2100 hr. The next day, 27 June, was the squadron's final day on Exercise Carte Blanche, and again saw scrambles to intercept enemy aircraft. Rex Boulton, flying XB732, managed to get a USAF F-86F kill on one mission – an unusual feat, as both the American F-86Fs and the Canadian Sabre 5s enjoyed a considerable performance advantage over the RAF Sabre 4s. Many of the squadron aircraft stopped to refuel at Wildenrath after this mission and then made the return trip to Brüggen later in the day. The squadron was back at base by 2000 hr. For John Oxenford the final day had been extremely busy: 'On the last day I think I flew four sorties, the final one being a short one from Geilenkirchen to Brüggen. That day I spent so much time in the air that the cockpit felt like home and all the cockpit drills and procedures became so automatic I did them almost unconsciously. Although very tired at the end of the day, I felt I could carry on flying indefinitely. The outstanding thing about our squadron during this exercise was that we didn't have a single accident.'

The squadron returned to a far busier airfield than it had left. From the beginning of July, Brüggen became the new home to 67 and 71 Sqns, both of which had just completed an armament-practice camp in Cyprus. With 135 Wg now comprising four Sabre squadrons, Brüggen became the hub of RAF Sabre operations. Fg Off Rex Boulton took part in an unusual exercise to help the new neighbours at this time. While on the trip back from Cyprus, two of the Sabres had damaged their drop tanks, and one Sabre each from 130 and 112 Sqn were tasked with ferrying out replacement drop tanks. Rex took XB851 and was accompanied by Fg Off Brown from 112. The mission did not go to plan. Departing Brüggen on 13 July the aircraft routed via Fürstenfeldbruck to Rome's Ciampino airport, where the drop tanks would be removed for use by the stricken aircraft. But, as Rex recalls, 'We tore one on turn-off of the runway on high-standing taxi lights. On return [to base] I had one tank and Brown was clean.' Thus, the return legs had to be short-ranged, and when they began the journey on 16 July the pair routed from Rome to Istrana and on to Wahn in Germany via Fürstenfeldbruck. After a night stop both aircraft returned to base the following day, though even then the excitement was not over: Rex Boulton flew the final leg with his undercarriage locked down after experiencing hydraulic problems.

Concurrent with the increase in aircraft at Brüggen, the squadrons began to reduce to a fourteen-aircraft unit establishment, and 130 Sqn began this process at the start of July. As mentioned above, the opportunity was taken to set off the loss of these aircraft by transferring out the more dog-eared examples, and thus it was that Flt Lt John Chick flew XB924 to Kemble on 29 July. This aircraft had been grounded with a cracked mainplane since May, and a 'one flight only' waiver was signed to get the aircraft back to the UK for repair. With two further Sabres in for long-term repair (XB929 and XB949), the squadron also gained two ex-4 Sqn Sabres at the end of the month, and seems to have got away with running above its establishment for a number of months: by the end of August the roster of aircraft comprised sixteen Sabres, rather than the usual fourteen.

Inevitably, this period was one of considerable upheaval, as acceptance inspections were required on newly arrived aircraft and those being ferried away also needed attention from the maintenance personnel. In addition, Fg Off Dickie Burden had also written off XB932 on 12 July, when he landed heavily in the undershoot area. On 22 July the aircraft were checked for aileron-hydraulic-line P-clip bracket cracks, and all bar two Sabres were found to be affected. The Sabres were again grounded on 11 August for inspection of fuselage upper fuel tanks for cracking, and two further aircraft required repair. On the same day, Flt Lt Chapman had a main undercarriage door come open in flight, and his aircraft, XB930, suffered Cat. 3 damage.

By 15 August, XB952 was the only serviceable Sabre on the squadron and, along with two 'almost serviceable' Sabres, it was sent to the harmonisation butts in preparation for a range-firing programme on the following day. Fortunately, this went off without a hitch and resulted in six successful sorties for an average of 16.3 per cent; 1,081 rounds were fired during the day. And there was also better news concerning aircraft serviceability. Those aircraft affected by fuel-tank cracks were declared fit for flight so long as cracks were 'slight' – however, these aircraft were restricted to straight and level flight only.

The squadron took part in Exercise Loco in a limited capacity at the end of August, flying as simulated bomber formations. The Sabres were limited to medium altitudes and were not allowed to take evasive action when intercepted. Most felt the whole thing to be unrealistic and something of a waste of time. A concerted effort was made to get in air-to-ground gunnery time during September, and a great deal of hours were flown before

This formation of 'B' Flight aircraft (blue circle with white code letter) was aloft during Exercise Battle Royal in September 1955 and comprised XB918/R, XB953, XB927/V and XB929/Q. XB927 was lost in Duncan Bracher's crash landing at Brüggen just a month later. Note also the complete lack of fuselage squadron markings at this relatively late date. (*John Oxenford*)

Exercise Beware, the annual UK air-defence test, which began at the end of the month. This was immediately followed on 1 October by Exercise Foxpaw, which saw eight Sabres airborne at lunchtime for a 35,000ft mission to the Lincolnshire coast and back. These sorties lasted nearly one and a half hours.

Following a number of incidents on the air-to-ground ranges, when gunnery began again at Monschau on 11 October, scores were not taken, and in the following days procedures were changed to make the ranges safer. By 19 October, control of the firing passes had been handed to the range officer, who would then tell each pilot when to begin firing and when to break off. Ultimately, dive angles were also reduced. During this period, though scores could not be assessed, the squadron would often programme long-range cross-country missions that culminated in firing passes on the range.

As 1955 drew to a close, the squadron began to turn its thoughts toward conversion onto the Hunter, and a number of lectures began on the new type. Sabre serviceability again took a nosedive and, among the usual gunsight problems experienced, new faults occurred with radio compasses and nose-wheel steering. Though a number of high-level cross-countries were completed, fog and mist for much of this period severely reduced the flying commitment.

Flown into Stansted on 12 April 1956 straight from assignment to 130 Sqn, XB929 is pictured there soon after. It was overhauled and passed to the Yugoslav Air Force. (*Author's Collection*)

A final Sabre detachment to Sylt began on 3 January 1956, the aircraft departing a day early after an unexpected gap in the weather arrived. Unfortunately, upon arrival at Sylt the squadron was grounded by fog on subsequent days, and an opportunity was lost on 6 January when flying was possible but a shipping check had not been completed on the range, and thus firing was out of the question. The squadron sat largely idle for ten days, awaiting the right conditions, with gunnery sorties being finally completed on the 13th, though, even then, the majority were cine only. By 16 January radar problems, crosswinds and snowfalls had curtailed activity again, and it was only on 26 January, with the runway semi-clear of snow, that glider-target sorties were planned. Unfortunately, after a landing accident involving a 112 Sqn Sabre, these were cancelled. A thoroughly dejected squadron returned to Brüggen on 27 January, having achieved little during its Sylt detachment – just forty-eight effective shoots in fact. Only 130 hours had been flown for the whole month.

But if January was poor, February was worse; ice and fog plus snow from mid-month resulted in just thirty-five missions being flown. On 2 February Sqn Ldr Mejor took XB949 aloft for the final flight of the day and was unable to get his starboard undercarriage locked down on returning to base. He had no option but to trust that the leg was in fact safe; but the aircraft's undercarriage collapsed as soon as it touched down and the aircraft sustained Cat. 3 damage. The fault was soon put down to a sticking undercarriage downlock pin; the squadron was grounded for rectification work and Sqn Ldr Mejor departed for some well-earned leave. At the end of March another potential problem was avoided when all Sabres were required to have their aileron actuators X-rayed; only XB928 was found to be unserviceable on this occasion.

Despite the poor start to the year, March also marked a change in fortunes, and a number of 'rat and terrier' missions were flown from the 8th onwards; these comprised aircraft flying out of the immediate area and performing low-level attacks while the rest of the squadron tried to intercept them. On 9 March a number of aircraft performed a recce mission on the Dieppe and Calais areas. One of the last Sabre missions for the squadron involved a four-ship that was tasked with intercepting a formation of DFLS Hunters inbound to Brüggen. Unfortunately, GCI became saturated with aircraft blips and proved of no use to the squadron; the Hunters were intercepted just south of base, and no claims could be made.

Meanwhile, Hunter lectures had begun in earnest on 4 February when Sqn Ldr Calvey of 229 OCU arrived to brief squadron personnel. The first Hunter for 130 Sqn was delivered on 27 March, followed by five more on 6 April, the day that the squadron became non-operational on the Sabre.

In turn the Sabres were ferried out to the UK, and by 11 April there were only nine remaining on the squadron, which by this time had eleven Hunters. With the emphasis now firmly on re-equipping, just forty-four Sabre sorties were flown in April 1956, and most of these were test flights prior to transfer out of the squadron. The final pair of Sabres on the squadron, XB949 and XB959, departed for Benson on 7 May and 14 June, respectively.

Brief note should be made of a short-lived squadron aerobatic team, which comprised Dave Brett as leader. Ray Chapman ('A' Flight commander), Bob Baker and John Oxenford also flew in the team.

Aircraft Assigned

Initial delivery, January to May 1954:

XB790, XB797/F, XB800/F, XB824, XB833, XB834, XB836, XB838, XB839, XB858, XB859, XB861, XB862/V, XB871, XB891, XB894.

All aircraft were slatted.

Second delivery, April 1954 to end of service:

XB648, XB732*, XB745/D*, XB851, XB852, XB916, XB918/R, XB921, XB922/X, XB924/E, XB927/V, XB928/G, XB929/Q, XB930/B, XB932, XB933/W, XB942, XB943/L, XB945, XB949/Z, XB951, XB952, XB953, XB954/U, XB959/V, XB961, XB975, XB981, XB985/V, XB986/D, XB987/H, XB988, XB991.

All '6–3'-winged from manufacture, except those indicated *, which were modified to '6–3' configuration during RAF service.

Markings – 130 Sqn

The squadron initially applied very simple markings to its Sabres; the white individual code letter was applied to a flight-coloured circle (red for 'A' Flight and dark blue for 'B' Flight) on the tail fin. Individual flight letters were 'A' to 'M' for 'A' Flight and 'N' to 'Z' for 'B' Flight.

When bar markings arrived, they were applied either side of the fuselage roundel and comprised a blue bar with a red elongated triangle superimposed, its short side towards the roundel. Each colour was separated by a thin white stripe, the whole bar being similarly treated.

Squadron Motto

Strong to serve.

CHAPTER FIFTEEN

147 SQUADRON

Though not a front-line unit, 147 Sqn figures prominently in the history of RAF Sabres, having been assigned the task of ferrying the aircraft to and from the user units. The squadron was formed concurrent with the disbanding of 1 (Long Range) Ferry Unit on 1 February 1953; it took over Sabre-ferrying tasks, and all personnel were transferred over 'on paper' from the ferry unit. The new squadron also inherited the three Sabre F. 2s and eight F. 4s previously flown by 1 (LR) FU. On 4 May the unit moved to RAF Benson, with Sqn Ldr T. Stevenson as its commanding officer.

The new squadron's first mission was to complete the delivery of aircraft on Bechers Brook 2; thirty-three aircraft were safely delivered, but the mission was marred by the loss of XB549 at Stornoway on 10 March. Fg Off Vindis experienced control problems on landing, and the aircraft was blown off its approach path, suffering an undercarriage collapse.

Aside from ferrying Sabres, 147 Sqn continued to train ferry crews, and further Sabres were assigned to the unit for this purpose. However, once the task had been taken over by the Sabre Conversion Unit in Germany, 147 Sqn began to lose its own Sabres. First to leave were the three Sabre F. 2s, which departed for Kemble at the end of June 1953. By the end of September the squadron only had a handful of Sabres left, and these were used to keep the unit's Sabre crews current on the type.

Peter Foard joined 147 Sqn soon after it was formed, and immediately began his Sabre conversion course. Then it was straight in at the deep end:

One of only three Sabre F. 2s operated by the RAF, XB531/B takes a rest between sorties at Benson. Note the tarmac ramp surface, which melted when fuel was spilt on it; a change to concrete hardstandings resolved the problem. (*Bruce Robertson*)

After several hours' familiarisation on the type, we were flown out to RCAF St Hubert by North Star or Hastings aircraft for further familiarisation prior to the ferrying operation. We would collect the new aircraft from Dorval airport across the St Lawrence. The route was up to Goose Bay, Bluie West 1, Iceland, then Scotland or Aldergrove down to Kemble, where the aircraft would be sprayed camouflage, prior to allocation to the squadrons.

Bluie West 1 in Greenland was interesting, as we had to fly up the fjord to reach the runway, as the rest of the surrounding area was mountainous; taking off also entailed flying down the fjord for the same reason. Sometimes when we were ready to take off, we had to hold until an iceberg floated out of the way of the take-off path. The immersion suits we had to wear 'sealed us up' for sometimes two legs of the trip. Trying to 'take a leak' could be quite an operation.

Peter's first ferry mission was Bechers Brook 6, when he flew XD717 across to Kemble, arriving there on 18 July 1953.

During 1953, 147 Sqn suffered a number of accidents, mainly associated with the hazards involved with ferrying brand-new aircraft in poor weather. On 1 March XB641 suffered Cat. 3 damage at Keflavik (possibly due to Flt Lt Hacke landing short at Keflavik), which necessitated repair by the maintenance unit at Kemble. On 5 April Sqn Ldr Cole was killed after his aircraft (XB610) hit high ground on approach to Kinloss; instrument failure after take-off was the principal cause. Back at Benson, on 16 May

Aside from being a useful colour reference for the all-black instrument panel, this view of XB544's cockpit also reveals that the g-meter (upper-left instrument) is registering more than 10g. Overstress was the result of the aircraft's incident on 16 May 1953. (*National Archives*)

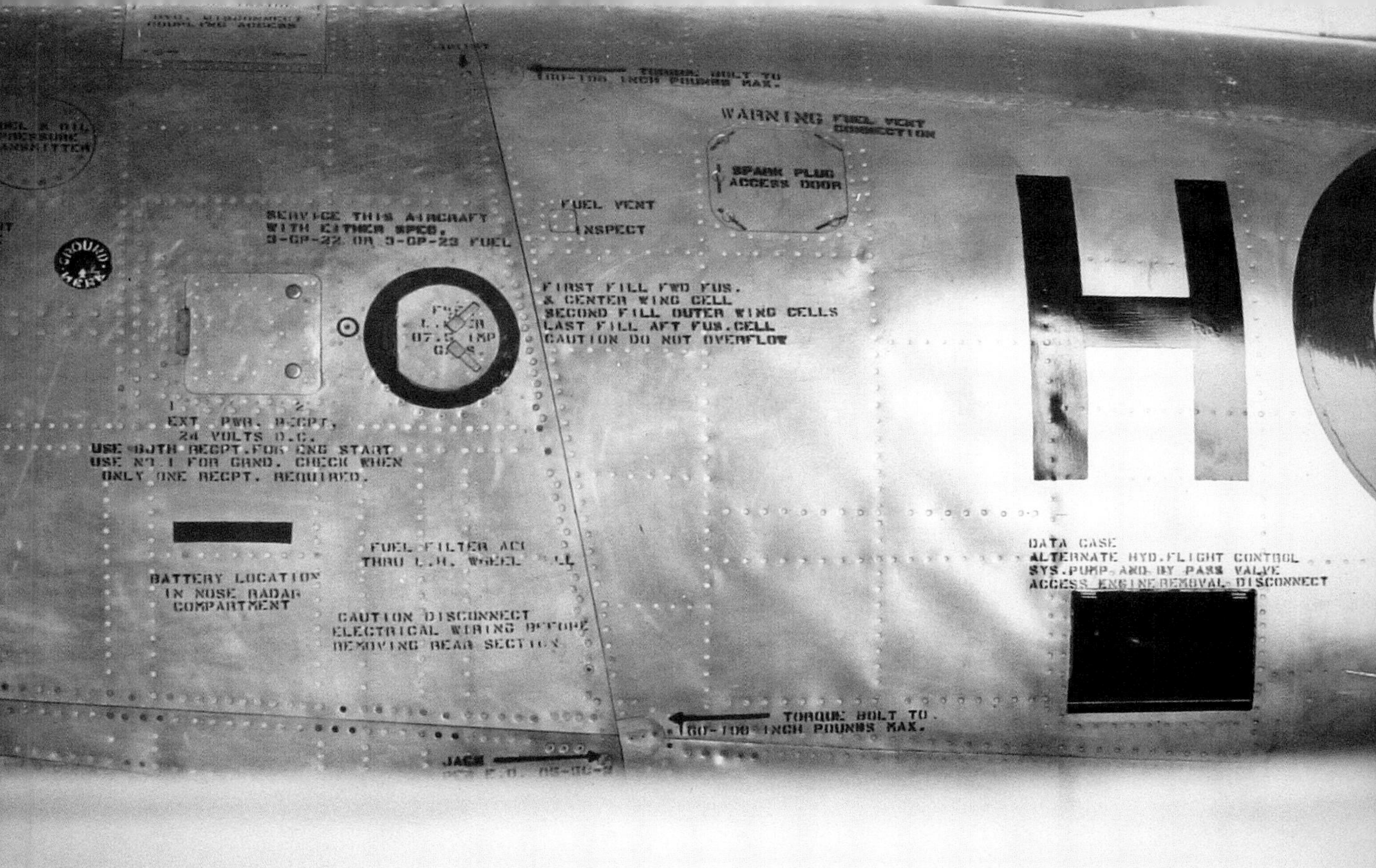

On 16 May 1953, a data-case door detached from XB544 during a flight from Benson; it struck the tailplane and led to an overstress of the airframe. P Off K.G. MacLeod recovered safely to base. Resultant skin wrinkling can be seen on this photograph, as well as the hole left below the 'H' by the errant door. (*National Archives*)

P Off K.G. MacLeod was lucky to escape with his life after an access panel came adrift on a local flight. The panel struck the Sabre's left-hand tailplane, causing a 10g overstress on the airframe – he landed safely at Benson, but his aircraft, XB544/H, was damaged beyond local repair. It was sent to Airwork for overhaul, but never returned to RAF service.

The summer brought no respite from these accidents: on 5 June Sgt Roderick was killed in XB863 near St-Félix-de-Valois, Quebec after becoming lost in cloud; it was his first Sabre flight in Canada. On 18 July P Off Butrym escaped from XB882 after his cockpit filled with smoke; he inadvertently fired the ejection seat near Dundee. Exactly one month later, the pilot of XD775 ejected at St Hubert after experiencing an elevator malfunction. Fg Off Cross survived another crash after XB925 lost power on approach to Kinloss on 28 September 1953. Finally, on 23 October P Off Garratt landed heavily at Benson in XB599. The aircraft had been allotted to 71 Sqn, but incurred Cat. 4 damage and was instead assigned to Airwork for repair.

Squadron pilots were also responsible for collecting stragglers from other Bechers Brook missions. On most ferry missions there were small incidents, and if any rectification was required the remainder of the flight would usually continue to the UK, leaving any stricken Sabres where they landed for rectification. Thus, on Bechers

A nice formation shot of Sabres on a Bechers Brook mission. Note also the red wingtip visible here and the natural metal surround to the roundel. (*Graham Elliott*)

Brook 5, for instance, nine aircraft were picked up along the ferry route that had been unserviceable on earlier missions. Other aircraft were damaged prior to delivery: XD128 (later re-serialled as XB989) was damaged at St Hubert on 23 November 1953 while being ferried by a Canadian pilot. It was returned to Canadair for repair three days later, finally flying out to the UK on Bechers Brook 11.

The Bechers Brook ferry missions were officially completed with the arrival of eleven Sabres at 33 MU, Lyneham on 19 December 1953; 368 Sabres had been ferried by 147 Sqn and its precursors. Further small batches of Sabres were ferried from Canada after this date, but the general emphasis for the unit now moved to the transfer of Sabres from maintenance unit to user squadrons. Ferry flights to the units in Germany had actually started in early 1953, and from 27 November 1953, 147 Sqn began to ferry Sabres to Fighter Command. Most of these missions routed through Benson, with refuel and route planning being carried out there prior to final delivery.

At the end of 1953, 147 Sqn pilots were responsible for ferrying most of the sixty RAF Sabres which had been loaned to Royal Canadian Air Force units. All had been overhauled by Airwork at Speke and were flown to 5 MU at Kemble, still bearing RCAF serial numbers. The first aircraft was 19454, which was flown Speke to Benson on 16 December, then to 5 MU on 21 December.

The final ferry flight of Sabres from Canada was carried out by 147 Sqn in July 1954. Two Sabres, XB761 and XB809, were flown from St Hubert to Chatham on 15 July, reaching Bluie West 1 the following day – XB761 was flown by Graham Elliott. The pair reached Kinloss on 20 July, finally bringing to a close this chapter of the RAF Sabre story.

Just less than a year later, the Sabres began to be withdrawn from 2 TAF units and mass ferrying began again. The first aircraft to return for overhaul were XB595, XB577 and XB597, the trio all coming from 26 Sqn. The pilots of 147 Sqn ferried these machines to Airwork at Ringway on 7 July 1955. Further aircraft were flown to Westland's overhaul facility at Yeovilton on 13 July, and from then on there was a mass exodus of Sabres from Germany.

On 17 August 1955, 147 Sqn suffered another loss: Fg Off K.G. MacLeod was ferrying XB700 to Yeovilton when it collided with a Navy Sea Hawk in the circuit there. Both pilots were killed; thankfully, it was the squadron's last Sabre loss.

On 20 June 1956, with the majority of Sabres transferred to the contractor organisations, 147's commanding officer led seven aircraft on a local fly-past to celebrate the unit's association with the Sabre. The last mass ferry flight from Germany had taken place on 15 June when seven Sabres were transferred from Geilenkirchen to Benson.

Ferry pilots during the early days gather at Abingdon in 1953. The three pilots at the left were the first to convert onto the Sabre – in Canada during August 1952. L–R: Sqn Ldr T. Stevenson, AFC, Flt Lt H.M. Deffee, Flt Lt H.F. Edwards, DFC, Flt Lt Sollom, Flt Sgt C.J.S. Howard, AFM, Flt Sgt J. Meecham, DFC, Sgt F.W. Burney and Flt Sgt W.H. Atkins. (*Larry Milberry*)

The formation was led by Flt Lt Burton. The last 2 TAF Sabre, XB670, was ferried into Benson on 21 June by Flt Lt Burton, and 147 Sqn's final Sabre flight took place on 25 June when Sgt Lackman transferred XB617 to Airwork at Speke. Graham Elliott was there right at the end; he had flown his last RAF Sabre flight on 22 June, taking XB973 to Speke for overhaul with Airwork.

However, 147 Sqn continued ferrying fighters for the RAF, notably Hunter and Swift aircraft. The unit was finally disbanded on 15 September 1958, when it amalgamated with 167 Sqn to form Ferry Squadron.

Aircraft Assigned

XB530/A, XB531/B, XB532/C, XB535/D, XB537/E, XB538/F, XB543/G, XB544/H, XB545/J, XB546, XB547/K, XB548, XB583, XB585, XB589, XB601/P, XB756, XB758.

All aircraft had slatted wings.

Markings – 147 Sqn

The squadron's aircraft were handed over initially in natural metal finish. Individual code letters were applied in black aft of the fuselage roundel. No other markings were carried. Later, a number of camouflaged aircraft were borrowed by the squadron, but these bore no individual markings.

Squadron Motto

Assidue portamus (We carry with regularity).

CHAPTER SIXTEEN

234 'MADRAS PRESIDENCY' SQUADRON

Operating from Oldenburg and commanded by Sqn Ldr Roy M. Chatfield, DFC, by late 1953, 234 Sqn was in the process of beginning conversion from Vampire fighter bombers to the Sabre. The process began in July when the squadron commander and OC 'A' Flight completed their Sabre courses at Wildenrath. However, although the first Sabres had been expected in early November, no other pilots were routed through the conversion course until 25 November, when nine crews travelled to Wildenrath and began tuition with Sabre Conversion Unit.

The first Sabre deliveries were delayed from mid-month by a thick haze in the Oldenburg area, and it was not until 27 November 1953 that XB735 and XB898 flew in to begin the changeover. This pair were followed by five more Sabres on the following day, but no further deliveries were made until the end of December. In the meantime the maintenance personnel started to perform acceptance checks on the newly arrived fighters, and also prepared the Vampires for ferrying out. The squadron flew its first Sabre sorties on 2 December, and further missions were completed on the afternoon of the following day. These early flights were devoted to individual-handling practice, so that crews could get used to the flying characteristics of the new aircraft. On 29 December, Fg Off C.V. Atkins went through the sound barrier, marking a first for the squadron.

Three more Sabres were delivered to 234 Sqn on 21 December, and this brought the squadron strength to ten aircraft. All of this batch were slatted, narrow-chord wing aircraft. However, before any further Sabres could be delivered, the squadron upped sticks and moved in its entirety to a new base at Geilenkirchen. Flying was stopped on 1 January 1954, and all personnel began the lengthy process of packing equipment for the move. The main party of the squadron moved to the new base on 4 January, but ice on the runway at Geilenkirchen meant that the Sabres could not fly across until better weather conditions arrived four days later. The first familiarisation flights from Geilenkirchen were completed on 13 January, followed by twenty sorties the following day. The squadron flew through the following weekend to take advantage of better weather, and settled relatively quickly into their new home.

By the end of January, with a hectic period now behind it, the squadron had finally begun to get to grips with the Sabre, though squadron strength stood at just sixteen until early March. Long-distance cross-country missions were undertaken on 2 February, enabling pilots to get used to fighter sweeps, and the squadron took up its first battle-flight commitment at the start of the month, despite two inches of snow on the runway. As the days wore on, more varied sorties were flown, such as a barrage exercise on 11 February, in which a squadron formation simulated an

The Sabre's intake could easily accommodate a full-grown man and, though it served as a handy backdrop for informal photographs such as this one of Tom Broomhead, it could also be a trap for the unwary. This shot also gives a good view of the nose checks applied to 234 Sqn Sabres: though the red background colour extended into the inner surface of the intake, the black checks did not. (*Tom Broomhead*)

incoming bomber raid; no interceptions were made against the Sabres on that occasion. Six days later, a number of formation let-down sorties were made, using straight-in approaches guided by the Wahn radio beacon and GCA. Emphasising the tactical role of the squadron, two army cooperation missions were completed on 24 February.

Almost inevitably, as the squadron was brought up to operational effectiveness a number of incidents occurred. On 18 February, while on a pairs take-off, number two in the formation failed to get airborne and ran into the overshoot area; only the wheels were damaged on this occasion. Five days later, as a section of four was carrying out a low-level strike, the formation leader, flying XB890, hit a bird, causing impact damage to the starboard side of the forward fuselage. Though the aircraft was safely returned to base, it had sustained Cat. 4 damage, requiring its return to the UK for repair; Fg Off A. Ross flew it to Dunsfold on 23 March.

Though larger than the Vampire it replaced, the Sabre was generally easy to work on, and large removable access panels allowed ground crews to get to key components. Note the mobile intake screen at the nose of XB838/P; it was essential in preventing foreign objects (and sometimes people) from being sucked down the intake during engine runs. (*Robin Brown*)

Snow was still present in March, and an expected involvement in Exercise Magna Flux came to nothing as a result of the weather conditions. Nonetheless, by 11 March barrage exercises were being flown, and on that day Valetta and F-84 aircraft were intercepted. On the following day, Fg Off Mike Langley, one of the Pilot Attack Instructors, flew to the Monschau range to plan a circuit in preparation for the squadron's first sorties there. Live air-to-ground firing at Monschau began on 18 March, though initially only experienced pilots were allowed to take part. On the first day, Fg Off Rawlinson, the Squadron Adjutant, hit a bird, causing damage to the wing of his Sabre. Fortunately, the following days were incident-free, and most pilots managed to complete live-firing sorties.

Night-flying missions started on 6 April, eighteen pilots being able to fly on this night alone. Though night missions were not often planned, they did help 234 Sqn's crews to become proficient at navigating in the dark; other Sabre squadrons did not take to it as easily. Also at the beginning of April, battle flight managed to obtain the services of four Vampires from 145 Sqn, and performed a number of interceptions against this easy prey. Tom Broomhead had arrived on the squadron during October 1953, fresh from training as a radar mechanic with 2 Radio School at Yatesbury: 'Along with 3 Sqn, we had to operate a battle flight. This consisted of two aircraft with pilots and ground crew sitting at the end of the runway all day at immediate readiness. A ground-crew man from every trade was involved, and our accommodation was a wooden hut to which our meals would be delivered at due times. To my knowledge we never had an incident, but it was exciting being at the "sharp end" of the Cold War.'

New revetments were completed at Geilenkirchen in late May and, on the 25th, pilots gave a demonstration, manoeuvring aircraft around these heavily built fortifications. Later in the year, Tom Broomhead was present when three Venoms from 16 Sqn arrived to carry out live attacks on these fixtures:

These [revetments] were frying-pan-shaped, with concrete walls, and with sandbags on top to raise the height, into which anti-blast shelters were incorporated. The revetments were connected to the perimeter track by new taxiways. We could park two or three Sabres in these and often did. However, one day [4 October] we were all instructed not to return from lunch and to stay in our billets until told otherwise. We learned that Venoms (from Wunstorf) were going to attack the revetments using rockets with concrete warheads. This they duly did, and it was exciting to watch them diving over our billet to release the rockets. Needless to say we didn't remain inside the billet. The revetments must have passed the test, for we continued to use them.

Barrage exercises and range firing at Monschau continued throughout June, and inevitably it was not long before the squadron lost its first aircraft, though thankfully not its pilot. On 29 June, Fg Off Pete Underdown, flying XB819/Z, suffered a fuel leak and flameout at 17,000ft while on a QGH mission. Unable to relight his engine, he was forced to put the aircraft down in a field four miles from the town of Jülich, and the impact destroyed the Sabre.

On 16 July the wing was briefed on the forthcoming Exercise Dividend, a test of the UK air-defence system. The Sabres of 234 Sqn, like so many others in 2 TAF, were tasked with flying missions to England, simulating bomber streams so that defending fighters could be vectored to intercept them. On the first day, 17 July, all missions were cancelled because of low cloud, and it was not until the following day that 234 Sqn finally took part. On that day, twenty-four sorties were flown against various coastal targets in East Anglia before the squadron stood down for two days. A dozen similar missions were launched on 22 July, culminating in a maximum-effort dawn attack on the 23rd, aimed at saturating the British defence network; a similar attack was completed the same afternoon. The squadron took no part in the final two days of Exercise Dividend due to bad weather. However, during the whole period very few interceptions had been made, despite the Sabres being restricted to relatively low speeds and altitudes.

Throughout this period the programme of range firing at Monschau continued, usually without incident. However, on 4 August Fg Off Shrimpton mushed into the ground on pulling out of his pass, causing damage to his Sabre's wingtip and tailpipe. He was fortunate to be able to regain control of the aircraft, and was escorted back to base for a formation landing; his escort gave Shrimpton accurate height and airspeed data as he brought the stricken aircraft in to land. The damage to XB807/Z – itself a replacement aircraft for XB819/Z, which had been lost less than two months earlier – was assessed as Cat. 4, and it was eventually returned to the UK for repair.

Considerable effort was now put into air-to-air gunnery, prior to the squadron's annual Sylt detachment. On 9 August, four Sabres took part in quarter attacks on a Lincoln bomber from the Central Fighter Establishment. During the following week, the squadron used its own Sabres to tow target flags, and also used radar to bring the guns to bear for the first time. Prior to the detachment, gunsights were calibrated and all pilots were required to fly cine sorties on the flag to assess their progress.

The advance party left for Sylt by road in the early morning of 19 August, with

Fg Off Dyckes in charge. The main rail party departed Geilenkirchen three days later but, though originally planned to fly out on the 23rd, poor weather at either departure or arrival point meant that it was not until 25 August that the sixteen Sabres made it into Sylt. By now the ground crews were well settled in, which meant that the first gunnery missions were flown that same day, enabling the squadron to recoup some of the lost time. The first to fire on the flag were the more experienced pilots, and the squadron then tried to get down to some problem-free gunnery. This didn't happen, recalls Tom Broomhead:

> One danger that was ever-present at Sylt was that of returning aircraft having ammunition in the guns. We were trained never to stand directly in front of the Sabres when taxiing and for marshalling and so on, and to wait until they had parked facing the earth bank. Then the trades would move in, usually led by the armourers, who would check guns clear. [On this occasion] the armourers had moved in first as usual and removed the panels to prepare for rearming, and at the same time a photographic-section airman had gone to the nose intake of the aircraft where the gun camera was located to recover the film. In clearing the guns a round was discharged which went into the earth embankment, but not before warming up the photographer's ear. He fell to the ground and it seemed he'd been shot, but it was a lucky escape. He said afterwards that he felt the heat as the round went past his head. New rules were introduced relating to clearing guns, and being in front of aircraft while this was being done was strictly banned.

Unfortunately, considerable problems were also experienced with gunsight serviceability, and on 6 September the station Prentice flew

With '6–3'-winged XB836 nearest the camera, these 234 Sqn Sabres display an interesting mix of old-style chequered intakes (XB794/V, third in line) and the newer red-trimmed type. Two of these machines also have unpainted replacement canopies. The photo was taken in August 1955. (*Robin Brown*)

Nice close-in view of the 234 Sqn aerobatic team led by Mike Langley. XB885/D is nearest the camera. (*Robin Brown*)

to Geilenkirchen to bring back more spares. In spite of these problems, Flt Lt Byrne managed to set a new high score of 36 per cent on 6 September, raising it to 40 per cent on the 13th. The squadron aircraft returned to Geilenkirchen on 17 September.

Immediately after arriving back at base, the squadron personnel began preparations for Exercise Battle Royal, deploying along with the aircraft to the dispersal revetments in the afternoon of 21 September. On subsequent days, ground-attack missions were flown against Wildenrath, and one more exercise sortie was launched on 24 September, but otherwise there was very little input for the squadron. The Sabres were returned to the hangar area at 1700 hr on 27 September.

During a period of enforced inactivity caused by poor weather in October, the squadron was introduced to the Hawker Hunter for the first time. A Martin-Baker ejection-seat rig arrived on a Queen Mary trailer, and all squadron pilots were given the chance to 'eject' themselves up the gantry. Turning back to their present aircraft, a number of pilots also went to Wildenrath on 12 October for lectures with the Sabre Mobile Technical Training Unit.

On 29 October, the squadron lost its second Sabre, again piloted by Fg Off Pete Underdown; for the second time, Underdown was fortunate to escape with his life. This time, his survival was nothing short of miraculous. Underdown had been tasked with performing a test flight on XB860/B, which had just been through 200-hour maintenance with ASF. The aircraft departed Geilenkirchen at lunchtime, and about two minutes after take-off the Sabre was seen at low level, flying at about 400kt. Suddenly it pitched nose up and then nose down; pieces of structure were seen to break away and the main part of the aircraft crashed into an orchard near Wintraak, Holland. Underdown was thrown through the canopy as his aircraft exploded, and came down, still in his ejector seat, on the lee side of a gentle slope. Though he had not initiated ejection or released his parachute, his gentle descending trajectory had matched that of the hill, and was further cushioned by the branches of a tree. Though seriously injured, Pete Underdown was soon recovering in hospital and was flown out to the UK on 20 December for rehabilitation. He would return to the squadron in October 1955 – nearly a year after his accident – and continue to fly the Sabre. Accident investigators soon found the cause of Underdown's crash: the elevator artificial-feel bracket had broken, causing undamped movement of the controls to overstress the aircraft.

The immediate result of Underdown's accident was the issuing of a preliminary warning signal on 3 November for inspection of the bracket assembly, with around fifty being found to be defective in 2 TAF alone. The effect on the squadrons was reduced somewhat, since the Sabres had in any case been grounded for a generator problem. The maintenance personnel of 234 Sqn were hard pressed to recover aircraft, but managed to get the first Sabres serviceable for air test on 4 November.

Unfortunately, the squadron then went through a spate of flying accidents and incidents, culminating in poor weather at the end of the year. On 10 November Flt Lt Keith Fitton had his port undercarriage leg collapse on landing, and his aircraft, XB615, was rendered Cat. 3. Two days later Fg Off Ross landed heavily while under GCA control and struck the boundary fence; his Sabre received only minor damage. On 18 November Fg Off S.R. West was more fortunate: he had a flameout at 4,000ft on a QGH, but despite the low altitude managed to relight his engine and landed safely.

Aside from the poor weather in December, flying was further restricted by the discovery of wing-attachment cracks in a number of aircraft. Less than 300 hours were flown on 243 missions. Conditions were even worse in January 1955, and though an air-to-ground programme was completed at Monschau on 4 January, along with eight night-flying missions, freezing rain on the following day and then further bouts of snow meant that very little flying was possible for much of the month. Snow again persisted throughout February but, on the odd day, flying was possible; an impressive 42 hours and 20 minutes of flying were logged on 18 February, for instance. During this period, aircraft began to be routed through the modification line, enabling the '6–3'-wing leading edge to be fitted. By the end of March, fifteen Sabres had been modified.

The squadron's new CO, Sqn Ldr Roger Emmett, took over on 7 March. Emmett had previously been the RAF's premier Meteor display pilot, and his arrival marked a change in fortunes for the squadron. On 24 March the first air-to-ground gunnery sorties for nearly three months were completed, and on this day alone 10,942 rounds were fired for only four stoppages. Four days later, a number of long-range cross-country sorties were flown – a first for many.

Exercise Sky High began at the end of April, and crews were briefed on the 23rd. First sorties were flown two days later, and most of these missions involved the Sabres operating against Canberra bombers, trying to intercept them before they passed out of the zone. Unfortunately, on all occasions these interceptions proved fruitless, because, though one section of Sabres managed to climb up to 47,000ft, the Canberras were routinely operating at 50,000.

From the start of May the accent turned to high-level battle formations in four-ship sections, Sqn Ldr Emmett changing the

Fire-picket duty did have its attractions. With the hangar empty of personnel, Tom Broomhead often took his camera on duty to capture illicit shots of the squadron's Sabres. XB817/U faces the camera, while the engineless forward fuselage of 873/Q is at the left, with its tail section at the right. (*Tom Broomhead*)

formations so that wing men were stepped back 10 degrees from the section leader to provide better cover; previously they had been flying 45 degrees back from the leader's wing. 'Bouncer' aircraft were used to validate the new formation, which did seem to be an improvement. On one of these sorties, the CO led the squadron's first formation supersonic bang.

June 1955 was a particularly busy month, which began with a large number of battle-flight interceptions, as well as barrage exercises against the US Zone. Two Sabres also went to Wahn on 14 June to demonstrate a 'refuel and rearm' to personnel there. But the main commitment for the month was to Exercise Carte Blanche, initial briefings for which took place on 18 June.

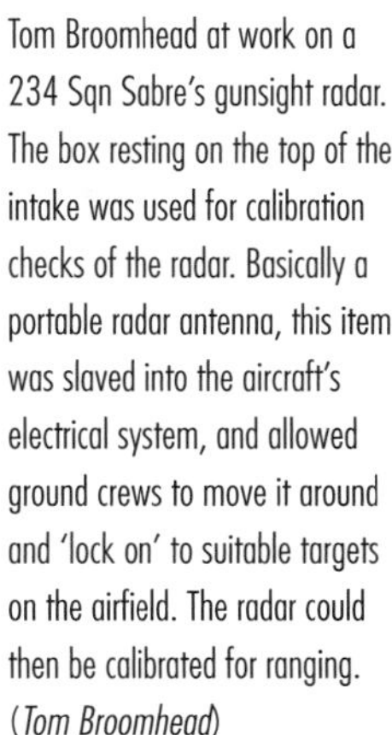

Tom Broomhead at work on a 234 Sqn Sabre's gunsight radar. The box resting on the top of the intake was used for calibration checks of the radar. Basically a portable radar antenna, this item was slaved into the aircraft's electrical system, and allowed ground crews to move it around and 'lock on' to suitable targets on the airfield. The radar could then be calibrated for ranging. (*Tom Broomhead*)

Carte Blanche's scenario involved two countries, 'Southland' and 'Northland', going to war, and Allied forces across Europe were split between the two sides. Initially, 234 Sqn would deploy to Beek in Holland to launch deployed air-defence missions against 'enemy' aircraft, which usually comprised USAF and Canadian Sabres. In addition, offensive-support sorties would also be required.

The advance party of the squadron left by road for Beek on 20 June, with a dozen Sabres and the rest of the squadron leaving on the 21st. No missions were flown on the next day, and the squadron took the opportunity to camouflage its positions and get settled in. The first sorties on Carte Blanche took place at 0525 hr on the morning of 23 June, and later that day a skittle run of twelve Sabres completed a fighter-sweep and radar-saturation mission. The squadron also looked after another eight Sabres that had diverted to Beek. On the following day, further skittle missions were completed, six Sabres diverting into Geilenkirchen before refuelling and returning to Beek later. Fog in the early morning of 25 June delayed the first missions, but eight Sabres soon left on a top-cover sortie for ground-attack F-84s. Eight further aircraft on a fighter sweep landed short of fuel at Wunstorf, and Fg Off Caldwell diverted into Hannover's Langenhagen airport. That same day the squadron prepared for another move, and the advance party left for Eindhoven.

After an interception sortie from Beek on the morning of 26 June, the Sabres flew into Eindhoven, briefly reuniting the squadron again. One section on this mission claimed 'kills' of a B-26 bomber as well as four F-86s. While the main ground party was making its way from Beek, the Sabres launched a further skittle sortie, three aircraft diverting into Geilenkirchen at the end of the mission. The next day, 27 June, was the final day of the exercise, and only a few interception sorties

Accident investigators looking into Pete Underdown's accident found this section of port wing more than half a mile from the main wreckage site. It enabled them to determine quickly that the aircraft had broken up in flight. (*National Archives*)

were flown before the aircraft finally returned to Geilenkirchen.

The tented area at Eindhoven was packed away, and the ground parties were back at base by lunchtime on 28 June. The squadron then stood down for a well-earned rest. It had flown 146 sorties on the exercise.

Upon returning to work on 30 June, the squadron was again the scene of frenzied activity, this time in preparation for deployment to Cyprus for an armament-practice camp. Compass swings, TABT inoculations and air tests were the order of the day, and khaki clothing was also issued, though a shortage of correct equipment required at least one run to the UK to pick up missing items. Ground equipment was taken by road to Wildenrath for loading onto Hastings transport aircraft there; ground crews and pilots not ferrying Sabres would also take the Hastings to Cyprus.

Twelve Sabres, along with the squadron Vampire, departed Geilenkirchen on 6 July, and routed via Fürstenfeldbruck to night-stop at Rome's Ciampino airport. On the following day the Sabres left for a refuelling stop at Larisa in Greece, though the Vampire was forced to return to Rome with a fuel-feed problem. The Sabres flew on to Nicosia in Cyprus, where they were greeted with cold beers by the resident crews of 73 Sqn. The Hastings transports arrived later in the day.

Air-to-air gunnery began on 8 July, initially by the pilots who had flown over in the Hastings, allowing the others to rest. By 13 July, the inevitable gunsight problems had already begun to affect the squadron's performance. The squadron's final day of live firing was completed safely on 20 July, by which time each pilot had registered only an average of three shoots each. Two days later, after saying their farewells, the ground crews departed in the Hastings for the journey home. The return of the Sabres would be far less straightforward and ultimately ended in tragedy.

Initially, things went well, with all twelve aircraft flying out to Eskisehir in Turkey on 23 July. Two Sabres then went unserviceable in Turkey, and Fg Off Scambler was left behind to look after them. The remaining aircraft departed for Rome, again routing through Larisa in Greece, but three more Sabres were left behind in Italy for various technical problems. The remaining seven Sabres made it back safely to Geilenkirchen on 24 July. Almost immediately, serviceability took a dive, with only four Sabres airworthy on 28 July and just one on the following day. Understandably, with so many aircraft spread across Europe, the main effort was put into recovering them all back to base. On 2 August, Fg Offs Foreman, Pintches and Phillips left for Rome by train to fetch the three aircraft there; only two made the trip back without incident, as Fg Off Foreman had to leave his Sabre at Munich after experiencing further problems. The other two from Rome arrived back on 5 August. The final stage of this sorry episode saw Fg Off Topham, recently posted in from 71 Sqn, depart for Turkey on 27 August to pick up XB735/W, the final aircraft to be recovered. Sadly, on 2 September, while ferrying this Sabre back to Germany, Fg Off Topham was killed when his aircraft struck a pylon on approach to Brindisi in Italy. His engine had suffered from fuel starvation and Topham had been making an emergency landing.

For the rest of the squadron, quite apart from Topham's accident, August was in any case a sorry month. Problems with split fuel tanks resulted in only three Sabres being serviceable by mid-month, and though a few sorties were flown on Exercise Loco from the 23rd, fewer than 300 hours were logged for the whole month. Most of these were put in by 'B' Flight, which seemed to be less affected by the problems.

During the month there had been an influx of pilots, including seven from 71 Sqn alone. Robin Brown had arrived with the unit in July 1955 via a more circuitous route. He had previously flown Meteor photo-reconnaissance aircraft with 79 Sqn at Gütersloh and Laarbruch before being posted to 2 TAF HQ at Rheindahlen as personal assistant to AVM 'Zulu' Morris. Brown was eager to get back to flying, and his route to the Sabre was somewhat unusual:

> Helped by my boss, who had spoken to Wg Cdr Ambrose, OC Flying [at nearby Wildenrath], and because he was away in Paris at the time, I was at a loose end and so managed to attend the Ground School at Wildenrath 'in my spare time'. I hung about the squadron crew rooms, mugging up on Pilot's Notes and drawing out the necessary flying gear, helmet, g-suit, so-called Sabre boots, etc. I was introduced to the cockpit and would have been allowed up on that day, 24th March, but for a crosswind that might have made landing tricky with a swept-wing aircraft. On Friday, 25th March I wrote in my diary 'Few people can have known less about the F-86 Sabre than I when I took off this morning. Once in the air there was nothing left to do but rush around the sky, trying to sort myself out. Came back to earth again about 12.30, not much wiser, and dashed off to the Mess to celebrate with a Coca-Cola. Found there was a possibility of flying again, so, even more nervously perhaps, at about 16.20 I tried again. I had been warned to be down by 17.00 with 100lb of fuel remaining. I landed in error at Brüggen. However, I taxied round and took off again and landed at Wildenrath without losing much time.'

'That was a good landing,' I was told by the 67 Sqn pilot when I climbed out. 'Not as good as the one I did at Brüggen,' I replied. I went back to Rheindahlen that night feeling completely tired out and drained. I even dreamed of flying that night, something I hardly ever did.

On 6th April I was able to take up a 71 Sqn aircraft without wing tanks, so was able to experience breaking the sound barrier, registering Mach 1.0 on the Machmeter. In July 1955, to my great pleasure, I was posted to 234 Sqn at RAF Geilenkirchen.

From 23 September, 234 Sqn took part in Exercise Beware, again testing the UK air defences by launching simulated bomber missions. On 25 and 26 September, fighter sweeps were sent out to the English coast in four-ship formations at 35,000ft. Like the previous year's effort, there was a worryingly small number of successful interceptions. The follow-on exercise, 'Foxpaw', saw pairs launched against the UK, this time at 30,000ft; none of these were intercepted either.

The squadron then began preparing for its next Sylt detachment, logging cine and flag sorties with a reflector flag, which had a spinning metallic reflector positioned about a quarter of the way up the tow cable from the flag. Results were good, these flags being towed from Jülich to Euskirchen. Packing for Sylt began on 5 October and the advance party left two days later. The aircraft, twelve Sabres and the Vampire, departed on 10 October. Unfortunately, thick fog at Sylt prevented any flying for four days, and even then it was still considered too misty for live firing. On 18 October the squadron was able to use the South high range, though XB578/C was damaged in a heavy landing on the same day. However, continued bouts of better weather enabled the squadron to get in some effective shoots despite this and the usual gunsight problems. On 24 October Fg Off Caldwell scored 72 hits out of 80 on the flag, establishing a circa 90 per cent score that remained a 2 TAF individual record.

The squadron moved to the Western range on 27 October, firing twenty miles off the coast of the island. By this point, pilots had averaged three shoots each, which was far less than expected. The List range was in use from 29 October, firing taking place from 6,000 to 10,000ft above the sea. An unprecedented number of seven successful shoots were logged in succession on that day. Individual scores ranged from 0 to 21 per cent. Poor weather at the start of November prevented many more meaningful sorties, and the customary rearm (operational turnaround) practice was cancelled. The squadron returned to Geilenkirchen on 10 November. Statistics for the detachment made depressing reading. Of 259 planned sorties, just 112 were successful; the remainder were cancelled by combinations of weather (40 cancelled), unserviceable gunsights (13), radar problems (18) and aircraft or flag unserviceabilities (41).

A further grounding came into force on 1 December, but by this time the weather was getting gradually worse, so the effect was less pronounced. Fortunately, there were bouts of better weather during the month, and on 13 December seventy-six air-to-ground sorties were flown, expending 16,715 rounds of ammunition for no stoppages. Night flying also took place, and most pilots flew five missions during the day. On 20 December Flt Lt May diverted into Brüggen with heavy engine vibration and low oil pressure in XB898/A; the rear bearing had failed. With a new engine fitted, XB898 returned to the squadron on 29 December. The year was rounded off by another fair-weather day on the 29th, when twenty cine quarter missions were logged.

An early start was made in the New Year of 1956, 'B' Flight managing to launch two battle-formation missions after lunch on 2 January

XB891 of 234 Sqn was 'zapped' with the USAF 494th Fighter Bomber Sqn's black cougar during a squadron visit. The black cougar was painted on either side of the fin against a red-painted area. (*David Watkins*)

before fog and snow closed in to prevent further flying for the next week or so. Aircraft were on standby on 12 January to intercept Canberra bombers on Exercise Argus, but these were again too high to be intercepted.

Further snow in February and March again precluded meaningful flying time and, though the airfield was 'green' on 5 March, a planned range programme at Monschau had to be cancelled because of low cloud. A number of instances of sticking flying controls during the early part of the year were finally put down to the wrong grease being used on the artificial-feel system. This was an embarrassing discovery for the ground crews, especially since on 6 March one of the maintenance personnel managed to drive XB838/P into the hangar door while towing it; the aircraft needed a leading-edge change. And though the squadron had fully converted to '6–3'-winged Sabres by this point, from the start of the year a number of slatted aircraft were transferred into the squadron as other 2 TAF Sabre squadrons began to convert onto the Hunter.

One final Sabre deployment began on 12 March, when eight aircraft departed for Chaumont in France on exchange with the USAF Sabre unit there. In return a number of F-86Fs from 494th Fighter Bomber Squadron arrived at Geilenkirchen and were looked after by the remainder of 234 Sqn. The crews at Chaumont flew sector recces on the first day, and on 13 March the two halves of 234 Sqn met in a dogfight, both formations using the same radio call signs; confusion reigned. On the following day, sixteen more sorties were made by the Sabres at Chaumont, but none from Geilenkirchen, due to unserviceability. The two squadrons returned to their respective bases on 19 March, 494th FBS leaving a special reminder of its stay by painting the fin of XB891 red, with the squadron's cougar emblem imposed on both sides. XB891 was one of the slatted aircraft that had been transferred in from 93 Sqn at the beginning of the month.

Flying was again curtailed on 6 April when all squadron aircraft were required to be sent to ASF for X-raying of their aileron actuators. They were back in action by 9 April, when air-to-ground sorties were flown at Monschau. These were controlled by personnel from 618 Signals Unit, who vectored the aircraft from 10,000ft over Aachen onto the range. On the next day a number of cross-country flights were made from base to Luxembourg, Frankfurt and Wahn, where GCAs were made. Further sorties were made to Wahn on 12 April, when nine Sabres left in poor visibility for an exercise for the benefit of ground-liaison officers from a course at Old Sarum. Sorties were then launched from Wahn, aircraft being vectored by a ground-contact team onto targets in the Königswinter and Bergisch-Gladbach areas. Further air-to-ground missions were flown at Monschau on 23 and 24 April, again using 618 Signals Unit to control the aircraft. These sorties were notable in using tracer for the first time. The second day's firing had to be stopped early after the woods around the range caught fire. Though no one mentioned it, this could well have been due to the tracer shells.

The squadron gained notoriety on 17 April when three Sabres intercepted a Russian Tu-104 airliner flying from London's Heathrow airport. It was thought that this aircraft was carrying Russian leader Bulganin back from a visit to the UK, and orders swiftly came down that interception of Tu-104s 'is not on'. Another unit, 71 Sqn, whose Sabres had also intercepted the Soviet airliner, received a similar order.

On 16 April a new era began for 234 Sqn. On that day, the Earl of Bandon, 2 TAF's new Commander-in-Chief, visited the squadron and informed personnel that 234 would be the first squadron in the wing to receive Hunters. This was confirmed on 30 April, when Wg Cdr Bob Weighill, the Wing Leader, revealed that conversion would begin in the next two weeks. As a kind of farewell to the Sabre, an eleven-ship 'balbo' was put up that day to mark the occasion.

Meanwhile, Sabre flying continued, though the emphasis seems to have changed into getting the most from the aircraft while they remained. At the end of April drop tanks were removed, and battle flight used its more

XB867/E carried Fg Off J.D. Anker's name on the canopy rail and was assigned to 'A' Flight. The aircraft was photographed shortly after arriving with Aviation Traders on 15 May 1956. (*Bruce Robertson*)

agile aircraft to maul any intruders. At the same time, a large number of Mach runs were completed.

Hunter lectures began on 3 May, and these concentrated on the new aircraft's hydraulic, electrical and engine-oil systems. The first Hunter arrived the same day, but was spirited away into Technical Wing to be used as a ground-training aid. On subsequent days the lectures continued, the squadron all the while maintaining battle-flight and flying-training commitments. The first Hunters for the squadron flew in on 7 May, and a further trio arrived on the 9th.

Some of the last Sabre sorties were flown on 10 May 1956, when cine exercises were completed; a further Hunter arrived on the same day to make a total of seven on squadron strength. By 14 May Sabre flying had been reduced to test flights only, and a number of aircraft were transferred to 3 Sqn as well as being assigned for overhaul in the UK. Thereafter, the squadron turned fully to Hunter conversion, and the days of the Sabre were effectively over. By the beginning of June, just four Sabres remained on the squadron. XB589 and XB827 departed for England on 13 June, and the final pair, XB792 and XB898, two days later.

Aerobatic Team

By the spring of 1954, Flt Lt Barry N. Byrne, who had taken over as 'B' Flight commander in May, had decided to form a Sabre aerobatic team; it flew one of its first displays at Maastricht in Holland on 11 June 1954. By that time, the team had already become well-organised and consisted of: Flt Lt Barry N. Byrne (leader) – later replaced by Fg Off Mike S. Langley; Fg Off A.R.D. 'Noddy' Newman (number two); Fg Off Dennis E. Caldwell (number three); and Fg Off John Rawlinson (number four).

The Sabres of 234 Sqn flew their entire display in a 'diamond four' formation, consisting of a full repertoire of aerobatic manoeuvres including rolls, loops and turns. The now Air Cdre Dennis Caldwell recalls the formation of the team:

> Barry Byrne initiated the team in 1954. Roger Emmett took over as CO from Roy Chatfield in circa Feb. 1955, but was not involved in the team; his fate was individual aeros in a Meteor, and [he] was in fact the Fighter Command display pilot before 1955. He died some years ago – I think around 1964.
>
> I was number three in the team during 1954/5. As regards displays, my logbook is less than explicit, but I remember ones at Maastricht in June 1954 and at Nicosia, Cyprus in July 1955. I believe we also gave a number of shows in the Geilenkirchen local area at various events.

The Cyprus detachment referred to by Dennis Caldwell began on 6 July 1955, and on the 13th Fg Off Langley led the team on a practice sortie over Nicosia, followed by another, two days later, when the team followed on from a solo Meteor F. 8 display by Sqn Ldr Emmett. These displays, though just practice sessions, got the team a write-up in the *Cyprus Mail* and *Times* newspapers.

Another practice display was flown on 18 July, followed by the real thing the next day. This team sortie was flown over Nicosia in front of the Governor of Cyprus. At the end of the display, Fg Off Fitton completed a fast fly-by in a solo Sabre.

The squadron's aerobatic team was operated on a far more formal basis than many of the other, mainly ad-hoc teams, as squadron pilot Robin A. Brown remembers:

> By the time I joined 234, the aerobatic team wasn't doing anything very much. Mike Langley did give me a trial for the team, but I wasn't any good at formation aerobatics so that came to nothing.

I joined 234 in July 1955, and I think the squadron detachment had just returned from Cyprus at the time. After that date, I don't recall it [the team] ever performing again. Mike Langley, 'Noddy' Newman, Dennis Caldwell and John Rawlinson were the backbone of the team, though, with, I think, one or two reserves.

On RAF squadrons at that time there were frequently temporary aerobatic teams, made up on pretty much an ad-hoc basis, if there were three or four pilots who felt capable of – or were interested in – attempting formation aeros. Sometimes these teams lasted only so long as the leader was on the squadron, after which they faded away, and I think this is what happened on 234.

The last Sabre aerobatic display was flown on 4 May 1956 over Geilenkirchen; with the arrival of Hunters, the team was idle for a while.

Aircraft Assigned

XB536/N, XB575/N, XB587/C, XB582, XB589/D, later T, XB614/J, XB615/H, XB642/S+, XB680/G, XB727/Y+, XB735/W, XB748/F, XB750/K, XB752/W, XB766/L, XB792/L+, XB794/V, XB803/Q, XB807/Z, XB817/U+, XB819/Z, XB827/H+, XB836/B+, XB838/P+, XB860/B, XB861/J, XB867/E+, XB872/R+, XB873/Q, XB885/D+, XB890, XB891/A, XB897/M, XB898/A, XB949*, XB975/K*, XB995/A*.

* = '6–3'-winged from manufacture.
+ = '6–3' wing (all conversions).

Markings – 234 Sqn

Initial markings for 234 Sqn comprised an individual code letter on the fuselage, forward of the roundel. These codes appear to have been different colours, probably red for 'A' Flight (early alphabet) and blue for 'B' Flight (late alphabet) with black outlines. The code letters were repeated on the forward nose-wheel door. The squadron's griffin marking appeared on a white circle on the tail fin. What really made 234 Sqn's Sabres stand out was the nose markings. On a scalloped area, the intake ring was painted in red and black checks, the scallop extending back to a point at the forward edge of the machine-gun blast panel. This area was bordered in a thin yellow band. The red treatment, though not the black checks, extended to the inside surface of the intake.

When bars began to appear either side of the fuselage roundel, these comprised a black bar, with red checks arranged in a diamond pattern. The individual code was then relocated to the tail fin and the griffin deleted.

The final variation of this colour scheme saw the nose checks replaced by a solid red section, still in the same scalloped area, outlined in yellow. Robin Brown was instrumental in reintroducing the squadron's griffin design, and by mid-November 1955 this was being applied on a white disc on the forward fuselage. Towards the end of squadron service, many aircraft gained pilot's names, in a variety of styles. Some aircraft carried the name in white on the canopy rail, others in white against a black oblong in the same position. A number carried the name on the fuselage side just below the canopy rail. In every case the name appeared only on the port (left) side.

Squadron Motto

Ignem mortemque despuimus
(We spit fire and death).

CHAPTER SEVENTEEN

MISCELLANEOUS UNITS

1 OVERSEAS FERRY UNIT

Based at Abingdon, just south of Oxford, 1 OFU was tasked with ferrying RAF aircraft throughout the world; once Sabres began to arrive in Britain, it also took up the role of training new pilots on the type. The unit was led by Sqn Ldr D.E. Bennett, who had commanded 1 OFU since 1 October 1952.

On 4 December 1952, 1 OFU began operations with three Sabre F. 2s: XB530, XB531 and XB532. These aircraft wore natural metal finish and were assigned squadron codes 'A', 'B' and 'C', respectively. Nine further Sabre F. 4s were earmarked for the unit straight off Bechers Brook 1, but one aircraft, XB534, was lost on the run in to Prestwick on 19 December 1952.

Flt Sgt A.P. Pugh had departed Keflavik at 1105 hr on 19 December as number two in Green Section, spaced five minutes behind the lead flight of the ferry mission. Pugh's flight was led by Flt Lt Harold F. Edwards with Flt Sgt William H. Atkins as number three. The weather forecast for the flight was good, with that at Prestwick being regarded as 'satisfactory'. However, once the aircraft approached Scotland the weather began to deteriorate, and a local storm in the Prestwick area added to this problem. Fuel was not critical as the flight reached the Prestwick beacon, but did not allow any room for diversion. During the descent to the airfield, both number two and number three aircraft lost sight of their leader in cloud; Flt Sgt Atkins called his leader to inform him that he would let down independently. No radio calls were heard from Flt Sgt Pugh, however, and at 1310 hr, Prestwick control tower was informed of a crash on the Mackeilston Farm at Crosshill, eleven miles south-east of the airfield. Pugh had been killed instantly as the aircraft flew into the ground at high speed on a bearing of 190 degrees. His aircraft had impacted on the lee side of a hill and exploded.

A subsequent court of inquiry was unable to find a positive reason for this accident, but postulated that Flt Sgt Pugh had probably lost sight of his leader in cloud, hit his wake turbulence and was unable to recover. This was the first accident to befall an RAF Sabre.

The remaining eight Sabres, led by Sqn Ldr Thomas Stevenson, arrived safely at Abingdon on 22 December and were immediately put to use training ferry pilots. This batch of aircraft comprised XB535, XB537, XB538, XB543, XB544, XB545, XB547 and XB548; they were assigned squadron codes 'D' to 'L', respectively (excluding 'I').

On 1 January 1953, 1 OFU was split into two separate formations: Ferry Training Unit and 1 (Long Range) Ferry Unit. The latter was tasked with ferrying aircraft, including the Sabres, and was commanded by Sqn Ldr Stevenson. Ferry Training Unit meanwhile undertook training of Sabre crews to support the ferry operation. On 4 January Sqn Ldr Stevenson left Abingdon with seven other pilots, bound for Canada and the commencement of Bechers Brook 2.

On 1 February 1953, 1 (LR) FU was disbanded, but 147 Sqn was concurrently formed to carry out Sabre ferrying tasks.

Aircraft Assigned

XB530/A, XB531/B, XB532/C, XB535/D, XB537/E, XB538/F, XB543/G, XB544/H, XB545/J, XB547/K, XB548/L.

All had slatted wings.

5 Maintenance Unit

Based at RAF Kemble in Gloucestershire, just south of the Cotswold market town of Cirencester, 5 Maintenance Unit (MU) became the primary aircraft storage and maintenance facility in the RAF. The first Sabres arrived at 5 MU in March 1953, and immediately a team of civilians from Air Service Training at Hamble began camouflaging the aircraft. In May of that year, thirty-two Sabres were painted by the AST team; they completed the camouflaging of all RAF Sabres in August 1954.

Commanding 5 MU during the first part of the Sabre period was Wg Cdr N.W. Wakelin. He had a single Sabre test pilot under his command, as well as a mix of civilian and service maintenance personnel. In June 1953 the unit test pilot was involved in providing Sabre ground instruction to personnel from 20 MU at Aston Down and 15 MU at Wroughton. It is presumed that this was a precursor to the arrival of Sabres at these units, but none are thought to have gone to either location.

Subsequent commanding officers of 5 MU were Wg Cdr W.N. Elwyn-Jones, who took over on 5 April 1954, and he was followed by Wg Cdr H.J. Rayner on 26 September 1955.

A number of Sabre repairs were accomplished at Kemble by detached staff of 34 and 49 Maintenance Units. With Sabres due to be withdrawn from RAF service, many of the aircraft stored at Kemble were flown out from mid-1955; they went to the civilian repair depots for overhaul. One of the last to leave was XB543, which departed for Ringway on 22 March 1956.

23 Maintenance Unit

Based at RAF Aldergrove in Northern Ireland, 23 MU dealt mainly with Fighter Command XD-serialled aircraft. Commanding officer during the Sabre period was Wg Cdr A.M. Stevens. The unit had received its first Sabres in August 1953, at short notice on a Sunday, just as Exercise Momentum finished. The unit did not have a long association with the type, however, and, when the final 2 TAF Sabres at Aldergrove were ferried out to Germany in November 1953, the remaining XD-serialled Fighter Command aircraft were transferred to MUs in England. Most went to 33 MU at Lyneham, with XD725 being the last to depart, on 14 June 1954.

32 Maintenance Unit

Two Sabres, XB579 and XB580, were transferred to 32 MU at St Athan in mid-April 1953 for special-fit modification. These aircraft departed during October and June 1953, respectively.

33 Maintenance Unit

Located in a complex of three blister hangars on the eastern side of RAF Lyneham, 33 MU was responsible for storage of RAF Sabres as well as certain modifications. Commanding officer during the Sabre period was Wg Cdr D.I. Fairbairn, who was replaced by Wg Cdr D.C. Sandeman, DFC on 19 April 1954. The majority of personnel at 33 MU were civilian aircraft technicians, recruited from the local community; most were ex-RAF.

A number of Sabres received the camouflage paint scheme at 33 MU, work

A 33 MU test pilot steps from his Sabre after a sortie. Taken on Lyneham's 'B' site, this photo shows a Fighter Command machine. (*MoD AHB*)

that was undertaken by a civilian working party from Air Service Training, Hamble. The AST team began work at 33 MU on 4 December 1953 and left on 18 December, having painted twelve Sabres by that time.

Sabre work was routine, though the odd incident punctuated life for unit test pilot Flt Lt W.D. Jarvis. On 27 March 1954, he was flying XD731 on a test hop when the undercarriage doors started to cycle. Though the doors were damaged, Jarvis managed to recover the Sabre safely to Lyneham. Repaired, it was later assigned to 66 Sqn. The arrival of Hunters in 1955 brought new problems. On 11 November an ejection seat fitted in one of the Hunters was accidentally triggered, causing serious injuries to Mr Dalton, an airframe fitter; Mr Lester, an electrician, was slightly injured. Both returned to work after recuperating from their lucky escape.

Some Sabre repairs were carried out at Lyneham by detached personnel from 49 MU at RAF Colerne. The final Sabre to leave 33 MU was XB754, which was dispatched to Ringway on 22 March 1956.

229 Operational Conversion Unit

Based at RAF Chivenor in Devon, 229 OCU was initially tasked with conversion training of pilots onto the Vampire fighter, these being flown by 'A' Flight. From 20 May 1954, with the arrival of its first six Sabres, the OCU nominally took over Sabre transition training from the Sabre Conversion Flight at Wildenrath in Germany. Back in July 1953, it had been decided that despite the impending arrival of '6–3'-wing conversion sets, all 229 OCU Sabres would retain their slatted-wing configuration on safety grounds. The '6–3' wing conversion degraded low-speed performance, and it was rightly deemed that students had enough to contend with without the need for them to be constantly on the lookout for the '6–3's often fatal stalling characteristics. The Sabres were assigned to 'B' and 'C' Flights.

The unit was soon sending sonic booms over the Devon countryside, and on 11 June visiting Air Cdre H.A.C. Hogan was treated to this event when Capt Rosencrans from 229 OCU took his Sabre through the sound

No. 3 Course, 229 OCU pose in front of XB644/B of 'B' Flight. Back row L–R: John Hardwick, Brian Scotford, Frank Rickwood, Dave Thornton, Taffy Heath. Front row: Ralph Owen, Cas Maynard, Jerry Thornally, Tom Henderson, Sam St Pierre. (*John Hardwick*)

barrier. At this time, dedicated markings were applied to the Sabres, comprising coloured wingtip and nose bands – white in colour for 'B' Flight and red for 'C' Flight. All aircraft carried a white letter code on the tail fin, with early alphabetical letters for 'B' Flight and later letters for 'C' Flight.

By the end of July, 229 OCU possessed twenty-four Sabres, but it was not until 8 August 1954 that the OCU finally began the first Sabre conversion class, with eleven officers on 1 Sabre Course at Chivenor. Each pilot would complete around eight 'familiarisation' flights in the Sabre, before moving on to close-formation, tail-chase, cross-country and battle-formation exercises. E.H. 'Ted' Roberts was one of those completing the first course:

I had completed the OCU course on Vampires (T. 11s and Mk. 5s) between January and March 1954 but, because of the re-equipping of squadrons, we were not immediately posted, but held at Chivenor completing 'refresher' training. Suddenly, in July 1954, we were told that the Sabres were on their way and, as we were all familiar with the local area, etc., we would form the first course.

It was all new to all of us, staff and students alike. We flew a few hours on Vampires as a lead-in to the Sabre part, at the same time sitting in a classroom, all going through Pilot's Notes. The staff instructors did their first trips and then stood on the wing roots while we started our Sabres. Our instructor then flew 'chase' with us while we wobbled off into the middle distance (the first time we had tried power controls).

I don't remember what we did on that first trip, but I do remember watching other people coming round finals with the 'smoke' billowing out as the power went on to check the descent when the flaps went down. I see that I completed 17 hr 35 min on the Sabre on the course, which included some 2 hours' actual instrument-flying. But, to my knowledge, no live firing. The final trip we did on the course was without drop tanks as a 'famil'. I recall we were told that we were officially not allowed to go supersonic, but that we were reminded how it was done (roll over and pull through) – oh, and by the way, it should really only be performed over the sea.

Ted's first solo was a one-hour flight in XB823. Other pilots on the first course were Sqn Ldr Glover, Fg Off Dennison and P Offs Blake, Gasson, Ferguson, Harryman, Holtby, Kelly, Kinnear and Pollard. Radio call signs for this group ranged from 'Dashpot 60' (Sqn Ldr Glover) to 'Dashpot 70' (P Off Pollard). This initial intake, 1 Sabre Course, completed its training at the end of September. Sqn Ldr Glover took over as CO of 20 Sqn and the other personnel on the course were split between 2 TAF and Fighter Command Sabre squadrons; Ted Roberts went on to 112 Sqn at Brüggen.

Subsequent Sabre courses overlapped each other, so that 2 Sabre Course had actually commenced on 5 September, again with eleven officers. By the end of August 1954, 229 OCU boasted a total of twenty-two aircraft, having lost one example each to the Air Fighting Development Squadron and Cat. 3 repair.

The unit had previously formed a Vampire aerobatic team, and the arrival of the Sabre saw this tradition continued. However, the Vampires were retained alongside the Sabres and, as late as August 1954, formation aerobatics were flown by the former. When it was formed, the Sabre team consisted of: Sqn Ldr Mike Calvey (solo); Fg Off John D. Bradley (leader); Fg Off Fred Hartley (number two); and Fg Off Pete Stott (number three).

John Bradley recalls one light-hearted moment from those days:

During the Battle of Britain Day, [18 September] 1954, we were lined up in front of the hangar and given the signal to start too early, and just as we turned, with our arse end pointing at the tower and the meteorological recording paraphernalia, we were told to hold. That evening, the BBC News reported Chivenor to be the hottest spot in the UK.

We flew whatever [Sabre] was available on the line and, due to the pressure of training students, it was difficult to get sufficient training time in. The ground crews at Chivenor were a great bunch and were always willing to work overtime to make the aircraft available.

At one stage, it was decided by the powers-that-be that the team should be vetted by a senior officer from Group Headquarters. Before we took off, we received a weather check, and he gave us base 4,000 and tops 6,000ft. We were comfortable with that, and went into our first loop knowing we would be clear on top, but things do change – when we went over we were still in solid clag. We carried on and finished the display, and were later told that the team could carry on.

Following the team's display for Battle of Britain Day, they immediately departed for Filton airfield, Bristol, where they gave a further aerobatic display.

Unfortunately, 2 Sabre Course lost one of its students, Fg Off Algy Longworth, in an accident on 23 October. He had been flying wing to instructor 'Bugs' Birley, and the pair had diverted to RAF Valley in North Wales because of bad weather. Birley managed to land safely at Valley, but of Longworth or his Sabre (XB711/S) there was no trace; it is thought that he crashed into the sea. Nine officers on the course finished their Sabre conversion on 13 November; 3 Course had started with a further eleven pilots on 4 October, and 4 Course followed hot on its heels a month later. By the end of 1954, thirty-nine pilots had successfully converted to the Sabre at Chivenor.

However, 229 OCU's use of the Sabre was short-lived, and the last of six courses was run from 3 January to 26 March 1955. The Sabres were replaced by the new Hawker Hunters, which had begun arriving during February. The last F-86 (XB813) departed for 5 Maintenance Unit at Kemble on 30 June that year. During the period they had flown the Sabre, 229 OCU had successfully converted fifty-eight officers and one airman/aircrew onto the fighter. The unit's aerobatic team immediately re-formed on the Hunter with its original members.

Aircraft Assigned

XB531, XB532, XB616/J, XB641/A, XB644/B, XB666/S, XB696/C, XB698/R, XB711/S, XB713/U, XB741/H, XB756/D, XB762/O, XB763/W, XB765/L, XB793/N, XB795/G, XB799/K, XB801/Z, XB811/P, XB813/M, XB821/E, XB823/F, XB825/T, XB835/V.

All had slatted wings.

Air Fighting Development Squadron

Part of Central Fighter Establishment, the Air Fighting Development Squadron (AFDS) at West Raynham was tasked with evaluating new fighter types and ensuring that their capabilities were made known to the fighter squadrons so that these aircraft could be used effectively.

As a result, on 4 May 1953 three Sabres were assigned to AFDS straight from delivery on Bechers Brook 4: XB622, XB666 and XB677. Two further aircraft were assigned by the end of 1953, and the unit's sixth and last Sabre, XB532, arrived on 16 July the following year.

XB666 was declared Cat. 3 (R) on 9 August 1954 after its nose undercarriage dropped out of its lock during a high-g manoeuvre. The undercarriage forced the nose door slightly open, whereupon it was wrenched off by the high-speed airflow. The aircraft, which was being flown by USAF pilot Capt D.O. Beck, was recovered safely to West Raynham, but permanently departed the unit for repairs.

At about this time the remaining Sabres were withdrawn from AFDS use, the last to go being XD781, which left for storage at 33 MU on 11 February 1955.

Aircraft Assigned

XB532, XB622, XB666, XB677, XD780, XD781.

All had slatted wings.

Aeroplane and Armament Experimental Establishment

As its name implies, the Aeroplane and Armament Experimental Establishment (A&AEE) at Boscombe Down in Wiltshire was mainly responsible for performing aircraft and armament trials on new military types. The unit had previously undertaken in-depth qualitative testing of the physical and flight characteristics of loaned F-86As, and would therefore also be involved once Canadair Sabres arrived for the RAF. As a result, XB733 was loaned to A&AEE on 22 July 1953 for comparative assessment and pilot familiarisation. The loan was planned to expire on 30 September 1954, but was subsequently extended. The aircraft retained its natural metal colour scheme and even carried the number 607 on its nose, a remnant of its Canadian serial number.

Comparative assessment was carried out during September 1954 when F-86E and

'F-86F' configurations were evaluated. For the purposes of this test, XB733 served as the F-86E, whilst XB992, briefly available to A&AEE for two weeks, was the 'F-86F' model by virtue of its '6–3' unslatted wing. Testing took in three distinct areas: qualitative control assessment, manoeuvre boundaries and straight stalls.

The A&AEE team's findings, though not as exhaustive as it would have liked, were nonetheless indicative of problems found out by others the hard way. In the qualitative control assessment the two aircraft were deemed as identical, though the report stated that, for both, 'Control forces were rather heavier than considered desirable on a fighter aircraft.' Moving on to manoeuvre boundaries, the aircraft characteristics were similar, though the 'F-86F' experienced buffet in the turn at slightly higher 'g' than the F-86E.

But it was in the stalling characteristics where large differences were noted. XB733, the F-86E, was flown in a power-off configuration with flaps and undercarriage up, whereupon very mild buffet was experienced at 110kt indicated. At 108kt the nose started to pitch up 5–8 degrees, followed by the wing drop associated with stall. XB992, in 'F-86F' configuration, was flown under the same conditions with power off, but first indications of the stall were experienced at 150kt when the aircraft pitched up. At 108kt the aircraft's nose dropped and could not be held up with full elevator input. This sudden onset of stall was characteristic of the '6–3' wing and took many lives before crews became fully aware of its nasty bite.

With tests completed, XB992 was returned to 33 MU at Lyneham on 28 September 1954. XB733 remained at Boscombe Down for some time, and was used to familiarise test pilots with the Sabre. It finally departed the unit, for 33 MU, on 4 March 1955.

Central Gunnery School (later Fighter Weapons School)

Tasked with training Pilot Attack Instructors (PAIs) for RAF fighter squadrons, Central Gunnery School (CGS) at Leconfield gained four Sabres in July 1954, and these aircraft were soon painted with individual letter codes in black, with white outlines, on either side of the fuselage.

Aside from training RAF pilots, CGS often hosted foreign students. Invariably, most of these aircrews had no prior experience of high-performance jets. On 13 August 1954, Flt Lt K.P. Miskra of the Indian Air Force undershot in XB810/D on landing at Leconfield after a 57-minute flight. The resultant heavy landing buckled the underside of the mainplane, causing Cat. 3 (R) damage. It was repaired on site and returned to service just a month later.

CGS transferred from Flying Training Command to Fighter Command on 1 November 1954 and was renamed the Fighter Weapons School on 1 January 1955. In April of that year the Sabres began to be withdrawn, XB546/B being the last to depart, to 33 MU, on 19 May 1955.

Aircraft Assigned

XB540/A, XB546/B, XB601/C, XB810/D.

All had slatted wings.

Command Support Unit

Located at Bückeburg in Germany, the Command Support Unit (CSU) was formed in January 1954 under commanding officer Sqn Ldr E.C. Gough with two instructors and twenty-eight pilots. A number of CSU pilots went through SCU conversion, though in May 1954 the unit was disbanded, with most of the pilots being posted to 2 TAF Sabre

One of only four Sabres flown by the Central Gunnery School at Leconfield, XB540/A was retired to Stansted for overhaul with Aviation Traders. (*A.J. Jackson Collection*)

squadrons. No Sabres were ever assigned to CSU at Bückeburg.

HAWKER

Not actually a military unit, Hawker Aircraft at Dunsfold was allotted XB551 on 25 March 1955 under Controller (Aircraft) charge from 5 MU and supposedly used on USAF 'Pacer' trials for an unknown purpose. A second machine, XB997, was assigned on 28 March 1955 and remained with Hawkers until returned to Kemble on 14 April. XB551 was placed Cat. 3 on 16 May 1955 and transferred to Airwork for rectification. XB675 was allotted to Hawker in its place from April 1955 to 12 September that year.

It is worth noting that, of the first pair of aircraft assigned, XB551 had the slatted wing and XB997 had the extended-chord '6–3' wing. This is undoubtedly significant, the presumption being that these machines were used in comparison tests between the two types. When XB551 departed in April 1955, it was replaced by another slatted machine.

ROYAL AIRCRAFT ESTABLISHMENT

The Royal Aircraft Establishment (RAE) based at Farnborough in Hampshire had for a long time been responsible for undertaking experimental aircraft programmes. Indeed, much of the work at Farnborough reflected similar research projects being tackled by the National Advisory Committee for Aeronautics (NACA, later NASA) in the USA. The first Sabres available to RAE were the Combined Test Project Agreement F-86As, which were assigned from April 1951 to November 1954. When that agreement ended, Sabres were by then available from the RAF, so it was only natural that RAE would continue its work into high-speed aerodynamics using these machines.

XB620 was allotted to Farnborough on 12 August 1953 and was flown from storage at 5 MU to RAE on the following day. The aircraft was placed on a twelve-month loan, and this was extended for another three months in November 1954. Ulimately, the aircraft was required for further work and did not depart Farnborough until 30 August 1955, again for storage at Kemble.

One such research project that involved XB620 was an investigation into the effectiveness of a rudder-tab spoiler. Previous evaluation of the F-86As at Farnborough had revealed that the effectiveness of the rudder tab fell off considerably at high speed, so RAE tried two different configurations to see if a remedy could be found. The two configurations of spoiler tested were both fitted at right angles to the aircraft centre line at the tab trailing edge. The first spoiler, with a 'T' cross-section, was attached to the trailing edge of the tab by means of arms reaching forward to a mounting point forward of the hinge line; it was 0.5in wide. The second version was of similar configuration but 0.88in wide. Both were used in concert with electrical potentiometers to determine rudder movement at various speeds. Results were as expected: the 0.5in spoiler gave 100 per cent more rudder deflection at low Mach numbers and 60 per cent more at transonic speeds. In turn, the 0.88in spoiler was generally 1.4 times more effective than the 0.5in version throughout the whole range. Rather curiously, this report was not submitted until April 1958, a good three years after the tests had taken place.

SABRE CONVERSION UNIT, FLIGHT

Though not officially formed until 1 April 1953, Sabre Conversion Unit (SCU) had actually received its first six Sabres on 16 March. The unit, based at RAF Wildenrath in Germany, had no commanding officer to start with, and few key personnel; in order to begin training 2 TAF Sabre pilots, Sqn Ldr Paddy Harbison (67 Sqn's commanding officer) took informal charge. The first six Sabres were XB591, XB592, XB602, XB603, XB616 and XB618. All were assigned straight off Bechers Brook 2.

Equipment was also in short supply, and the Kleine Brogel wing of the Belgian Air Force was kind enough to loan sets of American Type 6 parachutes and bone-dome helmets so that training could begin. First pilot to be checked out was Wildenrath's Station Commander, Wg Cdr J.E. 'Johnny' Johnson, DSO, DFC on 17 March. Next to receive conversion training was Wg Cdr Mike Le Bas, DSO, Wildenrath's Wing Commander Flying, who performed his first solo on 25 March. Initially, only experienced pilots were chosen for conversion, their training comprising two days of lectures and ground checks, followed by eight flying exercises over a 5 flying-hour period. A total of five pilots had successfully completed the course by the end of March. SCU thus came into being on 1 April having already put numbers on its balance sheet.

Sqn Ldr S. Daniels took over as SCU's first commanding officer and, on the day of the unit's official formation, Fg Off Fairhurst, the SCU Technical Officer, also soloed in the Sabre, having been granted dispensation (as a ground-based officer) to do so by AOC 83 Gp. From 2 April the first full course of conversion began with SCU, comprising three squadron pilots. The plan was that, after this squadron had fully trained its pilots, 67 and then 71 Sqn crews would then begin the SCU course. In bad weather, trainee pilots were given additional lectures and extra cockpit time to rehearse procedures. It should be remembered that no simulators or dual-seat Sabres were available to these airmen: their first flight in the Sabre was also their first solo.

With Wildenrath just visible to the right, this quartet of SCU Sabres still wear the Arctic-conspicuity red wingtips and tailplanes. This photograph was taken in the period May/June 1953; XB603 (foreground, left) was lost in a flying accident on 15 June 1953. (*Rex Boulton*)

Within a short period a steady stream of hopeful Sabre pilots began to pass through SCU – the first course was completed in the third week of April and the next course began lectures on the 20th of the month. Flying was, however, often interrupted. On 10 April four SCU Sabres were required to perform a fly-past over RAF Wahn for the Chief of Staff; this was the first public demonstration of the RAF's Sabres. On 27 April an urgent Special Technical Instruction had to be completed on all unit aircraft before flying could commence, and three days later the whole station ground to a halt so that Air Ministry photographers could take publicity pictures of the Sabres. SCU aircraft were utilised heavily to provide shots in a number of flying formations. By the end of April, twenty-nine pilots had been trained by SCU; 67 Sqn crews started their courses on 5 May.

SCU staff pilots had not only to be responsible for training 2 TAF pilots: they had other duties too. On 11 May crews took part in a formation-flying rehearsal for the Air Officer Commanding's annual inspection. Wg Cdr Le Bas led this practice sortie, and the inspection itself took place on 15 May. On 18 May 71 Sqn pilots began SCU courses, and four days later solo sorties began. These were not without incident. On 15 June

P Off Moss of 71 Sqn stalled XB603 onto the ground during an overshoot. Coming in too steep and too fast on his approach, Moss raised his flaps, causing the aircraft to sink. The pilot then advanced the throttle hard, which caused compressor failure and complete loss of power. XB603 slammed tail first into the runway; although Moss broke his back, he was later able to return to his SCU course, finally completing it in October. His aircraft, although initially assessed as repairable, was declared Cat. 5 (C) on 16 June and struck off. A more serious incident destroyed XB676 on the ground two days later when the aircraft's oxygen cylinders exploded and started a fire. No one was injured. C.R. 'Pop' Miles served with SCU as a corporal instrument fitter and remembers that the oxygen system did cause a few problems:

The first spot of bother I recall was that as instrument tradesmen we were responsible for charging the aircraft oxygen system. The Sabre system was 450psi, whereas we used the English charging trolleys, which were 1,600psi, and we had to turn the pressure regulator to the appropriate setting. This was not adhered to on at least two occasions to my knowledge, causing the front of the Sabre nose to be blown out by the aircraft-mounted oxygen bottles.

The Sabres that were on SCU were without any guns, so that made it relatively easy with no gunsights to worry about nor harmonisation and, with new pilots to the aircraft, very few defects came to our notice. It was only when the CO, Sqn Ldr Daniels, Flt Lt Martin Chandler and squadron engineer Flt Lt Fairhurst were involved did any defects really surface for our trade.

The pilots of 26 Sqn began to route through SCU from 26 June onwards; also during June Col de Moncheau, Wing Leader of the Belgian Air Force F-84 unit at Kleine Brogel, was converted onto the Sabre. However, the sortie rate in June decreased to a mere 138 (from 172 in May and 181 in April) for a total of 97.4 flying hours; only thirteen pilots were converted. There were many reasons for this, not least of which was the loss of two aircraft in accidents, another (XB726) which was loaned to the Wildenrath Wing for the Queen's fly-past in England, and a further two which were loaned to 67 Sqn from 17 June. The beginning of July saw Gp Capt Johnson lead three SCU Sabres to Wunstorf on what was ostensibly a formation-flying mission. However, arriving at Wunstorf on 4 July the pilots 'discovered' that a Command sports match was in full swing and decided to stay to lend their support.

Bill Bevan arrived at SCU in June 1953, as an experienced corporal electrician. He was overjoyed at his posting, having previously served on types such as the Prentice and Harvard IIB – hardly taxing for an electrician. However, life at SCU was not easy in the early days, and considerable skill and ingenuity was required to keep the aircraft flying:

On reporting to the Flight Sergeant (Electrical) in ASF Hangar, I was informed by him that I was posted to the Sabre Conversion Unit a couple of hangars away, and that I was to replace a corporal from RAF Geilenkirchen who had been working there awaiting my arrival. After a few enquiries the gentleman was pointed out to me and I went to meet the man I was replacing. He was overjoyed to see me, and at the same time handed me a cardboard box, containing some microswitches, nuts, washers and insulators. He said there was a problem with the hood/canopy actuator that he had not resolved, and the bits and pieces were from that system.

I told him I knew nothing about the Sabre, to which he replied, 'Join the club', or words to that effect. Having said that, he disappeared out through the hangar doors, and I never saw him again. I looked at the contents in the box, looked at the aircraft and with a sinking feeling in my stomach, went in search of the electrical workshop. A strong cup of coffee was needed. Such was my introduction to the Sabre. I was not alone in this. A number of new arrivals, all ex-apprentices, had been thrown in at the deep end with me. Fortunately for me the electrical workshop walls were covered with electrical wiring diagrams for the whole aircraft. Here, I must pay tribute to the instructors at Halton, who gave us the skills to read and understand these wiring diagrams.

From looking at the diagram for the hood system, I could see that the motor was a split-field series motor, so I decided to check out the windings before going any further. This check revealed that one winding was 'open circuit' and the problem I was looking for was resolved. Having found the problem, taking the corrective action was not easy and required the help of an airframe corporal. A serviceable motor was obtained and fitted. All microswitches, nuts and insulators were replaced. The whole system was tested a number of times and the aircraft declared serviceable, much to the delight of the flight sergeant in charge of SCU, who was running out of aircraft. I am convinced to this day that replacement of components was never really considered by designers or manufacturers of the Sabre.

July 1953 saw a further fall in pilot conversions, this time to a mere ten – mainly 234 Sqn personnel. From 24 July Exercise Coronet again took the SCU staff pilots away from their primary duties. Tasked with 'anti-rat' patrols, the flight flew eight sorties on the first day and kept up a similar effort until Coronet ended on 30 July. Sadly, further upheaval was on the horizon.

Runway repairs at Wildenrath began on 8 August, and all SCU Sabres were deployed to Brüggen for the duration. Pilot conversion was up, however, to nineteen and the unit returned to Wildenrath on 24 August. Incredibly, the whole of the station then stood down on 4 September so that demonstrations could be flown for Imperial Staff College visitors. Four SCU Sabres were loaned to 67 Sqn for a fly-past, and flight staff pilot Flt Lt Martin Chandler performed a solo aerobatic routine, while Flt Lt Wilson attempted to direct a sonic boom onto the station through a thick overcast. Training continued the following day, though the training nature of the mission meant that the Sabres did experience some rough handling. On 5 September, Fg Off Armstrong of 147 Sqn ferried XB587 out for repair at Dunsfold following a series of heavy landings which left it as a Cat. 4 (R) loss. It did not return to RAF service. On 24 September XB616 was also transferred Cat. 3 to Dunsfold, this time by P Off Pollock of 67 Sqn, after a nose undercarriage door detached in flight and damaged the aircraft's tailplane.

Another big exercise, 'Monte Carlo', began at 0500 hr on 10 September. SCU again performed anti-rat missions, flying fourteen sorties on the first day for a flying time of 8 hours and 25 minutes. Further early-morning starts were flown on subsequent days until 13 September, the final day, when a high-level sweep – declared as 'highly successful' – brought proceedings to a close. SCU flew a total of 38 sorties during Monte Carlo. Though the exercise inevitably took staff pilots away from their training tasks, twelve pilots from 3, 67 and 71 Sqns were trained during September, with courses generally being started every ten days, depending on weather and student proficiency.

Fighter Command had in the meantime been caught on the hop: Sabres had begun arriving with 66 Sqn before any pilots had been converted onto the type. As a result, squadron commander Sqn Ldr Dennis Usher, DFC and Flt Lt Jed Gray flew to Wildenrath on 2 December to take the SCU course. A further three pilots, including Flt Lt Barrey and Flt Sgt Volanthen from 66 Sqn, began training with SCU on 18 December. Their conversion was completed on 21 December, and a third Fighter Command pilot, Fg Off Wardell from 92 Sqn, who had been back-flighted by a head cold, completed his training on 8 January 1954. At the end of 1953, SCU strength stood at 6 officers, 15 senior non-commissioned officers and 122 airmen. At its peak, the flight 'owned' twenty-one Sabres.

The beginning of 1954 was heralded by the usual bad weather – three inches of snow fell on 4 January alone – but snow-clearing continued and, as long as the skies were relatively clear, so did training. Of sixteen flying days during the month, three were deemed suitable only for the experienced SCU instructors. And despite the needs of Fighter Command, 2 TAF's thirst for Sabre pilots was more urgent. Courses begun in January, concentrated on 112 and 130 Sqn crews; thirty-nine had passed out by the end of the month. Fighter Command pilots, mainly from 92 Sqn, were then slotted into the training programme during February. Two squadron commanders were also trained: Sqn Ldr Turner from 92 Sqn and Sqn Ldr Mejor from 130 Sqn. A Pakistan Air Force pilot, Sqn Ldr Hussain, was also put through the conversion process. He performed two solos on 2 March alongside a number of 4 Sqn pilots.

Emphasis changed during April 1954, with the completion of 2 TAF pilot training. The unit was also renamed, becoming Sabre Conversion Flight (SCF). The last few 93 Sqn crews were routed through SCF, and pilots from Bückeburg started ground courses. Their training continued into May. SCF's intended role as the 2 TAF Sabre training unit came to an end once Bückeburg's last crews had completed the course. Since responsibility for RAF Sabre training would then transfer to 229 OCU at Chivenor, it became one of the last SCF tasks to convert instructors from Chivenor. The first 229 OCU instructors started flying with the Flight on 11 May 1954, along with a few stragglers from Bückeburg and 93 Sqn. When the 2 TAF pilots completed their course on 19 May, Chivenor's pilots remained to carry out more in-depth familiarisation, such as practising battle-formation flying. Eight instructor pilots from 229 OCU passed through SCF for conversion during May.

The final SCF course started on 25 May. The final pilot to solo on the Sabre was Flt Lt Taylor, Wildenrath's Weapons Officer, who flew the Sabre on 12 June; however, none of this intake completed training. On 6 June 2 ATAF headquarters issued orders to disband the Sabre Conversion Flight. Thirty non-commissioned officers and airmen would be retained as a rear echelon to complete servicing of the unit's aircraft and to follow up their delivery to other units. Nonetheless, SCF pilots Flt Lt Watson and Fg Off Hastings were still able to act as airborne spares during a fly-past over Düsseldorf on 10 June, marking the Queen's Birthday. With the drawdown of operations, Fg Off B.P. Meade took over as CO in July; Meade had been medically grounded on 71 Sqn and was transferred across to close down SCF.

The first SCF Sabre to leave the unit, XB943, flew out to 130 Sqn at Brüggen on 14 June. A further aircraft was flown out to 5 Maintenance Unit on 24 June and the following day a further pair, along with the key personnel of the flight, were dispersed. By the end of June, eight Sabres had been ferried out, leaving thirteen at Wildenrath. Of this total, only two were deemed fully serviceable, the remainder being grounded for lack of spares. Though the SCF had officially disbanded, the flight's final Sabres – XB592 and XB618 – did not depart Wildenrath until October, when both were ferried out to

Black and white-trimmed, XB948 was the 138 Wing Leader's aircraft at Geilenkirchen. Wg Cdr Bob Weighill's name was painted in white on the canopy rail. (*Robin Brown*)

5 MU. During its existence, SCU/SCF had trained 353 pilots on the Sabre 4.

AIRCRAFT ASSIGNED

XB542, XB587, XB591, XB592, XB593, XB602, XB603, XB611, XB616, XB618, XB635, XB665, XB673/G, XB675, XB676, XB682, XB686, XB688, XB694, XB700, XB726, XB728/W, XB738, XB874, XB926*, XB935*, XB939*, XB943*, XB952*, XB953*.

* = '6–3'-winged from manufacture.

'PERSONAL' SABRES

A number of RAF Sabres were assigned to wing leaders, or became the personal mounts of station commanders on the various units where Sabres were flown. For completeness, these were:

Brüggen/135 Wing Leader. Wg Cdr G.B. Johns, DSO, DFC. Various Sabres assigned: XB702, XB893, XB945 and XB987. This last, a '6–3'-winged machine, wore the initials 'GBJ' angled downwards in white on the tail fin.

Geilenkirchen/138 Wing Leader. XB827 was initially assigned to Wg Cdr Clive Baker, then from March 1955, XB615 took over. Wg Cdr R.H.G. 'Bob' Weighill was assigned XB948 from July 1955; it was painted with black and white nose checks and had a black and white-checked tail band.

Jever/122 Wing Leader. Wg Cdr 'Hammer' West had XB948 assigned to him. This aircraft carried a red and white-checked tail.

Linton Wing Leader. Wg Cdr Lee Mailin flew XD763, coded 'LM'; the aircraft had been assigned from 66 Sqn to the station flight on 8 March 1954 for this purpose. When Wg Cdr Eric 'Ricky' W. Wright took over, he had XD763 painted with a 'sabre' design on the tail fin, with the initials 'EWW' superimposed. A lion rampant was painted on the nose, along with the words 'Linton Wing'.

Linton Station Commander. Gp Capt Mike Pedley was assigned XD736, coded 'MP', though the aircraft was nominally on 92 Sqn charge. It has been reported that when Gp Capt Dennis F. Spottiswode took over in April 1956 he had the aircraft recoded 'DFS'. If so, this would have been for a very short period: XD736 was allotted for overhaul at Westland on 25 April.

Oldenburg/124 Wing Leader. Wg Cdr Ian Campbell's Sabre was XB886, coded 'WL'.

Wildenrath/137 Wing Leader. Wg Cdr Mike Le Bas had XB619 and XB702 assigned to him. Wg Cdr C.F. Ambrose, DFC, AFC had taken over by 1955.

Wildenrath Station Commander. When the first Sabres arrived at Wildenrath, Gp Capt James Edgar 'Johnnie' Johnson was Station Commander. He soon selected XB616, a Sabre Conversion Unit aircraft, as his personal mount. On 19 August 1953, Johnnie Johnson was flying XB616 out of Sylt during 67 Sqn's deployment there. During the sortie, the nose undercarriage spontaneously extended and the resultant damage forced an immediate grounding. XB616 was assessed at Cat. 4 (Flyable) and was limited to 250kt. On

Wg Cdr Eric W. Wright flew XD763 when he was Linton Wing Leader. The aircraft had a stylised sabre on each side of the vertical fin, over which was imposed Wright's initials 'EWW'. On the nose, this aircraft carried a red griffin rampant along with the words 'Linton Wing' in white. Finally, the wing commander's pennant was painted on each gun-access panel. (*Eric Taylor via Bruce Robertson*)

Three key personnel in the early 2 TAF Sabre period were, L–R: Sqn Ldr Paddy Harbison (CO 67 Sqn), Gp Capt Johnnie Johnson (Wildenrath Station Commander) and Wg Cdr Mike Le Bas (Wildenrath Wing Leader). Mike Le Bas led the wing on its famous Coronation Review fly-past over Odiham. (*Paddy Harbison*)

31 August, Flt Lt Hicks of 67 Sqn ferried it back to Wildenrath via Oldenburg. It was then allotted for repair with Airwork in the UK.

The day after Johnnie Johnson's undercarriage incident at Sylt, XB686 was allotted to SCF, and Johnson took on this camouflaged machine as his next personal mount. To distinguish the aircraft, he had it painted with a red lower portion to the tail fin, red canopy rails and a red forward nose-gear door. The initials 'JEJ' were painted on the canopy rail and nose door.

It is not known whether Johnson's successor, Gp Capt R.J. Gosnell, had his own Sabre, but it seems doubtful. One occurrence seems to bear this out: on 1 July 1954, Gp Capt Gosnell flew to Bückeburg in a Sabre, but, inexperienced on the type, he failed to use the aircraft's aerodynamic braking on the airfield's short runway and overshot. The Sabre ended up in a ditch, sustaining Cat. 4 damage, and Sabre flights to Bückeburg were curtailed. Notably, Gosnell had not been flying a 'personal' Sabre, but a regular 71 Sqn machine, XB669.

CHAPTER EIGHTEEN

EXIT STAGE LEFT . . .

Inevitably, the arrival in service of indigenous fighters such as the Hawker Hunter spelled the end for the RAF's Sabre force. In preparation for this change, discussion had begun during July 1953 into the method of converting from one type to the other. US provision of Hunters for the RAF under the Military Assistance Program (MAP) was an early proposal: on 16 July Brig Gen Dan F. Callahan of the Military Assistance Advisory Group (MAAG) in the UK brought this up in a conversation with RAF Deputy Chief of the Air Staff, AM Sir Ronald Ivelaw-Chapman. Callahan put forward the idea that the RAF's Sabres could be replaced on a one-for-one basis by American 'offshore-funded' (MAP) Hunters when the time came. Ivelaw-Chapman stated that he was 'attracted to the offer'. This was something of an understatement, since it would mean the RAF getting its Hunters free of charge.

Further discussion took place, and on 18 August 1953 Air Cdre J.N.T. Stephenson for the RAF proposed a draft calendar for exchange. It predicted that 220 Sabres could be available for exchange in December 1954, 176 in March 1955 and 88 in June 1955. This proposal was put forward as Plan K1a. In a letter to Brig Gen Callahan on 21 August 1953, Ivelaw-Chapman agreed that the UK would accept responsibility for overhaul of all Sabres prior to handover to the US government.

Although the aircraft were owned jointly, but in differing percentages, by the US and Canada, the opinion of the British government was elicited as to which nation should receive the Sabres once they were back in US hands (agreement with Canada was later reached, transferring ownership of the Sabres entirely to the US government). On 21 May 1954, Air Cdre B.A. Casey at NATO transmitted the Air Staff's opinion concerning the disposal of Sabres, qualifying his statement by saying that the subject had not really been discussed at great length. In essence, the Air Staff thought that first choice would be the northern European countries (Norway, Denmark, Holland and Belgium), with the Turkish Air Force, the Italian Air Force and the Yugoslav Air Force as second choices.

On the same day as Casey drafted his letter, Mr R.C. Ayling at the Air Ministry formalised his department's official line in a letter to NATO chiefs. Ayling suggested that Norway should receive 54 aircraft, the Netherlands 138 and Belgium 153, making a total of 345 Sabres. This did not tally closely with US or Canadian ideas, however, and over the following months further exchanges were made to reach a satisfactory conclusion. The final decision was that the Sabres would be almost equally divided between Italy and Yugoslavia.

Discussion had meanwhile returned to the method of Hunter/Sabre exchange, and a meeting was convened at the Air Ministry in London on 18 May 1954 to discuss a draft memorandum issued by HQ, USAF Europe on behalf of the US government's MAP. The memorandum proposed that all remaining RAF Sabres would be exchanged for 350 Hawker Hunter aircraft being supplied under the offshore procurement programme. HQ USAFE estimated that at least 375 Sabres would be available for transfer and that discussions should begin to arrange for release of all Canadian- and US-furnished F-86E aircraft, spare parts, support equipment, test equipment, special tools and training equipment.

Responsibility for overhaul of the aircraft prior to handover to the USAF would rest with the United Kingdom, and all Sabres would be rehabilitated at UK expense. Outstanding mandatory 'technical-order compliances' and 'safety of flight' modifications would be embodied on all aircraft during overhaul, and engines that had run more than 200 hours since last major servicing would be subject to a complete overhaul. For engines having run between 50 and 200 hours since overhaul, a minor repair schedule would be put in place; engines with less than 50 hours' running would be accepted on the basis of an inspection. HQ USAFE calculated that a ninety-day overhaul period for each aircraft would be necessary, and laid down an initial calendar for assigning Sabres into the overhaul process (presuming a best-case scenario of 405 aircraft available):

No. of Aircraft	Quarter Ending
30	30 September 1954
30	31 December 1954
45	31 March 1955
65	30 June 1955
65	30 September 1955
65	31 December 1955
60	31 March 1956
15	30 June 1956

Chairman at the 18 May meeting was Air Cdre B.A. Casey, who opened by stating that no decisions could be taken without further detailed consideration. He also pointed out that the final figure of available Sabres was likely to be closer to 345 than the US estimate. This difference seems to have been due to an American perception that as many as ninety Sabres were currently in store; the British response was that by December 1954 only about twenty-five Sabres would remain stored. The meeting closed, and further discussions took place concerning the implementation of the exchange, as well as the process of completing the overhaul of the Sabres.

On 3 January 1955, Mr Lincoln Gordon, Minister of Economic Affairs, informed the Minister of Defence, the Rt. Hon. Harold MacMillan MP, that the former had been instructed to carry out the Sabre/Hunter exchange proposal. On 19 May Gordon contacted the minister again (though the post was now filled by Selwyn Lloyd) to inform him that a memorandum of understanding had been agreed with the US authorities on the Hunter/Sabre exchange. The memorandum broadly agreed with the suggestions set out by HQ USAFE during the previous year, though only 340 Hunters (rather than 350) would be supplied. The UK government in return would make every effort to ensure that not less than 360 Sabres would be transferred to the US government. Notably, the US government would not be obligated to assign more Hunters to the UK than the number of Sabres it received in exchange. A revised calendar for delivery of Sabres into overhaul was also appended, for a total of between 340 and 360 aircraft. It programmed for the first thirty Sabres being routed into overhaul in August 1955, then a similar amount each month, rising to fifty per month in January 1956. The final aircraft would go into the overhaul lines in June 1956.

The memorandum of understanding stated that delivery of the first fifty Sabres to new recipients (foreign air forces) must be completed during the quarter ending 31 December 1955. In this it signally failed: first deliveries were not made until early 1956. Overhaul of the Sabres was contracted to a number of established civilian companies, which are detailed below.

Part of the first batch of ex-RAF Sabres supplied to Yugoslavia from 1956, 11035 wears the standard 2 TAF colour scheme in which these machines were delivered. The first Yugoslav Sabres were based at Batajnica near Belgrade. (*Mitja Maruško*)

In autumn 1955, the RAF Sabre squadrons gradually began to convert onto the Hunter, allowing the overhaul process to begin. Concurrently, Sabres held in store with the maintenance units were also prepared for transfer. As agreed in August 1953, the aircraft would be overhauled before return to US control, and in most cases Sabres were allotted to overhaul organisations prior to flying out from their final RAF units. This enabled them to be positioned with the various civilian workshops by their ferry pilots. Once there, Sabres that had not received the '6–3' wing modification in RAF service were brought up to that standard, and after a thorough overhaul – sometimes of up to twelve months, rather than the ninety days planned for – emerged in freshly painted RAF camouflage, with whitewashable USAF markings, for their delivery flights. All export aircraft were redesignated F-86E(M) – the 'M' signifying 'modified'. The job of ferrying the Sabres to Yugoslavia and Italy was assigned to USAF pilots at various bases in Europe.

The first aircraft from overhaul were delivered to the Italian Air Force, (Aeronautica Militare Italiana – AMI) and this process began on 12 January 1956 with the delivery of 19544 (XB641) from Airwork at Dunsfold. In total, the AMI received 179 Sabres, with the last being delivered in 1957. The aircraft went on to serve with two wing-sized units – 2 Aerobrigata and 4 Aerobrigata – and were finally withdrawn from service in August 1965.

Yugoslavia, on the other hand, gained its aircraft in two distinct batches. The first gratis MAP delivery to the Yugoslav Air Force (Ratnog vazduhoplovstva i protivvazdusne odbrane – RV i PVO) began with the delivery of two aircraft to Belgrade on 21 May 1956. These Sabres were reserialled as 11001 and 11002 in the RV i PVO system, and all subsequent F-86E(M) aircraft delivered to Yugoslavia adopted consecutive serial numbers. By mid-1957, forty-three Sabres had been delivered to the RV i PVO, but on 15 July that year the Yugoslav government issued a statement that from the end of the year all US aid to the country would cease. Warming relations between Yugoslavia and the Soviet Union had led the US government to stop all free MAP aid, and that included the Sabres.

However, a solution was found that managed to circumvent this ruling: instead of being given the remaining aircraft, Yugoslavia would instead buy the Sabres, thus avoiding the MAP regulations. Supplied from similarly overhauled ex-RAF stocks, the Yugoslavs paid between $5,000 and $15,000 per aircraft and eventually managed to acquire a further 78 Sabres in this way, giving them a total of 121 aircraft. Serial numbers for these 'commercially acquired' Sabres commenced at 11044. In RV i PVO service the F-86E(M) were flown by 117 vp (vuzduhoplovni puk – aircraft wing) and 204 vp. They were withdrawn from use in 1971, though a few were then sold to the Honduran Air Force in Central America. This small group of original ex-RAF Sabres were finally grounded in the mid-1980s.

Not all of the RAF aircraft found a home, however. On 2 June 1959, Mr F. Cooper, Head of the S.6 Department at the Air

With its machine-gun armament reinstalled, 19774 reaches the end of its overhaul at Airwork's Speke facility. Previously XB886, strangely 19774 appears to have been allotted to Westland for overhaul. It later became 11097 with the Yugoslav Air Force. (*Keith Parker*)

Fresh from overhaul with Aviation Traders in August 1957, 19862 (XB774) awaits a test flight. This machine was delivered to the Yugoslavian Air Force on 5 October that year as s/n 11116. (*via Dave McLaren*)

Ministry, sent a loose minute to the RAF's Deputy Chief of the Air Staff detailing the final disposition of RAF Sabres. In it Cooper stated that 302 Sabres had been refurbished and returned to the USAF, and 52 were in the process of being broken up. Intriguingly, he also commented that one Sabre had been sent to 'a Dominion', as well as accounting for one aircraft that was still on loan to Bristol Siddeley for the Orpheus engine project. Presumably, the 'Dominion' aircraft referred to a second machine passed to Bristol Siddeley, this time for spares use.

The fifty-two Sabres detailed in the Air Ministry letter as undergoing the process of being scrapped had been declared surplus to requirements; all had been struck off charge on 18 December 1958. They had all been overhauled in anticipation of further foreign service, but, unlike those aircraft that found their way to Italy and Yugoslavia, the final fifty-two found no further use. The aircraft at Yeovilton and Stansted were scrapped *in situ*, but many of the Airwork Sabres were bought by the Staravia aircraft parts company. They found their way to Lasham in Hampshire,

This very unusual photograph was taken at Yeovilton on 28 July 1956 and shows ex-RAF Sabres midway through overhaul by Westland. The aircraft are in primer and have their RAF serials stencilled on the tail fins. Notably, all these aircraft have yet to receive the '6–3' wing modification necessary to bring them up to F-86E(M) export standard. L–R they are: XB801, XB821, XB767 and XD757. All were exported to either Italy or Yugoslavia. (*Peter R. March*)

where they languished until the company moved the airframes to nearby Church Crookham in 1963. For many years the Sabres could be seen there, gradually being reclaimed for spares. In 1970 the Church Crookham yard was closed and a few of the surviving Sabres made their way back to the airfield at Lasham. By the start of 1972, just two ex-RAF Sabres remained at Lasham: 19529 (XB626) and 19764 (XD762). These aircraft were finally broken up in 1973.

The main organisations involved with the overhaul of the ex-RAF Sabres were:

Airwork & General Trading

Airwork & General Trading (AGT) had been initially tasked with providing in-depth repair of RAF Sabres while in service. From 1953, the company began receiving Sabres at Dunsfold, and following structural repair, most were returned to squadron service. This process was generally a routine affair, but test-flying of these aircraft did prove hazardous. One such instance involved XB635, on 21 September 1954, which was on test following damage incurred at Sabre Conversion Unit in Germany the previous year. The Airwork test pilot experienced a violent 'flick' of his aircraft, followed by loss of control. He managed to recover, and it became obvious that the Sabre's nose door had inadvertently opened in flight. Airwork staff conducted a detailed investigation that revealed a nose-gear retraction bell crank had been incorrectly fitted. In this case, a visually similar port (left) side bell crank had been fitted instead of the correct starboard version. AGT's investigation revealed that, in such a case, full locking of the fairing doors in the 'up' position was not achieved, and their work in highlighting the problem prevented similar occurrences in service.

With the impending withdrawal of Sabres from RAF service, AGT expanded its operating base, and opened up Sabre overhaul facilities at Gatwick to the south of London, Speke near Liverpool, and Ringway on the outskirts of Manchester. Airwork now had four separate locations looking after these machines, and the overhaul of Sabres for export was arranged under contract 6/Acft/12466 for Speke and Ringway, with contracts 6/Acft/10370 and 12576 covering the Dunsfold and Gatwick operations.

Airwork's Speke facility was housed in a hangar on the northern side of the airfield, which had earlier been used to overhaul up to sixty Sabres loaned to the Canadians. The Speke operation was responsible for preparing these aircraft prior to RAF service. Overhaul of ex-RAF Sabres began to get going there in late 1955, and during the following year Keith Parker was detached to Speke as one of a few RAF personnel detailed to work alongside the mainly civilian workforce:

In the Summer of 1956, I was posted to RAF Hucknall in Nottinghamshire from 32 MU RAF St Athan. At that time RAF Hucknall was a school for the RAF Police as well as my future parent unit. Immediate events on arrival at Hucknall ensured that I was not going to have

Some of those that didn't make it. With deliveries to Yugoslavia and Italy fulfilled, any other overhauled ex-RAF Sabres were declared surplus at the end of 1958 and scrapped. Many of these airframes gravitated to Staravia at Lasham in Hampshire, and some lingered on into the early 1970s. The aircraft at the front is 19772 – XD770 with 66 Sqn. (*Author's Collection*)

any lingering memories of that station in any case. I arrived on station in the late afternoon in time to dump my kit in the transit quarters and get a meal: next morning I reported to the armoury to sign in, to be met with the remarks of 'Don't unpack your kit, you're being detached straight away. You are going to Liverpool', or words to that effect.

I was introduced to my civilian landlords, a Mr and Mrs Rose of Long Lane in Garston, Liverpool, and then taken on down to Liverpool airport to meet the management of Messrs Airwork Services, where I found that I was to be responsible for looking after the airborne armament requirements of the F-86 Sabre aircraft while they were being refurbished. I discovered that I was also to be responsible for a staff of one SAC to assist, who was already in place and also living in civvy digs.

The job basically required that the armament of six 'point fives' per aircraft be removed and locked away for safe storage while the F-86 aircraft were being refurbished; then later, after cleaning, etc., refitting these as required, plus later still, gunsight and gun harmonisation. There was no requirement that I can recall that stipulated our involvement with the aircraft's safety equipment (ejection seat, etc.).

The workmen all seemed to be friendly and helpful and, when asked, would explain what they were doing; but we were not, as one would expect, encouraged to interrupt their work.

I cannot now recall anything of the management, which probably goes to show how we were left very much on our own to do our RAF thing. I do recall being told that a number of the people working on the aircraft were not recognised craftsmen but were previously (aircraft) unskilled and locally trained for their particular tasks. A lot of drilling and riveting work went on in the hangar.

Some of the first ex-RAF Sabres to arrive at the Manchester/Ringway site flew in on 7 July 1955 and comprised XB577, XB595 and XB597, two 26 Sqn and one 20 Sqn aircraft, respectively. On 22 March 1956 the last pair, XB543 and XB754, were ferried in for overhaul. Denis H. Martin had served eight years in the RAF as an airframe fitter, and his first job after leaving the service was with Airwork at Ringway:

Airwork had recruited a fairly small team by poaching experienced staff from the two local major aviation employers, the Fairey Aviation Company and Avro, with a sprinkling of ex-RAF and ex-RN engineers. Very few of the team had any previous F-86 experience, but between us we had many combined years of aircraft manufacturing, maintenance and repair-technique basic know-how. We were supported by a small team of contract-administration and customer-liaison staff from Airwork's main base and the Air Ministry had AID (Aircraft Inspection Directorate) surveyors working on the site.

The aircraft were completely depanelled, engines were removed, and a full airframe visual inspection for damage and corrosion (I don't remember any corrosion) was carried out. I recall finding several cases of excessive play in the control surfaces attached to the horizontal stabiliser, which involved the replacement of the appropriate worn bushes/pins, etc. Some in-service skin repairs were deemed not up to the standard required by the repair manuals, so were redone. During the inspections I was interested to find that there was very little wire-locking of pipe unions, etc. compared to British aircraft, where every pipe joint or major attachment nut or bolt was double-twisted, wire-locked. From memory, the only wire-locked areas on the F-86 were the ring of bolts at the wing fuel pumps, the flying-control cable quick disconnects for fuselage removal, and the four rear-fuselage attachment bolts. Another pleasant surprise was the high standard of part-interchangeability, which far exceeded anything that British manufacturers were able to achieve at that time.

When the aircraft was back in one piece, full system-function checks/flyers range-of-movement checks/hydraulic main and alternate system tests and cockpit-pressurisation testing was carried out. If all was well the engine was ground-performance tested and the ship offered to the resident test pilot, Dave Hunt, who raised a few complaints from ATC due to his tendency towards exuberant flying habits, which were probably OK in 2 TAF but didn't go down at all well on a sober municipal airport. His Wartburg car was always parked outside the flight office on the airfield side of the hangar instead of in the official car park, and I seem to remember it got grit-blasted by a taxiing F-86 as it turned from the hardstanding onto the perimeter track. Another thing that pleased him was the couple of times that the dispatching mechanic forgot to return the gear-door safety servicing switch to the flight position, which meant that the inner doors stayed open after take-off. I'll guess that happened a few times in the RAF too.

The contract came to a premature end at Manchester towards the end of 1956. The hangar was on a short-term lease from Manchester Corporation, who refused to extend it. They were beginning the process of creating a major international civil airport, which wasn't helped by the Fairey company test-flying Fireflies and Gannets from their assembly works on the western side of the airfield, and the Royal Auxiliary Air Force 613 City of Manchester Sqn operating Vampires from a hangar on the north side, with Airwork making a lot of noise on the south side.

The distinction of delivering the first F-86E(M) to the USAF fell to AGT's operation at Dunsfold; it handed over 19544 (XB641) on 12 January 1956 and a second machine (19570/XB684) two weeks later. Both went to the Italian Air Force. The various AGT sites delivered their final Sabres in 1958 and, aside from a few surplus aircraft that were scrapped on site, this ended the company's association with this aircraft.

Aviation Traders (Engineering) Limited

Founded by entrepreneur Freddie Laker just after the Second World War, Aviation Traders (Engineering) Ltd (ATEL) centred its Sabre overhaul facilities at Stansted airfield in Essex. There, with a staff of mainly ex-RAF and Navy engineers, the company was eventually responsible for preparing 96 ex-RAF Sabres for export under contract 6/Acft/12467.

ATEL also set up an engine bay at Stansted, which was tasked with preparing stored engines for fitting into the Sabres. Many of these engines had been configured to fit into B-36 bombers, and thus much of the work involved stripping the ancillary components and building them up again to J47-GE-13 specification. Alan Cook worked for ATEL during the 1956–8 period, and offers a unique insight into the workings of the Sabre overhaul operation:

The aircraft were hangared and stripped down prior to inspection. Engines were removed and brought to the engine bay, whereupon jet pipes, exhaust cones and various pipework were all removed and labelled. The engines were then packed into pressurised containers. Silica-gel packs were added, then the containers were sealed and pressurised. They were then sent back to the USA for overhaul.

The overhauled engines that ATEL received were to B-36 specification, which entailed quite a lot of change to pipe runs and removal of some pipework. This had to be replaced with the pipework removed from the original aircraft engines. Of course, any parts that were time expired had to be replaced. Some of the pipes we found were just about impossible to procure. In such cases we had to make them up by hand. In the case of the armoured pipes, i.e. high-pressure hydraulic pipes, it was extremely hard work and very painful on the hands.

All the pipework was eventually grouped to the front of the engine into what were commonly known as 'islands', ready to be connected to various parts of the fuselage, i.e. fuel, oil, hydraulics, electric. Of course, everything had to be wire-locked. The turbine-disc nut had to be checked for torque loading with a rather large torque-loading spanner. Great care had to be taken while using this spanner, as misuse could cause a very nasty injury. The exhaust cone was then fitted, using, I think, eighty-seven $\frac{5}{16}$in AF bolts and self-locking nuts. These also had to be torque-loaded (another job that was a bit of a pain in the rear end). The jet pipe was then fitted and covered with insulating materials. These were metal objects filled with heat-resisting material. These had to be wire-locked in position to a set pattern of locking, using 18 SWG stainless-steel wire. This was another job which was painful to the hands, as they had to be really tight. We used to hang our full weight onto the wire for this job.

Then the throttle linkage had to be set up. This entailed the fuel system being filled with hot engine oil (70°C). The linkage was then set up using a special protractor and two gauges. When the linkage had been set up and checked, the oil was drained and the system flushed out. Of course, during the build of each engine, every operation had to be checked by an AID inspector so that nothing was left to chance. I do not remember the number of hours spent on these engine builds, but they were quite considerable.

First aircraft to arrive with ATEL were XB631 and XB710, which flew in on 28 July 1955; and the last of a total of ninety-six Sabres were ferried in for overhaul with ATEL at Stansted by the end of June 1956. Once the aircraft had been overhauled and brought up to F-86E(M) standard, test-flying was carried out by a Royal Auxiliary Air Force pilot from nearby North Weald. As he declared aircraft serviceable, and when two aircraft were available, a pair of USAF pilots from RAF Wethersfield flew the Sabres out to their final destinations.

Test-flying of the F-86E(M) aircraft began early in 1956, 19584 (XB698) being one of the first overhauled Sabres to take to the air, on 15 March. It was then assigned to the Italian Air Force and departed five days later. Final airborne departure from Stansted was 19692 (XB838), which flew out for eventual assignment to Yugoslavia on 27 January 1958. This left approximately twelve surplus Sabres; these were struck off charge in December and scrapped.

WESTLAND

Located in a specially built workshop on the western side of the Royal Naval Air Station at Yeovilton, Westland began receiving Sabres in the summer of 1955. The aircraft were all overhauled under contract 6/Acft/12465, and the first five aircraft (XB580, XB687, XB691, XB708 and XB796) were flown in by 147 Sqn ferry pilots on 13 July. Just over a month later, on 17 August, XB700 was lost in the circuit at Yeovilton while on delivery to Westland. The aircraft collided with a Navy Sea Hawk, killing both pilots.

Fortunately, there were no other incidents, and the last pair of Sabres, XB672 and XB959, were ferried in from Benson on 22 June 1956. This brought the total of Sabres under overhaul with Westland to ninety-one. The first aircraft to leave after overhaul was 19594 (XB708), which flew out on 14 September 1956. Overhaul and modification of the aircraft continued until late 1957, when, in anticipation of the forthcoming Sea Vixen fighter, the Navy decided to strengthen Yeovilton's runways. As a result, from November of that year, Sabres were transported to nearby Merryfield, where test-flying was completed.

Prior to this, a number of Sabres had been transferred to Airwork at Speke for completion of overhauls, though Westland did eventually hand over sixty-three Sabres to

The sole Orpheus-powered Sabre was XB982, which had initially been assigned to 92 Sqn. Retired to Westland at Yeovilton, the aircraft was then overhauled and modified to receive the Bristol Siddeley Orpheus 801 and Orpheus engines and flew as a test bed in this natural metal finish. It was withdrawn from use in 1962. (*Peter R. March*)

the USAF for export. Final airborne departure was 19795 (XD774), which flew away for service in Yugoslavia on 8 January 1958. That left twenty-one Sabres without a home, of which XB982 was converted to accept the Orpheus engine and was then delivered to Bristol Siddeley Engines. XB900 was also delivered to BSE for use as a spares source for XB982. The remaining aircraft were declared surplus to requirements at the end of 1958 and were subsequently scrapped.

Bristol Aircraft/Bristol Siddeley Engines Limited

Though not primarily involved in overhaul of the Sabres, Bristol Aircraft Ltd (later Bristol-Siddeley Engines (BSE) Ltd) was involved in the latter part of the RAF Sabre story. In the mid-fifties, BSE was busy developing its Orpheus 12 engine for use in NATO's new lightweight fighter aircraft, a competition that was eventually won by the Fiat G. 91.

In order to provide flight-test data for this engine, Bristol loaned ex-RAF Sabre 4 XB982, which had been overhauled by Westland and was modified to accept the Orpheus. The aircraft had been assigned to Bristol Aircraft under contract 6/Acft/14370/CB.9(a) on 4 March 1957, and was delivered to BSE's Filton airfield near Bristol during 1958. In deference to its test role, the aircraft wore a natural metal finish with basic RAF markings, similar to those worn on the original ferry flight from Canada. Uniquely for an F-86E(M), the aircraft wore its RAF serial number, XB982, rather than the Canadian serial number, 19873.

This Sabre, 19788 (ex-XB900) was transferred to Bristol Siddeley Engines at Bristol's Filton airfield in 1959 and used as a spares source for the Orpheus Sabre XB982. (*Peter R. March*)

Initially fitted with an Orpheus 801 engine, XB982 completed its first flight as such on 3 July 1958; Godfrey Auty was the pilot on this occasion. Once the Orpheus 12 test engine was available, XB982 returned to Westland for further modification. It returned to Bristol late in 1959 and made its first Orpheus 12-powered flight with Tom Frost at the controls on 10 November. Further flights were also piloted by Mike Webber and Harry Pollitt. With a more advanced design than the Sabre's usual J47 power plant, the Orpheus 12 featured variable compressor-inlet guide vanes and a two-stage turbine. Lighter in weight than the J47, the Orpheus 12 nonetheless produced 6,810lb thrust at sea level in the Sabre test bed. In a test programme accounting for 25 flying hours, the Sabre test bed proved the Orpheus 12 to be a safe and powerful engine.

XB982 ceased flying on 16 December 1959, and was put into storage at Filton. In 1962, the aircraft was scrapped, along with the fuselage from its spares aircraft, XB900/19788.

APPENDIX 1

LEADING PARTICULARS – CANADAIR SABRE F. MK. 4

Length:	37ft 6in
Heights:	14ft 7in (to fin tip)
	9ft 3in (to top of canopy)
Wingspan:	37ft 1in
Wing Area:	287.4ft^2 (slatted) / 302.3ft^2 ('6–3' wing)
Weights:	11,100lb (empty)
	17,750lb (fuelled, with two drop tanks)
Engine:	General Electric J47-GE-13
Thrust:	5,200lb static at sea level
Fuel Capacities:	362 imperial gallons internal (usable)
	200 imperial gallons external (two drop tanks)
Top Speed:	679mph at sea level
Stalling Speed (20,000lb all-up weight, wheels and flaps down):	125kt (slatted) / 135kt ('6–3' wing)
Service Ceiling:	47,200ft
Combat Radius:	320 miles
Maximum Range:	1,022 miles

APPENDIX 2

RAF SABRE SERIAL NUMBERS

Sabre F. Mk. 2

RAF s/n	RCAF s/n	Quantity	Notes
XB530	19378	1	replacement for XB530 ntu/19461
XB531	19384	1	replacement for 19462, w/o 22 Jan 53*
XB532	19404	1	replacement for 19463, w/o 5 Mar 53*

Sabre F. Mk. 4

RAF s/n	RCAF s/n	Quantity	Notes
XB533–XB550	19464–19481	18	
XB551	19663	1	(originally XB809)
XB575–XB603	19482–19510	29	
XB608–XB646	19511–19549	39	
XB647–XB650	19854–19857	4†	(originally XD102 to XD105)
XB664–XB688	19550–19574	25	
XB689	19457	1	replacement for XB689 ntu/19575
XB690–XB713	19576–19599	24	
XB726–XB744	19600–19618	19	
XB745	19635	1	replacement for 19619, w/o 28 Dec 53*
XB746–XB754	19620–19628	9	
XB755	19458	1	replacement for XB755 ntu/19629
XB756–XB760	19630–19634	5	
XB761	19459	1	replacement for XB761 ntu/19635
XB762	19636	1	
XB763	19629	1	replacement for 19637, w/o 2 Mar 54*
XB764–XB768	19638–19642	5	
XB769	19460	1	replacement for 19643, w/o 15 Jun 53*
XB770–XB775	19858–19863	6†	(originally XD106 to XD111)

RAF s/n	RCAF s/n	Quantity	Notes
XB790–XB805	19644–19659	16	
XB806	19461	1	replacement for 19660, w/o 9 Jun 53*
XB807–XB808	19661–19662	2	
XB809	19453	1	
XB810–XB815	19664–19669	6	
XB816	19454	1	replacement for 19670, w/o 12 Jun 53*
XB817–XB824	19671–19678	8	
XB825	19575	1	replacement for 19679, w/o 2 Mar 54*
XB826–XB834	19680–19688	9	
XB835	19455	1	replacement for 19689, w/o 27 May 53*
XB836–XB839	19690–19693	4	
XB851–XB855	19864–19868	5†	(originally XD112 to XD116)
XB856–XB868	19694–19706	13	
XB869–XB885	19732–19748	17	
XB886–XB888	19774–19776	3	(originally USAF 52-10227 to 52-10229)
XB889–XB900	19777–19788	12	
XB912–XB915	19789–19792	4	(originally XB901 to XB904)
XB916–XB961	19803–19848	46†	(originally XB905, XB941 to XB985)
XB973–XB977	19849–19853	5†	(originally XB986 to XB990)
XB978–XB999	19869–19890	22†	(originally XD117 to XD138)
XD706–XD730	19707–19731	25	(originally USAF 52-10177 to 52-10201)
XD731–XD736	19749–19754	6	(originally USAF 52-10202 to 52-10207)
XD753–XD771	19755–19773	19	(originally USAF 52-10208 to 52-10226)
XD772–XD775	19793–19796	4	
XD776–XD779	19797–19800	4	(originally USAF 52-10231 to 52-10234)
XD780–XD781	19801–19802	2†	(originally USAF 52-10235 to 52-10236)
Total		431	

Notes:

1. Aircraft marked * were loaned to the RCAF and written off (w/o) in service prior to return to the RAF.
2. ntu = not taken up; RAF serial allotted but not applied on aircraft.
3. Aircraft marked † had the '6–3' wing installed during manufacture.

APPENDIX 3

RAF SABRE LOSSES

Serial	Date	Unit	Pilot	Fatal/Non	Circumstances
49-1296	14 Aug '52	RAE	Flt Lt Ecclestone	N	Elevator runaway
XB534	19 Dec '52	OFU	Flt Sgt A.P. Pugh	F	Dived into ground on let-down into Prestwick
XB549	10 Mar '53	147 Sqn	Fg Off Vindis	N	Force-landed at Stornoway
XB610	5 Apr '53	147 Sqn	Sqn Ldr Cole	F	Engine failed 7 miles NE of Grantown-on-Spey
XB863	5 Jun '53	147 Sqn	Sgt Roderick	F	Lost control 6 miles NE of St-Félix-de-Valois, Canada
XB603	15 Jun '53	SCU	P Off Moss	N	Sank on approach to Wildenrath
XB676	17 Jun '53	SCU	n/a	N	Oxygen cylinders exploded on ground
XB882	18 Jul '53	147 Sqn	P Off Butrym	N	Inadvertent ejection 4 miles north of Broughty Ferry
XD775	18 Aug '53	147 Sqn	unknown	N	Stabiliser malfunction at St Hubert
XB683	17 Sep '53	67 Sqn	Flt Lt Wilson	N	Loss of control 6 miles from Liège, Belgium
XB949*	28 Sep '53	147 Sqn	Fg Off M. Cross	N	Engine failed on approach to Kinloss
XB690	6 Nov '53	67 Sqn	P Off Craig	N	Mid-air with XB730 near Mönchengladbach
XB730	6 Nov '53	67 Sqn	Fg Off A.F. Pollock	F	Mid-air with XB690 near Mönchengladbach
XB681	10 Feb '54	3 Sqn	Fg Off J.W. Tate	N	Landing at Geilenkirchen
XB643	24 Feb '54	3 Sqn	Fg Off J.A. Adair	F	Bad weather, Henri-Chapelle, Belgium
XB667	24 Feb '54	3 Sqn	Fg Off J.W. Tate	F	Bad weather, Henri-Chapelle, Belgium
XB866	24 Feb '54	26 Sqn	Flt Sgt J. Swales	F	Believed crashed into North Sea

Serial	Date	Unit	Pilot	Fatal/Non	Circumstances
XB912	4 Mar '54	112 Sqn	Fg Off L.R. Francis	N	Engine failed on approach to Brüggen
XB936	4 Mar '54	67 Sqn	P Off P. Rogers	N	Failed to get airborne
XB600	22 Mar '54	67 Sqn	Fg Off J. Law	N	Wheels-up landing at Oldenburg
XD722	6 May '54	66 Sqn	Flt Lt J. Gray	N	Flameout on landing at Langham
XD773	13 May '54	66 Sqn	Sgt K.P.D. Foard	N	Flameout on finals
XB648	3 Jun '54	130 Sqn	Fg Off W. Ireland	N	Slewed off runway at Brüggen
XB884	16 Jun '54	112 Sqn	Fg Off R. Mansfield	N	Control failure on test flight from Brüggen
XD711	16 Jun '54	66 Sqn	Fg Off J. Sweet	N	Mid-air with XD716 4 miles WNW of Hornsea
XD716	16 Jun '54	66 Sqn	Fg Off J. Rumbelow	N	Mid air with XD711 4 miles WNW of Hornsea
XB940	22 Jun '54	4 Sqn	Fg Off R. Gray	N	Fuel exhaustion, 8 miles east of Hamburg
XB819	29 Jun '54	234 Sqn	Fg Off P.J. Underdown	N	Forced landing 4 miles ENE of Jülich
XB647	8 Jul '54	4 Sqn	Fg Off J. Jack	F	Rolled into ground, Jever
XD707	22 Jul '54	66 Sqn	Fg Off J.D. Horne	F	Flew into Kinder Scout in cloud
XD730	22 Jul '54	66 Sqn	Flt Lt A. Green	F	Flew into Kinder Scout in cloud
XD758	22 Jul '54	66 Sqn	Fg Off G. Owen	N	Fire warning light 2½ miles NE of Helmsley
XB865	23 Jul '54	26 Sqn	P Off Stewart	F	Exploded and crashed 4 miles from Hude
XB638	5 Aug '54	20 Sqn	Fg Off H. Capewell	N	Hit ground at night, Oldenburg
XD768	10 Aug '54	66 Sqn	Fg Off J.M. Davies	N	Lost power on landing at Full Sutton
XD776	27 Aug '54	66 Sqn	Flt Lt J. Gray	N	Ammunition bay fire 12 miles SW of North Luffenham
XB734	3 Sep '54	26 Sqn	Fg Off R. Chase	N	Wheels-up landing at Oldenburg
XB627	7 Sep '54	67 Sqn	Fg Off G.E. Thomson	N	Emergency landing in field 3 miles S of Peer, Belgium
XD733	21 Sep '54	92 Sqn	Fg Off C.A. Grabham	F	Flew into high ground at night, Easingwold

Serial	Date	Unit	Pilot	Fatal/Non	Circumstances
XB899	22 Sep '54	20 Sqn	Flt Lt W.C. Kendall	N	Wheels-up landing at Schleswigland
XD771	29 Sep '54	92 Sqn	M/Plt E.S. Bannard	N	Engine failed, belly landing
XB937	8 Oct '54	4 Sqn	Fg Off K.A. Richardson	F	Dived into sea 9 miles SE of Sylt
XB988	19 Oct '54	130 Sqn	Fg Off C. Woodruff	F	Caught fire at night 7 miles NE of Kassel
XB711	23 Oct '54	229 OCU	Fg Off A. Longworth	F	Believed lost at sea
XB628	26 Oct '54	71 Sqn	Fg Off A.C. Jones	N	Mid-air with XB729 10 miles from Kronfeld
XB729	26 Oct '54	71 Sqn	Fg Off A.J. Chalkeley	N	Mid-air with XB628 10 miles from Kronfeld
XB860	29 Oct '54	234 Sqn	Fg Off P. Underdown	N	Exploded near Wintraak, Netherlands
XB927	29 Oct '54	130 Sqn	Fg Off D. Bracher	N	Engine failed on approach to Brüggen
XD772	29 Nov '54	66 Sqn	Fg Off G. Owen	N	Engine failed ½ mile east of Kelstern
XD713	29 Jan '55	92 Sqn	Fg Off E.S. Dodds	N	Tyre burst on take-off from Linton
XB760	4 Feb '55	71 Sqn	Flt Lt A.J.C. Taylor	F	Lost control in cloud, crashed 2 miles from Jülich
XB839	10 Feb '55	26 Sqn	Fg Off F.H. Rickwood	F	Dived into ground 8 miles from Oldenburg
XB623	24 Feb '55	26 Sqn	Fg Off Ferguson	N	Hit snow bank, Oldenburg
XD755	16 Mar '55	66 Sqn	Fg Off H. Armstrong	F	Stalled on approach to Driffield
XB634	5 Apr '55	67 Sqn	Fg Off M.J.C. Grant	F	Mid-air collision with Anson at Wildenrath
XD710	5 Apr '55	92 Sqn	Fg Off V.H. Hallam	N	Abandoned take-off from Acklington
XB615	3 May '55	234 Sqn	Sqn Ldr R. Emett	N	Wheels-up landing in field 1 mile from Pfaffendorf
XD780	14 May '55	92 Sqn	Fg Off D. Shelton-Smith	N	Stalled on landing at Linton
XB699	16 May '55	3 Sqn	Fg Off R. Taylor	F	Lontzen, Holland
XD712	16 Jun '55	66 Sqn	Fg Off L.M.P. Harryman	F	Broke up in dive
XB677	24 Jun '55	92 Sqn	Fg Off W.D. Cartwright	N	Failed to get airborne from Linton
XB633	26 Jun '55	3 Sqn	Fg Off M. Line	N	Wake turbulence at Eindhoven
XB950	5 Jul '55	112 Sqn	Fg Off M. Smith	F	Exploded 1 mile east of Heerlen, Holland

Serial	Date	Unit	Pilot	Fatal/Non	Circumstances
XB932	12 Jul '55	130 Sqn	Fg Off R. Burden	N	Undershot at Brüggen
XB880	15 Jul '55	71 Sqn	Sqn Ldr Cherry	F	Stalled on approach to Brüggen
XB548	3 Aug '55	93 Sqn	Fg Off E. Scott	F	Stalled on Meppen range
XB931	10 Aug '55	4 Sqn	n/a	N	Oxygen cylinders exploded during filling
XB808	16 Aug '55	20 Sqn	Flt Lt Kendall	F	Hit ground, Meppen range
XB700	17 Aug '55	147 Sqn	Fg Off K.G. MacLeod	F	Mid-air with Sea Hawk at Yeovilton
XB735	2 Sep '55	234 Sqn	Fg Off P. Topham	F	Hit pylon near Brindisi, Italy
XB822	1 Oct '55	93 Sqn	Fg Off J.S.C. Davis	N	Engine failed on test flight from Jever
XD729	25 Jan '56	66 Sqn	Fg Off L.J. Bradley	N	Lost power on landing at Linton

Note: One further Sabre, not initially assessed as a write-off, was later scrapped as a result of damage caused in service: XB612 with 3 Sqn, *c.* 25 November 1953.

APPENDIX 4

SURVIVING EX-RAF SABRES

RAF s/n	Location	Details
XB620	Grazzanize AB, Italy	
XB631	Turin/Caselle Airport, Italy	
XB697	San Pedro Sula AB, Honduras, derelict	ex-Honduran AF s/n 3010
XB710	Capua AB, Italy	
XB794	Village School, Kucure, Serbia	ex-Yugoslav AF s/n 11072
XB810	Capua AB, Italy	
XB812	Royal Air Force Museum, Hendon, UK	
XB814	Cameri AB, Italy	
XB820	San Pedro Sula AB, Honduras, derelict	ex-Honduran AF s/n 3009
XB826	A. Malignani Institute, Udine, Italy	
XB827	San Pedro Sula AB, Honduras, derelict	ex-Honduran AF s/n 3008
XB875	National Aviation Museum, Belgrade, Serbia	ex-Yugoslav AF s/n 11088
XB879	Polygon Bosnjaci Military Base, Serbia	ex-Yugoslav AF s/n 11090
XB894	Da Vinci Technical School, Pisa, Italy	
XB915	Italian Air Force Museum, Vigna di Valle, Italy	
XB934	San Pedro Sula AB, Honduras, preserved	ex-Honduran AF s/n 3006
XB954	Grosseto AB, Italy	
XB974	Polygon Bosnjaci Military Base, Serbia	ex-Yugoslav AF s/n 11112
XB978	San Pedro Sula AB, Honduras, derelict	ex-Honduran AF s/n 3002
XD723	Rivolto AB, Italy	
XD724	San Pedro Sula AB, Honduras, derelict	ex-Honduran AF s/n 3007
XD757	Subotica, Serbia, derelict	ex-Yugoslav AF s/n 11093
XD760	San Pedro Sula AB, Honduras, derelict	ex-Honduran AF s/n 3005
unknown	Chilean Air Force Museum, Los Cerillos, Chile	ex-Honduran AF s/n 3003?
unknown	Tegucigalpa Airport, Honduras, derelict	ex-Honduran AF s/n 3001
unknown	National Aviation Museum, Belgrade, Serbia	ex-Yugoslav AF s/n 11025
unknown	National Aviation Museum, Belgrade, Serbia	ex-Yugoslav AF s/n 11054

GLOSSARY

Barrage – Simulated bomber-raid exercise.

Battle Flight – Daylight duty whereby one flight was always at standby to intercept intruding aircraft. Scrambles launched by battle flight were often against known targets, but unknown 'bogies' were also encountered.

Beechers Brook/Bechers Brook – The air-ferry operation whereby most of the Sabres for the RAF were flown to the UK from Canada. Official documents use the terms 'Beechers Brook' and 'Bechers Brook' in almost equal measure to describe the RAF's epic Sabre-ferry operation. The correct spelling should be 'Bechers Brook', and for clarity this is the version used throughout this book.

Form D – Ground-attack exercise, usually against Army positions.

GCA – Ground-Controlled Approach.

GCI – Ground-Controlled Intercept.

Kingpin – Exercise which required bomber types – usually Canberras or V-Force aircraft – to simulate a Soviet raid on the UK. The fighter aircraft would be vectored onto a fixed point and from there directed against the bomber stream.

PAI – Pilot Attack Instructor.

PI – Practice Intercept.

QFI – Qualified Flying Instructor.

QGH – Controlled descent through cloud.

Rats and Terriers – Practice mission whereby aircraft ('rats') would depart base and return at low level to attempt to avoid interception by other fighters ('terriers').

Repair Categories – Aircraft damage/repair categories, such as 'Cat. 4', are mentioned at various points throughout this book. For reference, the categories mentioned in this book are as follows:

Cat. 3 (R) – Aircraft repairable on site, but beyond 2nd Line capability (usually repaired by civilian working party or within ASF).

Cat. 4 – Aircraft not repairable on site (usually dismantled for transport and repaired by civilian contractor).

Cat. 4 (Rehab) – Aircraft not repairable on site (allocated to rehabilitation centre). For the Sabres, this category was applied when they were withdrawn from RAF service. It enabled them to be ferried by air to the civilian contractor.

Cat. 4 (Flyable) – Aircraft not repairable on site, but allowed flight to repair depot.

Cat. 4 (R) – Category 4, repairable; same as Cat. 4.

Cat. 5 (C) – Aircraft written off and suitable for component reclamation.

Cat. 5 (Missing) – Aircraft missing.

SI – Servicing Instruction. An instruction issued at short notice to rectify a maintenance problem, but which requires regular compliance throughout the life of the aircraft.

Skittle – Exercise whose objective was to saturate 'enemy' radar, using as many aircraft as possible.

STI – Special Technical Instruction. A one-off instruction issued at short notice to rectify a maintenance problem. STIs were often issued as a result of accident investigations, or when serious defects were found at squadron level.

BIBLIOGRAPHY & SOURCES

PRIMARY SOURCES

Sabre 4 Pilot's Notes AP4503D-PN
USAF Credits for Destruction of Enemy Aircraft Korean War – USAF Historical Study 81, June 1963
Weight and Balance Data – Sabre 2 & 4 EO05-5C-8

Files held by The National Archives (Public Record Office):

3 Sqn	AIR 27/2724 & AIR 27/2877
4 Sqn	AIR 27/2725 & AIR 27/2878
20 Sqn	AIR 27/2693
26 Sqn	AIR 27/2604
66 Sqn	AIR 27/2627 & AIR 27/2792
67 Sqn	AIR 27/2627 & AIR 27/2792
71 Sqn	AIR 27/2628
92 Sqn	AIR 27/2636 & AIR 27/2677
93 Sqn	AIR 27/2636 & AIR 27/2803
112 Sqn	AIR 27/2643 & AIR 27/2758
130 Sqn	AIR 27/2705
147 Sqn	AIR 27/2647 & AIR 27/2820
234 Sqn	AIR 27/2662
229 OCU	AIR 29/2282
5 MU	AIR 29/2083 & AIR 29/2778
23 MU	AIR 29/2971
33 MU	AIR 29/2019
Comparison of Sabre and MiG-15	DSIR 23/20084
Hunter/Sabre exchange	AIR 2/10962–10965, DEFE 13/56
Operation Bechers Brook	AIR 8/1686
Provision of Sabres for RAF	AIR 8/1989, AVIA 54/899
Provision of Sabres for Fighter Command	AIR 20/9733
Sabre Conversion Unit, Flight	AIR 29/2412
Sabre Accident Reports	AVIA 5/32, AVIA 5/34, BT 233/131, BT233/152, BT233/220, BT233/222, BT233/231, BT233/238, BT233/246, BT233/258, BT233/280, BT233/285, BT233/293
Sabre Handling Appraisal (A&AEE)	DSIR 23/23038, DSIR 23/23054
F-86A Test Reports	AVIA 6/17976, AVIA 18/4278 to AVIA 18/4285

Accident records held at the RAF Museum, Hendon
Individual aircraft record cards held at the RAF Museum, Hendon

SECONDARY SOURCES

Books:

Caygill, P. *Jet Jockeys*, Crowood Press, 2002

Milberry, L. *The Canadair Sabre*, CANAV Books, 1986

Wagner, R. *The North American Sabre*, MacDonald, 1963

Magazines:

Allsopp, C. 'Life on Three', *Three's Company* (3 Sqn Association magazine) (February 2001)

Author unknown. 'A Tour of 2nd TAF', *Flight* (15 June 1956)

Dickinson, R.J.F. 'Fighter Operations with the USAF', *RAF Historical Society Journal* 21 (2000)

Fitchen, K. 'No More Night Flying after That', *RAF News* (25 May 2001)

Gunston, W.T. '2nd TAF Today', *Flight* (12 February 1954)

Oakford, 'Oake'. 'I Learnt about Flying from That', *Air Clues* (October 1987)

Staff. 'Farewell to the Sabre', *Flight* (25 May 1956)

Staff. 'First Line of Defence', *Flight* (3 December 1954)

Staff. 'Here and There', *Flight* (17 October 1952)

Staff. 'RAF Sabres Arrive', *Flight* (9 January 1953)

Staff. 'Sabres Across the Atlantic', *Aeroplane* (20 November 1953)

Tomkins, M. 'The Commonwealth's Contribution to the Korean War', *Air Mail* (RAF Association magazine) (January–March 2001)

INDEX